WOMEN'S POLITICAL DISCOURSE

Communication, Media, and Politics

Series Editor
Robert E. Denton, Jr., Virginia Tech

This series features a broad range of work dealing with the role and function of communication in the realm of politics, broadly defined. Including general academic books, monographs, and texts for use in graduate and advanced undergraduate courses, the series encompasses humanistic, critical, historical, and empirical studies in political communication in the United States. Primary subject areas include campaigns and elections, media, and political institutions. *Communication, Media, and Politics* books are of interest to students, teachers, and scholars of political communication from the disciplines of communication, rhetorical studies, political science, journalism, and political sociology.

Recent Titles in the Series

WOMEN'S POLITICAL DISCOURSE

A 21st-Century Perspective

MOLLY A. MAYHEAD &
BRENDA DEVORE MARSHALL

ROWMAN & LITTLEFIELD PUBLISHERS, INC.
Lanham • Boulder • New York • Toronto • Oxford

ROWMAN & LITTLEFIELD PUBLISHERS, INC.

Published in the United States of America
by Rowman & Littlefield Publishers, Inc.
A wholly owned subsidiary of The Rowman & Littlefield Publishing Group, Inc.
4501 Forbes Boulevard, Suite 200, Lanham, Maryland 20706
www.rowmanlittlefield.com

P.O. Box 317, Oxford OX2 9RU, UK

British Library Cataloguing in Publication Information Available

Library of Congress Cataloging-in-Publication Data
Mayhead, Molly A., 1961–
  Women's political discourse : a 21st-century perspective / Molly A. Mayhead and
Brenda DeVore Marshall.
    p.   cm. — (Communication, media, and politics)
  Includes bibliographical references and index.
  ISBN 0-7425-2908-8 (cloth : alk. paper) — ISBN 0-7425-2909-6 (pbk. : alk. paper)
  1. Women in politics—United States. 2. Political oratory—United States. I. Marshall, Brenda
DeVore, 1951– II. Title. III. Series.
HQ1236.5.U6M39 2005
320'.082'0973—dc22

2005020780

Printed in the United States of America

∞™ The paper used in this publication meets the minimum requirements of American
National Standard for Information Sciences—Permanence of Paper for Printed Library
Materials, ANSI/NISO Z39.48-1992.

Dedicated to
the courageous women who bring new voices to the political table
and
Ed and Ty, for your encouragement, patience, and support of women's rights.

There are thousands of talented women who should be in politics but are not. And it's our job to bring them in.

—HUBERT HUMPHREY, QTD. IN GERALDINE FERRARO, *MY STORY* 310

In 1892, J. Ellen Foster stood before the Republican National Convention at Minneapolis. "We are here to help you," she told the assembled men. "And we have come to stay."

—JO FREEMAN, *A ROOM AT A TIME:
HOW WOMEN ENTERED PARTY POLITICS* 37

A more inclusive view of the history of women shows them surmounting, sometimes one by one, a series of double binds whose roots are deeply embedded in the past. Women who unmasked one dilemma faced the next and challenged it, bumped into a third and pirouetted around it, confronted another, and denied it its power. In the process they enlarged the scope of science, changed laws, altered behaviors, and changed the political complexion of this country. If they do not disable themselves with the rhetoric of disempowerment and victimization, they will enter the twenty-first century able to stand, speak, dance, and redefine the world as the need arises.

—KATHLEEN HALL JAMIESON, *BEYOND THE DOUBLE BIND* 21

We'll have equity when gender is no longer an issue. When we're really measured on the basis of our brains and talent, we'll do just fine.

—MARY LANDRIEU, MIKULSKI ET AL., *NINE AND COUNTING* 58

Gender does not act as a filter, allowing some needs to pass only into female fields of vision while others fall only within a male field. It is not that differences are not there. It is, instead, that the presence of women in leadership itself can free us from stereotypical thinking.

—SUE TOLLESON-RINEHART,
"DO WOMEN LEADERS MAKE A DIFFERENCE?" 164

CONTENTS

CHAPTER THREE

Discourse from "A Woman's Place": Twenty-first-Century Rhetoric in the
U.S. House of Representatives   81

CHAPTER FOUR

Strangers No More: The Discourse of
Twenty-first-Century Women in the U.S. Senate   117

CHAPTER FIVE

Voices from All Directions: Women's Discourse in the
Twenty-first-Century State House   173

Acknowledgments

WE EXPRESS OUR GRATITUDE to the courageous women whose voices echo in the following pages and to countless others whose participation in electoral politics at the local, state, and national levels has altered the face of our government. Thank you for making a difference.

We offer our appreciation to the students who have joined us in the adventure of learning more about women's public discourse. Brenda extends a special thanks to the women in her spring 2004 course, Women's Political Voices, for their perceptive questions and "ah-ha" moments and to Aron Carleson for daring to venture forth into the fray. Appreciation goes to Carrie Elmore and Katie Dolph for assistance with the references and appendices.

For their work in securing interlibrary resources and encouragement of this project we thank the staff of Linfield College's Nicholson Library, including Frances Rasmussen, Jean Caspers, Kathleen Spring, and especially, Susan Barnes Whyte, director of the library, as well as the great staff of Hamersly Library at Western Oregon University.

Dialogues with our colleagues, past and present, often find their way into our thinking and writing without our explicit awareness. So, to those of you who have joined our conversations, thank you.

Brenda acknowledges the support of her faculty colleagues in Linfield's Department of Theatre and Communication Arts. Thank you Janet Gupton, Jackson Miller, Kate Hawkes, and Tyrone Marshall for "being there," especially in moments of crisis, and for the joy you bring to our work with students. Appreciation also goes to Vicky Ragsdale, academic secretary and box office manager extraordinaire, whose work in the department has allowed Brenda to devote more time to scholarly endeavors and less to matters of bookkeeping. On September 12, 2001, professor of religious studies, William Millar, faced the unenviable task of delivering a faculty lecture in the wake of 9/11. His thoughtful interrogation of Second and Third Space dialectics in ancient Israel shed light not only on the horrific events of the preceding day but also on the burgeoning ideas of rhetorical space expressed in chapter 1 of this book. Barbara Seidman, professor of English and gender studies, colleague, and friend, thank you for encouragement, for interrogative excursions into feminist theory, and for insightful comments about many of the ideas developed in this work. Brenda also extends appreciation to Vivian Bull, president of Linfield College, for her graceful and transformative leadership in service to others and for her advocacy on behalf of faculty, students, and liberal arts education. Thanks go as well to Marvin Henberg, dean of faculty, for his support of this work and Linfield's gender studies program. Molly thanks the best friends and colleagues in the world, Nick Backus, Claire Ferraris, and Emily Plec, for making West House a joyous place to work.

To our families, thank you. Molly thanks her parents, Janeen and Derek Mayhead, for their encouragement of and excitement about her work throughout her many years of education and teaching. Brenda thanks her aunt, Alene DeVore, for providing a role model for professional women; her siblings, Glenda Lakey and Verne DeVore, for their support and humor in the face of sadness; and her parents, Keith and Alberta DeVore, whose inspiration lives on in memories.

We express our appreciation to the Center for American Women and Politics, a unit of the Eagle Institute of Politics at Rutgers, The State University of New Jersey, for compiling both historical and contemporary data on the activities of women in politics. The archival and research work done at the center provides crucial information for those of us conducting scholarly investigations in this area.

We extend our gratitude to Robert Denton, series editor, for his advocacy for this project and for his unflinching dedication to scholarly works that interrogate the role of women's discourse in the public affairs of the United States. Our appreciation also goes to Brenda Hadenfeldt, acquisitions editor for communication and journalism at Rowman and Littlefield, for believing in this book and for her patience in the midst of life's interruptions. We also acknowledge the many members of the Rowman and Littlefield team whose work on this project has contributed to its success. Special thanks go to Jennifer Nemec, associate editor; Jane McGarry, copyeditor; Erica Fast and Bess Vanrenen, editorial assistants; Virginia Bridges, proofreader; and Piper Furbush, who designed the book cover.

Finally, we want to acknowledge that this is a completely coauthored book. Because each author contributes equally to our collaborative endeavors, we have elected to alternate the order of our names in those publications.

Introduction

> *Women populate half the democracy; we should occupy half the positions of leadership—both for gender equity and because women, a natural resource, should be mined for energy. . . . When I look at the issues we face, and when I think of the changes we need, I am as convinced as I have ever been that our future depends on the leadership of women—not to replace men, but to transform our options alongside them.*
>
> —MARIE WILSON IX–X

B Y ALL ACCOUNTS, women in the United States have made much progress in the last two centuries. We occupy the traditional "women's roles" as well as professional positions once considered unthinkable. In spite of our successes as doctors, lawyers, astronauts, college professors, CEOs, and even politicians, in the early years of the twenty-first century we still encounter many of the obstacles faced by our predecessors. As Joan Tronto observed in the waning years of the twentieth century, "Women remain almost entirely excluded from power in political, economic, and cultural institutions of importance in the United States, despite the small gains of 'the year of the woman' [1992]" (2). While some progress has been made to mitigate women's marginalization in the public sphere, more than a decade later Tronto's words still ring all too true.

Despite some progress, including women's accomplishments in the House, the Senate, and even the state house, the challenges facing women in the political arena remain substantial. "When it comes to women's leadership, we live in a land of deep resistance, with structural and emotional impediments burned into the cultures of our organizations, into our society, and into the psyches and expectations of both sexes" (Wilson xiii). Although women still confront numerous hurdles in electoral contexts, their presence in what continues to be perceived as masculine territory has begun to transform the political landscape and promises to continue to do so in the twenty-first century. Even though in the international arena the United States ranks sixtieth in women's political leadership (Wilson xii), in 2004, a record nine women held governorships, sixty women served as House members with an additional three women elected as delegates from Washington, D.C., Guam, and the Virgin Islands, and fourteen women occupied Senate seats. How have these women managed to beat the odds in their successful attempts to enter national politics? How do they manage to fruitfully participate in the political process once they gain entry into the sacred halls of the Congress and the state house?

The rhetoric politicians and their constituents employ creates our political world as we know it. Language, according to Ofer Feldman, constitutes political society. "In other words, the essence of politics is talk" (195). Echoing the thoughts of many scholars in the field of political communication and cultural studies, Christ'l De Landtsheer argues that "those who control [political] discourse control society" and that "politics is discourse and discourse is politics" (4). It becomes self-evident, then, that for women to make meaningful contributions to the shaping of political reality their voices must be included in the symphony of our national discussion of public affairs. We also know that even in the beginning of the twenty-first century, women's utterances often are muted, regarded as dissonant and thus, irrelevant, or silenced altogether as we orchestrate our political discourse. Equally evident is the fact that, however slowly, "the times they are a'changin." We suggest that a study of the political discourse employed by the women who have found their way into national politics and whose voices have been included in the political dialogue holds the key to answering the questions posed above and to advancing women's opportunities to transform the political landscape alongside their male colleagues. And, in an era in which on a daily basis weapons seem to speak louder than political talk, we are obligated to "take a positive look at political discourse because such discussion might directly affect the quality of the future" (Feldman 204).

According to former Vermont governor, Madeleine Kunin, once women gain access to the inner circle of politics, they tend to govern differently, or at least have different agendas than their male counterparts, because they have little in common with the traditional lobbyists and instead often work more closely with or for those outside the traditional sphere, those who are marginalized or disenfranchised (366). Madeleine Albright, who served as secretary of state in the Clinton administration, echoes Kunin's thoughts. "If women in government do their jobs," she advises, "they will improve the lot of women and girls everywhere. They will raise issues that others overlook, pass bills that others oppose, put money into projects others ignore, and seek an end to abuses others accept" (qtd. in Wilson 14). Research conducted by the Center for American Women in Politics at Rutgers University and the Women and Politics Institute at American University supports the observations made by Kunin and Albright. Since the 1980s, their studies have "consistently demonstrated that women legislators differ from their male colleagues in the issues they address, the positions they take, and the approaches they use in lawmaking. Thus, the Center contends, electing more women has a significant impact on what government does and how it operates" ("Final"). In her interpretation of this data Marie Wilson, founder and president of the White House Project, suggests that women in politics "tend to include diverse viewpoints in decision making, have a broader conception of public policy, and offer new solutions. Females," she continues, "define 'women's issues' more broadly than most of their male colleagues, and they put these issues at the top of the legislative agenda—bills dealing with children, education, and health care, for instance" (9–10). This, then, is the true benefit of bringing women into the inner circle of politics—the system acquires a diversity of interests and styles that can only serve to enhance and improve the way government operates.

Our book, *Navigating Boundaries: The Rhetoric of Women Governors*, provides an initial examination of discourse strategies and media coverage of selected women governors. As we conclude in that work, "Women in the United States continue to change the gubernatorial landscape and contribute to the increasing importance of this role at both the state and federal levels. Thus, the values and perspectives revealed in their discourse must merit our further investigation" (Marshall and Mayhead 124). The experiences and contributions of women elected to the House and Senate parallel those of women governors. With this in mind, we examine the discourse of women elected to serve in these three highly visible offices in order to accomplish several goals. First, this investigation extends previous discussions of women whose political rhetoric has not been studied systematically. Second, this study allows increased understanding of the development of women's unique approaches to governing as evidenced in their political discourse. Finally, the focus on key twenty-first-century women politicians models innovative approaches to governmental leadership in a post-September 11th world.

In order to investigate how women governors, senators, and representatives navigate the varied obstacles of the political system, our analysis draws from an ideographic approach to rhetorical criticism. Illumination of the contemporary and often covert private/public sphere duality women politicians negotiate and, we argue, transform, coupled with a search for new parameters characterizing the genre of women's political discourse, highlights a unifying thread for our work.

Chapter I features a discussion of the dichotomy of the public and private spheres. Tracing the early writings of key nineteenth- and twentieth-century feminists and political activists, the chapter provides a theoretical framework that illuminates the evolution of thinking about the socially constructed realities of the public and the private. Specifically, we introduce the concept of both Second and Third Space discourse that accounts for lived experience. We conclude that women in electoral politics in the twenty-first century are forging new strategies of integrating Second and Third Space realities in an in-between dimension that values a more androgynous approach to political discourse. The chapter concludes with a discussion of the significant role ideology plays in this new rhetoric.

In chapter 2 we provide an overview of women's political voices in the twentieth century. We have not attempted an exhaustive survey of the more than two hundred women who served in the U.S. House of Representatives, the U.S. Senate, and as governors of their states in the previous century. Rather, we have selected politicians in each group who gave voice to the issues of their decade or across decades. Collectively, the lives and discourse of these women exemplify the courage, knowledge, and leadership skills necessary to participate in a traditionally male world.

The discourse of women serving in the U.S. House of Representatives, the U.S. Senate, and governorships in the twenty-first century yields fertile ground for analysis in chapters 3, 4, and 5. These discussions interrogate the rhetoric of women who began their foray into electoral politics in the twentieth century as well as those elected to their current office after the year 2000. We seek to provide an illustrative sample of the diverse demographics, party platforms, and personal ideologies these politicians represent. Using a collection of their rhetorical texts, we explore ideographs the women incorporate into their public discourse to shape a space in which a new vision of policies and practices becomes viable.

Even in the twenty-first century our views about the role of women in elective office in the United States remain contradictory, as the opening paragraphs of this introduction suggest. Women still face both covert and overt obstructions to their participation in electoral politics. Yet, their presence in the U.S. House, in the Senate chamber, and in the state house, as well as other political bodies, has begun to facilitate significant modification in the governing process. With this work, born of the hope and fortitude expressed in the actions of the women whose voices echo in these pages, we offer our encouragement to those who endeavor to bring new insights to the political table.

A Space for Discourse   I

Despite their many contributions to public dialogue, the history of women's rhetoric is the story of an unending struggle to be heard and to be heeded in the face of the hostility of the church, the courts, the professions, and the press, supported by state and federal courts and legislatures.

—KARLYN KOHRS CAMPBELL, INTRODUCTION XIII

THE SLOGAN, *THE PERSONAL IS POLITICAL*, SERVED AS a rallying cry for women of feminism's second wave. To many feminists the phrase, first coined by Carol Hanisch in *Notes from the Second Year* (Hanisch 76; Humm 162), "argued that personal and intimate experience is not isolated, individual, or undetermined, but rather is social, political, and systemic" (Kramarae and Treichler 333). As Hanisch described the consciousness raising groups in which she participated she noted that "one of the first things we discover in these groups is that personal problems are political problems" (76). Catharine Mackinnon asserted that "the personal as political is not a simile, not a metaphor, and not an analogy. . . . It means that women's distinctive experience as women occurs within that sphere that has been socially lived as the personal—private, emotional, interiorized, particular, individuated, intimate—so that what it is to *know* the *politics* of woman's situation is to know women's personal lives" (535). Radical feminists contended that "distinctions between the personal and the public realms are fallacious" (Humm 162). Iris Young explained the concept in the following passage: "The feminist slogan 'The personal is political' does not deny a social distinction between public and private, but it does deny a social division between public and private spheres, with different kinds of institution, activity, and human attribute" (441). Charlotte Bunch summarized the concept rather succinctly: "There is no private domain of a person's life that is not political and there is no political issue that is not ultimately personal" ("Broom" 29). Long before the late 1960s and early 1970s, however, women understood that both the personal is political and its converse, the political is personal, underscored their comprehension of and participation in both the "woman's sphere" and the political world.

Even before the writers of the Declaration of Sentiments called for equality at Seneca Falls in 1848, small numbers of women had found their way into the public sphere via their social and political involvement in education. After all, those in the public sphere viewed public education, the education of children, that is, as an extension of the private sphere. Women had been responsible for the early education of their sons and often for the total education of their daughters. "Most early proponents of educating women argued that if a mother was going to raise sons, she had to be able to teach young children at home so that they would be prepared to enter a literate world" (Freedman 48). It followed then that women's early involvement in the public sphere and in the political arena could revolve around this "woman's issue" without creating too many suspicions. Individuals such as Judith Sargent Murray, Mary Wollstonecraft, and Frances Wright believed that "reason, if properly cultivated through education, could set men and women free" (Rossi 3). Reason, they surmised, "would lead the way to a progressively better social order, free of the superstitions that had in the past bogged down mankind" (3).

In the early years following the American Revolution, the citizens of this newly formed democracy found themselves grappling with the "egalitarian principles immortalized in Thomas Jefferson's Declaration of Independence" (Skemp 3). Issues of privilege, individual rights, and political participation as well as questions about the old social and political order permeated both intellectual and personal discussions. While often not as overt, concerns about traditional definitions of gender and expectations of and for women found their way into this dialogue. Historian Joan Cashin noted that following the Revolution men and women engaged in "dialogue, struggle, and contemplation about the meaning of gender and how men and women should relate to each other" (qtd. in Skemp 4). According to Sheila Skemp, "One of the most thoughtful and outspoken participants in that dialogue was Massachusetts-born poet, essayist, and playwright, Judith Sargent Murray" (4).

The *Massachusetts Magazine* published Murray's essay, "On the Equality of the Sexes," in 1790. In this groundbreaking work, Judith Sargent Murray claimed that women's intellectual abilities are equal to those of men. She believed that women are endowed with the qualities of imagination, reason, memory, and judgment. In the opening of the essay, Murray posed the following questions:

Is it upon mature consideration we adopt the idea, that nature is thus partial in her distributions? Is it indeed a fact, that she hath yielded to one half of the human species so unquestionable a mental superiority? I know that to both sexes elevated understandings, and the reverse, are common. But, suffer me to ask, in what the minds of females are so notoriously deficient, or unequal. May not the intellectual powers be ranged under their four heads—imagination, reason, memory and judgment. (Murray 177)

Murray argued that perceived deficiencies in women's intellect were not inherent but rather were a product of their limited educational opportunities. She believed that "we can only reason from what we know, and if opportunity of acquiring knowledge hath been denied us, the inferiority of our sex cannot fairly be deduced from thence" (178). In the spirit of the time, Murray contended that the education of women would not deter them from their traditional roles and household duties, but rather that the development of women's intellect would allow them to be happier and to create a more pleasant home for their husbands. She stated: "Nay, while we are pursuing the needle, or the superintendency of the family, I repeat, that our minds are at full liberty for reflection; that imagination may exert itself in full vigor, and that if a just foundation early laid, our ideas will then be worthy of rational beings" (179). Murray's ideas were "not only reminiscent of the views of philosopher John Locke, but anticipated the work of the English feminist Mary Wollstonecraft" (Skemp 176).

Mary Wollstonecraft, one of the most vehement advocates for the public education of females, wrote *A Vindication of the Rights of Woman* in response to Charles Maurice de Talleyrand's book, *A Report on Public Instruction*. Talleyrand proposed a new system of education for France in which French girls would be educated in public schools only until the age of eight. After that, they would spend the remainder of their years at home where their lives would be centered thereafter (Rossi 29). According to Alice Rossi, Wollstonecraft dedicated *Vindication* to Talleyrand, "urging him in a preface to revise his educational plan and not bar women from their democratic rights" (29). To Wollstonecraft, education meant equality between the sexes, with all of the concomitant advantages. Not only must women have access to education, they must have equal education. "But I still insist," she stated, "that not only the virtue, but the *knowledge* of the two sexes should be the same in nature, if not in degree, and that women, considered not only as moral, but rational creatures, ought to endeavour to acquire human virtues (or perfections) by the *same* means as men, instead of being educated like a fanciful kind of *half* being" (Wollstonecraft 39). Wollstonecraft was particularly concerned that females were only taught to be beautiful and pleasing, and not to be thinking, rational individuals.

Without exposure to and a chance to discuss issues, she stated, females find that the "truth is hidden from them, and they are made to assume an artificial character before their faculties have acquired any strength" (44).

Throughout her book, Wollstonecraft highlighted the problems with keeping women ignorant. For instance, when beauty fades and they become less attractive for men to gaze upon, men and society cease to value them (11). In addition, women often had to feign sickness or "delicacy" to secure their husband's affection (29). "Marriage will never be sacred," Wollstonecraft argued, "'till women, by being brought up with men, are prepared to be their companions rather than their mistresses" (165). Ultimately, Wollstonecraft suggested, women are simply "slaves to their bodies, and glory in their subjection" (44). So, women must be educated equally. "The conclusion I wish to draw is obvious," Wollstonecraft stated. "Make women rational creatures, and free citizens; and they will quickly become good wives and mothers" (178). And, of course, they will be productive members of society as well.

As one of the first truly radical thinkers and activists, Frances (Fanny) Wright held the notion that society could be improved only through equality in education. Having observed the events in the French Revolution, she argued that education could eliminate both class and gender differences. In the early 1800s, she traveled around the United States giving a series of lectures in which she advocated education for all citizens. The country could not realize its full potential, she suggested, until education was available to everyone. "Until women assume the place in society which good sense and good feeling alike assign to them," she posited, "human improvement must advance but feebly" (Wright 44). Knowing that men fought the American Revolution for concepts such as liberty and equality, Wright observed that equal rights "cannot exist without equality of instruction" (46). "Equality is the soul of liberty," she continued. "There is, in fact, no liberty without it—none that cannot be overthrown by the violence of ignorant anarchy, or sapped by the subtilty [sic] of professional craft" (46).

Wright specifically criticized parents who believed their daughters should be educated differently than their sons. "We see men," she stated, "who will aid the instruction of their sons, and condemn only their daughters to ignorance" (Wright 52). According to Wright, while parents believed that their sons should receive extensive and diverse educations, conversely, for their "daughters, little trouble or expense is necessary. They can never *be any thing*; in fact, they *are nothing*" (52). Parents had a duty, Wright posited, to make sure their children, regardless of their sex, received an education. "Their duty is plain, evident, decided," she stated. "In a daughter they have in charge a human being; in a son, the same. Let them train up these *human beings*, under the expanded wings of liberty. Let them seek *for* them and *with* them just knowledge" (53); "encouraging, from the cradle upward," she continued, "that useful curiosity which will lead them unbidden in the paths of free enquiry; and place them, safe and superior to the storms of life, in the security of well regulated, self possessed minds, well grounded, well reasoned, conscientious opinions, and self-approved, consistent practice" (53). This search for knowledge, Wright concluded, held vital importance to "our world prosperity, to our happiness, our dignity. . . . we must throw it open to both sexes—to all ages— to the whole family of humankind" (62).

Following on the heels of Frances Wright, the women of Seneca Falls and the many who joined them in the campaign for suffrage found ways to create and contribute to the late nineteenth- and early twentieth-century public debates about women's roles and rights. It was no coincidence that the Declaration of Sentiments called for educational opportunities for women as well as the elective franchise. These women understood that education and the freedom to express one's beliefs on the public platform and at the ballot box were fundamental to their success in what society dubbed their own "woman's" space and to their participation in the affairs of their communities and the nation. In "Why Women Should Vote," Jane Addams argued that "if woman would keep on with her old business of caring for her house and rearing her children she will have to have some conscience in regard to public affairs lying quite outside of her immediate household" (105).

Without the ability to prevent or control conception, the right to vote or even work outside the home would have little impact on women's lives. The discourse and efforts of one of the greatest champions of birth control, Margaret Sanger, underscore this intersection between the personal and political. Her activities in the birth control movement spanned five decades (Rossi 521) and included lobbying Congress and the courts, several arrests, the opening of family planning clinics, and the publication of several documents including her "militantly feminist journal" (Sicherman and Green 625), *The Woman Rebel,* which began in 1914 (Sanger, *Margaret* 106), and the sixteen-page pamphlet, *Family Limitation* (Rossi 519).

Sanger's motivation for and interest in participating in the birth control movement were rooted in a number of personal experiences and observations. As one of seven children, she believed that her family often had to struggle to survive. She was particularly concerned about her mother who was often in very poor health. "In Margaret's memory," reports her most recent and acclaimed biographer, Ellen Chesler, "her mother was forever cooking, cleaning, or sewing in a futile effort to bring order to her chaotic household. But constrained by poverty and poor health," she continues, "Margaret's mother did little more than exacerbate their problems" (40). In addition, Sanger recognized that few women had access to birth control information, and the inability to plan or prevent pregnancies only served to hold them back politically and economically. As she states in her autobiography, a woman must be allowed to develop all her potentialities. "Feminists were trying to free her from the new economic ideology but were doing nothing to free her from her biological subservience to man, which was the true cause of her enslavement" (Sanger, *Margaret* 107).

Perhaps the most significant event in Sanger's career involved a young mother named Sadie Sacks, for it was this woman's situation that caused Sanger to abandon her nursing career and endeavor to provide contraception information to anyone who needed it. Sadie Sacks lived with her husband and three infants on New York's Lower East Side. According to Sanger, the children were loved, but it was a struggle to take care of them on the husband's meager salary. Sadie had become pregnant again and had "taken various drugs and purgatives" which made her extremely sick (Sanger, *My Fight* 51). Mrs. Sacks begged Sanger, who had nursed her back to health, for information on contraception. Sanger turned to Mrs. Sacks's doctor who merely laughed and said, "tell Jake [the husband] to sleep on the roof" (53). Several months later Jake phoned Sanger imploring her to come to his apartment because his wife was extremely ill. She had taken drugs to end another pregnancy and this time she died (54). After that incident, Sanger wrote, "I would never go back again to nurse women's ailing bodies while their miseries were as vast as the stars. . . . I resolved that women should have knowledge of contraception. They have every right to know about their own bodies" (56). After decades of work, Sanger was gratified to see the historic 1965 Supreme Court decision *Griswold v. Connecticut*, which guaranteed a woman's right to privacy. This encompassed the right to use contraceptives. As Margaret Sanger neared death, her granddaughter asked what she wanted said at her funeral. "Margaret said she hoped she would be remembered for helping women, because women are the strength of the future. They take care of culture and tradition, and preserve what is good. That, she hoped, would be her remembrance" (Chesler 468).

As the preceding examples illustrate, since their first forays into the public sphere, women have understood the synergistic intersection between the personal and the political. Knowing this, since the mid-nineteenth century literally thousands of women have navigated the boundaries between the public world of politics and the personal world of their more private lived experience. As female politicians of the twentieth century have demonstrated by occupying the office of governor, inhabiting the U.S. Senate chamber, and holding seats in the House of Representatives, elected women officials elucidate the importance, and inevitability, of linking the two spheres in which they live their lives.

In her book, *Living a Political Life*, Madeleine Kunin provides the implicit argument that any woman can participate in politics. Often the exigence spurring this involvement occurs at the boundaries of the political and the personal. For example, a mundane sidewalk provided the impetus for Kunin's entrance into politics.

Watching her daughter, Julia, walk to school one day in 1966, she noticed that the child had to walk along the street as cars whizzed by. Horrified by the potential for an accident, she began lobbying the local Board of Aldermen and spoke one night at a meeting. Her motion calling for sidewalk construction was tabled indefinitely, but she was not daunted by her defeat and, as she said, she learned that she "could stand up and speak before an angry crowd, that [she] could say what she believed, not through self-conscious effort, but by becoming less self-conscious" (82). She felt so strongly about the need for sidewalks, however, that the entire family moved to Dunbar Road where she soon discovered that her children would have to cross an unmarked railroad track on their way to and from school.

Again, Kunin lobbied the Board of Aldermen who this time authorized a study of the alleged hazard. After two weeks of discussions and observations, and a near collision between an alderman and a railroad car, two flashing lights were installed at the crossing. Kunin did not merely revel in her success; she learned something from the entire experience. She writes:

> These two red lights illuminated the rewards that came with risk. The once-distant and impenetrable structure called the political system had responded to my en-treaties. For the first time I became aware of my potential political effectiveness. The success at the railroad crossing enlarged my sense of possibility and strength-ened my optimism; my efforts had achieved practical results. This is how I began to lay the groundwork for living a political life. The belief that as an individual I could have an effect on an impersonal political system was essential to my growth. It made me believe that I could change the world. (83)

Similarly, Maryland Senator Barbara Mikulski began her foray into politics fighting with local government. In her case, however, she fought against plans to build a sixteen-lane highway right through her neighborhood. Having earned a master's degree in community organization, Mikulski knew how to mobilize forces. In order to be successful, she states, "We had to do our homework. We had to build coalitions that would increase our power. The first step," she continued, "was joining forces with the black community on the west side. This was in the af-termath of the civil rights riots, and at that time it would have been impossible for the Polish neighborhoods on the east side and the black neighborhoods on the west side to work together. . . . I knew differently. We were facing a common threat" (Mikulski et al. 30). Senator Mikulski reports that the two sides came to-gether to create a citywide group called MAD—Movement Against Destruction. And, she concludes, "the highway forces didn't know what hit them" (31).

Like Madeleine Kunin, Barbara-Rose Collins, the first African American woman elected to Congress from Michigan, became involved in politics because of her child. Concerned about the quality of education afforded her daughter in the neighborhood school Collins herself had attended, she complained to school officials who "looked upon her as an intrusive, unwanted nuisance" (Gill 139). In order to dissuade Collins from continuing her quest for a better school system, an administrator contacted her employer to inquire about the amount of time she spent away from her job in order to pursue this cause. Despite this intrusion, Collins chose to continue her efforts rather than succumb to intimidation. As she noted: "That [the phone call to her supervisor] would have done one of two things: gotten me fired or reprimanded, but it would also remove a concerned parent from the school system. So when they asked me to run for school board, I didn't want to, but I did" (qtd. in Gill 139). She won the election and endeavored to "restore the schools to the standards of excellence that she remembered from her childhood" (Gill 140).

As these brief vignettes illustrate, historically women have entered the public arena to address issues in what traditionally has been viewed as the private sphere. These women's lived experiences support Homi Bhabha's stance that the "recesses of the domestic space become sites for history's most intricate invasions" (9). From Bhabha's perspective, in the resulting displacement "the borders between home and world become confused; and, uncannily, the private and the public become part of each other" (9). Bhabha and other cultural theorists refer to this "new" space as the "in-between space" (38), a site that allows a new dimension of understanding.

Drawing on the work of Edward Soja and Henri Lefebvre, archaeologist James Flanagan proposes three perspectives on space. He describes First Space as perceived or empirical space, "the space of the physical world" (29). Second Space exists as conceived space (29). According to Soja, "second space epistemologies are immediately distinguishable by their explanatory concentration on conceived rather than perceived space and their implicit assumption that spatial knowledge is primarily produced through discursively devised representations of space, through the spatial workings of the mind" (78–79). Those in power in the Second Space project on First Space a hierarchical ordering of experience within that expanse and thus, create the normative (Millar 4–5). In this schema, "Third Space becomes the space of the marginalized, the silenced, the rendered-invisible ones, the place where difference gathers as a result of our Second Space decisions. Until, that is, someone challenges the system with an utterance . . . bringing voice to Third Space, rendering it visible" (5). While all of these layers of space exist simultaneously in any given moment and context, within a patriarchal infrastructure Second Space gains primacy while Third Space perspectives are silenced, and hence, made invisible most of the time. Thus, it is the Second Space or "public" sphere interpretations of First Space experience that define and guide our collective endeavors. Historically, the private or "woman's sphere" has existed within the

Third Space and hence, has not been valued for its potential contributions to our comprehension of experience in the First Space despite the mutual influence each has on the other. As Third Space voices penetrate their own spatial boundaries "rendering visible" Third Space experience, they simultaneously move beyond that location toward, but not into Second Space. From the vantage point of this "in-between space," the discourse metamorphoses Second and Third Space language into a rhetoric that while formed from both is neither hegemonic nor marginalized but which by its very nature transcends each. From this transformation emerges the possibility for new interpretations of First Space lived experience.

"Private and public" Bhabha argues, "develop an interstitial intimacy. It is an intimacy that questions binary divisions through which such spheres of social experience are often spatially opposed" (13). This interrogation refutes the typical Western patriarchal either/or notions of existence and illustrates the need for a combinatory metaphor that accounts for the blending of the spheres. Many women, while understanding and experiencing the binary impulse, also appreciate a more synergistic comprehension of the world in which existence can been seen as a "both/and" phenomenon. We argue that since their earliest involvement in politics women not only have negotiated these binary boundaries, they have attempted to create a new site in which the personal and public spheres, specifically the political arena, transmute into an increasingly androgynous in-between space—informed by a synergistic understanding of the inability to segregate these dimensions of human existence. In this in-between space, "the original binary choice is not dismissed entirely but is subjected to a creative process of *restructuring* that draws selectively and strategically from the two opposing categories to open new alternatives" (Soja 5). Martin Heidegger advocates a similar perspective in his suggestion that "a space is something that has been made room for, something that is cleared and free, namely within a boundary, Greek *peras*. A boundary is not that at which something stops but, as the Greeks recognized, the boundary is that from which something *begins its presencing*" (154).

It is at the intersection of the Second and Third Space boundaries, in the in-between space where public and private spheres become one, that women's voices and actions have challenged the Second Space interpretations of politics, "a discursive event" (Bhabha 23). In their interrogation and incorporation of both private and public views, women have contributed to a revisioning of the political landscape. Thus, it is this in-between space that allows a reframing of Second and Third Space ideology. We suggest that by the mid-nineteenth century women's political discourse began to frame this "new" political site as a more androgynous arena in which both masculine and feminine views of the world could be heard and acted upon. Moreover, this reconfiguration is transformative, not simply integrative (Freedman 7). And, we argue, this both/and perspective promises to be the salient feature of women's political discourse in the twenty-first century.

Since this in-between space finds its inception in public discourse, rhetorical theories and practices provide frames through which we may investigate its nature. As Nan Johnson notes, one can treat these rhetorical endeavors as "cultural sites where we can observe the interdependence of codes of rhetorical performance and the construction of conventional identities" (1). If, as Johnson argues, "the boundaries around rhetorical space have been actively patrolled for as long as it has been undeniably clear that to speak well and write convincingly were the surest routes to political, economic, and cultural stature," (2) then we can assume that the navigation and morphing of those boundaries may indeed create a new in-between rhetorical and cultural space.

Practitioners' use of rhetorical space, and scholars' conceptions of it, have evolved over time. Until the Grimké sisters' foray into antislavery debates in the early nineteenth century, society considered the public forum to be the domain of males. Certainly, women were loath to speak in public for fear of appearing too masculine and of violating societal norms. Scholars and biographers actually perpetuated this male-female dichotomy, suggests Johnson. "Post bellum biographical treatments of women orators," she contends, "reinscribe the dominant nineteenth-century cultural assumptions that a woman's rhetorical status depended upon whether or not she performed gender appropriately when speaking or writing" (112). In her pioneering work, Lillian O'Connor evaluated the work of nineteenth-century women orators against the traditional Aristotelian standards of rhetorical proof. She concluded that "the analysis of the extant texts brings to light the fact that the women who most skillfully exemplified all three modes [*ethos, pathos,* and *logos*] were those speakers whose familiarity with the rhetorical standards can be definitely established and in whose public utterances there is an expressed interest in correct practices of good public speaking" (225).

In her analysis of the persuasive discourse of many of these same nineteenth-century women, Karlyn Kohrs Campbell described a "feminine rhetorical style" that valued women's ways of knowing and allowed women speakers to succeed in the face of the double bind they encountered at the podium. That is, they could not be seen as "too" masculine in their appropriation of "rational," "traditional," and "non-emotional" modes of argument and yet, they had to rise above the expectation that they were incapable of embodying these very qualities. According to Campbell this feminine style was not, and is not today, "exclusive to women, either as speakers or as audiences" (*Man* 12).

Rather than envision rhetorical space as gendered, it is important to think of it, instead, as "framing certain kinds of opportunities that reflect the ways a culture has defined where significant cultural conversations take place" (N. Johnson 175). The women we discuss in the following chapters have entered into and reshaped this rhetorical space and bring to it issues that cross gender, racial, and class boundaries. They have created an in-between discourse site where it is not only appropriate to discuss topics that once were considered masculine or feminine only, it is *imperative* for them to do so. This process, believes Iris Young, is a process of liberating public expression, which involves "lifting formerly privatized issues into the open of public and rational discussion" (443). Access to this space matters as well. The space and expression itself can be considered public only when "third parties may witness it within the institutions that give these others opportunity to respond to the expression and enter the discussion" (440). The contents of these discussions are inherently political, for they "raise and address issues of moral value or human desirability of an institution or practice whose decisions affect a large number of people" (440). Quite simply, as Pratibha Parma states, the "appropriation and use of space are political acts" (qtd. in hooks 152).

In order to ensure a political system that includes the myriad voices relegated to the Third Space, we must identify and understand the strategies women politicians have and continue to use to both inhabit and act from the interstitial regions between Second and Third Space or between the public and the private spheres. From both a domestic and global perspective we believe women, who have understood the multiple binds of gender, race, and class, are positioned to provide leadership for those marginalized in the Third Space as well as those whose visions have been constrained by Second Space hegemonies.

Third Space discourse, while using the "language" of First and Second Spaces, sounds alien to those in the dominant culture, just as hegemonic symbols often signify little for those in the Third Space. This problem of translation exemplifies the notion that rhetoric can and does create reality and, consequently, quite literally shapes our ability to function within the world we fashion from our understanding of that reality. Rhetoric, thus, becomes "an important way in which individuals create worlds, perspectives, and identities" (Foss, Foss, and Griffin 7). According to Sonja Foss, Karen Foss, and Cindy Griffin:

> Understanding how rhetoric functions allows us to make conscious choices about the kinds of worlds we want to create, who and how we want to be in those worlds, and the values we want those worlds to embody. The study of rhetoric, then, enables us to understand and articulate the various ways individuals create and enact the worlds in which they choose to live. (7)

The rhetorical analysis of women's political discourse, as we propose in the preceding discussion, promises to elucidate the ways in which women contribute to the creation and enactment of an "in-between, public/private" space that privileges a nonessentialist view of men and women. In so doing, these women contribute to the evolution of a more androgynous style of political discourse with rhetorical options available to both female and male politicians and ordinary citizens.

Our interrogation of the discourse of women politicians in the twenty-first century finds its impetus in the twentieth-century study of a feminine rhetorical style identified by Karlyn Kohrs Campbell, as mentioned above. In her analysis of the rhetoric of nineteenth-century female reformers, Campbell concludes that "a woman who spoke displayed her 'masculinity'; that is, she demonstrated that she possessed qualities traditionally ascribed only to males. When a woman spoke," Campbell continues, "she enacted her equality, that is, she herself was proof that she was as able as her male counterparts to function in the public sphere" (*Man* 11). In order to soften the societal outcry against their participation in the public dialogue, these women developed a rhetorical style that "emerged out of their experiences as women and was adapted to the attitudes and experiences of female audiences" (12). These experiences epitomized women's roles as mothers and housewives and embodied women's primary means of acquiring knowledge. That is, at least in the earliest examples of women who defied the prevailing norms, these women applied the principles of craft-learning they encountered in acquiring the skills to function successfully in the home to their work as public speakers. They mentored each other and combined "expert advice with trial and error" (13). This process, argues Campbell, produced a discourse with specific characteristics:

> Such discourse will be personal in tone . . . relying heavily on personal experience, anecdotes, and other examples. It will tend to be structured inductively. . . . It will invite audience participation, including the process of testing generalizations or principles against the experiences of the audience. Audience members will be addressed as peers, with recognition of authority based on experience . . . and efforts will be made to create identification with the experiences of the audience and those described by the speaker. The goal of such rhetoric is empowerment. (13)

Campbell's work suggests that women understood the multiple binds they faced as they stepped into the public arena and that they were sufficiently astute and resourceful to successfully function within those strictures.

Jane Blankenship and Deborah C. Robson expand Campbell's work in an interrogation of more contemporary women's political discourse. They, too, argue that a "distinctive 'feminine style' of women's political discourse . . . not only exists, but its legitimation is expanding through its use by both women and men in positions of power" (353). They identify five characteristics of this feminine style:

1. Basing political judgments on concrete, lived experience;
2. Valuing inclusivity and the relational nature of being;
3. Conceptualizing the power of public office as a capacity to "get things done" and to empower others;

4. Approaching policy formation holistically;
5. Moving women's issues to the forefront of the public arena. (359)

Blankenship and Robson assert that based on these features, "the typical line drawn between private and public spheres has been redrawn" (363).

Drawing on Campbell's scholarship, Blankenship and Robson's study, and other previous work in the field of women's rhetoric, we propose to examine twenty-first-century political discourse from an ideological perspective. Teun A. van Dijk, in his work, *Ideology: A Multidisciplinary Approach*, defines ideology as a belief system that portrays a group's "fundamental social, economic, political, or cultural interests" (69). Present in statements reflecting these ideological beliefs are what Michael McGee has termed "ideographs." He defines the ideograph as:

> an ordinary language term found in political discourse. It is a high-order abstraction representing collective commitment to a particular but equivocal and ill-defined normative goal. It warrants the use of power, excuses behavior and belief which might otherwise be perceived as eccentric or antisocial, and guides behavior and belief into channels easily recognized by a community as acceptable and laudable. (15)

Ideographs "exist in real discourse" (McGee 7) and are easily recognizable and believable. So ingrained are they in a society's psyche, the fundamental logic of the ideographs is unquestionable (6–7). They appear in public argument and provide structure and meaning for the society. As Celeste Condit and John Lucaites suggest, the "central, organizing elements for any rhetorical culture are its 'ideographs'" (xii). "An ideograph," they continue, "is a culturally biased, abstract word or phrase, drawn from ordinary language, which serves as a constitutional value for a historically situated collectivity" (xii). Much like the narratives that often contain them, "ideographs represent in condensed form the normative, collective commitment of the members of a public, and they typically appear in public argumentation as the necessary motivation or justifications for action performed in the name of the public" (xii–xiii). Examples of contemporary ideographs are limitless and include words like *liberty, freedom, equality, democracy, family,* and *terrorism,* to name just a few. Ideographs such as these function as "agents of political consciousness" (McGee 7).

Ideographs present in public discourse reveal the "structures of public motives which have the capacity to both control power and to influence (if not determine) the shape and texture of each individual's reality" (McGee and Hogan 427) and consequently, of a collective political view. We are interested particularly in the ability of the ideograph to operate simultaneously and independently in the hegemonic Second Space, the silenced and marginalized Third Space, and the regions in between.

In the following chapters we examine the discourse of several prominent women politicians to illustrate the evolution of women's political discourse from simply "feminine" in style and content to a more gender-neutral rhetoric that occupies an androgynous in-between space. While it would be incorrect to assume that either masculine or feminine discourse is "superior," we argue that the morphing of these rhetorical approaches into a discourse shaped from the language of old but with potential for a new "presencing" provides for a more effective and more realistic way to examine the public argument of these elected officials. We believe the use of an ideological perspective enables us to interrogate twenty-first-century political discourse by key women leaders to elucidate principles of an androgynous political landscape and, thereby, contribute to an enhanced understanding of women's changing involvement in the political arena.

Echoes from the Pioneers
Women's Political Voices
in the Twentieth Century

2

> *When women comprise more than half of the population, why are there so few of them in public office? I have thought about this a great deal. . . . Is there something in our national mores that makes us think that women are unable to help direct the ship of state? We trust them to manage a home, rear children and live within a budget, but not to make the laws that vitally affect the family. . . . A woman who dares to expose herself to the electorate will have more days of frustration and heartache than any other combatant. Her family will be criticized, the length of her skirts will be cause for comment, and her every remark will be weighed for its veracity. But the goal is worth the race. To be a participant in governing the country is ample reward. If it is an elective office she has sought and won, she will find a self-fulfillment each time she responds to a roll call.*

—MAURINE NEUBERGER, FOREWORD XII–XIII

OUR UNDERSTANDING OF WOMEN'S POLITICAL DISCOURSE in the twenty-first century must necessarily find its grounding in the work and rhetoric of females who pioneered women's foray into electoral politics. That work, in turn, owes its debt to the women of the nineteenth century who fought for women's rights to participate in, and thus, speak in the public sphere. As indicated in chapter I, these foremothers challenged entrenched societal strictures prohibiting women's participation as citizens of a larger community beyond their own homes as they fought for equality and rights even within that private sphere.

In the twentieth century, one hundred seventy-eight women served in the U.S. House of Representatives, twenty-seven successfully sought election to the U.S.

Senate, and seventeen became state governors. Because these ladies paved the way for contemporary women engaged in electoral politics, we provide glimpses of the rhetoric of a few of them to contextualize our analysis of women's political discourse in the twenty-first century. Their words and deeds, woven into the tapestry of the history of American public address, demonstrate that women's commitment to issues of public importance transcend party affiliation, special interests, and most importantly, the private sphere.

Women in the U.S. House of Representatives

Jeannette Rankin (1917–1919 and 1941–1943)

Before the U.S. Constitution guaranteed universal suffrage, voters in the West elected the first woman to the U.S. House of Representatives. The state of Montana granted women the right to vote in 1914. Two years later, Jeannette Rankin, running on a Progressive Republican ticket, won the race for a U.S. congressional seat and became the first woman "elected to any national office in the United States" (McGinty 32). During her two terms in Congress, from 1917 through 1919 and then again from 1941 through 1943, and throughout the almost ninety-three years of her life, Rankin "fought against war and the diminution of human beings" (Kaptur 21). She was the only member of Congress to oppose the United States' entry into both World War I and World War II as well as the only one to vote against the country's participation in World War II.

Even many of her detractors, who often criticized Jeannette Rankin's political stance, admired her perseverance and moral conviction. Senator Lee Metcalf posited in his eulogy that "while history may not agree with Miss Rankin's views, it will applaud her courage and sense of duty. She was a public servant who voted conscientiously and independently" (United States Cong. Senate 65). The pioneering spirit of the western frontier, which many argue generally recognized the contributions of women more than did society elsewhere in the country, helped shape Rankin's political and moral worldviews. In addition to her western heritage, Rankin enjoyed the privilege of an education not often afforded young women of her era. In 1902, she received a bachelor of science degree in biology from the University of Montana. Following graduation she taught school for a brief time but found the work "tedious" (Kaptur 23). Searching for a new purpose, she traveled to Boston and later to San Francisco. In both of these cities she witnessed firsthand the predicament of the poor, especially women and children. These experiences, according to Kaptur, "motivated her to discover ways to make life more humane for others" (23). Still uncertain about the direction of her life, in 1908 she attended the New York School of Philanthropy, now the Columbia School of

Social Work, and in 1909 entered the University of Washington (Sicherman and Green 566). There Rankin joined the Washington state campaign for suffrage and met Minnie J. Reynolds, a journalist and former suffrage campaigner from New Jersey, who influenced her views on suffrage and pacifism and convinced her to incorporate the quest for peace into her work for the suffrage movement (Sicherman and Green 566; Anderson 103). These events facilitated a turning point in Rankin's career and forged the foundation for her life's work.

In 1911, Jeannette Rankin began a more formal phase of her political career as she urged the Montana legislature to adopt suffrage for women. On February 1, Rankin, the first woman to speak before this august body, addressed the members of the state House of Representatives. Senators, who had refused to attend as a formal body, adjourned their own session providing the unofficial opportunity for most of them to join their colleagues in the House (Josephson 27–28; Giles 45). In order to negotiate the double bind women faced when participating in the public sphere, Rankin attempted to justify women's inclusion in state, and consequently, federal, government as an issue of "fairness" while not disrupting entirely the expectations these legislators held for women in the private sphere. Continuing her testimony on behalf of the women of the country, Rankin stated:

> It is not for myself that I am making this appeal, but for the six million women who are suffering for better conditions, women who should be working amid more sanitary conditions, under better moral conditions, at equal wages with men for equal work performed. For those women and their children I ask that you support this measure. (qtd. in Giles 46)

Like many of her suffragist colleagues, Rankin argued that in all fairness women were entitled to the vote because they paid taxes, and she reminded her audience of the tyranny of taxation without representation. As she did in her subsequent speeches, Rankin employed the technique of using illustrations of women's experiences in the private sphere, which were affected by decisions made in the public sphere, to argue for women's representation in government. Understanding the pressures these male legislatures faced from their constituents as well as the constitutional issues, Rankin concluded her speech by acknowledging, "We are not asking you gentlemen to decide this great question. We are merely asking you to leave it to the voters" (qtd. in Josephson 29). In large part due to Rankin's leadership and exhaustive efforts, the citizens of Montana granted women the right to vote on November 3, 1914.

Still intent on the need for a federal amendment and surmising that a female member of the U.S. Congress could help push a national suffrage bill through the legislative process, Jeannette Rankin announced her intention to run for national office in 1916. "We reasoned," she said, "that the men would find it difficult to vote against the women in their home states when a woman was sitting with them making laws" (qtd. in Stineman 127). In her campaign, Jeannette Rankin relied on the system she had developed and the networks she had forged with women throughout the state as they worked for women's suffrage. According to Kathryn Anderson, she "perfected the infamous street corner speech" to gain access to voters male candidates could reach in more formal settings that were off limits to women (109). In 1916, Montana had two at-large House seats, which required Rankin to run a statewide campaign. She won the election by 6,354 votes despite a state Democratic landslide in the presidential election (Kaptur 25).

Disregarding a long-standing rule prohibiting comment during roll-call voting, Rankin delivered her first congressional speech, which was a mere two sentences long, on the House floor on April 6, 1917, as part of her vote against the entry of the United States into World War I. "Gripped by a fear of offending votes desperately needed to secure the passage of the suffrage amendment and by a desire to express a woman's horror of war and her principles against it" (T. Harris 116), Rankin determined to wait until the second roll call to cast her vote. Knowing she could no longer postpone her decision that was certain to raise controversy and perhaps end her political career, Rankin stood and said: "I want to stand by my country, but I cannot vote for war. I vote no" (qtd. in T. Harris 116–17). Harris argues that "in the first part of an unprecedented remark during roll call, Rankin established her patriotism; and, when she concluded, 'I cannot vote for war,' she proved her womanhood" (117). Rankin "voted against the war because she saw it as her duty to oppose hostilities," Clara Bingham notes. "If war could be stopped, then it would be women, Rankin believed, who would stop it" (Bingham 9). With this vote, Rankin began her long public career of opposition to war and violence as a means of settling disputes. Throughout her life, "she remained steadfastly committed to peace, despite personal sacrifice, public scrutiny, and criticism" (J. Cook 92).

Returning to her commitment to woman suffrage, Rankin and five other representatives cosponsored a resolution providing for federal suffrage on the opening day of the Special Session of Congress in April 1917. With the assistance of Representative John Raker, Rankin successfully argued for the creation of a thirteen-member woman suffrage committee to consider the resolution. As she was considered the authority on the issue, the Republican caucus endorsed Rankin as the ranking minority member of the committee (Chamberlin 10). Because of her recognized leadership on the issue, in the committee hearings on January 10, 1918, Jeannette Rankin opened the House debate on the woman suffrage amendment. Speaking of the hardships the country faced in the midst of war, Rankin asked: "Might it not be that a great force which has always been thinking in terms of hu-

man needs, and that always will think in terms of human needs, has not been mobilized? Is it not possible that the women of the country have something of value
to give the country at this time?" ("Floor Statement on Woman" 770). Rankin then
describes the work women have done in various facets of society, noting that
"women have done all that they were allowed to do, all that the men planned for
them to do. But," she insists, "through all their work they have pleaded for the political machinery which would enable them to do more" (770). After carefully
grounding her arguments in the illustrations of women's past and potential service
to the country, Rankin turns her attention to the specific issue at hand. "Shall our
women, our home defense, be our only fighters in the struggle for democracy who
shall be denied federal action?" she inquires (771). "How can people in other countries who are trying to grasp our plan of democracy avoid stumbling over our logic
when we deny the first steps in democracy to our women? May they not see a distinction between the government of the United States and the women of the
United States?" (771). Continuing her discussion of democracy, Rankin argues
that "in our hearts we know that desire [for equality] can be realized only when
'those who submit to authority have a voice in their own government'—whether
that government be political, industrial or social?" (771). Finally, Rankin ends her
speech with the following memorable passage:

> Can we afford to allow these men and women [the people of the nation] to doubt
> for a single instant the sincerity of our protestations of democracy? How shall we
> answer their challenge, gentlemen? How shall we explain to them the meaning of
> democracy if the same congress that voted for war to make the world safe for de-
> mocracy refuses to give this small measure of democracy to the women of our
> country? (772)

Congresswoman Rankin cast her vote in favor of the Nineteenth Amendment.
However, her term had expired when both the Senate and the House finally passed
the legislation and sent it to the states for ratification.

Redistricting in Montana effectively prevented Rankin from winning another
term in Congress, so she unsuccessfully campaigned for a seat in the U.S. Senate
in 1918. Following her defeat, she turned to nonelectoral political work and spent
much of her time lobbying Congress on behalf of women's rights and peace. In
1941, at the age of sixty, she returned to the House of Representatives and, once
again, refused to vote to send U.S. troops to war. "At the first roll call she spoke
her 'nay' in a firm, clear voice. She again violated protocol by adding, 'as a woman
I can't go to war, and I refuse to send anyone else'" (Jeansonne). Although she honored her campaign promise, illustrated by the slogan "prepare to the limit for defense, keep our men out of Europe," after her refusal to vote for war almost no
one supported her for standing by that pledge (Stineman 127).

Throughout her two terms in office and in her role as an activist citizen Rankin advocated for the common people and for women and children in particular. Rankin could "speak their language, listen to their problems, and most important, offer some hope" (T. Harris 148). By her actions in Congress she illustrated that "women were as well qualified as men to hold office and help make the laws of the land" (Josephson 101). Through her networking "from the ground up," her ability to persuade her listeners with statistical evidence gathered from thorough investigation, common-sense anecdotes, and a passion for fairness and for the issues of a democracy that truly represented all of its people, Jeannette Rankin "set in motion the political journey for women that has become a twentieth [and twenty-first] century odyssey" (Kaptur 31).

Edith Nourse Rogers (1925–1960)

With a congressional career that spanned thirty-five years, Edith Nourse Rogers served in the House of Representatives longer than any other woman in history. Elected from the Fifth District in Massachusetts in 1925, Rogers also became the first woman to chair a major congressional committee, Veterans' Affairs (Sicherman and Green 587). Early in her legislative career she focused primarily on issues affecting New England; in the thirties, forties, and fifties she honed in on foreign affairs and veterans' legislation, and rose as one of the first U.S. legislators to speak about the threat Adolph Hitler posed to the world (588–89). Ultimately, she consistently and vehemently lobbied for veterans' organizations, and most notably authored the bill to establish the Women's Army Corp and coauthored the document that later became the G.I. Bill of Rights (Schenken 584). In 1942, *Current Biography* evaluated her work stating, "Representative Edith Nourse Rogers is bringing her considerable powers increasingly to bear on the American war effort. Once again," the article continued, "with the patriotic fervor that characterized her labors during the First World War, she is championing 'preparedness' and the fullest utilization of man and woman power in order to win the Second World War" ("Rogers"). She died of a heart attack three days prior to what would have been her nineteenth primary election. A male-dominated history seems to have neglected the contributions of Edith Nourse Rogers, but her legacy lives on in her words, preserved in the *Congressional Record*, as the following discourse samples indicate. She most notably incorporates metaphor and repetition when presenting her points.

In one of her earliest speeches, Rogers advocates a significant buildup of the U.S. Navy to prevent any surprise attacks on the Panama Canal. She begins by stating a theme that is recurrent in many of her speeches, *peace through strength*, as exemplified in this quotation: "It is because I desire peace so much for our country and for all of the world that I want an adequate Navy as a part of our national defense and in order to help make world peace" (Rogers, "Does" 18). She uses a metaphor, that of police, to explain her rationale for increasing the size of the Navy fleet. "I believe much of the hysteria against the naval preparedness program is due to a lack of understanding of what an adequate Navy really is," she states. "Perhaps the time will come when the world will be so well behaved that we shall need no policemen, but we shall have them to keep law and order until that time. If a policeman at the present time is too old or is disabled," she elaborates, "he is replaced by an able-bodied man. This naval police program in large measure is one of replacements" (18).

When reading Rogers's speeches, one gets a sense of her overwhelming nationalism. From her perspective, America could do no wrong. It works to provide and preserve world peace, she argues, and never acts as aggressor. In a floor speech written to decry the splitting of Berlin into East and West segments, Rogers continues to advance this theme of *America the good, America the protector*. This theme meshes with her other premise that peace can exist only through strength. Answering possible critics of U.S. foreign policy, Rogers states in her speech, "The Berlin Crisis":

> In the entire history of human affairs, never has one nation worked so consistently and beneficially for the improvement of mankind as has the United States of America. No nation has been so liberal with its substance. No nation has contributed so much of its material and human and spiritual resources to help people in all lands. No nation has given so much of its life and leadership. No nation possesses such a record of unselfishness. No nation can challenge this record of America. It stands alone. (3789)

History does not seem to remember Rogers as a particularly significant player in U.S. politics. Yet, one must be impressed by her patriotism and her certainty, albeit perhaps naiveté, in the infallibility of U.S. foreign policy. In retrospect, she was ahead of her time in the kinds of criticisms she envisioned being launched at the United States.

Clare Boothe Luce (1943–1947)

As one of Rogers's congressional contemporaries in the 1940s, Clare Boothe Luce had one of the most distinguished careers of any woman in the public eye. Initially a writer by trade, Luce penned popular Broadway plays and later traveled to Europe as a journalist for *Life* magazine to write about World War II ("Luce, Clare Boothe," *World* 1618). She collected enough material to craft a book, *Europe in the Spring*, "in which she called for American patriotism and immediate action against

Hitler" (1618). She grew "very disillusioned with Mr. Roosevelt's foreign policy" (1618) and switched to the Republican Party when she married Henry R. Luce, then president of Time, Incorporated. Clare Boothe Luce actively entered the political arena when she worked aggressively in Wendell Wilkie's presidential campaign in 1940. In the summer of 1942, Luce successfully became the candidate for the Fourth Connecticut Congressional District, which she served until 1947. She introduced numerous bills in Congress, such as one that would "authorize the admission and naturalization of East Indians and Chinese on the same quota percentage as nationals of other countries . . . a bill to establish a bureau in the Department of Labor to insure workers equal pay for equal work . . . and a resolution 'favoring the creation of appropriate international machinery'" within the United Nations for the control and reduction of weapons, especially atomic bombs ("Luce, Clare Boothe," *Current*). When General Dwight D. Eisenhower received the Republican nomination for president, Luce actively campaigned on his behalf, delivering forty-seven radio and television speeches in support of his candidacy ("Luce, Clare Boothe," *Current*). After his election as president, Eisenhower rewarded Luce with the Ambassadorship to Italy in March 1953 ("Luce, Clare Boothe," *Current*). Upon her death in 1987, an article in the *New York Times* noted that "the complexities of her character are as numerous as the facets of her career" (qtd. in "Luce, Clare Boothe," *World* 1618).

Luce spoke often about foreign affairs and post–World War II policy. Her "maiden" speech in Congress, delivered on February 9, 1943, garnered attention for her statement that "much of what [Vice President] Mr. Wallace calls his global thinking is, no matter how you slice it, still 'globaloney.' Mr. Wallace's warp of sense and his woof of nonsense is very tricky cloth out of which to cut the pattern of a post war world" (Luce, "America" 334). Toward the end of this speech, Luce demands a clear policy governing the use of air space. Specifically, she states:

> The time has come for the administration to redefine clearly what it believes our air policy is, or should be. Then it is up to the people to decide that they approve of it, and the State Department to negotiate those policies with all United Nations countries, in a generous manner, a manner consistent with our new and grave responsibility as the world's leading air power. And above all, it is for us here to review laws and make appropriations which will implement this responsibility forcefully. ("America" 336)

In a speech she delivered to the Union League of Philadelphia slightly more than one year later, Luce outlined her idea of an effective foreign policy. "The primary objective of future U.S. Foreign Policy must be to bind a constellation of peace loving, well populated, industrialized nations together in order to discourage and forestall the rise of aggressive, industrialized power combinations either in Asia or Europe" (Luce, "The Search" 554). She concludes her speech by saying, "we may well be God's chosen nation, but it rests on us to prove it, by our wisdom in providing for the common defense, and in aiding and abetting everywhere the causes of Freedom-loving and Peace-loving nations" (554). The tenor and tone of these foreign policy speeches suggest that Luce was committed solely to working out problems in a collaborative manner. These speeches, however, belie the partisan approach she took when discussing domestic affairs. Her speech, "A Greater and Freer America," delivered to the Republican National Convention, sharply criticizes the Democratic administration and its handling of World War II. She says, in part: "The last twelve years have not been Republican years. . . . It was not a Republican president who dealt with the visibly rising menaces of Hitler and Mussolini and Hirohito. Ours was not the administration" that promised peace. "This terrible truth cannot be denied," she continues. "These promises, which were given by a Government that was elected again and again and again because it made them, lie quite dead" (587).

Edith Green (1955–1974)

Edith Starrett Green, considered "one of the most powerful women ever to serve in Congress" ("Green, Edith Starrett: Obituary" 631), represented the people of Oregon's Third District from 1955 to 1975. During these tumultuous twenty years she "became one of the country's most effective champions of educational legislation" and an advocate for women's rights (Tolchin 32). Not surprisingly, she often was called "Mrs. Education" because of her dedication and expertise in educational matters (Engelbarts 77). Green credited her political longevity for much of her influence in the House, arguing that "no woman would ever have any power in Congress were it not for the seniority system" (Tolchin 32). Despite this realistic assessment, Green's expertise in the field of education, her oratorical skills, and her diligence won her the respect of her congressional colleagues, even as a newly elected representative.

A daughter of teachers, Green embarked on a career in education because her parents and other adults persuaded her that electrical engineering and law, her first choices, were not appropriate fields for women (Kaptur 112) and that "nursing and teaching were professions where women might be allowed to make meaningful contributions" (Stineman 53). Following studies at Willamette University and Monmouth Teachers College, now Western Oregon University, as an English and education major, Green received a teaching certificate and taught in the Salem school system for eleven years (M. Rosenberg 8–9; Doherty 9). She then attended the University of Oregon where she completed a B.S. degree in 1939, and she later completed a few graduate courses in speech communication at Stanford (Doherty 9; Chamberlin 256). Green received some financial assistance from her family but also worked to put herself through school and ended her education at Willamette because her money ran out (Kaptur 112; M. Rosenberg 9). This experience influenced Green's view of financial support for education and motivated her to work for federal financial assistance for college and university students.

Edith Green exhibited her penchant for leadership at Salem High School where she held student body offices. During her junior year in 1926, she won a statewide contest and was named Oregon's Outstanding High School Girl (M. Rosenberg 8). Here Green continued her interest in debate, nurtured at home by friendly competition with her brother, Robert. She was a participant in the first cross-country debate between Salem, Oregon, and Salem, Massachusetts (Doherty 8). In 1927, Green was named valedictorian of her class and "received recognition for her scholarship, debate, and her captaincy of the tennis team" (M. Rosenberg 8). She continued her debate activities at Willamette University where, as she recalled, she spent "many hours in research, preparation and practice debates" (qtd. in Doherty 8) and at Monmouth College (M. Rosenberg 8). The skills she acquired during these years served Green well throughout her political life.

In the mid-thirties, Green began her overt political activity by making campaign radio speeches on behalf of Governor Charles H. Martin (M. Rosenberg 10). Entered in a statewide speech contest sponsored by the Democratic Committee in 1938, she "won an award for her address on 'The New Deal in the History of the Northwest.' It was altogether fitting, even prophetic," according to Marie Rosenberg, "that the award should have been named in honor of Nan Wood Honeymoon, Oregon's first Congresswoman" (10). Green's style "almost personifies her reform measures—articulate, reasonable, lucid," Hope Chamberlin suggested. "On the House floor or in the committee hearing room, her position is imposing" (Chamberlin 255). According to Yvonne Franklin, a Washington correspondent for the *Oregonian*, "Edith Green gives rousing speeches. They are the kind that keep members glued to their leather chairs in the House Chamber" (qtd. in Chamberlin 256). Her high school and college debating experience gave Green the skills to stand her ground with her male colleagues. Reporter Maxine Cheshire described Green's remarks as "a rapid-fire attack that was nevertheless delivered in a well-modulated ladylike voice" (qtd. in "Green, Edith Starrett" 227). Calling Green's skills as a floor manager "legendary," Chamberlin interpreted her style in presiding over hearings as deliberately inquisitorial ("Green, Edith Starrett" 252, 255). "The representative whose perennial campaign slogan is 'You Get Straight Answers from Edith Green,'" she argued, "expects her questions to be answered just as frankly" (255).

After she resigned from teaching in 1941, Green worked in radio broadcasting, became active in the Parent-Teachers Association, and campaigned on behalf of the State Basic School Support Bill (M. Rosenberg 13). She even returned to teaching for three years but once again retired to devote more time to the Oregon Congress of Parents and Teachers Associations. She worked for the Children's Bill Committee and helped guide the bill through the legislative session and a successful referendum campaign in 1950. Throughout the decade of the forties, Green found herself increasingly involved with the politics of Oregon education.

In 1952, Edith Green decided to stand for elective office and intended to run for the state senate. Pressured by a group of Democratic Party organizers and friends, at the last minute Green filed for secretary of state. "It was a good race," she said, "even though I lost and it became quite significant at a later date" (qtd. in M. Rosenberg 19). Although she lost the election, Green carried Multnomah County in her race against the incumbent Republican (M. Rosenberg 19). This set the stage for Green's 1954 race for the U.S. Congress from the Third Congressional District. This time she was successful. Campaigning on an education platform, she defeated the TV newscaster (later governor) Tom McCall, winning by 9,608 votes (Chamberlin 256).

Edith Green entered the halls of Congress at a historic time. In 1954 the Supreme Court declared segregation unconstitutional in its *Brown v. Board of Education* decision, and in 1958 the Soviet Union launched the satellite Sputnik, spurring a frenzy in the United States to equal and surpass science education in the USSR. These two events converged to bring education to the forefront of public discussion and legislative action. Her experiences in education propelled Edith Green to the center of many of these debates. In her first term, Green was appointed to the Committee on Education and Labor on which she served until her final term when she moved to a seat on the Appropriations Committee (Kaptur 113). She became the second ranking member of the Education and Labor Committee as well as the chair of its special Subcommittee on Post-secondary Education.

Like Jeannette Rankin's, the first bill Green introduced in the House succeeded. On January 24, 1955, she sponsored the Library Services Bill to "promote the extension of public library service in rural areas" ("Green, Edith Starrett" 226). Green argued that rural library services would mean a better-informed citizenry. Even at this early stage in her congressional career she made it clear that "the provisions of this bill shall not be so construed as to interfere with state and local initiative and responsibility in the conduct of public library services" (226). President Eisenhower signed the bill into law on June 19, 1956 (226).

On May 26, 1955, Representative Green introduced the Equal Pay for Equal Work legislation. "This bill which would require the payment of equal pay for work of comparable character requiring comparable skills," she declares, "is designed to remove a serious injustice to both men and women workers in our Nation" ("Floor Statement on Equal Pay" 7172). Should Congress adopt the bill, she suggests, "it would add another cornerstone to our structure of equal justice and would fortify the rights of all workers, regardless of sex to equal treatment" (7172). Expanding her assertion that the legislation benefits both men and women, Green contends that "there are still glaring and shocking examples of women receiving rates of pay far less than men for equivalent work. This not only lowers the standards for pay for women," she continues, "but by setting women up as unfair competitors to men, it undermines the pay standards of men, also" (7172). Introducing another argument in favor of the legislation, Green explains that "in view of the tremendous increase in the number of women in gainful employment and the great changes in industrial and commercial activities, this legislation for equal pay becomes necessary. . . . I think it is high time," she proclaims, "that women workers are treated with full and equal employment rights" (7172). Green had done her homework and knew the major criticisms with which others would attack the bill. So, employing the skills she acquired in debate, she refuted these critiques before her colleagues had an opportunity to voice them. For example, she states: "It has been said that such legislation as I have introduced is impractical because it is not possible to find an equation between work of women and men unless they are on exactly the same job. That is not true," she explains. "In personnel practices generally, methods are utilized for measuring and establishing job ratings. In one form or another they are called job-evaluation systems" (7172). Although it took eight years for Congress to enact the bill, Green counted this legislation as one of her most important career accomplishments.

In February 1956, Congresswoman Green joined other members of the House in urging President Eisenhower to "declare that he would not allocate Federal funds to any public school system defying the U.S. Supreme Court ruling prohibiting segregation" ("Green, Edith Starrett" 227). Instrumental in passing the national Defense Education Act, Congresswoman Green authored the 1963 Higher Education Facilities Act, the Green Amendments to the 1965 Vocational Rehabilitation Act, and the 1965 Higher Education Act. Green fought ferociously for educational funding; for her there was no more important issue than preparing the country's youth for the future. She introduced and advocated for legislation creating the federal work-study program and other grant programs for students. In a lecture at Harvard University in 1964, Green expresses her assumptions about the nature of education. "And we live in a world, thank goodness, where there are still many who believe that education is not the mere training of shoemakers and tanners and nuclear physicists, but is for the formation of the complete individual, his abilities fully developed and his potential made clearer and more available to him" ("Federal" 3). She unflinchingly advocated for federal support of all levels of education as indicated in the following passage:

> In discussing the role of the Federal government in education the question is not whether there should be federal assistance, both financial and nonmonetary in character. That question was decided in the affirmative during the fledgling years of our nation. The questions of importance today are what kind of assistance from the federal level there should be—where and how the federal assistance should be applied and, of course, why. ("Federal" 5)

Green maintained that "if we are to progress as a nation, we must devote more attention and additional resources to education" ("Federal" 9). Failure to do so, she argues, will be catastrophic. "Young people must be prepared not for the twentieth century but for the twenty-first century in which they will be living most of their adult lives," she argues. "And we must provide the kind of an education that will make it possible for them to find the answers to questions we cannot even imagine" (10).

Edith Green wore the liberal label when she entered Congress. However, her support for "liberal" issues was not automatic. "Because of her discriminating analyses of pending legislation and her independent voting habits, Green frustrated the Democratic party leadership and was criticized by others outside the party" (Larson 486). Yet, in the House she "command[ed] great respect because of her eloquence, her extraordinary command of information and her reputation for hard work" (Wides 26). A Republican colleague, Congressman William Steiger, remarked, "she is respected during debate, for her timing, eloquence, ability to know the mood of the House and to speak appropriately given that mood" (qtd. in Wides 26). Former Senator Mark Hatfield described Green as a "powerful congresswoman who could 'switch people's votes on the floor through the power of her intellect and her ability to persuade.' People listened to her, he said because 'when Edith Green spoke, she spoke from the heart as well as the mind'" (qtd. in Larson 486).

Patsy Mink (1965–1977 and 1990–2002)

Described as the "most prominent woman in Hawaiian politics since Queen Liliuokalani," Patsy Mink entered the U.S. House of Representatives in 1965 as the first woman of color and the first woman of Asian–Pacific Islander descent in the history of the institution ("Mink, Patsy T[akemoto]" 253; "Firsts"). She also claimed the distinction at the time as the "youngest member of the Congress representing the youngest state in the Union" (Lamson, *Few* 98). Finding herself in Washington, D.C., in the midst of the social upheavals of the 1960s, she advocated for civil rights and against the conflict in Vietnam. "What I bring to Congress," she declared, "is an Hawaiian background of tolerance and equality that can contribute a great deal to better understanding between races" (qtd. in "Mink, Patsy T[ake-moto]" 253). Mink served in the U.S. House from 1965 to 1977 and again from 1990 to 2002. Throughout the decades in which she represented the people of Hawaii, Mink remained a "champion of civil rights for women and minorities and of governmental support of educational opportunities" (United States Cong. House 171). Recalling her childhood fascination with President Franklin D. Roosevelt's "fireside chats," in an interview with the *New York Post* Patsy Mink stated: "It occurred to me that one had to find a reason for one's existence. It seemed to me that possibly the highest achievement is to find a place in life that permits one to be of service to his fellow men" (qtd. in "Mink, Patsy T[akemoto]" 254).

Born in the small sugar plantation town of Paia, on the Hawaiian island of Maui, Patsy Mink attended Maui High School where she served as president of the student body in her senior year and garnered academic honors as class vale-dictorian ("Mink, Patsy T[akemoto]" 254; Mink, "Change" 137). Her father was one of the earliest graduates of the University of Hawaii and instilled in Mink and her brother the importance of education (Mink, "Change" 137). Determined to become a physician, Mink attended the University of Hawaii in Honolulu. She spent her junior year at Wilson College in Chambersburg, Pennsylvania, and at the University of Nebraska before returning to Hawaii to complete her studies ("Mink, Patsy T[akemoto]" 254). She earned a BA degree in zoology and chemistry in 1948 from the University of Hawaii (Schenken 444). During her senior year, Mink applied to medical schools. "I must have sent away applications to at least a dozen of them," she remembered. "Every one came back with a rejection. Most said that they did not accept female students. I was absolutely dumbfounded" (Mink, "Change" 139). Friends finally convinced Mink to try other avenues, so she applied to two law schools: Columbia University and the University of Chicago, which accepted her. "This was the turning point in my life," she said. "I literally turned from defeat and disillusionment that I could not become a doctor, to an entirely new adventure—that of becoming a lawyer" (139). She graduated from the University of Chicago Law School in 1951 and returned to Hawaii to practice law. As only the second woman of Asian ancestry admitted to the Hawaii bar, Mink's "ambition was simply to be a practicing attorney—one of the best," she asserted (qtd. in Chamberlin 309). More discrimination awaited her, however. None of the law firms would hire her. Telling her to "stay home and take care of your child" (Chamberlin 309), the law firms blatantly refused to hire her because she was a woman, a wife, and a mother (Mink, "Change" 140). With no other avenues open to her, Mink opened her own law office. And, as she waited for clients, "she became involved with the community, the Democratic Party, and the drive for statehood, all of which led to seeking political office for herself" (Chamberlin 309). The experiences of having educational and professional opportunities closed to her because she was a woman forever influenced Mink's view of the world and the nature of her public service.

In addition to her law practice, Patsy Mink taught business law at the University of Hawaii from 1952 to 1956 and from 1959 to 1962 ("Mink, Patsy T[akemoto]" 254; Engelbarts 100). Mink's political career began with her involvement with the Democratic Party. She was a founder and first president of the Oahu Young Democrats and went on to become the first territorial president of the Hawaii Young Democrats. She participated in the platform committee of the 1960 Democratic National Convention, and "her influence added to the weight of the civil rights plank in the platform that year" ("Mink, Patsy T[akemoto]" 254). Elected to the Territory of Hawaii House of Representatives in 1956, the Hawaii Territorial Senate in 1958, and the Hawaii State Senate in 1962, Mink focused on improving education and labor reform, especially in areas affecting women such as equal-pay-for-equal-work legislation ("Mink, Patsy T[akemoto]" 254; Engelbarts 100). On her second attempt, she succeeded in winning a U.S. House seat in the 1964 election and in five subsequent campaigns. In May 1972, Patsy Mink entered the Oregon presidential primary. Mink cited two reasons for her run for the nation's highest office. "Without a woman contending for the Presidency, the concept of absolute equality will continue to be placed on the backburner as warmed-over lip service" and "my candidacy offers a real and tangible [political] alternative, based—if any one word can be singled out—on humanism" (qtd. in Chamberlin 313). Rather than run for a seventh term in the U.S. House in 1976, Mink turned her attention to the U.S. Senate (United States Cong. House 172). Failing to triumph in that election, she maintained an active role in local and state government and politics until she returned to the U.S. House in 1990. She continued to represent Hawaii in the House until she died from pneumonia on September 28, 2002 ("Death" A19). During her twelve terms in Congress, Mink became a leader in progressive approaches to legislation on "welfare and other anti-poverty matters, health, civil rights, education, and housing" ("Mink, Patsy T." 645). Other issues she supported included abortion rights; Title IX, legislation that she helped draft and guide through the House debates; special education programs such as student loans, bilingual education, child care, and Head Start; labor reform; and women's rights ("Mink, Patsy T." 645; United States Cong. House 172). She advocated against capital punishment and, as noted above, she opposed President Johnson's policies in Vietnam ("Mink, Patsy T." 645; Stineman 113).

Although she focused on a variety of issues during her tenure in Congress, Representative Mink always fought for civil rights and equal opportunity for everyone, especially those whose rights had been ignored for too long in this country. Her discourse reflected this agenda. She noted that as a woman in Congress, she had to "represent all the women who have no [female] representative here" (qtd. in Schultz and van Assendelft 148). Joining in a commemoration of the pioneer work of Susan B. Anthony and Jeannette Rankin, Mink states: "To Susan B. Anthony and Honorable Jeannette Rankin, we express our profound admiration and sincere appreciation; and while doing so, we use the paths they have trod to discover new avenues for expanding and achieving greater opportunities for women in all aspects of American life" (Mink, "Floor Remarks Commemorating" 4816). Praising President Johnson's 1967 Executive Order on Equal Employment Opportunity, Mink argues that "this Executive order requires employers to follow the President's own policy of choosing the most qualified person for a job—regardless of their color, religion, or sex. The day is surely not far away," she continues, "when women will share with men the full equality of citizenship and opportunity our laws promise" (Mink, "Floor Remarks: President" 29588). She endorsed the 1965 National Vocational Student Loan Insurance Act stating that the legislation would "close a gap in our educational program that has gone unnoticed too long. It would give recognition to today's 'forgotten man,' the young student of earnest endeavor who has decided upon his life's work, has determined the shortest route toward it and is willing to do everything in his power to get the education he needs for success" (Mink, "Floor Remarks on the National" 14121). After discussing the obstacles these students face "because their families cannot afford to finance their educations completely," Mink tells her colleagues that "it is indeed unfortunate that these students have been neglected for so long, and that they do not enjoy the financial opportunities open to those who wish to go to college. This bill," she contends, "would go far to correct that neglect, and would open the doors of education to many who have left school too early and now realize their mistake" (14121). Mink supported the Economic Opportunity Amendments of 1965 and in particular continued funding for Job Corps. On behalf of the legislation she declares: "I am extremely enthusiastic about this program, because it is founded on the basic notion that through education and training every individual can ultimately realize his own capacity and potential for growth" (Mink, "Floor Remarks on the Economic" 17603).

In the 1990s, Representative Mink continued her advocacy for those relegated to the margins. Speaking in support of the Family Stability and Work Act, she maintains that "what was a reform effort has now turned into a savage effort to cut away needed funds for our most vulnerable children in order to pay for the tax cuts for the wealthiest in America" (Mink, "Statement on Behalf"). She argues that "for most of this century America has stood tall as a country that helped its poor, and fed its children, and nursed its sick. . . . America is about having the greatness to offer help where needed. I rise today," she proclaims, "because I passionately reject the meanness that I see and hear. I reject that the poor are less deserving of our love and affection" ("Statement on Behalf"). In testimony before the Senate Committee on Governmental Affairs, Congresswoman Mink lashed out against the English Language Empowerment Act of 1996. "What this bill really is doing," she avers, "is to confine, to restrict the programs and opportunities for people who are not proficient in English from participating in all the fullness and richness of this society. It really degrades the whole notion of our open society, accessible to everybody legally within its borders" (Mink, "English"). Furthermore, she asserts, "if we want to empower all these individuals in our community, regardless of what their ethnic origin is or where they come from, it seems to me that we have to find ways in which to embrace them, not to leave them out" ("English"). In closing her remarks, Mink declares the act "is not an empowerment. It is denial" ("English"). Later, Mink spoke against the House version of legislation intended to proclaim English the official language of the U.S. government. In the beginning of her speech, she refutes the various claims made to support the bill. She specifically questions the argument that "this nation is threatened by 'division among linguistic lines'" (Mink, "Statement of U.S."). She complains that the bill "is touted as a way to bolster the national unity" and expresses her fear that it will create divisiveness instead ("Statement of U.S."). "The strength of our nation," she asserts, "has always been its diversity. The right of each person to seek information from their government should not be limited by restrictions on the provider. To forsake immigrants this right," Mink argues, "is to deny the very principle on which this country was built, which is free and open access to our elected officials and our government" ("Statement of U.S."). She concludes that the act's "clear message of 'English Only' is still exclusionary to those who do not speak English, implying that they are somehow less American than those who do. Whether or not it is its intention," she attests, "linguistic elitism often gives way to the social forces of resentment and intolerance, and this bill panders to the wave of anti-immigrant sentiment that has become increasingly prevalent" ("Statement of U.S.").

Described as a "liberated woman long before the movement had a name" (Chamberlin 309), Congresswoman Mink possessed the ability to identify the heart of an argument and the intellect and passion to effectively advocate or refute the claims made within it. Always polite, she brought both candor and persistence to her work on behalf of opportunity and dignity for all. Although she was small in stature, her voice still echoes loudly and clearly through the social legislation she helped mold. And, the image she painted of an inclusive nation still illuminates our journey toward that goal.

Shirley Chisholm (1969–1983)

At times, critics and supporters alike called Shirley Chisholm "headstrong, pugnacious, egotistical, expedient, power-hungry, peevish, and pushy" (Chamberlin 322). Certainly no one could deny the passion and commitment that this first black woman to serve in Congress brought to the office and all of her political endeavors. Born in Brooklyn in 1924, Chisholm lived with her grandparents in Barbados where she attended school. She received her BA from Brooklyn College in 1946 and her MA from Columbia University in 1952 (United States Cong. House 44). After working as a teacher and childcare center director, Chisholm began her political career in the New York State Assembly, serving there from 1965 to 1968 when she decided to run for the U.S. Congress. She had the distinction of becoming the second African American to be elected to this state legislative body and the first from Brooklyn (Chamberlin 327).

Using the motto "Unbought and Unbossed," she won the Democratic primary House seat in the Twelfth District. Campaigning ferociously, she went on to defeat her Republican opponent, James Farmer, in the general election by a 2.5 to 1 margin. The district Chisholm represented consisted primarily of minorities and the poor, and her concerns for her constituents are reflected clearly in the legislation on which she spent the most time and effort. "Her legislative strategy," according to Esther Stineman, "was to co-sponsor bills vital to her constituency—education for minorities, welfare bills. . . . Of necessity" she concentrated on the "problems of the chronic poor: high unemployment, inadequate housing, the lack of medical and drug treatment facilities, understaffed schools with minimal resources," and the like (Stineman 29). Chisholm's work and her votes consistently embodied "her unflagging commitment to the fiery issue of equal rights—for women, blacks, and other oppressed Americans" (30). While some representatives flood Congress with a deluge of bills, Chisholm presented only a few bills but they were of "great importance. The most necessary, on child care centers, passed congress, but Nixon axed it by his veto" (Engelbarts 107). Chisholm held little love for President Nixon, criticized him often, and increasingly voiced her opposition to his policies, "voting against 65 Nixon-issue roll calls" (106). She frequently attacked the military-industrial complex and introduced legislation to end the draft, arguing that money could be better spent on domestic programs here at home (Kaptur 151). Chisholm saw her role in Congress as pragmatic—she wanted to improve the lives of those in need. "I can use my position to help people who elected me," she states (Chisholm, *Unbought* 103). She goes on to add that she could use her office "to apply pressure to the federal machinery to try to save programs and get new ones, to secure grants for my district, and to fight discrimination" (103). As she commented, she did not see herself as a "lawmaker, an innovator in the field of legislation. America," she observes, "has the laws and resources it takes to insure justice for all its people. What it lacks is the heart, the humanity, the Christian love that it would take. It is perhaps unrealistic to hope," she muses, "that I can help give this nation any of those things, but that is what I believe that I have to try to do" (104). Chisholm served in the House of Representatives until 1983.

In 1972, Chisholm campaigned for the office of president of the United States (Kaptur 150). In the formal announcement of her candidacy, Chisholm states: "I stand before you today as a candidate for the Democratic nomination for the Presidency of the United States. I am not the candidate of black America, although I am black and proud. I am not the candidate of the women's movement of this country, although I am a woman, and I am equally proud of that. I am not the candidate of any political bosses or special interests," she concludes. "I am the candidate of the people" (Chisholm, *Good* 71). In later assessing her run for the presidency, Chisholm states: "I ran because someone had to do it first. In this country everybody is supposed to be able to run for president, but that's never been really true. I ran *because* most people think the country is not ready for a black candidate, not ready for a woman candidate. Someday. . ." (3). She also wanted her campaign to serve as a wake-up call to the country. She kept stressing "the principle that our government cannot keep on being primarily responsive to the privileged white upper classes but must serve the human needs of every citizen" (161). She felt her candidacy accomplished something important. "The next time a woman of whatever color, or a dark-skinned person of whatever sex aspires to be President, the way should be a little smoother because I helped pave it" (162). Although her quest was a long shot, she captured 151.25 delegate votes. "No other woman candidate had ever been given so many votes at a major party convention," Chisholm recalls (123). Her run for the nation's top office gained her "much favorable national exposure and won millions of admirers for her directness, dignity, and good sense" (Braden, *Representative American Speeches: 1972–1973* 79).

Both the public and her colleagues considered Representative Chisholm an "effective speaker and a skilled debater" (Thonssen 68). She easily built rapport with audiences with her forthright, blunt style of speaking (Braden, *Representative American Speeches: 1972–1973* 79), although she had a "commanding and imperious presence, holding herself like a queen with her back as straight as a ruler" (Nan Robertson qtd. in Braden, *Representative American Speeches: 1971–1972* 27). Her maiden speech in Congress, daring and clearly articulating her priorities, laid the groundwork for dozens of noteworthy addresses to follow. In these remarks, Chisholm announces that she intended to "vote No on every money bill that comes to the floor of this House and provides any funds for the Department of Defense. Any bill whatsoever," she warns, "until the time comes when our values and priorities have been turned right side up again, until the monstrous waste and the shocking profits in the defense budget have been eliminated and our country starts to use its strength, its tremendous resources, for people and peace, not for profits and war" ("It Is Time" 68–69).

Social and economic inequities provided the impetus for Chisholm's key legislation. She often detailed the problems of inequality at length and consistently argued that a fundamental shift in national priorities must take place before serious reform could occur. Specifically, she called for a decrease in defense spending and an increase in social programs. Previous failures to do so, she reasoned, resulted in serious problems for the country:

> The real price we pay is in shoddy consumer goods, rotting cities which can no longer pay their share of taxes, increased property taxes in suburban areas to pay for the declining revenue base in the older parts of cities, and collapse of school systems because tax payers revolt and say they have had enough. And the basic reason, the underlying cause, of this cycle is the fundamental lack of balance in national priorities. If the priorities were set by the people for a change, some of this imbalance would be removed. (Chisholm, "Economic Injustice" 36)

Although she claimed that she served as the representative of the people, Shirley Chisholm often focused on the plight of women, for she believed that discrimination still ran rampant in society. She championed equal pay and equal opportunities for women and supported the Equal Rights Amendment. In her blunt, forthright way, for instance, she pointed out that the workforce fostered inequality. "The factors that have narrowed our opportunities are multiple and complex," she states. "There are restrictive hiring practices. There is discrimination in promotion" (Chisholm, "Economic Justice" 188).

In a floor speech supporting the ERA, for example, she documents the inequality women face in higher education. Citing a study done by the Center of Manpower Policy in the Sociology Department at George Washington University, she points out that "it is almost unheard of for women to reach the rank of Full Professor at a major American university" ("Floor Statement on the Equal Rights Amendment" 35315). In her blunt way Chisholm states, "Let me say that I would like to point out to the gentlemen that it is not a question of whether or not we are going to snip clitoral imperialism or smash male oppression. The question is whether or not in reality we are going to accord to the women of this country equal rights" (35315).

Chisholm uses the topic of discrimination to encourage women to enter politics in order to better their world. "American women must stand and fight," she argues. "Be militant even—for rights which are ours. Not necessarily on soapboxes should we voice our sentiments," she elaborates, "but in the community and at the polls. We must demand and get day care centers, better job training, more opportunities to enter fields and professions of our choosing and stop accepting what is handed to us" (Chisholm, "Economic Justice" 192). In explaining her decision to run for the presidency, she states that she did so because she felt that "the time for tokenism and symbolic gestures is passed. Women need to plunge into the world of politics and battle it out toe to toe on the same ground as their male counterparts" (Chisholm, "Women" 80). Chisholm also recognized, however, that campaign issues had to be broad based and appeal to a wide audience. In speaking to the National Women's Political Caucus Convention in 1973, she warns, "if we are to succeed in uniting ourselves and in attracting the typical woman who is likely to be a housewife and mother who likes living in suburbia, we are going to have to make a concerted effort to articulate issues so that everyone will want to be identified with and active in the movement" (83).

Shirley Chisholm lived her life according to her own standards, truly "unbought and unbossed," a slogan she said was an expression of what she believed she was and what all candidates could be (Chisholm, *Unbought* 190). Her blunt style and clear examples connected with audiences, and the speeches she delivered throughout her life provided passionate testimony to her commitment to improving the lives of the poor and minorities, those who do not have the power to make a change. While she was cognizant that she was the first black woman to run for the presidency, and the first to serve in Congress, she offered the following: "I hope if I am remembered it will finally be for what I have done, not for what I happen to be. And I hope that my having made it, the hard way, can be some kind of inspiration, particularly to women" (12). As the Center for American Women and Politics noted on the occasion of her death in January 2005, Chisholm "never refused an opportunity to speak to and inspire other women, especially young women. . . . Whether in Congress, as a presidential candidate, or as a voice of conscience even after her retirement, she was a model of candor and courage" ("In Memoriam").

Barbara Jordan (1973–1979)

Few political events of the twentieth century can rival the Watergate Scandal for importance. Key images and discourse from that time still remain etched in the public's minds, and a congresswoman from Texas, Barbara Jordan, remains one of the most vivid figures. Her statement at the impeachment hearings of then-president Richard M. Nixon gained her much-deserved notoriety, but her training as a rhetor who could make a difference began long before her speech on a hot July day of 1974.

As the daughter of a Baptist minister in Houston, Jordan frequently memorized and recited Bible verses while growing up. In high school she decided she wanted to be "Girl of the Year" and believed that public speaking skills could help her attain that goal (Henry 233). She went on to compete in the national oratory finals of the United Ushers Association where she took first place with her speech regarding the necessity of higher education ("Jordan"). At Texas Southern University she became a champion intercollegiate debater and then later received her LLB from Boston University Law School. She returned to Houston to practice law ("Jordan"). She first became interested in a political career while working as a volunteer in John F. Kennedy's campaign in 1960 where she "helped manage a highly organized voting drive that served all forty predominantly black precincts in Houston" ("Jordan"). She ran for the state House of Representatives in 1962, lost, ran again, and lost again. In 1972, she successfully campaigned for a seat in the U.S. House of Representatives (Henry 234). Two years later she "burst onto the national stage" with her opening remarks at the House Judiciary Committee hearings on the possible impeachment of President Nixon. Her performance received positive responses from both the press and the public. "Her booming voice with her elegant articulations" (235) resonated with everyone. She had a "deep rich voice that has been likened to the imagined voice of God" ("Jordan"). Rhetorical critics have identified "key rhetorical features of her statement" such as "detailed research, the speech's compelling structure, and her confident delivery" (Henry 235). Because of her impressive performance at the Impeachment Hearings, she received countless requests for subsequent speaking appearances (236), delivering the Keynote Address at the 1976 Democratic National Convention.

The content of Jordan's impeachment address and her convention speech reveal her strong belief in the principles of a democratic nation. In the former speech, for instance, she states, "My faith in the Constitution is whole; it is complete; it is total. And I am not going to sit here and be an idle spectator to the diminution, the subversion, the destruction, of the Constitution" (Jordan, "Statement"). She invokes the words of James Madison when she intones, the "president is impeachable if he attempts to subvert the Constitution" ("Statement"). The culmination of what she had witnessed at the hearings led her to conclude, "If the impeachment provision in the Constitution of the United States will not reach the offenses charged here, then perhaps that 18th century Constitution should be abandoned to a 20th century paper shredder" ("Statement").

The uniqueness of a black woman delivering the Democratic Convention Keynote Address was not lost on Jordan. In fact, she uses her presence as the first black woman addressing the convention as evidence that "the American Dream need not forever be deferred" (Jordan, "Democratic" 225). Several statements in the first third of the speech attest to her belief in the promise America's government holds for all citizens. For instance, she states:

We believe in equality. . . . We believe that the people are the source of all governmental power. . . . We believe that the government which represents the authority of all the people, not just one interest group, but all the people, has an obligation to . . . remove obstacles emanating from race, sex, economic condition. . . . We have a positive vision of the future founded on the belief that the gap between the promise and reality of America can one day be finally closed. ("Democratic" 226–27)

Jordan's speech also reveals the importance she places on the concept of uniting, rather than dividing, people. She suggests that "a spirit of harmony will survive in America only if each of us remembers that we share a common destiny. If each of us remembers when self-interest and bitterness seem to prevail, that we share a common destiny. I have confidence," she concludes, "that we share a common destiny" ("Democratic" 228).

Geraldine Ferraro (1979–1985)
While history and the public most often remember Barbara Jordan for her impeachment speech and as the first black woman to address the Democratic National Convention, Geraldine Ferraro often receives recognition because she was the first female vice-presidential candidate on a major party ticket. Born in 1935 to Italian immigrant parents, Ferraro grew up in the Bronx and in Queens. She attended night classes at Fordham University Law School while teaching in the Queens public school system. She was admitted to the New York State Bar and later to the United States Supreme Court Bar. In 1974, she accepted a full-time job as an assistant district attorney, where she gained a reputation as a "tough prosecutor" ("Ferraro, Geraldine A."). In 1978, she successfully ran for a seat in the U.S. House of Representatives. Her "talent, willingness to work hard, and party loyalty have made her the 'favored daughter' of the democratic establishment" ("Ferraro, Geraldine A."). Speaker of the House, Thomas "Tip" O'Neill, became her friend and mentor and helped her attain key committee positions, including chairperson of the 1984 Democratic platform committee. This won her almost instant party prominence and made her a top contender for a spot as Walter "Fritz" Mondale's running mate in the 1984 election ("Ferraro, Geraldine A.").

When Ferraro gave her acceptance speech at the Democratic National Convention on July 19, 1984, the world, and Ferraro herself, knew the enormity of the situation. An editorial in the *Washington Post* said that her dual task was to be herself yet create "a whole new idea of what a woman may become in this country" ("And the Ferraro" A20). As Ferraro stated, "It was the most important speech I would ever make, and I wanted it to express my thoughts perfectly" (Ferraro and Francke 7). The address focused on themes of the *American Dream* and of *fairness*, or *playing by the rules*. She literally included something for everyone: the economically challenged, women, the working class, immigrants, the elderly, and rural and urban audiences all received some mention in her remarks. Her speaking style in this speech, and in most campaign appearances, was considered "breezy and colloquial" (V. O'Donnell 50). She "typically spoke with directness and energy . . . and did not shy away from the confrontational and antithetical. Even more consistent, however, were her arguments from definition and her movement from 'statistical' to human terms, in which she drew on the personal and anecdotal" (Blankenship 204).

One of the most touching moments in Ferraro's speech occurs when she links her past to the future of America. This implicitly invokes the notion of the *American Dream*. Ferraro states: "Tonight the daughter of a woman whose highest goal was a future for her children talks to our nation's oldest party about a future for us all. Tonight, the daughter of working Americans tells all Americans that the future is within our reach—if we are willing to reach for it" (Ferraro, "Acceptance" 729). She then explicitly suggests: "Our faith that we can shape a better future is what the American dream is all about. The promise of our country is that the rules are fair. If you work hard and play by the rules, you can earn your share of America's blessings" (729). Ferraro spends the bulk of her speech attacking the unfairness of the Reagan administration's policies, contrasts Reagan with Walter Mondale, and concludes with the following statement. "To all the children of America, I say: The generation before ours kept faith with us, and like them, we will pass on to you a stronger, most just America. Thank you" (732).

Patricia Schroeder (1973–1997)

The First Congressional District in Colorado elected Patricia Schroeder to the House of Representatives in 1972. It was the first time the state had ever sent a woman to Congress ("Schroeder"). Although few people had heard of her at the time of her election, she became nationally known and popular, both for her activism as well as her outspokenness ("Schroeder"). She is perhaps best known nationally, however, for her "exploratory run for the presidency in 1987" (Jerry and Spangle 395). One of her classic remarks in the House became legendary and served to demonstrate to all women that they, too, could be part of national government. Schroeder reports that during her first day on Capitol Hill a male colleague asked how she could be a mother of two small children and a member of Congress at the same time. She responded, "I have a brain and a uterus and I use them both" ("Schroeder"). Rather than settle for an insignificant committee assignment, Schroeder lobbied her way onto the Armed Services Committee, which controlled approximately 40 percent of the national budget. She often attacked what she viewed as excessive military spending, arguing that the United States did not need to have the capability to destroy an enemy fifteen times over when only five times would suffice ("Schroeder"). Schroeder consistently sponsored bills that focused on consumer, environmental, and welfare issues and was particularly popular with liberal organizations ("Schroeder"). She was an early supporter of legalized abortion and the criminalization of obstructing access to clinics (Robin Morgan 41).

E. Claire Jerry and Michael Spangle analyzed Congresswoman Schroeder's rhetoric for a chapter in Karlyn Kohrs Campbell's anthology, *Women Public Speakers in the United States, 1925–1993: A Bio-Critical Sourcebook.* They noted a number of attributes in the style, content, and delivery of her speech. Stylistically, Schroeder relies on analogies, metaphors, and examples to reach the audience (400–401). Jerry and Spangle found Schroeder particularly adept in her ability to "transform issues from a small arena to a national concern" (403). In tandem with that ability, Schroeder can convert issues "by framing her positions as 'real' in contrast to the 'new smoke and mirrors' of the opposition who survey society with the 'nostalgic rearview mirror'" (404). With her quick wit and fearless commitment to get things done, Schroeder is best known for her sound-bite-friendly one-liners that become big hits in the news media and popular culture. Calling President Ronald Reagan the "Teflon president" because criticism never stuck to him is perhaps her most famous line. What follows is a quick sample of Schroeder's biting statements, illustrating her ability to paint vivid pictures in the minds of the audience as well as reduce her opponents or their pet projects down to size.

In a scathing attack against the "trickle down" economic policies of the Reagan-Bush administrations, she pointed out that only the rich were benefiting, and that "the American taxpayers are being trickled on, and the man at the sprinkler is George Bush" (Schroeder, "Trickled On"). When the George Herbert Walker Bush administration attempted to use Racketeer Influenced Corrupt Organization (RICO) to clean up the savings and loan scandal, she found the effort "underwhelming. Worse, the attorney general is lobbying to gut the RICO law so that even corrupt thrift executives currently under investigation will be let off the hook. What does Bush have to say? 'Wave the flag—burn the taxpayer'" (Schroeder, "Wave" H3507). In criticizing the administration's plan to spend forty-eight billion dollars on the B-2 bomber before testing it, she called the act "flyaway robbery" (Schroeder, "Flyaway"). And finally, reminiscent of her moniker for President Reagan, Schroeder dubbed President George H. W. Bush the "Revlon President" for "the Bush presidency is all dressed up and [has] nowhere to go" (Schroeder, "The Revlon"). After leaving politics in 1996, Schroeder later became the president and CEO of the Association of American Publishers (Gold). In 1998, she released a memoir of her experiences in Congress titled *24 Years of House Work and the Place Is Still a Mess.* As of

2003, she heads New Century/New Solutions, an "outside the box think tank, for the Institute for Civil Society in Newton, Massachusetts" (Robin Morgan 41). Although she left electoral politics, she still serves to inspire young women to enter the fray. In her article, "Running for Our Lives: Electoral Politics," she asks, "Why aren't you running for public office? I'm serious" (28). She then states that women are well educated and hard working and could "grab the controls" rather than sit in the bleachers wringing their hands (28). After a lengthy discussion of her experiences in Congress, Schroeder explains ways women can be more effective in politics. For instance, women should establish voting clubs to discuss key issues and candidates (38). Women also should use resources more wisely. Rather than writing lengthy letters of complaint to a man in power, they should go to a copy shop and print "'*Did you know Senator X voted against the Civil Rights Act!?!*'—or whatever. Then mail one to Senator X" along with a note stating that five hundred of these flyers had just been mailed to his constituents (38). Finally, she suggests, the Left needs to become more media savvy and purchase some cable stations (40). Schroeder ends her call to action by posing a question to her readers: "So. Are you wringing your hands? Or rolling up your sleeves?" (40).

Women in the U.S. Senate

Rebecca Latimer Felton (11/21/22–11/22/22)

Five years after Jeannette Rankin won election to the U.S. Congress, Rebecca Latimer Felton entered the history books as the country's first woman senator. In October 1922, Georgia Governor Thomas Hardwick appointed her to fill the seat left vacant by the death of Senator Thomas Watson (M. Martin 12). Hardwick, who had voted against the Nineteenth Amendment, thought the appointment might gain him favor with the women voters. He also made it quite clear that Felton's tenure in the Senate would end before she could serve because the Congress would be in recess until after her replacement was elected (Chamberlin 19–20). In accepting the appointment, Felton, an ardent supporter of suffrage and women's rights, clearly stated the importance of the governor's action. "The biggest part of this appointment," she suggests, "lies in the recognition of women in the government of our country. It means, as far as I can see, there are now no limitations upon the ambitions of women. They can be elected or appointed to any office in the land. The word 'sex' has been obliterated entirely from the Constitution" (qtd. in Chamberlin 20). And, the spirited eighty-seven-year-old had every intention of taking her rightful seat in the Senate.

With the assistance of Senator-elect Walter F. George, who agreed that Felton would present her credentials first, and a vigorous campaign launched by the women of Georgia on her behalf, Felton was sworn in as a member of the Senate on November 21, 1922 (Chamberlin 22; M. Martin 12). During her two-day tenure, Felton did not have an opportunity to cast a vote. However, she did deliver a short speech recognizing the importance of her appointment for the women of the country. "When the women of the country come in and sit with you though there may be but a very few in the next few years," she declared to the gentlemen of the Senate, "I pledge you that you will get ability, you will get integrity of purpose, you will get exalted patriotism, and you will get unstinted usefulness" (qtd. in Chamberlin 36). Her prophetic words still serve as a rallying cry for the women who follow in her footsteps.

Hattie Wyatt Caraway (1931–1945)

"My idea of this job is to do my level best to represent the people of my State, not only in matters of legislation but in all matters where I can be of service" (Caraway, *Silent* 138–39). These words, taken from her personal journal, express the conviction with which Hattie Caraway approached her work as a member of the U.S. Senate. Given a temporary appointment to take her deceased husband's seat, Hattie Caraway took the oath of office on December 9, 1931, becoming the nation's second female senator. In January 1932, Caraway won the special election to fill the balance of Senator Thaddeus Caraway's term, which expired in March 1933 (Hartmann, "Caraway" 370; L. Young 285). Thus, she earned distinction in the historical annals as the first woman elected to the U.S. Senate. Most thought her fame and political career would end when the term expired and that she would return to her place in the home. But her tenure in the political limelight did not end in 1933. "What did happen is that a determined woman struggled through a maze of discouraging circumstances to achieve—not just be assigned— her own seat in the Senate, and performed the functions of that office with sufficient capability to survive" two full terms as a U.S. senator from the state of Arkansas (Kincaid 31).

Born on a small farm, Hattie Caraway spent most of her childhood in Hustburg, Tennessee, where her limited educational opportunities were "supplemented by listening to the political discussions around the cracker barrel in her father's store" (L. Young 284–85). She attended Ebenezer College in Hustburg and then transferred to Dickson Normal College in Tennessee where she earned a BA degree in 1896 (Hartmann, "Caraway" 369–70). Following her college graduation, she taught school before she married Thaddeus Caraway, whom she had met at Dickson, in 1902 (L. Young 285; Hartmann, "Caraway" 370). The couple settled in Jonesboro, Arkansas, where Caraway "cared for the children [three sons], tended the household and kitchen garden, and helped to oversee the family's cotton farm" (Hartmann, "Caraway" 370). After her husband's election to the U.S. House of Representatives, the family maintained a second home in Riverdale, Maryland. Caraway did take some interest in her husband's work, but retained her focus on their children and homemaking, avoiding much of Washington's social and political life (370). Even after Thaddeus Caraway won election to the U.S. Senate in 1920, she adhered closely to the theme of *a woman's place is in the home* and rarely made public or even social appearances (Tolchin 15). Hattie Caraway was not an early feminist and had avoided the public debates over suffrage. After the passage of the Nineteenth Amendment, Caraway recalled that she simply "added voting to cooking and sewing and other household duties" (qtd. in Hartmann, "Caraway" 370).

On May 9, 1932, just in time to meet the filing deadline for the August Democratic primary, Hattie Caraway stunned and dismayed her senatorial colleagues and politicians in the state of Arkansas. On the same day she became the first woman to preside over the Senate, she announced her intention to seek a full term in that august body. Her journal entry for that day contains the following reflection about her historic moment. "Made history. Presided over the Senate while Mr. Glass was speaking. It was snap judgment and I was scared. Nothing came up but oh, the autographs I signed" (Caraway, *Silent* 121). She then turns her attention to the announcement she had made. "Well, I pitched a coin and heads came three times, so because the boys wish, and because I really want to try out my own theory of a woman running for office I let my check and pledges be filed" (121). Caraway told reporters: "The time has passed when a woman should be placed in a position and kept there only while someone else is being groomed for the job" (qtd. in Hartmann, "Caraway" 370). With campaign assistance from Louisiana Senator Huey Long and support from the women voters of Arkansas, Caraway won "decisively" in what at that time was "the heaviest primary vote ever recorded in the state" (L. Young 285). With her victory in the November general election, she earned a full six-year term in the Senate, becoming not only the first woman elected to the Senate, but also the first woman elected in her own right. Caraway successfully sought reelection to a second term in 1938 but lost to Congressman J. William Fulbright in the 1944 election. President Franklin D. Roosevelt appointed the former senator to the Federal Employees' Compensation Commission in 1945, and President Harry Truman named her to the Employee's Compensation Appeals Board in 1946. She served on the board until she suffered a stroke in January 1950 (Hartmann, "Caraway" 370). She died later that year.

Although she supported much of the legislation proposed by the Democrats and the Roosevelt administration, Caraway also had an independent streak. She voted her conscience and on behalf of her constituents in Arkansas. From her husband, Caraway "inherited an interest in flood control, distrust of lobbies, and opposition to isolationism" (L. Young 285–86). Caraway helped many workers find "employment in the difficult depression years, and actively assisted many Arkansas communities in securing numerous grants and loans for assorted public works projects" (Kincaid 10). She generally supported labor and the President's New Deal legislation (Sarkela, Ross, and Lowe 181). Opposing war in principle, Caraway argued for military preparedness as the path to peace and voted for the Lend-Lease Bill of 1941 (Engelbarts 121; Sarkela, Ross, and Lowe 183). Veterans could always count on her support (United States Cong. House 42). She remained a staunch advocate for states' rights. In 1943, she became the first woman in Congress to cosponsor, and thus endorse, the Equal Rights Amendment to the Constitution (Sarkela, Ross, and Lowe 182; L. Young 286). "She introduced no major legislation but, always unobtrusively attentive to the interests of her constituents, sponsored a fair quota of public and private bills of direct concern to Arkansas" (L. Young 286). She served on the Committee for Agriculture and Forestry and the Committee on Commerce. She gained distinction as the first woman to chair a Senate committee when she was elected to head the Committee on Enrolled Bills (United States Cong. House 42). In addition to the "firsts" already mentioned, Senator Caraway was the first woman to conduct Senate hearings and the first woman to become a senior U.S. senator (Tolchin 15; Engelbarts 121). Caraway believed that "men and women legislators should not be differentiated on the basis of sex" (Sarkela, Ross, and Lowe 183) and that there was "no need to set women apart from serious consideration as qualified legislators" (L. Young 286).

Senator Caraway brought to her office a "realistic understanding of the duties of a legislator and a practical desire to test the range of her own competence" (L. Young 285). Although she was diligent in her labors for her constituents, hers was a quiet voice in the Senate. As Diane Kincaid suggests, "she was so rarely vocal on any subject . . . that silence became her trademark, and she became known as 'Silent Hattie,' or 'The Woman Who Holds Her Tongue'" (28). She made only fifteen speeches on the Senate floor during her thirteen-year tenure in Congress (Kincaid 29). When asked about her silence, Caraway once replied: "I haven't the heart to take a minute away from the men. The poor dears love it so" (qtd. in Kincaid 29). Kincaid argues that "for Sen. Caraway, silence was more than a natural tendency, reinforced by social sanctions and compounded by inexperience. It was a deliberately self-imposed shield against the ever-present possibilities of misunderstanding, criticism, and ridicule" (Kincaid 31). R. L. Duffus reported in the *New York Times Magazine* that "though she listens instead of talking, she exerts an influence in committee through her votes" (Duffus 4). When Hattie felt compelled to speak, her remarks exemplified her belief that "both women and men needed to be rational thinkers when it came to government" (Sarkela, Ross, and Lowe

183). "Her own verbal style was simple and straightforward, reinforcing her stated preference for commonsense reasoning, and the no-frills 'back-home, back-bone kind of women'" (183). And, as the following examples of her discourse illustrate, Caraway utilized a traditional mode of rational argument in her speeches as she unequivocally stated her opinion on the issues of the day.

In her radio address on the Lend-Lease Bill, Caraway speaks out about the role of women in the debate on the war in Europe and her own position as the only female senator. Caraway criticizes those who seek to defeat the bill suggesting they have succumbed to the "slimy hands of Nazi propagandists [who] have been at work" writing to the legislators ("Lend-Lease" 184–85). She states:

> I am the only woman Member of the United States Senate. Because of that fact, I have received a great many communications against the bill that would not otherwise have come to me. They urge that because of my sex I should, in support of their views, vote against this proposed legislation. I stated when I entered the Senate that I saw no reason for differentiation between men and women who serve in legislative capacities. There should be equal responsibility among them with a view toward equal service to achieve identical goals. (185)

Caraway then iterates her belief in the need for rational thinking and discussion of the issue. "Let us view this matter without emotions," she suggests. "Let there be borne by all the desire alone to have what is best for the United States" (185). In this speech Caraway also argues that peace follows from preparedness. "No bully is apt to attack one who is prepared," she contends. "I believe," she continues, "that the enactment of this bill into law will do much to prevent our being drawn into the conflict" (184). Speaking of the Selective Service Act, she affirms that "if the United States is forced into war, that measure will help protect our boys by making them better prepared" (184). For those who fear the passage of the bill will lead the nation into war, Caraway reminds the listeners that she has "as much interest in keeping this nation out of war as anyone. I have two sons already in the military service" (187). Near the end of the speech she again insists that "it is my firm belief that the pending measure, if enacted into law, will do much to keep the war from our shores" (187). Caraway closes the address drawing on her own credibility to engender goodwill among the people. "As a representative of a sovereign state, as an American mother, as one who has been a constant advocate of peace, as one who believes that humanity is at stake and that some measure must be taken to safeguard it, I will cast my vote for the lend-lease bill" (187).

Lobbying for support of legislation to provide federal aid to public education in 1943, Caraway contends that no measure that has come before the Senate during her tenure "will affect our future more than will the pending measure, which has for its purpose the proper educational training of our greatest national assets, the American youth of today and tomorrow (Caraway, "Floor Statement on Federal Aid" 8410). To reinforce her argument that this investment in education is necessary, Caraway claims "illiteracy in the United States is high in comparison with illiteracy in the countries of our two major enemies—Germany and Japan" (8411). She then presents data indicating that Germany has "no illiteracy" and that "Japan claims to have less than 1 percent" while the "percentage of illiteracy in the United States, according to the latest available figures, is 4.3 percent" (8411). She also reminds her colleagues that "the number of men in the United States who have been rejected for military service for lack of even an elementary education has been alarming" (8411). In the following passage, Caraway refutes the argument that the amount of funding called for in the bill is excessive:

> Mr. President, we have appropriated billions of dollars for war. The purpose of these appropriations was to preserve the future safety of our Nation. Certainly the amount carried in this bill is but small in comparison with the other great sums expended for that purpose. While it may be small in money, it will be great in benefits which will accrue.
>
> We have spent millions of dollars for the improvement of agricultural crops; and yet, if we do not pass this measure we will overlook the crop of greatest value to our future—our young people. (8411)

In words reminiscent of our own era, Caraway remarks that "the time may have been when it was not so necessary to have a proper education. That time is no more. . . . We must not fail to give each American boy and girl an equal opportunity to be educated" (8411). While she may not have spoken frequently, Caraway's carefully measured comments exuded commitment and an in-depth understanding of the issues.

Despite her silence, "Caraway's defiance of the Arkansas establishment in insisting that she was more than a temporary stand-in for her husband enabled her to set a valuable precedent for women in politics" (Hartmann, "Caraway" 370). Her "diligent and capable attention to Senate responsibilities," Susan Hartmann maintained, "won the respect of her colleagues, encouraged advocates of wider public roles for women, and demonstrated that political skills were not the exclusive property of men" (370).

Margaret Chase Smith (1949–1973)

One of the most active women in Congress, Margaret Chase Smith served in both the House and the Senate. Her legacy includes several firsts: "She was the first woman to serve in both chambers of Congress, the first woman to win election to the Senate in her own right and go on to serve, and the first woman to have her name placed in nomination for president at a major party convention" (Ponessa). The state of Maine elected her husband, Clyde, to Congress in 1936, and Smith accompanied him to Washington to work as his secretary. While there, a woman's club invited her to speak on "The Experiences of a Congressman's Wife in Washington" (Smith with Lewis 66). As Smith writes in her autobiography, "Though I knew my place as Clyde's wife, and though I knew it was important to Clyde to cultivate the women's vote for him, I had never been a feminist. But I was somewhat rebellious to the idea of restricting the talk to the social life of Washington, D.C." (66). Instead, Smith discussed the need for a strong U.S. Navy. When her husband died of a heart attack two years later, Smith ran to succeed him and was able to garner the support and endorsement of Guy Gannet, an influential journalist, because of her strong stand on military defense. She won the election and served eight years in Congress; in 1948, Smith was elected to the U.S. Senate, and remained there until 1973. In 1950, she drew national attention for her excoriating speech opposing Senator Joseph McCarthy and his investigations of alleged communists.

In this speech, Smith reminds her colleagues of the importance of democratic principles. She begins by indicating that these are not partisan issues. She states: "I speak as a Republican. I speak as a woman. I speak as a United States Senator. I speak as an American" (Smith with Lewis 13). She later assails the McCarthyites as "those who, by their own words and acts, ignore some of the basic principles of Americanism: The right to criticize; the right to hold unpopular beliefs; the right to protest; the right to hold independent thought" (14). She again shows that the issues cross both sides of the congressional aisle when she argues, "As an American, I am shocked at the way Republicans and Democrats alike are playing directly into the Communist design of 'confuse, divide, and conquer.' As an American," she continues, "I don't want a Democratic Administration 'Whitewash' or 'cover-up' any more than I want a Republican smear or witch hunt" (16). She finished this extraordinary speech by reading the "Declaration of Conscience" which she drafted; six other senators had signed it.

William Lewis reports that the "aftermath of the Declaration is essentially the story of Senator McCarthy's campaign of retaliation against Senator Smith" (Smith with Lewis 18). However, her speech "produced the heaviest mail Margaret Chase Smith ever received" and prompted "an 8 to 1 favorable ratio" (18). *Newsweek* wrote about her and increased speculation that she might someday run for the vice presidency. In what is perhaps revealing of the time period, Smith also received numerous accolades after the speech. "She was selected as one of the Ten Best Tailored Women of the world, the best tailored in Government. She was selected as one of the Six Best Dressed Little Women. She was offered a commission as a Lieutenant Colonel in the Air Force Reserve" (21).

Much like Cal Ripken in baseball who set a record for consecutive games played, Smith set a record for the most consecutive roll-call votes, casting 2,941 from 1955 to 1968 (Ponessa). Her commitment to participating in congressional votes, however, hurt her final campaign as she traveled less than her opponent and subsequently, lost the race. During her tenure in Congress, Smith worked tirelessly on issues such as national defense and voted for progressive ideas such as Social Security and civil rights. Her endeavors earned her respect throughout the country. Her presidential campaign provides an interesting, if often overlooked, historical footnote about her reputation. The *San Diego Union* stated that she would "have to be taken seriously" by the other candidates (qtd. in Smith with Lewis 362). Ultimately, she arrived at the Republican National Convention on July 12, 1964, with only sixteen delegates committed to her candidacy (Smith with Lewis 380). As the editor of the South Carolina paper, the *Mirror*, writes: "This distinguished woman never really had a chance to be her party's standard bearer, but the *Mirror* is glad she campaigned for the nation's highest office. It gave millions of Americans a televised glimpse of one of this country's greatest public servants" (qtd. in Smith with Lewis 390).

Margaret Chase Smith's commitment to public service illustrates the confluence and duality of the public and private spheres. In exhorting the graduating class of Westbrook Junior College in 1953 to "make the best of these years" (Smith, "Woman" 657), she implores the women to think for themselves and to protect democracy. She states: "Too few people in this country realize that too many people in this country are defaulting their thinking to demagogs [sic] and that we are closer to surrendering our freedom than most of us are willing to admit" (658). She adds that "women, just like men, have the role of voting, of thinking, of articulating—of taking a stand and expressing their beliefs" (658). However, she then continues her speech by identifying what she considers the key role for women: "The most important role of the woman in defense of Democracy is her traditional role as homemaker. . . . I wish that there were more women holding top positions in democracy," she continues (658). "But in that wish I regard the role of homemaker for women as being far more important than the role in public office. . . . Since woman is the homemaker—the keeper of the home— she is the key individual of our democracy at the grassroots level. In that respect," she elaborates, "woman is the primary and basic governor of our democracy for our governing starts right in the home" (658). Being a housewife, Smith concludes, is patriotic. "Whether you enter public service or not, there is no finer role that you can play in the defense of democracy and our American way of life than that of wife, mother, and homemaker" (659). Several times in her autobiography Smith made it clear that she never considered herself, nor did she want others to consider her, a feminist. But her speeches and her public service indicate that she at least recognized the importance of women being both seen and heard outside of the home. She certainly helped pave the path for other brave women to follow.

Maurine Neuberger (1960–1967)

One woman Smith influenced, Maurine Neuberger, secured a U.S. Senate seat from 1960 to 1967. Born in Cloverdale, Oregon, in 1907, Neuberger began her life of public service as a teacher. While teaching in Portland in 1936, she met Richard Neuberger, then a writer interested in government and politics ("Neuberger"). After he finished military duty, they were married in 1945. Neuberger became involved in politics working on her husband's state senate campaign in 1946. Although he lost in 1946, he won in 1948. Maurine Neuberger successfully ran for a seat in the Oregon House of Representatives two years later, and in 1951, they became the first husband and wife team in the country's history to serve concurrently in both houses of a state legislature ("Neuberger"). "During her two terms in the Oregon Legislature, Maurine Neuberger became known as a friend of the housewife" (Cahn 82) and focused primarily on legislation dealing with consumer and educational issues ("Neuberger"). In one of her biggest battles she attempted to repeal a milk control act that prevented stores from selling below the home delivery price (Cahn 82). Although she lost the fight in the legislature, she took the issue directly to the voters through the initiative process. They repealed the milk control law. Her most memorable "legislative coup was the repeal of a long-standing law banning the sale of colored oleomargarine" (82). Neuberger took a mixing bowl and a pound of margarine onto the House floor to demonstrate the messiness of coloring the margarine at home. "If it's legal to put artificial coloring into maraschino cherries, catchup [sic], Cheddar cheese, and even into your butter," she argues, "why should it ever have been illegal to do the same thing with margarine" (qtd. in Cahn 82). After the legislators received a deluge of letters from the public, and newspapers published stories about the stunt throughout the state, the law was repealed ("Neuberger").

Maurine Neuberger skillfully campaigned and won reelection in 1952 and 1954. After serving until 1955, she decided to go to Washington, D.C., to work with her husband who had been elected to the U.S. Senate in 1954. She operated as his unpaid political partner and research assistant. On March 9, 1960, her husband died suddenly of a cerebral hemorrhage. Neuberger had to decide quickly whether to meet the March 11 deadline to file for her own candidacy. Numerous influential people, including Senator Margaret Chase Smith, urged her to become a candidate ("Neuberger") and several thousand Oregonians signed petitions to place her name on the ballot (Cahn 81). Encouraged by the level of support, Maurine Neuberger entered the race, won the primary, and then defeated former governor Elmo Smith by 68,000 votes in the general election. She campaigned on a variety of issues, including medical aid for the elderly, federal aid to education for teachers' salaries, an improved federal housing program, a strong civil rights program, and support for the United Nations ("Neuberger"). Her husband always believed that his wife's "candor was the quality that made her so popular with the voters" (Cahn 81). The press often attributed her success to the "warm, forthright, and modest manner with which she appeals to voters. There is . . . a refreshing candor about her that seems to flow from a relaxed sureness about her own standards of political morality" ("Neuberger"). While in the U.S. Senate she sponsored legislation to make it easier for taxpayers to deduct expenses for child care, supported immigration law reform, advocated stronger controls on cigarette advertising and the printing of warning labels on cigarettes, and sponsored a bill to establish the Oregon Dunes National Seashore (Tolchin 178). After leaving the Senate, she lectured on consumer affairs and the status of women and taught American government at several prestigious universities. Maurine Neuberger died on February 22, 2000. Her arguments regarding regulation of cigarettes provide the best understanding of her rhetorical style, as the following examples illustrate.

In 1963, Neuberger authored the book, *Smoke Screen: Tobacco and the Public Welfare*. She states that the work reflected her belief that the "moral and intellectual poverty that has characterized our approach to the smoking problem must no longer be shrouded by the press-agentry [sic] of the tobacco industry, nor the fancy bureaucratic footwork of government agencies charged with responsibility for guarding the nation's health" (Neuberger, *Smoke* xiii). She published the book after more than a year of intense research, combing the reports of the surgeon general and the Royal College of Great Britain that detailed the harms of cigarette smoking. After she began advocating for warning labels on cigarettes, the *Oregonian* published an editorial criticizing her of "big brother" aspirations and worried the next step would be prohibition. Neuberger responds that nothing could be further from the truth. She argues that she operates as a champion of free choice, but the choice must be informed. "I had always believed that educating a consumer to the proved dangers of a product, then leaving him to the choice of consuming it or not, was the very antithesis of prohibition," she states (*Smoke* 116). She links her research, and her book, to the idea of public policy. As she states in the conclusion:

> Since I am not a doctor I can't justify this book as an authoritative treatise on the medical aspects of smoking (which it is most assuredly not), nor can I claim any special insight into the economic, sociological, or even historical aspects of the smoking phenomenon. But I am a legislator, and I do make a modest claim to be at home with questions of government responsibility. And, since this book

culminates a year-long period of relatively intense study and contemplation of the smoking problem, I hope that my conclusions would be of some use to those who are called upon to chart the course of national policy with respect to smoking; namely the Surgeon General's Committee on Smoking. (*Smoke* 119)

The next year, in a floor speech, Neuberger cites the Surgeon General's Report on Smoking as a "massive, unequivocal, and unimpeachable scientific indictment of smoking" (Neuberger, "Cigarette" 512). She then proposes the Cigarette Advertising and Labeling Act that required, among other provisions, a warning label on cigarette packages. Unlike many of the early suffragists, Neuberger was fortunate to see her legislative proposals enacted. Because of her steadfast commitment to consumer affairs, the tobacco industry now meets significant regulatory standards.

Nancy Landon Kassebaum (1978–1997)

Following Maurine Neuberger's departure, voters in the states did not elect a woman to a full term in the Senate until the end of the seventies. When the state of Kansas elected Nancy Landon Kassebaum to the U.S. Senate in 1978, she became the first woman to reach the chamber on her own, without first serving as the widow of or replacement for an ailing husband ("Kassebaum" 191). Born in 1932, to Alfred Landon, a former presidential candidate, and his second wife, Theo, Nancy grew up as a typical teenager in the Midwest with few aspirations outside the home. She attended the University of Kansas where she majored in political science. It was there she met her husband, Philip Kassebaum. She pursued a master's degree in diplomatic history at the University of Michigan, writing her thesis on the division of Poland at the Yalta Conference ("Nancy" 198). Kassebaum recalls that she "enjoyed politics and public policy so much that there were times in high school and college when I mused about becoming actively involved as a candidate. But it was a daydream. A fantasy" (qtd. in "Kassebaum" 191).

As her marriage began to disintegrate in the 1970s, Nancy Landon Kassebaum's actions turned that daydream into a reality. After she received a legal separation from her husband, she accepted a job as a caseworker for Kansas Senator James B. Pearson ("Kassebaum" 191). When Pearson chose not to seek reelection in 1978, Kassebaum considered running for the vacant seat. "I believed that I could contribute something, that I had something to offer," she recalls. "But I would not have gone through with it if I had not thought I had at least a credible chance of winning" (qtd. in "Kassebaum" 191–92). Her only previous electoral experience was as a member of the Maize, Kansas, school board.

Kassebaum swept through the primaries and easily won the general election ("Nancy" 198). Her slogan, "A Fresh Face: A Trusted Name," resonated with a state whose citizens fondly remembered her father. As she once stated, "It has been said I am riding on the coattails of my dad, but I can't think of any better coattails to ride on" (qtd. in "Nancy" 198). Her personal wealth also aided her campaign, as she contributed more than one hundred thousand dollars to it. Because of her lack of direct political experience, "there was widespread expectation in Washington that she would be a political lightweight" (Richter 77). She proved to be quite capable, however, and served on a number of prestigious committees, including the Banking, Housing, and Urban Affairs Committee, the Budget Committee, the Commerce, Science, and Transportation Committee, and the Special Committee on Aging. She later served on the Foreign Relations Committee and chaired the African subcommittee of the Foreign Affairs body.

As a Republican, Nancy Kassebaum was generally conservative, but not rigidly so. She "defies pigeonholing. In general, she's conservative fiscally, liberal on some domestic social issues, conservative on others, a frugal internationalist, a moderate feminist, and a careful student of her constituents' interests" (Richter 83). She has called for a "mature foreign policy . . . one that is hospitable to the combination of principles with pragmatism, one willing to live with contradictions, to play an active role without excessive costs, to pursue arms control without any illusions about détente" (qtd. in "Kassebaum" 193). She took a moderate stance on "women's issues," urging passage of the Equal Rights Amendment and supporting abortion rights. "She chose to define women's issues broadly, as major public issues of fairness, equity, the economy, and national security" (Richter 86). One issue that separated Kassebaum from feminists was the draft: Kassebaum fought for female draft registration, for she believed that "each sex is legally equal in all obligations of citizenship" (87). Her approach to foreign and domestic policy reflects her pragmatism, as the following excerpts from two of her speeches illustrate. In a floor speech decrying U.S. policy toward Africa, for instance, she states:

> Earlier this summer, President Moi ordered the imprisonment of dozens of prominent lawyers and human rights activists, including Gitobu Imanyara, editor of the now banned *Nairobi Law Monthly*, and two former Cabinet ministers who had spoken out for democracy, Charles Rubia and Kenneth Matiba. Mr. Rubia and Mr. Matiba remain in jail, held without charge. As human rights conditions deteriorate, the United States government continues to supply Kenya with nearly $50 million in aid. . . . Mr. President, I believe that the situation in Kenya has reached the point where we must send a clear and firm message to the Government in Nairobi that we will not tolerate the continued suppression of basic human rights and civil liberties. In order to convey our strong disapproval of the current policies, I support the cessation of all military aid and economic support funds to Kenya until the human rights situation improves. (Kassebaum, "Deteriorating")

Kassebaum's speech to Kansas State University in 1996 reveals similar passion, clarity, and pragmatism. She has a keen sense of what she believes the role of government should be. Government should be effective, not intrusive. "Half a century of growing federal power and rising national debt cannot be reversed in a single Congress not even, perhaps, in a single decade," she reports. "But I am confident those trends will be reversed over time because the demand for that change does not flow only from Congress and the Republican party," she continues, "but from the most basic power of our democracy—our citizens" (Kassebaum, "The Intersection"). In discussing the need for balancing social programs with fiscal responsibility, Kassebaum intones, "the voters are not demanding that we abandon families in poverty, cut off health care to the needy, or turn our backs on the elderly and the disadvantaged. To the contrary," she explains, "most people are distraught not because we are doing these things, but because we are doing them poorly. What people are demanding," Kassebaum concludes, "is a more effective approach that produces real results" ("The Intersection"). Nancy Landon Kassebaum spent eighteen years in the Senate pursing that ideal.

Carol Moseley-Braun (1993–1999)

"Each person makes a difference in shaping the climate of opinion from which policy will emerge. Each of us has a role to play in directing the course our country will take. Our challenge is to reach outside of our private lives to shape our community" (Moseley-Braun, "Standing" 108). Carol Moseley-Braun, the first African American woman elected to the U.S. Senate, the first female senator from Illinois, and the first African American Democratic senator, has dedicated her public career to molding more harmonious and inclusive communities (Moseley-Braun, "About Carol"). After her swearing-in ceremony, the senator from Illinois acknowledged the historical moment as well as her desire to "be more than a symbol. I am—by definition—a different kind of senator. I am an African-American, a woman, a product of the working class," she admits. "I cannot escape the fact that I come to the Senate as a symbol of hope and change. Nor would I want to, because my presence in and of itself will change the U.S. Senate" (qtd. in "Moseley-Braun"). Carol Moseley-Braun's words have proven prophetic.

Born into a middle-class Chicago family in 1947, Moseley-Braun has recognized her parents' influence on her personal and political life. Her father, a police officer and "a consummate renaissance man, a musician who mastered seven instruments and spoke several languages," and her mother, a medical technician, "encouraged their children to pursue excellence, embrace opportunity and follow their dreams" (Moseley-Braun, "About Carol"). After her parents divorced in 1963, Moseley-Braun, her mother, and her brother and sister lived with her grandmother in a "Chicago neighborhood, known as Bucket of Blood, that was marked by its 'crushing poverty'" ("Moseley-Braun"). This experience of living in an environment "among 'people who are really trapped and don't have options'" strengthened her commitment, "instilled in her by her parents, to try to improve society" ("Moseley-Braun"). Moseley-Braun recalled that her "parents were always philosophizing about how to bring about change. To me, people who didn't try to make the world a better place were strange" (qtd. in "Moseley-Braun").

Carol Moseley-Braun attended Chicago's public schools. Her realization of the intersection of the public and private spheres emerged during her high school years. For example, "she staged a one-woman sit-in at a restaurant," which refused to serve her because of her race ("Moseley-Braun"). Visiting a beach that had been declared "for whites-only" she endured the insult of having stones hurled at her ("Moseley-Braun"). Moseley-Braun graduated from the University of Illinois-Chicago with a bachelor of arts degree in political science ("Moseley-Braun"; Moseley-Braun, "About Carol"). As a university student she "marched with the Reverend Martin Luther King, Jr., in a Chicago civil rights demonstration" and, during 1968, worked on one of Harold Washington's campaigns for reelection to the state legislature ("Moseley-Braun"). Moseley-Braun earned a law degree from the University of Chicago Law School in 1972 (Moseley-Braun, "About Carol"). While in law school she met her future husband, Michael Braun (Gill 150). In 1973, she joined the Chicago United States Attorney's office as an assistant attorney. Focusing on civil and appellate law, "her work in housing, health policy, and environmental law won her the [U.S.] Attorney General's Special Achievement award" (Moseley-Braun, "About Carol"). She left this position in 1977 to begin a family.

Even as a stay-at-home mom, Moseley-Braun maintained her interest in public issues, concentrating her activism on local environmental matters, especially the fight to preserve one of Chicago's few bobolink habitats (Moseley-Braun, "About Carol"; Marks, "Quest"). Her neighbors observed Moseley-Braun's energetic commitment to the issues and many of them urged her to run for public office. Inspired by her supporters, Moseley-Braun ignored the voices urging her not to enter the 1978 race for a seat in the state House of Representatives. She remembered the advice offered by some of those opposed to her campaign. "They said, 'You can't possibly win, the blacks won't vote for you because you're not part of the Chicago machine, the whites won't vote for you because you're black and nobody's going to vote for you because you're a woman.' So I said, 'OK, where do I sign up for this job?' That tipped my scale and I put my hat in the ring and won" (Moseley-Braun qtd. in Marks, "Quest"). During Moseley-Braun's decade-long tenure in the state legislature, reporters Frank James and Hugh Dellios of the *Chicago Tribune* suggested, she transformed herself "from political ingénue to veteran Cook County politician, one who knows how the power game is played" (qtd. in "Moseley-Braun"). Representing a diverse district, Moseley-Braun championed education, civil rights, and governmental reform (Moseley-Braun, "About Carol"). More specifically, she advocated universal health care, welfare reform, gun control, and programs for minorities and women. She sponsored a bill prohibiting the state from "investing in funds in South Africa until apartheid was abolished" and introduced legislation to "ban discrimination in housing and private clubs" (Gill 150). In 1983, Chicago Mayor Harold Washington selected her as the "city's floor leader in the legislature, a position that required her to spearhead legislation that supported the city's housing, education, budget, and other municipal needs" (150). Moseley-Braun's colleagues elected her assistant majority leader of the Illinois House, the first African American and the first woman to serve in that capacity (150). For her leadership in the state House, during each of the ten years she served, Carol Moseley-Braun won the "Best Legislator" award from the Independent Voters of Illinois-Independent Precinct Organization and her colleagues recognized her as "the conscience of the House" (Gill 150; Moseley-Braun, "About Carol").

Following her departure from the state legislature, Carol Moseley-Braun won a bid for recorder of deeds for Cook County. With this triumph she entered the state's history books as the first African American and the first woman elected to an executive office in the Cook County government (Moseley-Braun, "Standing"). The position had its challenges. Inheriting an office described as "in a state of considerable disarray," Moseley-Braun sought the advice of a panel of experts and implemented many of their suggestions ("Moseley-Braun"). By the end of her term, "the deed recording system had been modernized, an ethics code had been established, and the lowest pay grades . . . had been eliminated" ("Moseley-Braun").

In the fall of 1991, dismayed by the Clarence Thomas confirmation hearings and looking for new challenges, Carol Moseley-Braun announced her intention to unseat incumbent U.S. Senator Alan J. Dixon in the 1992 election. Listening to the senators interrogate Anita Hill convinced Moseley-Braun that the Senate "absolutely needed a healthy dose of democracy, that it wasn't enough to have millionaire white males over the age of fifty representing all the people in this country" (qtd. in "Moseley-Braun"). Despite a campaign that featured "no money, no organization and no political backing," she triumphed in the Democratic primary, defeating her two opponents with 38 percent of the vote ("Moseley-Braun"; Gill 152). This win characterized Moseley-Braun as a "national celebrity and a symbol" of the Year of the Woman ("Moseley-Braun"). The impetus from the primary win catapulted Moseley-Braun to victory over her opponent, prominent Illinois businessman Richard Williamson, in the general election despite "campaign mishaps and a serious scandal involving a reimbursement owed to the state Medicaid program" (Gill 152). The electorate endorsed Moseley-Braun with 53 percent of their ballots, including 95 percent of the votes from African Americans, almost 50 percent from whites, and 58 percent from women ("Moseley-Braun"). Following the election, Moseley-Braun noted that her success said "clearly to the country that the time for coming together is at hand. We're going to start writing a new chapter in our politics, a new chapter in our history" (qtd. in "Moseley-Braun").

Following her swearing-in on January 3, 1993, Senator Carol Moseley-Braun joined Senator Dianne Feinstein on the Judiciary Committee. The irony was not lost on those who had shared Moseley-Braun's dismay over the treatment of Anita Hill by the all-male Judiciary Committee. During her one term in the Senate, she also served on the Banking, Housing, and Urban Affairs Committee, the Special Committee on Aging, as well as the Finance Committee, where she became the first woman listed as a permanent member (Gill 148; Neuman, *True* 100). According to her 2004 presidential campaign web site, Senator Moseley-Braun's legislative work was far ranging. She led the debate on the "nation's crumbling schools"; advocated for the brownfields tax law to bolster environmental remediation; endorsed tax policies that assisted widows, students, and the poor; supported laws to enact a balanced budget amendment; and offered a "consistent and strong voice for equal opportunity, the prevention of discrimination on the basis of race, gender, or sexual orientation, reproductive freedom, and social and economic justice" (Moseley-Braun, "About Carol"). In the summer of 1993, Senator Moseley-Braun "captivated the nation with a rare show of political passion and courage. With tenacity and persuasive oratorical skills, she moved the Senate beyond ordinary debate . . . when she launched a filibuster over the passage of the United Daughters of the Confederacy (UDC) amendment to the National Service Bill" (Gill 152). According to LaVerne Gill, this event "introduced Senator Carol Moseley-Braun to the nation and introduced the Senate to the meaning of diversity" (152).

Senator Moseley-Braun sought reelection for a second term in 1998. From the beginning of the race, charges of ethical violations, mismanagement, misuse of campaign funds, and poor judgment plagued her campaign. She lost the election by two percentage points to a wealthy and conservative Republican who hired Karl Rove to lead his attack against the senator (Marks, "Quest"). The Federal Election Commission, the Internal Revenue Service, and other agencies involved in the probe of Moseley-Braun's actions eventually cleared her of all allegations. In spite of that, the ghosts of the complaints still haunt her, as evidenced by their resurrection in the 2004 presidential primary campaign. "To this day . . . she carries an inch-thick dossier, one that she says outlines and discounts each charge" (Marks,

"Quest"). Following her defeat, President Clinton appointed her to the Department of Education as a special consultant on school construction ("Moseley-Braun"). In 1999, the president nominated Moseley-Braun to serve as the U.S. Ambassador to New Zealand and Samoa. Despite Senator Jesse Helms's efforts to revisit the former charges of wrongdoing on her part, she won confirmation by a ninety-eight to two vote of the full Senate (Marks, "Quest"). Upon the completion of her ambassadorial assignment, Carol Moseley-Braun returned to Alabama to "rehabilitate and rescue her family farm" (Moseley-Braun, "About Carol"). During that time, she started her business consultancy, began a business law practice, and began to teach political science (Moseley-Braun, "About Carol"; "A Return"). In 2003, Moseley-Braun once again entered the political fray as a contender in the Democratic presidential primary. She withdrew from the race in January 2004 and returned, once again, to life outside the public limelight.

Described as an "orator in the tradition of America's major debaters" (Gill 162), Carol Moseley-Braun proved early in her political career that she was a speaker "capable of winning battles against opponents and colleagues without alienating them" (James and Dellios qtd. in "Moseley-Braun"). In her maiden speech on the floor of the Senate chamber, Moseley-Braun paid tribute to Supreme Court Justice Thurgood Marshall and in so doing gently put her colleagues on notice that she intended to pursue issues of equality in her senatorial work. Speaking of Marshall's death, Moseley-Braun laments that it is "nonetheless hard to conceive that a heart as mighty and as courageous as his is no longer beating" ("Tribute" 124). "Thurgood Marshall," she proclaims, "epitomized the best in America; he was, in fact, what this country is all about" (124). She then details some of the discrimination Marshall faced in his lifetime. "After all," she contends, "he himself was very aware of the fact that the United States did not, and in too many instances still does not, live up entirely to its founding principles. . . . He knew," she insists, "that racial inequality was incompatible with American ideals, and he made it his life's unending fight to see that this country's ideals became true for all of its citizens" (125). Senator Moseley-Braun then highlights the work Marshall accomplished. He "played a key role in creating a rebellion in America, a rebellion not of violence, but of law. What Marshall did," she argues, "was to use the U.S. legal system to bludgeon and destroy state-supported segregation" (125). Summarizing his accomplishments, she attests that "he was a man who worked and fought to make a difference; he was a man who did make a difference. . . . His life was the most convincing evidence that change is possible" (126). Near the end of the speech, Moseley-Braun challenges her colleagues to keep Marshall's spirit alive by continuing his efforts on behalf of equality. "I share his view," she begins. "Elimination of racism is not just an interest of African-Americans, but of all Americans. Only then will we be able to tap the full potential of our people. Only then will we live the greatness of the American promise. . . . I hope we will all remember Marshall," she implores, "by dedicating ourselves to the principles and goals he dedicated himself to: making American opportunity available to every American" (126–27). In the concluding statement of her remarks, Moseley-Braun identifies the agenda she plans to pursue during her tenure in the Senate. "I am proud," she declares, "to have the opportunity, in some small way, to continue his work, and to try to build on his legacy" (127).

In July 1993, Moseley-Braun cemented her reputation as a champion of minorities, particularly African Americans. Earlier in the year, the Judiciary Committee had voted thirteen to two to deny the United Daughters of the Confederacy the right to continue placing the Senate seal on its logo, which contained the Confederate flag. On the day in question, Moseley-Braun, who was attending a confirmation hearing, learned that Senator Helms had "attached an amendment to President Clinton's service bill that would renew the logo's patent" (Peterson 88). Furious, she returned to the Senate chamber to speak against the amendment. "I submit to the body," she states, "that the Judiciary Committee . . . recognized how singularly inappropriate it would be to renew the patent for the United Daughters of the Confederacy and it is singularly inappropriate for this amendment to be accepted" (Moseley-Braun, "Getting Beyond" 94). With no small degree of emotion, Moseley-Braun declared: "I have to tell you this vote is about race. It is about racial symbolism. It is about racial symbols, the racial past, and the single most painful episode in American history" (94–95). After reiterating that the symbol in question was indeed the Confederate flag and elaborating on its meaning, she argues that "the issue is whether or not Americans, such as myself, who believe in the promise of this country, who feel strongly and who are patriots in this country, will have to suffer the indignity of being reminded time and time again, that at one point in this country's history we were human chattel. We were property. We could be traded, bought, and sold" (96). Near the end of her remarks, Moseley-Braun proclaims: "If I have to stand here until this room freezes over, Madam President, I am going to do so. Because I will tell you, this is something that has no place in our modern times. It has no place in this body. It has no place in the Senate. It has no place in our society" (98). She closes the speech stating that "the fact of the matter is that there are those who would keep us slipping back into the darkness of vision, into the snake pit of racial hatred, of racial antagonism and of support for symbols—symbols of the struggle to keep African Americans, Americans of African descent, in bondage (99). This debate, according to Gill, "resonated as a historic reminder of the new rules of engagement brought about by the cultural, racial, and gender symbolism stemming from Carol Moseley-Braun's rhetoric on the Senate floor" (163).

Women Governors

Nellie Tayloe Ross (1925–1927)

Five years after the ratification of the Nineteenth Amendment, the citizens of the state of Wyoming welcomed their first woman to the governorship. Nellie Tayloe Ross became the first woman in the country's history to serve as the governor of a state. In her personal memoir of Ross, Julia Freeborn suggested that it was "fitting indeed that Wyoming, the first state in the Union to grant the ballot to women, should be the first commonwealth to choose a woman as its Chief Executive" (1). Ross's husband, Governor William B. Ross, died in office, just twenty-one months after his inauguration. This event set the stage for Nellie Tayloe Ross's election to fill the remainder of her husband's term. Freeborn briefly described the circumstances of her election:

> Almost immediately [after William Ross's death] friends approached Mrs. Ross with the suggestion that she allow her name to be presented to the voters of Wyoming as a candidate to fill out her husband's unexpired term, since, under the statutes of the state, it would be necessary to select his successor at an early special election. At first this proposal seemed to her impossible of acceptance, but, gradually out of her sorrow, there came the desire to carry out his program and plans, with which she was so familiar. And so, out of the strength that sometimes comes through grief and bereavement, came the opportunity for a woman to enter and [sic] untried political field, in a country where women's ability is highly thought of and readily acknowledged. The large majority given Mrs. Ross at the polls showed the confidence the electorate was willing to place in a woman's fitness to occupy this high post. (1–2)

Following her election, Ross became a "recognized political figure" and "received considerable attention from her contemporaries" (Pierce 31).

Born near St. Joseph, Missouri, Nellie Tayloe Ross attended both public and private schools in Missouri and Kansas. She enrolled in a kindergarten teacher's training school in Omaha, Nebraska, from which she received her teaching credentials in the late 1890s (Murdock 918–19; Dubois and Brown). Following graduation, Ross taught school in Omaha for two years. During this time, she met William Bradford Ross on a trip to Tennessee. The couple married in 1902 and moved to Cheyenne, Wyoming, where William Ross established a law practice (Murdock 919; Dubois and Brown). In her autobiography, Ross "portrayed herself as an intellectual partner to her husband and the successor to his political goals" (Pierce 38). As William Ross established himself as a political leader in the state, Nellie Ross increasingly functioned as his political confidant, sometimes assisting with his professional duties, including speech writing (38). This relationship continued when William Ross assumed the governorship. Ross "recounted having discussed his 'problems and plans' for the state and helping him write speeches under deadline pressure" (39). Ross explained to the readers of her autobiography that "her husband was like a mentor to her and that her assistance to him served her interests as well as his" (39). She also noted that the couple's habit of reading the classics out loud contributed to her ability to speak from the public platform (39).

In her inaugural address on January 5, 1925, Ross paid tribute to her husband and stated that her purpose was to continue the programs and policies he had established and envisioned (Murdock 919). Ten days later, in her message to the legislature, she indicated that the preparation of the address had "been facilitated not alone by such knowledge of the state's problems as I had the privilege of gaining during the past two years from association with the Governor, my husband, but also by the extensive notes which he had already assembled and designated to be embodied in his message to you" (N. Ross, "Message" 26). The legislators adopted many of the issues she presented to them in this address and throughout her term, including the enactment of bills promoting coal mine safety regulations, child labor laws, new banking codes, tax fairness, and relief for farmers. They did not support her legislation to strengthen Prohibition (Murdock 919; Dubois and Brown). T. A. Larson, a renowned Wyoming historian, argued that "Mrs. Ross proved to be a good governor who gave the state a respectable, dignified, and economical administration" (qtd. in Murdock 919).

In 1926, the Wyoming Democratic Party nominated Ross for a second term. With only 1,365 votes separating them, she narrowly lost the race to Republican Frank Emerson, the state engineer (Murdock 919; "Gubernatorial Vote"). Political observers at the time concluded that although the "issue of the appropriateness of a woman as governor was raised during this election," it was not a determining factor in the outcome. Rather, they argued Ross "lost the election less because of her gender than because of the dominance of the Republican party in the state and concerns about the state's economic stagnation" (Murdock 919).

Nellie Tayloe Ross's work in the political arena did not end with the expiration of her gubernatorial duties. In 1926, while she was still governor, the Wyoming Democratic convention endorsed her as a vice-presidential candidate for Al Smith; on the first ballot at the national convention, she received twenty-five votes (919). A popular lecturer on the Chautauqua circuit, Ross traveled the country speaking about her experiences as a woman governor and the need for women to participate actively in the political process. She served as a vice chairman of the Democratic National Committee and headed the national Democratic Party's women's activities from 1929 to 1932 (919). She supported the candidacy of Franklin D. Roosevelt for president and directed the campaign for the women's vote on his behalf (Dubois and Brown). In 1933, President Roosevelt appointed Ross director of the U.S. Mint. As a result of this position, she became the first woman in the United States to have her likeness imprinted on a Mint metal and on the cornerstone of a government building (Dubois and Brown). One of the first women appointed to such a high post, Ross served four successive five-year terms directing the Mint from the Great Depression through World War II and into the postwar period (Murdock 919). She oversaw the automation of the Mint's production process and reduced operation expenses ("Nellie"). After her retirement in 1952, Ross lived in Washington, D.C. She died there in 1977, at the age of 101 (Murdock 919).

During her term as governor, Ross understood the uniqueness of her position and the responsibility she shouldered to provide a positive role model to "vindicate the fitness of women to hold high executive office" (N. Ross qtd. in Murdock 919). Although she believed women should maintain their roles as wives and mothers, she also advocated for women's greater participation in the political arena as informed voters and officeholders. These themes found expression in many of her speeches as illustrated in the following examples. Speaking to the Woman's Democratic Club of Kentucky in the early 1930s, Ross contends: "It is a significant fact that the extension of full suffrage to women and the exercise of that privilege by them has come at the very time when the principles of representative government are being undermined both at home and abroad. It is of the highest importance, therefore," she insists, "that the women of America who desire to participate to the full in the affairs of government should first acquire a complete understanding of the meaning of the American form of government" (N. Ross, "Women" 1). Ross bemoans the fact that it is difficult to find both men and women willing to endure the "political vituperation which seems to be the common lot of every person who aspires to public office of an elective character" (8). She argues that "well qualified patriotic women could render invaluable services to their communities by developing a mind for public affairs and allowing themselves to be nominated for positions in the State legislatures, in city councils and in Congress" (9). Ross offers the following comments about the women serving in the U.S. House of Representatives:

> It is a sign of political development and, I think of continued improvement of our public standards that there are today in the National House of Representatives more women members than ever before. The seven women who occupy seats in congress will, I am confident, render an excellent account of themselves by studious attention [to] the responsibilities which are placed upon them. If for no other reason than that they recognize the fact that all other women will be judged by their failures and success, they will give the best that is in them. (9)

Governor Ross delivered an address at the National Women's Democratic Club Dinner in Washington, D.C., on March 7, 1925, in celebration of the organization's first anniversary. Although she allocates much of the speech to praises of the Democratic Party, she does offer observations on the meaning of women's suffrage for women and for the country. She states:

> Universal suffrage marks a new era in the history of the women of America and opens to them the door of unbounded possibilities of service. Now that she has the ballot, what use is she to make of it? If universal suffrage is to mean only an increased number of votes divided along certain party lines, directed by masculine opinion—rendering more duplication in fact, it will not result in any definite service to the country. If this were to be the end and aim of woman's suffrage, we might very well have allowed the old order to continue. The truth is this change has brought to woman not only vastly increased opportunities, but a corresponding measure of responsibility to exercise her influence and to employ her ballot in such a spirit of consecrated service as to place the politics of the Nation on a higher plane than has heretofore been known. (N. Ross, "Address" 3)

As she urges women to take an informed and active role in the public sphere, she also admonishes them to make a difference by bringing their unique perspectives to the table. "Now that she has for the first time been admitted to a seat at the council table, it is not only vital," she attests, "but highly consistent that her voice shall be the voice of humanity. In effect," she continues, "she must speak a new language in politics." ("Address" 3–4). Assuredly, the words of Nellie Tayloe Ross echo in the rhetorical in-between space of the twenty-first century.

Ella Grasso (1975–1980)

Elected to lead Connecticut's state government in 1975, Ella Tambussi Grasso earned her place in the historical annals as the state's first woman governor and its first head of state of Italian heritage. She also became the first woman in the nation to occupy a state's highest position without the benefit of succeeding her husband. A popular and effective politician who never lost an election in twenty-eight years in public service (Schultz and van Assendelft 98), Grasso believed that "public service—working for the people—is the noblest profession" (Chamberlin 340). Always proud of her working-class heritage, she devoted her entire adult life to the embodiment of that belief. "I realized early on," she commented, "that if I was concerned with problems, the best way of getting them solved was to be part of the decision-making process" ("Grasso" 1975 174).

A daughter of Italian immigrants, Ella Grasso entered the world in Windsor Locks, Connecticut, in 1919, one year before women in the United States earned the rights of full citizenship with the ratification of the Nineteenth Amendment to the Constitution. Her parents valued education and managed for their daughter to attend private schools in Windsor Locks and Windsor ("Ella"). An excellent student, Grasso received scholarships to Mount Holyoke College, where she won election to Phi Beta Kappa in her junior year and graduated *magna cum laude* in 1940 with a BA degree in sociology and economics ("Grasso" 1975 173). In 1942, she earned a master's degree, again in sociology and economics, from Mount Holyoke ("Ella"). Later in 1942, Grasso returned to Windsor Locks to marry Thomas Grasso, a teacher whom she had known for most of her life (Lamson, *Few* 216). Grasso's educational experiences convinced her to enter public service ("Ella"). She also indicated that the League of Women Voters played a major part in preparing her for a role in public life. "I can't imagine a better apprenticeship," she said. "The League is a perfect training ground. It teaches you to understand issues, to formulate programs, and to learn legislative procedures" (qtd. in Lamson, *Few* 216). During World War II, Grasso served with the Federal War Manpower Commission in Connecticut as the assistant director of research ("Grasso" 1975 173). She left that position in 1946 and worked actively on campaigns for the state Democratic Party until she entered public office.

Ella Grasso began her foray into electoral politics in 1952, when she won election to the House of Representatives in Connecticut's General Assembly. She was reelected in 1954 and served as the assistant house leader during her second term. As a state legislator, Grasso worked to eliminate an outdated county governmental structure, reform the municipal court system, initiate state offices for the mentally handicapped and for consumer protection, and pass housing legislation banning discrimination on the basis of race, religion, or nationality ("Grasso" 1975 174; Lamson, *Few* 221). The voters of Connecticut elected Grasso secretary of state in 1958. Winning two additional terms with "slate-leading pluralities," Grasso served in this office until 1970 and became "one of the best known politicians in the state" ("Grasso" 1975 174). According to Esther Stineman, she "displayed a finesse in political matters unequaled by other contemporary female politicians" (50).

During her tenure as secretary of state, Grasso also labored diligently for the Democratic Party. She chaired the state platform committee for many years. From 1956 to 1958, she worked as a national Democratic committeewoman and became a member of the national platform committee in 1960. She cochaired the resolutions committees at the national conventions in Atlantic City and Chicago ("Grasso" 1975 74; E. Rosenberg 427). Like others in Chicago in 1968, Grasso's attention focused on the war in Vietnam. She helped craft and "push through a minority report opposing continued United States involvement in Vietnam," and she joined "those who walked out of the convention in protest against the riot-provoking tactics of the police" ("Grasso" 1975 174). According to colleagues, Grasso became the "conscience of the Democratic Party" (Lamson, *Few* 19).

Ella Grasso successfully campaigned for a seat in the U.S. House of Representatives in 1970, despite her misgivings about leaving her family to spend the weekdays in Washington. Drawing on her popularity and campaigning on issues such as inflation, unemployment, and withdrawal from Vietnam, she defeated her Republican challenger with 51 percent of the vote. In her reelection bid two years later, she "increased her margin of victory eleven times, receiving 47,507 more votes than her opponent" ("Grasso" 1975 174). As a U.S. congresswoman, Grasso served on the Education and Labor Committee and the Veterans Affairs Committee. She assisted with the passage of the Emergency Employment Act of 1971 and supported the Emergency Education Act of 1971, the Fair Labor Standards Amendments of 1971, and the Education Act of 1972. Although her voice was heard on important issues in the congressional halls, Grasso became increasingly "frustrated with a system in Washington that left new legislators virtually powerless" ("Ella"). She did not seek reelection to the House and instead returned to Connecticut to work more directly with the people of her state.

Heartened by polls indicating she could win the governorship of Connecticut by a wide margin, Grasso decided in January 1974 to enter the gubernatorial race. She "trounced other Democratic hopefuls" in the spring primary and received the Democratic Party's nomination by acclamation in July ("Grasso" 1975 174). Not many issues emerged in the campaign, but Grasso focused on the state's economy, especially her predecessor's sales tax increases and the state's huge deficit. She defeated her opponent with a margin of almost 200,000 votes.

Despite her challenger's attempt to make it an issue and the scrutiny her candidacy naturally brought to the campaign, gender played a minor role in the race. Although she received a great deal of national media attention as a woman candidate, Grasso "tried to disassociate her sex from her qualifications for governor" ("Grasso" 1975 174). "The judgment will be made of me as an individual," she commented, "on the basis of what I have accomplished in my career in public life and on the basis of what I'll be saying to the voters" (qtd. in "Grasso" 1975 174). Although she recognized the obstacles other women in the political arena faced, Grasso believed she had escaped many of those travails. "It has been my good fortune," she noted, "not to experience any discernible discrimination, even from the earliest days of my public career" (qtd. in Stineman 51). Grasso supported many, although not all, of the ideals of the women's movement, but she did not actively engage in its rhetoric. In fact, a devout Roman Catholic, she quietly opposed legalized abortion, one of the major planks of the feminist agenda ("Grasso" 1975 174; Schultz and van Assendelft 98). She did, however, believe that "as a public servant" she was "bound to the duty of respecting the legality of abortion as upheld by the Supreme Court ("Grasso" 1975 174). Despite her ambivalence on some issues, Grasso recognized the many ways in which she had benefited from the issues advanced by the women's movement. "It's done a great deal in a short time to provide equal opportunity for women. . . . Whereas four years ago I might have had some difficulty in advancing a viable candidacy as a woman, it's a non-issue at this time. I give silent thanks for that" (qtd. in "Grasso" 1975 174).

On her inauguration day, Governor Grasso faced a "state in disarray" with a looming budget deficit of more than seventy million dollars ("Grasso" 1975 174; "Ella"). Employing various strategies, including raising the sales tax, implementation of the state lottery, increased gasoline tax, reorganization and streamlining of state operations, limitations on welfare and financial aid to cities, and rigorous regulation of public utilities augmented by an overall improvement in the economy, Grasso eventually guided the state to sound economic footing and even a budget surplus ("Ella"; E. Rosenberg 427). At one point, when the General Assembly refused to collaborate with her to find viable solutions to the problems, she laid off 505 state employees. Most of these workers regained their positions as the economy improved ("Ella"). To emphasize her commitment to fiscal responsibility, Grasso returned to the state her own salary increase of $7,000 (E. Rosenberg 427). During the great blizzard of 1978, which paralyzed the state for days, Grasso took charge of the relief effort to help the state's citizens recover from the devastating effects of the storm (E. Rosenberg 427; "Ella"). Following this event, the public "believed that it had not just a politician but a pro-active, caring, compassionate woman as governor" ("Ella"). In the face of all the economic difficulties, Grasso managed to continue state efforts to assist the elderly and the mentally handicapped and to "uphold the Connecticut tradition of no income tax" (E. Rosenberg 427).

In a "testament to both her political shrewdness and her immense appeal," Governor Grasso easily won reelection in 1978, garnering 189,000 more votes than her Republican challenger ("Ella"). What promised to be an exhilarating second term for the governor and the state soon disintegrated into disappointment as economic turmoil once again invaded the state and cancer ravaged Ella Grasso's body. Unable to continue her duties as governor, Ella Grasso resigned on December 31, 1980. She lost her struggle with cancer in February 1981 ("Ella").

Transparency and *accessibility* of government emerged as the major themes of Ella Grasso's political career, regardless of the office she held at any given time. As secretary of state, she converted her office into a "'people's lobby,' where people could come to seek or give advice" (E. Rosenberg 427). When she served in the U.S. Congress, Grasso installed a toll-free phone line in her office. Dubbed the "Ella Phone," it provided "around-the-clock service for residents in the 47 towns and cities of her district" (Chamberlin 340). "It's my way," she commented, "of bringing government closer to the people and the people closer to the government" (qtd. in Chamberlin 340). Governor Grasso initiated an "open door" policy for her own office and those of her staff in the state house. She created a consumer ombudsman and with the legislature instituted "right to know" or "sunshine" laws ensuring open meetings and full disclosure of records throughout the state government ("Grasso" 1975 175; E. Rosenberg 427). In a break with political practice, she refused to fill state positions on a patronage basis. Rather, the hiring process utilized a "strict evaluation of skills" (E. Rosenberg 427). "People expect skills," she insisted. "Purely political appointments of persons with no credit other than party affiliation are no longer part of our modern politics" (qtd. in "Grasso" 1975 176).

Governor Grasso's discourse embodied her commitment to public service and to solving problems for the people. She never lost sight of her definition of politics: "the art of the possible" (Grasso, "Commencement Address"). For Grasso, "the possible" often resided in a spirit of cooperation embraced by people coming together to work in a transparent manner on behalf of those for whom they serve. These ideals guided her work, as the following samples from her political rhetoric illustrate. Grasso begins her 1975 inaugural address by noting that "many influences in our lives, and many aspirations of our hearts and minds, have combined to bring us here together" ("Inaugural Message" 61). The governor reminds her colleagues in the legislature that "despite the limited financial resources of our State and the need to tighten our belts, we must not forget the reason government exists: to provide necessary human services to the people. . . . Most important," she tells her audience, "we must insure that the services we provide people—help people" (63). Grasso insists that "we will work with—and for—all our people. We will afford equal opportunity for all our citizens, as we affirm the rights of every individual" (63).

Throughout these remarks, Grasso also addresses the issue of openness in the government. "Last July," she states, "when I accepted my party's nomination for governor, I said that 'the business of Connecticut can be conducted openly, compassionately and efficiently—with prudence and economy. It can; it must; and so it will.' Today, as I stand before you, my conviction is stronger still" ("Inaugural Message" 64). Addressing the topic more directly, Grasso declares: "Ours will be an open government. The Governor's office and all state agencies will be open to all citizens to discuss their problems, answer their inquiries and act on their complaints" (62). She then vows that her administration "will present to the people of Connecticut all the facts in our possession so that they too can understand and participate in the hard decisions ahead" (62). She states further that "the Governor and agency heads will go to the people throughout the

State" (62) to provide all citizens with an opportunity to voice their opinions. To guarantee the people have access to the workings of the government, Grasso promises that the "'right-to-know' law will be rewritten and strengthened to ensure that the processes of local and state government will be totally open to public view and constructive public criticism" (62). Governor Grasso also pledges to work collaboratively with her colleagues in the General Assembly. "I intend to maintain to the best of my ability the most open and cooperative relationship with the Legislature in our State's history. I intend to seek your counsel on a continuing basis," she assures her audience. "We will evaluate programs you develop as well as programs I suggest so that we may, in our combined judgment, most effectively meet the needs of our people" (64). As she did so often in her speeches and in her work, Governor Grasso returned the focus of her inaugural address to the people of the state.

Confronted with an enormous budget deficit and other economic woes, Governor Ella Grasso spent much of her time in office working to put the state's fiscal house in order. However, in the face of great economic challenge, she never forgot that the well-being of the Connecticut people shaped the purpose of her work and remained the top priority of her government. Despite her many years in elective office, Ella Grasso never lost sight of the goal of public service—working for the people.

Madeleine Kunin (1985–1991)

"Don't cry," she told herself. "Stay in control" (Kunin 3). If she cried, she thought, she would be viewed as weak, and her tears would be "taken as a sign of defeat, proof that [she] had not been tough enough to handle the strains of political life" (5). On April 3, 1990, Madeleine Kunin, governor of the state of Vermont, held a press conference to announce that she would not seek a fourth term of office. Her six years in office had been notable for several respects. She was the first woman governor of that state and the first Democratic governor since the Civil War. Lamenting her decision not to run for reelection, the *Burlington Free Press* praised her many political accomplishments. The paper claimed that she led the most "energetic government . . . since the 1960s, compiling a record rivaled by few men." Kunin's decision was "too bad for Vermont politics. Kunin sees government as a benevolent force. Under her prodding," the article continued, "lawmakers increased spending on childcare and education, and enacted broad environmental protections. From the Housing and Conservation Trust to trash management to job training for low income women, Kunin and lawmakers increased state government's presence in the state. Even in this year's hard times," the editorial suggested, "she proposed new jobs for government to do" (qtd. in Kunin 33–34). In addition to her policy accomplishments, Kunin increased the number of women involved in various levels of state and local government. During her tenure, for instance, the "number of women serving on state boards and commissions rose from 24 percent in 1983 to 40 percent in 1990. Forty-one percent of the state's top managers were women. She appointed Vermont's first female Supreme Court justice, two female Superior Court judges, and a female environmental judge" (qtd. in Kunin 33).

Kunin brought a unique management style to the governor's office. Stephen Terry, former newspaper editor, noted that her style of government was different from those who are strong willed. "Madeleine is not that way," he stated. "She is a consensus builder" (qtd. in Melvin 1A). Kunin, herself, characterized her leadership style as nonauthoritarian, a style that would allow others to thrive. She worked to build consensus and adopted a policy of mediation rather than confrontation (Kunin 372). At times this didn't prove successful. Some constituents and staff members thought she was too conservative in her actions, calling her "extremely cautious . . . even to the point of second guessing her appointees" (Graff 2B). Likewise, some Democrats criticized her for being neither aggressive nor progressive enough. Because of these criticisms from both sides of the political spectrum, Kunin had to work hard to make her vision and her message clear. Her policies and positions had to be explained in depth. She needed a term with a clear vision (Melvin 1A).

After relinquishing the governorship, Kunin continued to live a public and political life. She held visiting academic positions at both Dartmouth and Harvard and founded the Institute for Sustainable Communities at the Vermont Law School ("Kunin, Madeleine [May]"). In addition, "she served on the three-person committee that advised President Bill Clinton on the vice presidency and on the Presidential Board of Directors" ("Kunin, Madeleine [May]"). President Clinton named her deputy secretary of education, and she held that position from 1993 to 1996 until he appointed her ambassador to her native Switzerland ("Kunin, Madeleine M."). Prior to her work in the Clinton administration, Kunin penned her political autobiography, *Living a Political Life*. In this book, she documents her struggles and successes in navigating the treacherous political boundaries as she campaigned for and claimed various political offices. Since she is one of the few elected women officials to have written about her experiences, her words provide a unique insight into the world of politics. As a rhetorical artifact, Kunin's autobiography serves to both empower and instruct women who seek a career in politics. Specifically, she accomplishes the following. First, she demonstrates that women can prepare for politics by tapping into common, everyday experiences. Second, her discourse provides a living testimony of the importance of bringing women into the inner circle of politics. Finally, she documents the skills necessary to challenge the male-dominated power structure. Her book, therefore, constitutes a very important argument: women can and must enter politics.

As discussed in chapter 1, Kunin used her experience lobbying local government as the springboard for her political career. As a homemaker, Kunin was involved in a number of community activities, and her recounting of these experiences provides another facet of her argument that women can use their common activities and experiences as preparation for a public and political life. Committee and PTA meetings, for instance, as well as informal get-togethers with other mothers, can provide a foundation for later political experiences. As Bookmen and Ann Sandra Morgen suggest, "Women develop leadership skills and organize themselves in ways that emerge from, or are consistent with their responsibilities, interests, and relationships as women" (316). Kunin describes her community and family involvement this way:

> I was unknowingly preparing for a political life. . . . None of the activities I engaged in met the definition of "political," but they taught me political skills. The difference between community activities and political action is simply one of scale. Similar motivations are required. When I was eventually elected to public office, I discovered that I was far better prepared than I had anticipated. I had underestimated the enormous amount that I had learned in the community and was unaware of my ability to transfer my knowledge into public life. (Kunin 74)

These are just a few of the activities and experiences Kunin recounts in her book. By detailing her personal, everyday experiences in her autobiography, Kunin articulates a political vision that all women can access. She shows readers that no special training is required to enter politics, and that the route to do so, once open exclusively to males, has been paved for women. These examples serve not only to inform women of their options but also to persuade them to tap into their own experiences and forge their own paths to political success. In describing this process, her writing also encourages women to bring other women into the inner circle of politics, and she instructs women to become part of that inner circle in significant ways themselves.

Bringing women into the inner circle of politics proved advantageous on several levels. First, it provided personal and political support for Kunin herself. She found strength in her working relationships with her women colleagues, which in turn bolstered her esteem and supported her belief that women could make a significant difference in politics. "Any political administration becomes a family and develops a special and enduring camaraderie," she notes. "In a woman governed administration, such as mine in Vermont, this traditional political bonding was magnified by the knowledge that we women were doing it differently; we were inventing ourselves," she continues, "gazing out on a vast political landscape with the curiosity of explorers. Always in the backs of our minds," she concludes, "we were sobered by knowing that, whatever we did, our deed would outline the shape of things to come for other women" (Kunin 9–10). As Kunin and the women in her administration worked together, they found a way to blend the traditional male ways of governing with the "newly emerging female political styles" (10). "I soon learned," Kunin discloses, "that not only did my female cohorts need me, but I needed them. The presence of women in key places at critical times made me feel less alone, alien, and bizarre in male political terrain. I discovered that we could communicate as women in a secret and often silent language that was easily understood and created among us a feeling of shared conspiracy" (10–11).

By creating a woman-centered administration, Kunin benefited not only herself but the status of women as well. She recognized that she carved a place for women in the history of Vermont. More than that, however, women no longer had to struggle to find the courage to speak, to ask men for a place at the podium. Instead, the women themselves could frame the debate and exert control (Kunin 16). In essence, Kunin normalized the position of women in state government. She observes that the gender barriers that have prevented women from acquiring power must end. Because men have occupied the positions of power, they have worked together to shape the system. Women, she says, in order to have a similar impact, must be dispersed throughout the power structure in significant positions (366). Kunin credits this approach in her own administration for having a great impact on how policy was made (366).

Power for power's sake alone did not interest Governor Kunin in the slightest. Instead, she wanted to do something with the power the governor's office bestowed upon her. As she puts it, "the greatest power conferred upon" her was the "power to set the agenda and frame the debate" (Kunin 381). Certainly, this allowed her to move within the inner circle of politics and bring other women with her, as discussed above. But it also allowed Kunin to determine and focus on issues she believed were important, such as education and the environment, that had received short shrift from the previous governor.

Madeleine Kunin's autobiography, *Living a Political Life*, serves to encourage and persuade women to become involved in politics. By discussing her personal experiences, the formation of an inner circle, and the acquisition of power, Kunin illustrates key issues women should consider and strategies they should adopt in their quest for political office. Her autobiography provides an honest account of her struggles and successes in a male-dominated field, and as such invites all women to examine their political potential. To that extent, Kunin, therefore, provides the means for women to change their worlds.

Barbara Roberts (1991–1995)

Approximately seven months after Kunin announced she would not seek re-election, across the country the state of Oregon elected Barbara Roberts as its first woman governor. Roberts began her political career as many women do—lobbying state legislatures advocating for a personal cause. In her case, Roberts worked to improve programs for her autistic son. She later served on the Parkrose District School Board and the Mt. Hood Community College Board before her election to the Oregon House of Representatives in 1981 ("Gubernatorial History"). In 1984, she was elected secretary of state and became the first Democrat elected to that office in 114 years ("Gubernatorial History"). During her term as governor, 1990 to 1995, Roberts was recognized as a strong advocate for public education, human rights and services, environmental management, and streamlining state government.

Roberts won the election without a mandate from the citizens; she barely defeated Republican David Frohnmeyer in a bitter three-way race. In the same election, Oregonians adopted Measure 5, a property tax limitation that had the potential to thrust the state into a catastrophic budget crisis. Measure 5 capped property tax rates and shifted the burden for paying for public schools onto the state general fund. Costs of state services, coupled with this education obligation, resulted in a projected shortfall of $1.2 billion in the 1993–1995 biennium, and $2.5 billion in 1995–1997. As we have argued previously, Roberts attempted to include citizen participation in crafting a response to the budget problems the state faced (Marshall and Mayhead 93). While laudatory at face value, the approach Roberts adopted proved ineffective. Meaningful tax reform, Roberts's main goal of her tenure, did not occur, and the state had to continue to limp along without adequate funding for many of its programs.

To deal with the looming budget problem, Roberts launched what she called the Conversation with Oregon. It was designed to give citizens a role in crafting a budget and at the same time attempted to ascertain what services they felt government must provide. She elaborates her rationale for establishing the Conversation with a press release:

> Traditionally, politicians would turn to polls and advertising to push a tax reform plan. But neither of those shopworn approaches would have helped Oregon work through its budget troubles and find a solution that works. That's why we designed the Conversation. We are giving people the information and the power to help us answer the most critical question Oregon faces: What kind of future do we want for our state? What level of public services do we want and need? And finally, how are we going to provide for those services? (Roberts, "Press Release" n.p.).

More than ten thousand people attended the town-hall style meetings in approximately nine hundred gatherings held around the state. The meetings revealed nothing very significant, other than that people knew little about how government works and few if any wanted a property tax. Although she tried to tout the Conversation as the basis for meaningful tax reform, the press and legislators were unimpressed with the effort. Wayne Thompson argued in an editorial that "Roberts does not recognize the disaster that lies ahead for state agencies once Measure 5 builds up to its head of steam in the mid-1990s. But to deal with it she proposes little more than a statewide public relations effort" (B6). Ultimately, neither her approach nor her tax plan resonated with the public or the legislature. Citizens did not like the plan because they felt it was a back-door attempt at a sales tax; legislators were angered that they had been left out of the decision-making process (Mapes E1).

In several speeches, Roberts attempted to demonstrate that she had the best interests of the citizens in mind. Specifically, she agreed with the premise that government was not doing a good job and needed to be changed. For instance, in her second "State of the State Address," she intones, "You have lost confidence in your political leaders. You don't believe we hear you any more. Well, I listened, and I heard you. Oregonians are frustrated. You don't think we spend your tax dollars well. You want a more efficient government. You want better delivered services" (3). She never really defends state government in any of her speeches; instead, she seems content to evaluate it and find it deficient. "We are truly looking at the purpose of state government," she says in a speech to the Portland Metropolitan Chamber of Commerce. "Not just to save money," she continues, "but to define government's role in today's society" (Roberts, "Remarks" 3). She attempts to show that she is a governor of action by discussing the budget cuts she has made, including the lay-off of thousands of state workers. "We are cutting 4,000 state positions by July 1993. 4,000 state jobs that will be gone—now and in the future. That means more than 1,000 state workers will be laid off in just over 15 months. No Oregon governor has ever moved forward so aggressively to cut back the size of state government" (4).

Luckily for the state of Oregon, the early 1990s disappeared, to be replaced by a time of soaring state revenues fueled, in part, by a burgeoning technological industry. Oregon mirrored the rest of the country in the improvement of its financial outlook. Four thousand state workers did not lose their jobs, as Roberts had predicted. Certainly, Roberts should receive some credit for trying an innovative and inclusive approach in seeking a solution to Oregon's budget crisis in the early part of that decade. But her "solution" was too vague and her predictions unsubstantiated. Ultimately, beaten down by the press and a public that did not want to pay any more taxes, Roberts did not seek reelection in 1994.

Ann Richards (1991–1995)

In approximately one decade, Ann Richards left obscurity as a county commissioner to become one of the most famous politicians in the United States and the first woman governor of Texas since Miriam "Ma" Ferguson more than fifty years before ("Richards" 468). Born Dorothy Ann Willis in 1933, Ann grew up in Lakeview, Texas, a small town near Waco. She lived in what she called "the lower edge of the middle class" (468). Her father taught her that she could accomplish anything she set her mind to (469). She enrolled in Waco High School as Ann Willis and excelled in extracurricular activities such as debating and Girls State, a mock governmental session. She was chosen to represent Texas at Girls Nation (469). She fielded several offers of debate scholarships and eventually settled on Baylor University. After completing her degree in speech and government, she later attended the University of Texas and attained her teaching certificate. While at Baylor, she married David Richards in her junior year.

After the birth of their first child, the family moved to Dallas where Richards assisted her husband, who served as a Democratic precinct chairman; she also participated in other campaign-related activities and helped to establish the North Dallas Democratic Women organization ("Richards" 469). When the family moved to Austin, Richards realized she was tired of doing menial campaign tasks and thought she was done with politics. But when Sarah Weddington asked her to sign on as a campaign manager for her state legislature bid, Richards was hooked (469). Local party officials began to take notice of her skills and asked Richards to run for county commissioner when her husband declined the offer (469). Despite concerns about what a political life might do to her marriage, and with her husband's encouragement, she decided to run. She subordinated her role as wife and mother to a political career (469). Her fears regarding the fragility of marriage proved true, and she and David Richards divorced in 1984.

Prior to that, in 1982, Ann Richards was elected state treasurer ("Richards" 470). While serving in that capacity, "She catapulted to fame and national prominence as a result of her keynote address to the 1988 Democratic National Convention" (Mullaney 359). She cashed in on her political capital, publishing a campaign autobiography, *Straight from the Heart*, and entered the race for the Texas governorship in 1990 (359). She won a bitter three-way race in the primary, narrowly defeating two male opponents who ran campaigns in which mud-slinging was commonplace. Securing only 39 percent of the vote, she was forced into a run-off with Jim Mattox, and she "emerged victorious with fifty-seven percent of the vote" (360). She faced Clayton Williams in the general election, a man who hurt himself with self-inflicted political gaffes, such as the time he said something to the effect that rape is like bad weather. Relax and enjoy it (361). Richards defeated Williams with a 51 to 49 percent upset ("Richards" 471). She immediately went to work on issues such as insurance industry regulation, lobbyist ethics, hazardous waste disposal, and the reorganization of state agencies (471). "Welcome to the first day of the New Texas," she stated at her inaugural (471). Although generally popular, Ann Richards lost her reelection bid to George W. Bush in 1994.

Unlike other states, "Texas governors have few formal powers and the office itself is constitutionally weak." Therefore, "their power stems from style, ability to persuade, and popular appeal—all strategies that Richards appeared to have mastered" (Mullaney 361). Richards's style is very colloquial, very personal, and very "feminine" as defined by rhetorical scholars discussed in chapter 1. A sampling of some of her most famous addresses provides a taste of the unique flavor of her communication.

Ann Richards frequently uses concrete examples to illustrate points. In her "State of the State Address," for instance, she recounts the tale of the gift left for her in the Governor's Mansion:

> When I moved into the Governor's Mansion the other day, I found a gallon of honey waiting for me. Attached to it was a hand-written note on a scrap of paper. The hand that wrote the note was old and shaky. It was written by a man who worked all his life but didn't mind sharing some of the fruits of his hard labor. The note said, "we believe we finally have a governor who cares about the ordinary people and the poor." ("Remarks" 10)

Richards uses personal anecdotes liberally throughout her speeches. In her keynote speech, for example, she regales her audience with a story from her youth. "You know, tonight I felt like I did when I played basketball in the eighth grade. I thought I looked real cute in my uniform and then I heard a boy yell from the bleachers, 'make a basket birdlegs'" ("Keynote" 1). She could take a political issue and make it personal, as she does when attacking President Reagan's behavior during the Iran-Contra scandal. In criticizing him, she says, "The only answer we get is, 'I don't know,' or 'I forgot.' But you wouldn't accept that answer from your children. I wouldn't" (3). Her most famous sound bite at the Democratic National Convention forever immortalized her: "Poor George," she said of President George H. W. Bush, "he can't help it—he was born with a silver foot in his mouth" ("Richards" 470).

"Ann Richards became governor of Texas partially because she utilized a rhetorical style that appealed to voters" (Kaml 80). Her use of examples and humor served her well in all levels of campaigning. With wit and fortitude, Ann Richards forever changed the face of politics, in Texas and the United States.

Christine Todd Whitman (1994–2001)

When inaugurated as the fiftieth governor of New Jersey on January 18, 1994 ("Christine"), Republican Christine Todd Whitman wasted no time in invoking the spirit and philosophy of former president Ronald Reagan, as she surmised in her speech to the state: "Our problems are not the product of great global economic shifts or other vast, unseen forces. They are the creation of government" (qtd. in "Whitman").

Christine Todd Whitman possessed an extensive political pedigree, as both parents actively worked for the Republican Party. Her father, Webster B. Todd, served as a Republican state chairman; her mother, Eleanor Todd, was vice chairperson of the Republican National Committee, chaired the New Jersey finance committee of George H. W. Bush's campaign for the presidential nomination in 1980, and served on the New Jersey Commission on Higher Education ("Whitman"). Christine Todd Whitman first ran for public office in 1982, winning a seat and serving for five years on the Somerset County Board of Chosen Freeholders, which is similar to a board of county supervisors ("Whitman"). In 1988, New Jersey Governor Tom Kean appointed her as president of the New Jersey Board of Utilities, a position she held until her resignation in 1990 ("Whitman"). At this time, she declared she would run for the U.S. Senate.

Her opponent that year, Senator and former basketball great Bill Bradley, initially garnered 98 percent name recognition among voters; conversely, only 10 percent of the voting public knew Whitman's name ("Whitman"). "It seemed at first she would only be token opposition to Bradley" ("Christine"). However, New Jersey Governor Jim Florio, a Democrat, had so incensed the people of his state by breaking a promise not to raise taxes that the citizens transferred their anger to Bradley ("Whitman"; "Christine"). Whitman captured 49 percent of the vote and narrowly lost the election to Bradley. Emboldened by the close race, and wanting to capitalize on her newly established notoriety, Whitman began contemplating a run for the governorship. She began writing a weekly newspaper column and hosting a biweekly radio talk show ("Whitman"). She defeated two opponents in the primary and set her sights on Florio.

Florio proved to be his own worst enemy. After his "tax program went into effect, New Jersey dove into a recession deeper than that being experienced by the rest of the country" ("Christine"). Although she trailed at the polls by twenty points at one time, Whitman successfully fanned the flames of anger toward Florio by constantly reminding the citizens how bitterly angry they were toward him ("Whitman"). Whitman narrowly defeated Florio by a slim 25,628 ballots cast out of 2.5 million ("Whitman"). Whitman's campaign, however, generated criticism for its numerous rumors of scandal. When she released her tax returns, for instance, the documents indicated that she and her husband had cleared $3.7 million the previous year, making it hard for her to claim that she was a "regular person" ("Christine"). More damaging, however, was her campaign manager's claim that he had engineered the suppression of African American votes by bribing ministers to refrain from endorsing Florio. Democrats called for the election to be decertified, but after a federal and state investigation into the accusations, and after her campaign manager recanted his statement, Whitman was cleared of all charges ("Whitman"; "Christine").

Whitman successfully enacted her budget plan in the first two years of her term, reducing state income taxes by 30 percent ("Christine"). She also attracted the attention of the GOP who chose her to give the rebuttal to President Clinton's State of the Union Address in 1995; she was the first-ever governor selected to do so ("Christine"). Peter Jennings stated: "She is one of the fastest rising stars in the Republican Party . . . a tax cutting Republican on the move" ("Introduction"). President George W. Bush appointed Christine Todd Whitman to head the Environmental Protection Agency in 2001.

A brief survey of Whitman's speeches reveals her commitment to sound governmental policy and to rational decision making. She defends the job governors do, for instance, in a speech to the National Press Club of Washington, D.C. She says the personal behavior of politicians doesn't really matter to the average family and that citizens should look to their governors for true leadership. "I'm proud of what governors across the United States are accomplishing for the families we serve," she gushes. "I'm confident that as the scandal [of the Monica Lewinski incident] recedes into the background of American political life, people will see that our nation still has plenty of outstanding leaders who not only care about their real-life concerns but are making an impact" (Whitman, "Republicans"). As EPA chief she supported President Bush's environmental policy by stating that "taken together, the President's budget helps communities across America address their most pressing environmental priorities. It provides the funds," she continues, "and sets the priorities—my Agency needs to meet its mission of protecting our environment and safeguarding the public health. It is this Administration's first instalment [sic] on our pledge," she concludes, "to leave America's air clearer, water purer, and land better protected than we found it" (Whitman, "Statement"). The final example illustrates her stated commitment to examining issues in their entirety. She says to the 1995 graduating class at Deerfield Secondary School that "each of us here today—and this goes double for those of us in public life—needs to reexamine our commitment to listen to the other person's point of view. It doesn't matter whether you're on the left or right of the political spectrum," she adds. "Each of us owes one another a measure of civility to enhance and enoble [sic] the level of public discourse in this country—whether or not we agree with what we hear" (Whitman, "Deerfield Commencement").

Christine Todd Whitman led the state of New Jersey through tough economic times and catapulted to fame in the Republican Party with her rigid adherence to strict budget policy and a style that reminds people of "a compelling blend of Princess Diana and Margaret Thatcher" (qtd. in "Whitman"). No matter what people thought, few could disagree that she "proves that a woman can enact leadership powerfully and competently" (Sheeler 122).

Conclusion

The women whose lives and discourse we have examined in this chapter span every decade of the twentieth century in which women occupied electoral office. As their own words illustrate, the discourse of female politicians has both reflected and shaped key issues of the times. Alongside their male counterparts from 1917 through 1999, women debated, with compassion and insight, the national economy, America's role in the global order, struggles for equality and civil rights, education, and war. While these women brought remnants of the private sphere into the national conversation, it is clear that their knowledge was not limited to these matters. Their gradual shift from private sphere concerns to public space discussions of national and foreign policy helped erase previous constraints and paved the way for a new era of women's political participation in the twenty-first century.

Discourse from "A Woman's Place"   3
Twenty-first-Century Rhetoric in the
U.S. House of Representatives

> *If we're actually going to succeed, we've got to do our homework, because we've got to elevate the conversation or the debate on an intellectual level, since we're going to lose on the muscular level. Most women realize that if we're going to be successful, if we're going to make our sisters proud, then we have a lot of work to do on three of these fronts: changing the image of Congress; beefing up issues that women should be represented in; and being a part of every decision.*

—REPRESENTATIVE KARAN ENGLISH, QTD. IN MARGOLIES-MEZVINSKY 69

O N OCTOBER 8, 1991, A GROUP of seven women from the United States House of Representatives climbed the steps of the Senate building to speak in opposition to the nomination of Clarence Thomas to the Supreme Court. A law professor, Anita Hill, had recently testified that Thomas had sexually harassed her while she had worked for him. Still cameras flashed and news cameras rolled film; microphones and tape recorders were pointed at the representatives (Boxer, *Strangers* 30). A photo forever immortalized the women climbing those steps; some refer to the image as a woman's Iwo Jima (33). When the representatives knocked on the door of the Senate chamber, they were denied access to their colleagues. A Senate staff member told them, "we don't let strangers in" (34).

It seems almost unconscionable that a group of women with decades of political experience between them could be denied access to an avenue of decision making. Eventually, they did meet with Majority Leader George Mitchell and ultimately did express their concern that an individual with a record such as Justice

Thomas's could be appointed to the country's highest court. After the Hill testimony, the women representatives were flooded with telegrams and phone calls, imploring them to do something about the Thomas nomination (Boxer, *Strangers* 39–40, 55–60). These constituents, many from states not represented by these seven congresswomen, felt that the women in the House understood the issue of sexual harassment like no male politician could. The Representatives acted on behalf of all women of the country in hopes that justice and equality could prevail.

As the number of women in the U.S. House of Representatives increases, their impact on government increases as well. Cindy Simon Rosenthal posits that "the consideration and accommodation of feminalist concerns have altered the agenda, changed the content of policy debate and affected legislative outcomes regarding reproductive policy, cancer and health care, welfare reform, civil rights, and criminal and economic affairs. In no small part," she adds, "public policy advances have been achieved because of the commitment to surrogate representation—the sense of obligation felt by congresswomen to act for women beyond their geographic constituency" (Rosenthal 446). We do not argue in this chapter, or anywhere else in this book for that matter, that women in the political arena operate solely for the benefit of women. However, Rosenthal's observation does highlight the impact that women in Congress can and do have on the lives of all citizens—female and male alike.

To date, voters have sent seventy-nine women to the U.S. House of Representatives during the twenty-first century. In addition, three women have represented Washington, D.C., Guam, and the Virgin Islands. In 2004, sixty women served in the House along with the three delegates from the U.S. commonwealths. To provide a better understanding of the nature of women's political rhetoric in this new century, we analyze the discourse of six of the more colorful and passionate representatives in the following pages.

Nancy Pelosi

"We all have an enormous responsibility to the American people to articulate and fight for issues of concern to our great country," said Nancy Pelosi in a letter to her Democratic colleagues soon after being chosen House minority leader (qtd. in "Pelosi, Nancy"). Initially elected from California's Eighth District (San Francisco) in 1987, Congresswoman Pelosi won her eighth full term to Congress in 2002. She spent her time in the 106th and 107th Congresses working hard to help her party regain control of the House (Ferrechio). She also campaigned hard to gain the seat as minority leader, and when she won, became the first woman to hold the highest ranking position in House history. Before being elected to that post, she served as House Democratic whip for one year. Pelosi comes from a political family, as her father was Baltimore's mayor for twelve years. She recalls that her life was about campaigns ("Pelosi, Nancy"). After earning a BA in political science from Trinity University, she married Paul Pelosi and moved to San Francisco in 1969. There, she did volunteer work for the Democratic Party and eventually served as state party chairwoman. As the Representative from the Eighth District, her constituents include many environmentalists, gays, and immigrants. She is considered one of the most liberal members of Congress ("Pelosi, Nancy"). As such, she often fights losing battles on a range of issues, including "education, abortion, health care, and crime. But she perseveres, returning each year with undiminished enthusiasm for the same causes—with particular attention to the needs of San Francisco's large homosexual population" (Foerstel, "Rep. Nancy Pelosi").

When the Democrats selected her as minority leader, the Republicans met the choice with glee, sneering about the "California Liberal." However, Pelosi herself states, "I'm a non-menacing progressive Democrat. . . . I don't think [the Party] chose me as an outspoken San Francisco liberal. I think they chose me as a person who can lead the caucus to victory, as a person who can build coalitions among the various segments of our caucus and as a person who represents various points of view within the caucus" (Ferrechio). Pelosi is determined to unite her party and communicate its message to the American people. She states that the Democrats must put forth "clear and credible proposals legislatively and . . . build consensus—our three C's" (R. Cohen, "Pelosi's Fixed"). Pelosi "really has argued that on critical issues the party really needs to be unified, and she's been able to deliver" (Allen). Her overriding priority is to win back the House (R. Cohen, "Pelosi's Fast").

Colleagues give Pelosi high marks for achieving her goal of party unity. Representative Anna Eshoo says that Pelosi "understands in a very broad and deep way what leadership is, and the kind of leadership that succeeds" (qtd. in R. Cohen, "Pelosi's Fast"). "She is skilled in understanding the needs of members" (R. Cohen, "Pelosi's Fast"). Pelosi attempts to connect with her colleagues and supports their legislative efforts. Representative Jan Schakowsky states: "She exudes a sense of pride in our ability to be winners. She devotes meticulous attention to each individual member" (qtd. in R. Cohen, "Pelosi's Fast"). Representative Diana DeGette of Colorado observes, "Nancy's leadership has brought a breath of fresh air. She is trying to engage the entire caucus. . . . If we hope to take back the House, we need to have a discipline to speak with one voice to the American people" (qtd. in R. Cohen, "Pelosi's Fast").

Clearly, Congresswoman Nancy Pelosi possesses key leadership characteristics, which make her qualified to assess the leadership traits of others. In focusing on the nature of President George W. Bush's leadership, Pelosi frequently invokes the use of the term *president* as her most common ideograph. This word conveys a deep and traditional meaning for the American people. It has in the past meant leadership, as the president is both the leader of his (or her) own party as well as the nation. In addition, the president is seen as the individual who unites the American public in policies foreign and domestic. Finally, the term *president* is often treated as almost synonymous with respect. However, Pelosi turns the traditional meaning of *president* upside down. Her use of the ideograph instead shows President Bush's lack of leadership and illustrates her belief that he divides Americans from each other and the world. Ultimately, her constant criticism of Bush morphs the term *president* from one meaning respect to one deserving derision.

In her June 26, 2003, speech advocating a bill to extend benefits to military veterans, for instance, Pelosi points out that the Bush administration opposes such a plan. She begins by asking, "If we were to ask any military commander present at those [4th of July] ceremonies, what is the most important aspect of leadership? The answer would be: first, take care of the troops" ("Pelosi Statement on Military"). She adds: "Sadly, that leadership is lacking from President Bush and from the Republicans in Congress" ("Pelosi Statement on Military"). When Democrats proposed a resolution to increase the amount of money for troop equipment that the president and Republicans opposed, Pelosi had this to say about Bush: "Our bill urges that intelligence deficiencies be immediately remedied. It takes steps to correct the Bush Administration's failure to plan adequately for the post war occupation of Iraq" ("Pelosi Statement on Democratic Resolution").

She consistently attacks President Bush's lack of leadership on a variety of key issues. Pelosi claims that Bush has done a great disservice to women by cutting programs designed specifically to help them. She uses the term *leadership* in an ironic way when stating, "under the leadership of President Bush and Attorney General John Ashcroft, the Violence Against Women Office has been systematically weakened. Just within the last two months," she continues, "the policy department of the Violence Against Women Office disappeared, and the Director of the office has no access to the Attorney General or the President and no seat at the table to affect the policies of this Administration with concern to violence against women. This is one of a series of actions by this Administration to diminish the importance of women's issues" (Pelosi, "We Must"). President Bush's poor leadership also has harmed the environment, according to Pelosi. In a statement that demonstrates both Bush's bad leadership and his tendency to divide Americans, Pelosi reports that "ever so quickly, the Bush Administration is reversing more than three decades of bipartisan progress on the environment. Just this week," she notes, "the Natural Resources Defense Council released a report documenting the Administration's most recent actions to undermine environmental protection. The report describes 150 assaults on our environmental safeguards just since January 2003. When it comes to the environment," she concludes, "special interests trump the public interest every time for the Bush Administration" (Pelosi, "Bush Administration Reversing").

Pelosi often sounds most strident when evaluating Bush's actions toward Iraq. She consistently argues that the "President" is a model of incompetence and poor planning, and thus a weak leader. She also explicitly contends that his actions have divided Americans into two classes. These themes become quite apparent in her "pre-buttal" to his State of the Union Address in January 2004. She states, in part, "When President Bush disregards allies and international institutions; when he rejects global treaties without debate or alternative; when he makes assertions without evidence—as he did in the State of the Union last year; and when he embraces a radical doctrine of pre-emptive war; then he squanders our international credibility and moral authority" (Pelosi, "Pelosi and Daschle"). Pelosi also points out that President Bush's domestic policy is misguided as well, claiming that "President Bush and Republicans in Congress are focused on a different set of priorities—looking out for corporate interests rather than middle-class Americans. Mr. President," she adds, "America's families are hurting. But you are not helping. In fact, you are making it harder for American families to prosper. Yours is a government of the few, by the few, for the few" (Pelosi, "Pelosi and Daschle"). After President Bush's press conference on Iraq in April 2004, for instance, Pelosi intoned, "From the outset, the President's Iraq policy has had little basis in reality. In a country supposedly brimming with weapons of mass destruction, none has been found. Our troops continue to be met with rockets, not roses, as the Bush Administration claimed, and we have lost more than 670 lives" (Pelosi, "President's Resolve"). She repeats an often-levied criticism of the Iraq War, that Bush chose to go it alone rather than acquire international support—another sign of a lack of leadership. "As signs of progress," she states, "the President pointed to making greater use of the United Nations and involving nations in the region more fully, but he ignored the fact that the situation on the ground would likely be much more favorable today if these steps had been taken before the war started" ("President's Resolve"). Ultimately, she concludes that "The President's resolve may be firm, but his plan remains woefully inadequate" ("President's Resolve").

Bush's economic policies receive stinging criticism from Pelosi as well. Pelosi frequently argues that Bush has misled the American people and, worse, his policies actually harm them. These accusations do not call to mind the qualities of good leadership. She attacks his much-vaunted "No Child Left Behind Act" by pointing out that it actually makes budget cuts in needed areas. Education is the most important economic investment a country can make, Pelosi suggests, "and that is why the cuts in education proposed by the President and Republican leadership are so devastating" (Pelosi, "President's Education"). She ridicules the

White House's publication of photos of President Bush surrounded by children as misleading, as mere photo opportunities, for "the reality is that within weeks of signing the 'No Child Left Behind' act, the President submitted a budget that leaves millions of children behind. The President's budget stops six years of steady progress in federal support to local schools dead in its tracks" ("President's Education"). Pelosi excoriates Bush for the loss of American jobs. "Our manufacturing sector is critical, but after three years of President Bush, it is in crisis," she states. "Our country is hemorrhaging manufacturing jobs. Since taking office, President Bush has lost 2.8 million good-paying manufacturing jobs. . . . One million jobs have been shipped overseas" (Pelosi, "Our Manufacturing"). In an ironic tribute to former President Ronald Reagan, Pelosi asks the American people, "Are you better off" than you were four years ago? (Pelosi, "Are You"). She answers, no. "Under President Bush and the Republican Congress, most Americans have suffered. If you are a taxpayer, you are not better off. We went from a budget that was in balance in 1999, the deficit was zero, and on a path to a $5.6 trillion surplus to one now that is half a trillion dollars in debt this year alone" ("Are You"). In addition, Pelosi points out the significant cuts to education, higher education, and the significant increases in gasoline prices. "Clearly," she concludes, "we are not better off since President Bush took office" ("Are You").

Congresswoman Nancy Pelosi has little respect for President George W. Bush and his administration. While she doesn't come right out and call him an idiot, she does consistently point out where he has failed as a leader. Pelosi uses the ideograph of *president* derisively to show all of the shortcomings of Bush's foreign and domestic policies. She uses the phrase "President Bush" synonymously with failure and poor leadership. In this way she has transformed the ideograph *president* into a term of contempt in a particular context. Doing this has mixed ramifications for Pelosi. Her discourse seems polemic and has little chance of uniting Democrats and Republicans. She does not seem to operate in a bipartisan manner, at least when it comes to the issues of Iraq and the U.S. budget. News analysis and biographical discussions, as mentioned above, denote her as a liberal. However, her steadfast commitment to true Democratic principles, particularly in the area of social programs, has helped her create party unity. Finally, it is important to note that she speaks in terms neither masculine, nor feminine. Her issues and her language span gender and class boundaries. Essentially, she speaks the language of politics that mediates Second and Third Space discourse.

Diana DeGette

"Every so often in this body, I think it is important to talk about facts. Instead of legislating by an anecdote, I would like to actually look at some facts today," Di-

ana DeGette tells her congressional colleagues in a floor debate on healthcare issues ("House Floor Remarks on Help"). Representative DeGette, from the First
Congressional District of Colorado, often encourages her colleagues in the House
to focus on the evidence as they deliberate policy issues. Her reputation for delv-
ing into details and concentrating on complex issues remains legendary. "Since she
began her political career in the Colorado legislature, DeGette hasn't hesitated to
take on—and pass—complicated, controversial and fiendishly complex laws"
(Ryan Morgan). A former colleague in the Colorado Senate, Mike Feeley, says that
the congresswoman "takes a very intellectual approach to her work" (qtd. in Ryan
Morgan). He also suggests that "she is not afraid of diving into something complex, she's not afraid of hard work and she's not afraid of making the arguments
that are necessary" to create and promote legislation (qtd. in Ryan Morgan). Para-
phrasing DeGette's comments, Ryan Morgan, a staff writer for the *Denver Post*, reports that she is "proudest of the laws she's sponsored concerning children, health
care and the environment" and that "her real strengths lie less with the votes she
casts and more with the influential position she's won within her party and the
House" (Ryan Morgan). DeGette contends that although her position in the party
may be "less tangible" than her voting record, she has "really grown into a leadership role. I'm now very high up in the Democratic whip organization," she continues, "where I help try to persuade my colleagues on voting on bills" (qtd. in
Ryan Morgan). In announcing her bid for reelection to a fourth term in 2002,
DeGette describes the mission driving her political activism. "It's my job in Washington to be the voice of these neighbors, these communities, these families," she
tells her constituents, "not the privileged, wealthy few, but the people who work
hard and don't have the lobbyists and contributions and political connections"
(DeGette, "Congresswoman").

DeGette's commitment to the common people preceded her entrance into
politics. A fourth-generation Denverite, Diana DeGette entered the world on a
military base in Tachikawa, Japan, in 1957 ("DeGette"; DeGette, "Congresswoman"). During most of her childhood, however, she lived in the Denver area.
Following her parents' divorce, DeGette contributed to the family's income by
working after school (Hawkings and Nutting 178). "She recalls being profoundly affected, at age 10, by the news coverage of the assassination of the Rev.
Dr. Martin Luther King, Jr., which broadened her horizons and instilled in her
an interest in the civil rights movement" (178). She attended Denver's South
High School and graduated *magna cum laude* from Colorado College in 1979 with
a bachelor of arts degree (DeGette, "Congresswoman"). DeGette later attended
the New York University School of Law from which she earned her JD in 1982.
Named a Root-Tilden Scholar, she also received the Vanderbilt Medal and the
Jack Kroner Award during her tenure in law school (DeGette, "About Diana").

Following her return to Denver in 1982, DeGette served as a deputy state public defender until 1984 (DeGette, "Congresswoman"). She then went into private practice, where she focused on employment litigation and civil rights law
(Schenken 187), specializing "in cases of discrimination based on disability, sex
and age" until 1996 (Hawkings and Nutting 178). As an advocate for the people of Denver, however, DeGette determined she could accomplish more in the
public arena than in private practice. She believed "she could have a more direct
impact on public policy in the legislature than as a litigator" (Cook and Greenblatt). "I felt I could serve my constituents on a broader scale [in politics]," she
declared (qtd. in Ryan Morgan).

Diana DeGette began her political career participating in local party politics
and in 1992, won election to the Colorado House of Representatives "where she
was surprisingly productive for a member of the minority" (Barone and Cohen
313). Most notably, as a first-year legislator, she authored and won passage of the
"bubble bill," which requires "protesters to stay 8 feet away from anyone within
100 feet of the entrance" to an abortion clinic (Hawkings and Nutting 178;
Barone and Cohen 313). "The clinic access bill, which was the first [of] its kind
in the country, withstood court challenges all the way to the [U.S.] Supreme
Court," Feeley claims (qtd. in Ryan Morgan). The 2000 decision to uphold the
legislation occurred, according to Feeley, "largely because of the work that Diana
did at the beginning, making sure it balanced constitutional rights" (qtd. in Ryan
Morgan). She also sponsored a Voluntary Cleanup and Redevelopment Act "to
encourage businesses and citizens to clean up the environment" as well as a bill
that safeguarded accident victims' families from contact by lawyers for thirty days
following an incident (Barone, Cohen, and Cook 305). DeGette, who served as a
member of the Judiciary, Local Government, and Legal Services Committees
(DeGette, "Congresswoman"), resigned from the Colorado House in 1996 to
concentrate on her campaign to win the U.S. House seat vacated by Congresswoman Patricia Schroeder.

Not surprisingly, the campaign drew national media attention as both the Republican and Democratic parties coveted the post Schroeder had held for twenty-
four years. DeGette, considered the early front-runner in the Democratic primary,
"overcame a tough primary challenge from former Denver City Councilman Tim
Sandos" to advance to the general election (Cook and Greenblatt). DeGette's Republican opponent, Joe Rogers, an African American, secured the endorsement of
an influential group of African American ministers who usually supported Democratic candidates. DeGette, on the other hand, received the backing of Denver
Mayor Wellington Webb, as African American Democrat (Hawkings and Nutting
178; Cook and Greenblatt). In what political analysts consider the most liberal
district in the state, DeGette won the election by 17 percentage points with 57

percent of the vote (Hawkings and Nutting 178). In subsequent elections, DeGette has illustrated her staying power by amassing 67 percent of the vote in 1998, 69 percent in 2000, and 66 percent in 2002 (177). Labeled "feminist, organizationally adept and legislatively creative," Representative DeGette has proven "a worthy successor to Schroeder" (Barone, Cohen, and Cook 305).

DeGette brings to Congress eclectic interests that embody the diversity of the First Congressional District and its citizens. Representative DeGette, appointed to the Energy and Commerce Committee, enjoyed a propitious entrance into the halls of Congress in 1997, as "the only freshman Democrat named to an exclusive House panel in the 105th Congress" (Hawkings and Nutting 177). She has continued membership on this committee throughout her four terms in office and currently serves on four subcommittees: Oversight and Investigations; Health; Commerce, Trade and Consumer Protection; and Environment and Hazardous Materials (DeGette, "About Diana"; Hawkings and Nutting 177). Using the Energy and Commerce Committee assignment and "her status as the successor to Patricia Schroeder," DeGette has "made her presence felt on a broad array of topics: the budget, public housing, abortion rights, gun control, healthcare and tobacco regulation" (Hawkings and Nutting 177). The environment in general and wilderness issues in particular receive her rapt attention as well. Her pro-consumer views emerge in her intense interrogation of alleged corporate wrongdoing in scandals surrounding giants such as Enron and Denver-based Qwest Communications. DeGette's description of Qwest reveals her impatience with a company she believes has harmed citizens. "In the waning days of the go-go Internet boom, a group of cowboys by the name of Qwest came riding into town and they acquired US West," she proclaims. "Their bad business decisions have had a significant impact on our local economy, the local workforce and the community as a whole" (qtd. in Hawkings and Nutting 177). In addition to her committee work, DeGette cochairs the Congressional Diabetes Caucus, the largest congressional member caucus. Its mission "is to increase awareness of diabetes and to promote greater research into diabetes and diabetes-related complications" ("Congressional Diabetes"). She cochairs the Bipartisan Congressional Pro-Choice Caucus as well and zealously attacks the current administration's assaults on *Roe v. Wade*. Since January 2003, following her three-term appointment as regional whip, Congresswoman DeGette has served as the Democratic floor whip (DeGette, "About Diana").

No other group of constituents receives the consideration DeGette concentrates on the children of her district and, by extension, the children of the nation. Early in her congressional career, DeGette decided that "few other lawmakers were focusing on those issues [children's needs] or could bring to the task her personal perspective as a parent of two young daughters" (Hawkings and Nutting 177).

From health issues and domestic violence to gun control to education, she advocates for the welfare of the country's youngest citizens. Healthcare legislation and research have emerged as DeGette's top priorities. For example, she has lobbied successfully for the passage of an amendment that "created 'presumptive eligibility' for Medicaid for poor families with children," has gained House approval of a policy "to ensure that organ-transplant legislation recognizes the needs of children" (Barone, Cohen, and Cook 305), and has won enactment of a law requiring that medical devices intended for use on children "be reviewed by pediatric experts before they are put on the market" (Hawkings and Nutting 177). As DeGette calls for the expansion of research to find cures for diseases, including diabetes, that affect children and adults, she simultaneously advocates for stricter controls for investigations involving humans.

Much of Representative DeGette's available discourse reflects her concern for healthcare practices and research. Her rhetorical strategies in these contexts often rely on the primacy of the rational. As she explains in the quotation from a debate on healthcare reform cited previously, she wants to work with facts, not anecdotes. Criticizing the privatization of Social Security, DeGette calls on those who support the plan to "read the GAO report [and] look at the facts" (DeGette, "Cuts"). In her discussion of health matters, DeGette often expresses her perspective in the ideographs *science* and *science over politics*. The motifs *protection* or *conservation* also permeate DeGette's discourse on a variety of issues ranging from the environment to civil liberties.

Cochair of the House Congressional Diabetes Caucus and the mother of a diabetic daughter, DeGette highlights the need for funding to continue research, including embryonic stem cell programs, focused on this and other chronic diseases. In a 2002 statement to the Appropriations Subcommittee on Labor, Health and Human Services, and Education, she outlines the progress made in diabetes research despite the fact that "since 1987, the percentage of the entire NIH budget devoted to diabetes has fallen by more than 20 percent while diabetes has grown by over 50 percent" (DeGette, "FY 2003"). DeGette argues that "the need for increased funding comes at a crucial time as various studies and statistics reveal that both diabetes as well as obesity has nearly tripled in the last 30 years within the United States, particularly within communities of color" ("FY 2003"). Asking members of the subcommittee to avoid playing politics with this important issue, DeGette reminds them "that now is not the time to cut programs that focus on research, education and prevention of this epidemic" ("FY 2003"). In a June 2004 e-Newsletter to her constituents, the Congresswoman discusses the "Stem Cell Research Enhancement Act," legislation she introduced "to expand federal government support for embryonic stem cell research" (DeGette, "DeGette Report 7"). She explains to her readers that "this critical medical research holds the potential to develop treatment or cures for diseases including Parkinson's, diabetes and cancer as well as spinal chord [sic] and other nerve injuries" ("DeGette Report 7"). DeGette declares that "government policy—not scientific limitation—is now holding stem cell research back" ("DeGette Report 7"). Describing the ramifications of the bill, she says it "will allow for the development of new stem cell lines and allow science, not government policy, to determine the advancement of research. This is not about politics," she argues. "It is about science, medicine and hope" ("DeGette Report 7"). DeGette, in an August 2004 news release, urges the congressional leadership to "put sound policy over politics and allow the full House to consider the bipartisan proposal to increase federal funding for embryonic stem cell research" (DeGette, "House Should Put Science").

Congresswoman DeGette's speech at the 2004 Democratic National Convention provided an international, albeit partisan, platform for her views on scientific research and politics. Although her remarks were targeted, in part, for a narrow persuasive goal, DeGette did not deviate from the resolve she brings to the same issues in her House floor speeches. Commenting that "stem cell research has been embraced by liberals and conservatives, by those who are pro-choice and those who are pro-life," she argues that "some would rather put politics before sound science" (DeGette, "U.S."). She urges the nation to "provide the government support necessary for stem cell research instead of heeding the call of political extremism over scientific exploration" ("U.S."). She reminds her audience that "our government was created by and for the people. Manipulation of science for political goals," she maintains, "fails that goal" ("U.S."). Referring to "more than 60 of our nation's top scientists, including forty-eight Nobel Prize winners," DeGette says "they're warning that we cannot politicize science when we plan policy on global warming, on emergency contraception, and on embryonic stem cell research" ("U.S."). She claims these scientists see hope in the Democratic candidates, "hope that science will once again come first, that policy will come before politics and that lives will be saved" ("U.S."). She declares "it is time for America to have a president who puts scientific discovery ahead of political calculation" and "we must put the full weight of the government behind scientific discovery" ("U.S."). Despite its cloaking in the rationalistic language of *science*, DeGette's agenda for scientific research finds it grounding in her desire to protect others from the ravages of disease and thus, links directly to the second ideograph, *protection*, which pervades much of her discourse.

DeGette often testifies that among her "top priorities in Congress are improving the quality of our nation's health care system and making the system more accessible and affordable for all Americans, especially children" in order to protect their physical well-being. "I am proud of my efforts," she continues, "to improve the ways we treat and cure diseases and to expand health care coverage for millions of children who previously went uninsured" (DeGette, "Issues: Health"). She cites the need for "protecting American laboratories' access to stem cell research" because "a lack of research may delay development of treatment and therapies for a variety of diseases" ("Issues: Health"). DeGette believes "that it is important that Congress both encourage expansion of research in these emerging areas of medicine and work with the medical community to establish safeguards to protect patients taking part in clinical trials of these new therapies" ("Issues: Health"). In the House floor debate on the Pharmaceutical Market Access Act, DeGette tells her colleagues that "we have a duty to protect the people of this Nation" (DeGette, "House Floor Debate"). She claims, "This legislation will harm patients. It will harm the children, and it will harm the elderly. It lacks the necessary guarantees of safety and we should not subject the American people to it" ("House Floor Debate"). She argues that although "proponents of the bill say that the quality of the drugs will be protected," she has "not heard one Member on either side of the aisle say how that will happen" ("House Floor Debate"). She closes her remarks by reminding her audience, "We were elected to preserve the health and safety of the people we represent, over 600,000 each. Let us not sacrifice that fundamental right for a convoluted bill that is not even guaranteed to do what it is supposed to do" ("House Floor Debate").

As she works to protect the well-being of the country's citizens, DeGette simultaneously focuses on the health of the environment. Accusing President Bush of "flip flop[ping] on protecting America's forests," she calls upon him to "keep his promise and keep the rule that preserves roadless areas in our national forests" (DeGette, "Bush"). In a report to her constituents, she notes that "for several years, I have worked with Coloradoans to protect some of our last remaining wilderness lands that do not have roads, towns, or other development on them, from disappearing (DeGette, "DeGette Report 6"). She discusses her attempts to persuade U.S. Interior Secretary Gale Norton to "stop issuing new [oil and gas drilling] permits until the land under existing lease has been explored. . . . The surplus of unused drilling permits," she avers, "gives the Interior Department the ability to balance exploration without compromising the conservation of wilderness areas" ("DeGette Report 6"). Concluding her report, DeGette contends that "it is essential that we find a balance that allows us to continue energy exploration on federal lands and conserve our invaluable wilderness" ("DeGette Report 6").

A staunch advocate of the guarantee of constitutional rights, Representative DeGette lobbies for the protection of civil liberties and equality for all U.S. citizens. Announcing her 2002 reelection campaign, she observes that "we have the opportunity to protect our basic rights—the worker's right to organize and bargain, a woman's right to choose, the right of each childe [sic] to get a good public education" (DeGette, "Diana"). She promises her neighbors in Colorado's First Congressional District that "I will continue to lead the fight to ensure that the US [sic] Constitution protects all of your rights, regardless of your race, ancestry, sexual orientation or religion" (DeGette, "DeGette Report 1"). In a discussion of the USA Patriot Act, DeGette denounces the House Republican leadership for defeating a measure that would have established limits on the information the government could obtain from library and bookstore records. "This plan would have struck a critical balance between gathering intelligence information and protecting our basic Constitutional rights," she declares (DeGette, "DeGette Report 8"). "This was a sad day for protection of our Constitutional rights and for democratic fair play," she attests. "I will, however, continue to fight every day to protect your civil liberties and make sure that we remain the beacon of freedom we must in order to win the war on terrorism" (DeGette, "DeGette Report 8").

DeGette's concern for women's rights, especially reproductive freedom, remains a major tenet of her legislative platform as demonstrated in a January 2003 column. "As co-chair of the Bipartisan Pro-Choice Caucus in Congress," she says, "I have lead [sic] the fight to protect the full range of reproductive choices for women against this angry, dogmatic and moralistic anti-choice majority in Washington, D.C." (DeGette, "Overturning"). In a floor debate on the Lofgren Amendment to the Unborn Victims of Violence Act of 2003, she reemphasizes her view that the bill "is nothing but a poorly disguised vehicle to undermine *Roe v. Wade*" (DeGette, "House Floor Remarks on Unborn"). She explains to her colleagues that "the majority of Americans are pro-choice, and they depend on us to protect a woman's right to choose. . . . They depend on us to pass legislation that will protect their reproductive freedom," she postulates, "and they depend on us to know the difference between legislation that truly protects women and legislation that is discussed as something that it is not, like, for example, the bill that is before us now" ("House Floor Remarks on Unborn"). She continues her assault on the bill claiming that "we are not fooled by this legislation," and "our constituents will not be fooled by this legislation" ("House Floor Remarks on Unborn"). DeGette contends that "if Members of the House really care about taking steps to protect pregnant women and punish the people who commit horrible acts of violence against them, we will all join together and vote for the Lofgren substitute" ("House Floor Remarks on Unborn").

Congresswoman Diana DeGette's political discourse clearly embodies the concept of the in-between space. As she infuses traditionally private sphere concerns, such as children's health, with the language of public sphere rationality, in this case the primacy of science, she morphs the boundaries between Second and Third Space perceptions of lived experience. In advocating for the protection of constitutional rights in various facets of our existence, she wraps those private sphere activities within the cloak of public sphere constitutional rhetoric. Through the use of both of these ideographs, *science* and *protection*, DeGette exemplifies the notions that the personal is political and that the political is personal, and therefore, our government must function in a new, gender-neutral space if it is to succeed.

Barbara Lee

"Our deepest fears now haunt us. Yet I am convinced that military action will not prevent further acts of international terrorism against the United States. This is a very complex and complicated matter" (Lee, qtd. in Perine). Representative Barbara Lee, from the Ninth Congressional District of California, cast the lone dissenting vote against authorizing President Bush to use whatever force necessary to retaliate the September 11, 2001, attacks on the World Trade Center ("Lee" 64). She received death threats and subsequent twenty-four-hour police protection for taking a stand and maintaining her unpopular position. Even before the 9/11 attacks, however, Lee had established herself as an antiwar, antiviolence advocate. According to the *Almanac of American Politics*, she has consistently opposed military action and resolutions supporting U.S. bombing raids in places like Serbia. She also criticized President Bill Clinton's bombing of Iraq in December 1998 (Barone and Cohen 191).

According to Keith Perine, "Lee's politics are shaped by early exposure to discrimination. Her mother initially was refused treatment at an El Paso hospital while in labor with her. Barbara later attended a segregated high school where a small riot ensued when she was chosen for the cheerleading squad (Perine). While a student at Oak Mills College, Lee worked on Democrat Shirley Chisholm's campaign for the presidency as a class project (Perine). She later received a master's degree in social work at Berkeley and cofounded a health center in the area. She spent fifteen years on Congressman Ron Dellums's staff (Perine). Lee served from 1991 to 1997 in the California State Assembly. During that time, she focused on heightening awareness of the problems facing African Americans ("Lee" 63). When Dellums announced his retirement, Lee successfully ran for his seat and became a member of the U.S. House of Representatives in 1998. She has been reelected easily, carrying an 85 percent to 15 percent margin of victory over her last opponent who criticized her antimilitary stance (Barone and Cohen 191).

During her tenure as a U.S. congresswoman, Lee has "worked to form bipartisan coalitions to seek affordable health care and housing, equal access to quality education, and jobs, and she is a leader in the fight against HIV and AIDS, having secured over $5 million for HIV/AIDS services in Alameda County, California" ("Lee"). She "stands at the far left of the ideological political spectrum" and wants to reduce the country's stockpiles of weapons and sharply cut Pentagon spending (Barone and Cohen 191). Working with Congressman Henry Hyde, she helped increase support for international HIV/AIDS programs from $469 million to $535 million. After visiting Cuba, she called for the end of America's forty-year embargo of the island (191).

Representative Lee has won numerous awards, including the Wayne Morse Integrity in Government Award and the Sean McBride Prize from the International Peace Bureau. She has been named Public Elected Official of the Year by the National Association of Social Workers ("Lee"). In October 2003, the American Public Health Association gave its public Health Legislator of the Year Award to Lee for her ongoing efforts to combat AIDS as well as for her work to form coalitions to address health care, housing, education, and employment ("Baldacci"). Her most recent congressional committee membership includes a seat on Financial Services, working specifically in the areas of housing and community opportunity. She also holds a seat on the International Relations Committee, primarily focusing on Africa and Europe (Barone and Cohen 189). She is the chair of the Progressive Caucus and whip for the Congressional Black Caucus (B. Lee, "U.S. Congresswoman").

"My primary mission," Representative Lee says, "is to improve the lives of the people in the 9th Congressional District and to promote for Americans and all the world international security through peace" (B. Lee, "U.S. Congresswoman"). Her public statements indicate her belief that the world and country cannot become better places, however, when decision making and subsequent policies are flawed. Her floor speeches are noteworthy for their articulation of her concerns of *priorities* and of *equal opportunity*. She consistently criticizes the Bush administration, for instance, for having misplaced priorities that privilege military spending over necessary social programs. "I am extremely disappointed in the details of this budget," notes Lee. "On issues that are of the greatest importance to millions of Americans, this budget calls for policies that represent misplaced priorities. I call on my colleagues to fight against this blueprint that will turn back America years, if not decades" (B. Lee, "Congresswoman").

Rising in support of a bill that would increase and extend community block grants, Lee argues that "this bill should be about people not politics. . . . The truth is we are in an ongoing struggle for human dignity, basic human rights and real people living in poverty which this bill has provided resources and support to" (B. Lee, "Improving"). She then provides additional justification for the bill, once again asking her colleagues to consider what is important: "Our challenge and our obligation to eliminate poverty and guarantee basic human rights and dignity to all men and women must be championed not only by this bill but by some real money and attention" ("Improving"). Lee skillfully ties her theme into another national priority, peace and justice. "The centerpiece of this debate should be," she intones, "where there is justice for all men and women, we find peace and respect for human dignity and rights. Today this country needs leadership that will ensure and protect that dignity and our basic and most treasured human rights" ("Improving").

One of the causes closest to Lee's heart is the prevention and treatment of AIDS. As mentioned above, she has directed significant energy and resources to combating the deadly disease. She frequently points out that the effort to fight AIDS, nationally and globally, must be significant, must be a fiscal priority. As she says in a floor speech supporting World AIDS Day, "United Nations Secretary General Kofi Annan and global AIDS experts estimate that it will take $7 billion to $10 billion annually to launch an effective response. The United States should contribute at least $1 billion to this fund as the wealthiest and most powerful country on Earth. The human family," she concludes, "is at stake. We can and must do more" (B. Lee, "Supporting").

Barbara Lee has never wavered in her belief that her dissenting vote against authorizing the president broad discretionary powers to respond to the attacks of September 11 was the right thing to do. In an article for the *San Francisco Chronicle* later reprinted by *Black Scholar*, she explains her rationale in detail. Her priority is protecting the country's interests—and she is unconvinced war will accomplish that. Other solutions must be a priority before war. Lee states:

> I am not convinced that voting for the resolution preserves and protects U.S. interests. We must develop our intelligence and bring those who did this to justice. We must mobilize—and maintain—an international coalition against terrorism. Finally, we have a chance to demonstrate to the world that great powers can choose to fight on the fronts of their choosing, and that we can choose to avoid needless military action when other avenues to redress our rightful grievances and to protect our nation are available to us. (B. Lee, "Statement")

In a floor speech titled "Presidential Mistakes," Representative Lee launches a litany of attacks against the Bush Administration's spending priorities. She criticizes his "support" for his own No Child Left Behind Act, saying, "What has happened to Leave No Child Behind: 9.4 billion-plus underfunded. Leave No Child Behind has been a shame and a disgrace" ("Presidential Mistakes"). She points out that under the Clinton administration, AIDS initiatives operated effectively, but "since President Bush came in . . . programs continue to be 600 million-plus underfunded" ("Presidential Mistakes"). Finally, she directly attacks the Bush administration in general, stating that "I think we must once again communicate directly to the American people what we know and that is the fact that

their tax dollars are going from misplaced priorities of waging war rather than securing peace, waging a PR campaign to try to instill in the American people these
notions of facts that they want us to believe. They are really distortions put mild
and, in fact," Lee concludes, "a way to boost the foundation and the debate and
the rationale for waging war which, unfortunately," has cost many people their lives
("Presidential Mistakes").

Because of their significant opposition to the Bush Administration's proposed
2005 budget, the Congressional Black Caucus (CBC) drafted and proposed an alternative. In rising to support their bill, Congresswoman Lee states that they did
so "to discuss the misplaced priorities and the misallocated resources found in the
Republican Budget" (B. Lee, "Investing"). Her speech bluntly outlines some of
the problems with the priorities Bush has set. "During this debate and for weeks
prior to today," she claims, "we have made a clear case for why and how the Republican budget sacrifices our children, our senior citizens, our security, our environment, and our economy in order, really, to advance monied interests and to
promote tax breaks for the wealthy" ("Investing"). Conversely, Lee states, "unlike
the Republican budget, the Congressional Black Caucus substitute has its priorities really in the right place. It is based on fairness. It is based on fiscal responsibility. And it is based on the values that we hold dear" ("Investing"). An
examination of the CBC bill reveals that it increases funding to fight AIDS, increases funding for local law enforcement programs, extends more aid to Haiti,
strengthens Environmental Protection Agency provisions, creates housing vouch-
ers for the poor and homeless, and increases funding for a variety of educational
programs ("Investing").

The misplacement of priorities has a direct impact on the lives of Americans.
Barbara Lee voices particular concerns with making sure that individuals have the
opportunity to live the best life possible, and it is her focus on the concept of *equal
opportunity* or the lack thereof, that we now examine. In her first speech in Congress,
for instance, Lee informs her colleagues that she intends to "continue to challenge
those policies which continue to widen the gap between the rich and the poor" (B.
Lee, "Accepting"). She later adds that she brings to Congress a fundamental principle that Congress "provide, and should provide, equal opportunities for everyone, and shatter the walls of discrimination based upon race, national origin,
gender, age, disability, and sexual orientation" ("Accepting").

To further support the CBC's alternate budget proposal, Lee focuses on the
lack of opportunity under the Republican plan and the opportunities created by
the CBC. Specifically, the Bush proposal curtails the opportunities of minorities. "The insidious nature of this Bush Budget," Lee warns, "is that so many of
these efforts and programs which have been eliminated or cut affect the African

American, the Latino, and the Asian Pacific Islander communities. They affect low-income individuals, poor people" (B. Lee, "Investing"). However, according to Lee, with the CBC budget, there is abundant opportunity. She states:

> There are no jobs out there; but if in fact we created an infrastructure, development initiative, if we invested in our economy by investing in health care, if we invested by establishing the National Affordable Housing Trust Fund to increase the production of affordable housing in the country, we would be able to create jobs by creating an investment in our country and in our communities for areas that people need. ("Investing")

Representative Barbara Lee has been compared to Jeannette Rankin and also to her hero, Wayne Morse, for her antiwar stance. While comparisons are interesting, what is important to note about Representative Lee is her steadfast commitment to her stated priority—improving the lives of those in her district, her country, and the world. She uses the combined ideographs of *priority* and *equal opportunity* to illustrate what is wrong with current policies and to provide a glimpse into what could be a better way of doing the nation's business. She unflinchingly sticks to her principles and through her actions and her discourse demonstrates a keen political ability to fight for those most in need.

Judy Biggert

"I didn't realize how important seniority was," states Judy Biggert of her experience as a U.S. Representative from the Thirteenth District in Illinois (Barone and Cohen 567). Initially elected to Congress in 1998, Biggert had originally pledged to serve only three terms, a promise she abandoned in October 1999 (567). Biggert lived the life of the archetypal "soccer mom" and "car pool mom," having coached a team near her hometown. Technically, she began her political career as a local PTA president (Schribman), but her personal web site suggests that "a lifetime of community service prepared Judy for the challenges of public office," since she "served for four years as Chairman of the Village of Hinsdale Plan Commission and for four years as a member of the Steering Committee of the Hinsdale Citizens for Property Tax Accountability" (Biggert, "Meet Judy"). In addition, she has "served as the Chairman of the Hinsdale Assembly of the Hinsdale Hospital, Chairman of the Hinsdale Antiques Show, and as member of the Board of Directors of Salt Creek Ballet" ("Meet Judy").

Judy Biggert's legislative career commenced in 1992 when she "was elected to the Illinois House of Representatives to serve the newly created Eighty-first District" (Biggert, "Meet Judy"). While in the statehouse, she worked on economic initiatives such as "tort reform, state tax cuts, and balanced budgets" ("Meet

Judy"). She also worked to protect women and families and won the title "Woman of the Year" in government because of those efforts ("Meet Judy"). Perhaps most noteworthy of her tenure in state government was her "ability to negotiate and create consensus among her peers" ("Judy Biggert").

Biggert began running for the U.S. House of Representatives in 1997. She won the March primary by a 45 percent to 40 percent margin and the general election 61 percent to 39 percent (Barone and Cohen 567). *The Almanac of American Politics* reports that she supports abortion except for "late term" procedures, opposes gun control, and consistently supports Bush Administration positions (566–67). Analysis also suggests that she focuses on local issues such as health and juvenile crime. She has not been successful in moving into party leadership positions at the national level, hence her observation about seniority (567). Her web page reports, however, that she successfully introduced two pieces of legislation in her first term: "The Cybertipline legislation made it easier to report and track down computer based sex crimes against children, and the other was a bill that led to increased penalties for traffickers of club drugs such as Ecstasy" (Biggert, "Meet Judy").

Representative Biggert speaks to a wide variety of audiences on an equally wide range of topics. But one theme consistently occurs: the problem of *quick fixes* and the benefit of *long-term solutions*. Except in one instance, she privileges the latter and condemns the former, as the following excerpts from her addresses illustrate.

In a floor statement reprinted as "Biggert Opposes Court-Stripping Legislation" on her web page, Representative Biggert presents her opposition to the Marriage Protection Act. She argues that "proponents of this bill one day will deeply regret their actions. What may seem today a 'quick fix' to some very challenging issues will undoubtedly come back to haunt them" ("Biggert Opposes"). She goes on to add that the bill will "undermine the very law this Congress passed in 1996 to protect marriage [the Defense of Marriage Act stating that marriage is between one man and one woman]. At the same time, it will undermine the Constitution and the separation of powers" ("Biggert Opposes"). Instead, Biggert exhorts her colleagues to have faith in the long-term, time-honored solution of the Constitution of the United States, stating "I urge my colleagues to have faith in the constitutionality and merits of the DOMA they so rightly supported in 1996, and reject the 'quick fix' H.R. 3313" ("Biggert Opposes").

A House resolution commending Afghan women received Judy Biggert's support. In rising to explain her position, Biggert once again invoked the concept of long-term versus short-term solutions. After praising Congress's passage of the Afghan Women and Children's Relief Act, she suggests: "This was an important first step that provided immediate assistance. Now, however, it is time to look beyond the short-term and provide long-term assurance that the women of Afghanistan will never again be targeted for abuse by their government and forced to live under such horrific conditions" (Biggert, "Floor Statement").

The U.S. war in Iraq and its concurrent war on terror also deserve a long-term solution, according to Biggert. In her defense of Bush policies, she states: "Simply put, we must—and we will—sustain our effort to root out terrorists in other countries and we must deny al Qaeda members the chance to regroup and reload its weapons of terror" (Biggert, "War on Terrorism"). Later in this speech on homeland security Biggert explains that terrorism "is a complicated and difficult problem that did not arise overnight, nor will it be solved overnight" ("War on Terrorism"). She warns the audience, "I think we should be prepared for the long haul. As President Bush said last September, this will not be a short-term effort, but terrorism will be defeated" ("War on Terrorism").

Two years later, Biggert is still urging support for the Bush policies, which now include a full-scale war in Iraq. Specifically, she calls for patience in building a new democracy in Iraq, a process that takes a long time and great effort. No quick fix will work. "Now, there is no doubt that completing these steps will not be easy," she suggests. "But George Bush has stayed the course, reminding people that this will not happen overnight. I like to remind people, too, that restoring democracy and completing reconstruction in Germany after World War II took nearly seven years and yet we haven't been in Iraq seventeen months" (Biggert, "Judy's Remarks to the Hinsdale").

It is interesting to note that in one instance Representative Biggert actually advocates a quick solution to a perceived problem. She supports President Bush's preemptive strike against the country of Iraq. In supporting the action, Biggert eschews the long-term solution of investigation and containment in favor of overthrowing the Iraqi government. In response to critics of the war, she argues: "Now to those who say we should have given Hans Blix and his team more time [to find weapons of mass destruction], I say this. I frankly do not know what that could have accomplished except to give Saddam more time to stall, conceal, and continue developing weapons to use against us, his own people, and his neighbors" (Biggert, "Judy's Latest Statement").

Domestic issues also benefit from long-term effort and solutions. In the area of juvenile crime, for instance, Biggert details the work needed to reduce youth violence and drug use. When speaking at the Bolingbrook Citizen Police Academy Commencement Ceremony, she revealed the problems with curtailing club drugs like Ecstasy, stating that drug dealing "penalties were a joke, providing virtually no deterrent . . . so I introduced legislation that increased the maximum sentences for trafficking Ecstasy and other club drugs. Recognizing the importance of local efforts," she continues, "I included money in the bill to provide grants for local law enforcement or non-profit organizations to run school and community based education, abuse and addiction programs regarding Ecstasy and related drugs" (Biggert, "Judy's Remarks at Bolingbrook"). Similarly, youth violence can only be solved by a lengthy, concerted effort, she states. "After several months of work," Biggert reports, "we concluded that reducing youth violence requires a combination of responsible parents, solid prevention programs, good schools, and mental-health services" ("Judy's Remarks at Bolingbrook").

Representative Judy Biggert from the Thirteenth District of Illinois supports and debates a plethora of issues both foreign and domestic. While she is often recognized for her work on women's issues, she has entered the complete political fray, discussing such issues as gay marriage, youth violence, and the U.S. war in Iraq. Her ideograph of *long-term solutions* is imbued with cautiousness and conservatism, except where, in the case of the U.S. invasion of Iraq, it is not convenient to do so. Biggert's use of the *long-term* concept gives the impression that she is the rational policy maker and that others proposing different solutions are the ones rushing to a dangerous or at least troublesome outcome.

Tammy Baldwin

"In a democracy we decide what's possible" (Baldwin, "Harvey"). Tammy Baldwin's brief but profound statement aptly describes her passion and purpose in politics. Regardless of the issue, Representative Baldwin, from Wisconsin's Second Congressional District, promotes citizen and legislative participation in open and honest discussion. "The thing I love the most about this job," she declares, "is that moment you connect with someone and they figure out their vote matters, their voice matters, their participation matters" (qtd. in Conniff, "Tammy"). Lauren Azar, her partner, describes Baldwin's "deep-seated hopefulness for our community, for people, for government. And, her commitment to youth is absolutely phenomenal. It's all about access," she continues. "This government is their government" (qtd. in Ocamb). Given her push for a government of, by, and for the people, she often finds herself at odds with the current administration's attempts to bypass congressional debate, particularly on matters of foreign policy and divisive domestic matters. Baldwin, a staunch supporter of the Bill of Rights and the fundamental concept of separation of powers, often argues on the House floor for adherence to the system of checks and balances guaranteed in the U.S. Constitution.

Baldwin cemented her place in history when she won the 1998 congressional race and became the first woman sent to the U.S. House of Representatives by Wisconsin voters. Additionally, Baldwin's election catapulted the nation's first non-incumbent, openly homosexual candidate into the halls of Congress. When asked in an interview if she felt pressured because of the significance of her election,

Baldwin replied, "No, I feel just delighted and proud because I think I understand the symbolic importance. . . . What I feel more than anything else," she continued, "is that if I do my job well to represent all of the people in the Second Congressional district, and work really hard on the agenda that we've spelled out, that I'll do more to challenge stereotypes that people might have about progressives, about young people, about women, about lesbians" (qtd. in Conniff, "Tammy").

Tammy Baldwin's commitment to a life in politics came as no surprise to those who know her. "She was almost born for the job," suggested freelance writer Karen Ocamb. Born in 1962 in Madison, Wisconsin, the center of the district she now represents and "one of the heartbeats of the anti-Vietnam War movement in the 1960s," Baldwin "accompanied her student mother to anti-war demonstrations on the University of Wisconsin campus" (Ocamb). Following the divorce of her parents, Baldwin's maternal grandparents, both of whom taught at the university, helped raise her. They instilled within her "a commitment to political causes" and encouraged her "to be aware of the world around her" (Ocamb). In middle school, Baldwin learned about "the impact public service can have on people's lives" (Baldwin, "About Tammy"). A member of the student council, Baldwin "served on an outreach committee to improve relations with neighbors of the school" ("About Tammy"). She describes this experience as "a great exercise in problem-solving and in seeing how a small group of people can effect positive change. I really loved the experience," she says, "and it put me on the career path I'm following to this day" ("About Tammy"). Baldwin graduated first in her class of 510 students at Madison West High School and then earned a BA degree in 1984 from Smith College, where she majored in political science and math ("About Tammy"; Barone and Cohen 1742; Hawkings and Nutting 1104). Following graduation, she returned to Wisconsin and worked as an intern in the office of Governor Tony Earl before she entered the University of Wisconsin Law School ("About Tammy"). Baldwin completed her law degree and passed the bar in 1989. She practiced law from 1989 until 1992. Describing her work as an attorney, Baldwin notes that "approximately a third of my practice was in civil rights; advocating for people denied housing opportunities, advocating for people terminated from jobs or who failed to receive a promotion for a variety of factors—sexual orientation or race or HIV status" (Neff). While in law school, Baldwin made her first foray into electoral politics.

In 1986, at the age of twenty-four Tammy Baldwin won election to the Dane County Board of Supervisors. During her four terms on the board, Baldwin established and chaired the Dane Country Task Force on AIDS, served briefly on the Madison City Council, completed her law degree, and in November 1992, ran for state assembly (Schenken 55; Baldwin, "About Tammy"). She served as a member of the Wisconsin Assembly from January 1993 until January 1999, when she began her tenure in the U.S. House of Representatives. On the board and in the state assembly, Baldwin represented the university district, which included a constituency many politicians failed to consider important. Given her proclivity to advocate on behalf of the marginalized, Baldwin embraced this population. "I had built an early career trying to get people to take young people seriously" and to recognize "that the student constituency was not just a transient group passing through the community," Baldwin notes. Students are "citizens who deserve to have a voice in public policy making," she continues. "So we spent a tremendous amount of attention getting young people to take part in the democratic process and feel ownership of it" (qtd. in Ocamb). Baldwin's consideration of the student population exemplifies the focus of her public endeavors. "And that is the very essence of who I am [as] a politician" she declares, "getting the voice of people who are often overlooked heard" (qtd. in Ocamb). As a state assembly person, Baldwin achieved victories on several legislative issues, including "providing protection for whistle blowers who report elderly abuse," granting collective bargaining rights for state public defenders, and regulating the life insurance industry (Ocamb). Although she also worked for more liberal social causes, her efforts in these areas garnered less success (Ocamb).

In the 1998 Democratic primary on her way to the U.S. House of Representatives, Baldwin employed many of the strategies that had proven successful in her previous campaigns for local and state office. In addition, she focused on her sex, making it "central to her campaign" (Canon and Herrnson). "While positioning herself as a policy-oriented candidate, she repeatedly pointed out that Wisconsin had never sent a woman to Congress and ran television ads saying that 'Tammy Baldwin will take on the issues that most congressmen won't'" (Canon and Herrnson). In her broadcast advertising, Baldwin targeted women with ads, which "were broadcast during television programs that attracted largely female audiences" (Canon and Herrnson). She focused on issues that "topped women's concerns, including equal pay for equal work, protecting Social Security, quality education, combating nursing home abuse and health care reform" (Canon and Herrnson). As she had done in her previous campaigns, Baldwin "mobilized young voters," especially Generation Xers (Canon and Herrnson). Ads aimed at this population appeared on "MTV, Ally McBeal and other shows with large student audiences" (Canon and Herrnson). While Baldwin did not make homosexuality an issue in the campaign, not surprisingly, others did. In the early days of the campaign, the local press almost always "describ[ed] her as 'Tammy Baldwin, the first lesbian member of the state assembly'" (Canon and Herrnson). Her two Democratic opponents in the primary and five of the Republican primary candidates did not spotlight this topic. Ron Greer, one of the Republican contenders, however, attacked Baldwin's sexual orientation throughout the campaign. For example, in one of his fund-raising letters "he labeled Baldwin 'a left-wing lesbian'" (Canon and Herrnson). As one would expect, such negative tactics "mobilize[d] Madison's politically active gay community and drew the attention of homosexuals nationwide, many of whom responded by contributing to Baldwin's campaign" (Canon and Herrnson). In addition to financial contributions from the Victory Fund, Baldwin amassed support from EMILY's List (Barone and Cohen 1742). Baldwin, who raised more money than her two Democratic competitors, won the primary with 37 percent of the vote (Canon and Herrnson; Barone and Cohen 1742).

In the general election, Baldwin faced Republican Josephine Musser. Explicit gender issues moved from the center to the sidelines in the campaign as the two women vied for the congressional seat. Baldwin reframed topics of particular concern to women as more gender-neutral family issues. Both Baldwin and Musser overcame one of the hurdles that often impedes female candidates; they each garnered substantial financial support. In fact, the $1.5 million Baldwin raised broke all records for the amount of money spent in Wisconsin U.S. House races (Canon and Herrnson; Barone and Cohen 1742). "Baldwin's candidacy," according to Michael Barone and Richard Cohen, "roused the enthusiasm of Madison liberals in a way not seen in years" (1743). Her campaign messages accentuated the idea that "she was a different kind of candidate who had vision" by focusing on her youth, political experience, and "commitment to bipartisan solutions to national problems" (Canon and Herrnson). She created a human face for "her vision by framing Social Security, protection for the elderly and workplace fairness issues around the experiences of her 92-year-old grandmother and 2-year-old cousin" (Canon and Herrnson). Baldwin also guided her campaign down the information highway through her innovative use of the World Wide Web. Her web site included the now familiar campaign data as well as voting information for her constituents (Canon and Herrnson). The site proved especially popular among the student and young adult population. More than three thousand volunteers, many of them students, joined Baldwin's campaign efforts (Canon and Herrnson). With a "well-oiled campaign organization" (Canon and Herrnson), Baldwin defeated Musser, winning 52 percent of the vote (Hawkings and Nutting 1104). Political scientists argue, "This campaign demonstrates that modern elections cannot ignore grassroots organization and get-out-the-vote efforts" (Canon and Herrnson). In the 2000 election, she overcame a strong challenge from a University of Wisconsin history professor and eked out a victory with only 51 percent of the voters' support (Barone and Cohen 1743; Hawkings and Nutting 1105). The incumbent Baldwin won easily in the 2002 contest. Finding favor with 66 percent of the voters, she triumphed over Ron Greer, who once again attacked her sexual orientation (Barone and Cohen 1743).

An outspoken liberal, Representative Tammy Baldwin enjoys membership in the Progressive Caucus, one of the most liberal bastions in the House (Hawkings and Nutting 1104). She serves on the House Judiciary and Budget committees. The issues on which she concentrates encompass a broad range of social concerns, often focused on those groups and individuals whose voices she feels have been muted or silenced. While she works diligently for her Wisconsin constituents, her vision encompasses national and international matters. Health care reform remains one of her principal goals. In this area she promotes universal coverage with a single-payer system and has sponsored the Health Security for All Americans Act to ensure that all citizens of this country have access to adequate health care. (Schenken 55; Barone and Cohen 1743; Hawkings and Nutting 1104). Baldwin has sponsored legislation to create a federal office and center to study health issues related to military service (Barone and Cohen 1743; Hawkings and Nutting 1105). She has fought to expand the definition of hate crimes to include violence perpetrated against individuals based on their gender, sexual orientation, or disability. During her first term in Congress, Baldwin assisted with the victorious endeavor to reauthorize the Violence Against Women Act (Baldwin, "About Tammy"). Representative Baldwin also advocates for protecting Social Security and Medicare; augmenting support for education including nutrition programs for children, Head Start, financial aid for higher education, smaller class sizes, and computer technology; reducing the cost of prescription drugs for seniors; safeguarding the environment; and, guaranteeing equitable treatment for Wisconsin's farmers ("About Tammy"; Schenken 55; Barone and Cohen 1743).

Tammy Baldwin's public rhetoric embodies her personal and political philosophies and ideals. In speaking with her constituents in Wisconsin as well as her colleagues in the House, she formulates a discourse focusing on *cooperation not confrontation* in an atmosphere of governmental *transparency not secrecy* that enhances individuals' *freedom*. These three ideographs permeate Baldwin's discussion of the issues facing the nation and the state of Wisconsin and exemplify her approach to accomplishing the business of the government.

Whether she speaks of builders and destroyers, constructiveness versus destructiveness, working together or building coalitions, Tammy Baldwin believes in working cooperatively, not confrontationally, with others to achieve results beneficial to the people of this country. As a state assemblywoman, she developed a "reputation for reaching across the aisle and building coalitions" (Conniff, "Tammy"). When asked in an interview how she might handle potential aggressive comments or personal attacks from colleagues in the House, Baldwin replies that she "recognize[s] that there's going to be something, some day, that I need to work with them on, and that burning bridges is probably not a good practice" (qtd. in Conniff, "Tammy"). Responding to a question about how the country might effect meaningful changes in the healthcare system, she replies: "I think one works both within the institution of Congress as well as outside. . . . Outside the institution, we need to build a stronger coalition. . . . I think we can build a coalition that has business at the table" (qtd. in Conniff, "Tammy"). Baldwin's comments are not just empty words. For example, she has extended a hand across the congressional aisle to work with Republican Bob Barr to prohibit distribution of drug recipes over the Internet and to cosponsor a bill with Republican Melissa Hart to enjoin distributors of offensive materials from tampering with consumer products (Barone and Cohen 1743).

Now in her third term in office, Baldwin frequently employs the *cooperation not confrontation* ideograph in discussions centered on the war in Iraq. Prior to the war, she argues in October 2002 that "working with our allies and other nations to address this threat [weapons of mass destruction] is the appropriate way to proceed. . . . Absent an imminent threat, we must exhaust our other tools before hauling out the machinery of death and destruction," she attests. "There are realistic alternatives between doing nothing and declaring war" (Baldwin, "Statement on Use"). Continuing her assault on the House resolution authorizing the president to declare war on Iraq in a unilateral first strike, Baldwin suggests the resolution "undermin[es] the ability of the world community to maintain peace and security" and that the "precedent set by a 'go-it-alone first strike' would shape the future of this century. . . . And how we will speak with any moral authority to other sovereign nations who seek to 'take things into their own hands' against other states they see as threats?" she asks ("Statement on Use"). On March 6, 2003, Baldwin once again addresses the issue of a preemptive attack on Iraq in a speech on the House floor. "I and many others around the world are shocked and dismayed by the unilateral, confrontational approach that the Bush Administration has taken in the world arena," she proclaims ("Iraq"). "We have time to work together with the international community," she declares, "to collectively address the threat of Iraq" ("Iraq"). She speaks about the ways in which "the world came together in solidarity with our loss" following the attack on 9/11. "It should have been crystal clear," she laments, "that fighting terrorism and protecting American security would require friends and allies; cooperation, not confrontation. Yet," she proceeds, "the Administration instead engaged in a single-minded drive to achieve its Iraqi objectives at any cost instead of developing a policy to deal with Iraq by working with our allies, by working with the world community" ("Iraq").

Following the president's decision to attack Iraq, Representative Baldwin endorsed a House resolution in support of the troops on March 26, 2003. In these remarks she also calls for the reconstruction of Iraq after the war and urges the president to "rebuild our relations with the nations of this world so that we might once again work closely together to avoid war and maintain peace in solving global challenges" (Baldwin, "Statement on Support"). Speaking in support of a supplemental appropriations bill on April 3, 2003, Baldwin reiterates her earlier appeal for the nation to address the diplomatic wreckage created by President Bush's decision to invade Iraq. "I believe that we must take immediate responsibility for rebuilding strong trusting relationships with the international community—relationships that have been strained and damaged when this administration turned away from pursuit of a diplomatic resolution to this problem" (Baldwin, "Statement on Supplemental"). She decries what she sees as the country's movement away from democratic principle and commitment to finding "peaceful solutions to world disagreements and conflicts. The United States was seen as a constructive force in the world," she concludes. "Right now we are seen by many as a destructive force in the world" ("Statement on Supplemental"). In an impassioned plea, she asks for the restoration of a more constructive foreign policy:

> I stand here today to urge this President and this Congress to return to our tradition of constructiveness rather than destructiveness. We should be builders rather than destroyers. . . . I urge Members and citizens to join me in the effort to become constructive as a nation once again. . . to become builders once again. . . . We must rebuild and restore our relationships with our allies and our friends around the world. Our long-term security rests in working cooperatively in a world community with international standards and laws, seeking peaceful solutions to the many challenges we face. ("Statement on Supplemental")

Concluding her remarks, Baldwin communicates her "hope [for] the rebirth of our true vision of America, in which we reject the 'go-it-alone' mentality, reject preemptions and endorse the hard work of building and growing a peaceful world" ("Statement on Supplemental").

Baldwin reiterates many of these ideas in October 2003, when the House debated yet another appropriations bill for Iraq. For instance, she repeats the sentence: "It should have been crystal clear that fighting terrorism and protecting American security would require friends and allies; cooperation, not confrontation" (Baldwin, "Statement on Iraq"). And, she reemphasizes the idea that the United States is now seen as a destructive force when historically the country has been seen as a constructive force ("Statement on Iraq"). "Many around the world are shocked and dismayed by the unilateral confrontational approach that the Bush Administration has taken in the world arena. I share their concern," she tells her colleagues in the House ("Statement on Iraq"). Urging Congress and the president to "return to our tradition of constructiveness rather than destructiveness," she once again reminds her audience that "we should be builders rather than destroyers" ("Statement on Iraq"). Baldwin clearly opposes the president's policy, "or rather lack of policy" ("Statement on Iraq"), and decries the secrecy with which that policy has been negotiated and implemented.

In her speeches on the House floor, Representative Baldwin frequently reminds her colleagues that one of the functions of Congress is to ensure that the peoples' voices are heard in this democracy and that they understand what the government does and how it goes about its business. She relies upon the *transparency not secrecy* ideograph as a rhetorical strategy to communicate this idea. In her statement at Attorney General Ashcroft's hearing before the House in June 2003, Baldwin tells the attorney general "the American people are properly concerned about the authority and actions of the Department of Justice and other agencies. My constituents," she reminds him, "have a right to know about the safeguards that secure their liberty" ("Statement at Attorney"). While she and those she represents agree there are legitimate uses of these powers, they also recognize "there is a perception among many American citizens that these terms are being proffered not only in legitimate contexts, but also to prevent scrutiny of government actions" ("Statement at Attorney"). She asks, "What is the answer to our citizens' concerns about government secrecy, about abuse of power, about corruption?" In response to her own question she suggests, "in a democracy the burden is on our government to provide the assurances demanded by the people. And I believe," she continues, "there is only one way to alleviate our fellow citizens' concerns: we must bend over backwards to make our government transparent. We must give our citizens as much information as possible" ("Statement at Attorney"). Speaking about the increased use of Executive Privilege since September 11, 2001, Baldwin contends that "while I understand the fears that prompted some of this secrecy, it is a trend that must be reversed" ("Statement at Attorney").

Baldwin assumes the responsibility of her position as a U.S. representative is to engage actively in the government's business and to ensure the checks and balances inherent in our democratic system operate effectively. "I have taken an oath to protect and defend the Constitution of the United States," she tells her colleagues. "I cannot, and will not, simply delegate the responsibility to the President of the United States" (Baldwin, "Statement on Support"). In response to the criticism she and others have received due to their interrogation of the president's policies, Baldwin submits that "some will say that questioning the Administration in a time of war is unpatriotic and dangerous to the war effort. My oath compels me to disagree," she argues. "A democratic country must always have a debate, must always have questions raised, and Congress must never become a rubber stamp" ("Statement on Support"). Acting on her statements, Baldwin often questions the appropriations bills, especially those offered in support of the Iraqi War. She expresses specific concern about the bill debated on the House floor on October 16, 2003, and the lack of openness it represents. "The bill could have been improved in many ways, but there are two changes that I believe are essential," she contends. "First, the bill should require a detailed report from the president describing how funds in the previous war supplemental have been spent, how funds appropriated in this bill will be spent, and the level and types of funding needed for future years for both military and reconstruction activities" (Baldwin, "Statement on Iraq"). She proceeds with the discussion decrying the bidding practices, or lack thereof, in expending funds allocated in previous legislation. "The bill should require that Congress be notified of non-competitive contracting, require a report from the General Accounting Office on accountability, and tighten public disclosure requirements," she argues ("Statement on Iraq"). Baldwin then lists the various contracts that have been awarded without these practices. "We need to make sure that every cent of the $20 billion for Iraq reconstruction is awarded fairly and openly," she attests ("Statement on Iraq"). Baldwin asks: "What is wrong with the House voting on these and other amendments? I wish someone would tell us. Unfortunately," she exclaims, "the Republican House leadership used procedural roadblocks to prevent debate on most of these alternatives and improvements [to the appropriations bill]. . . . It is time for some accountability" ("Statement on Iraq").

Representative Baldwin uses the ideograph *freedom* in a variety of contexts. From concerns about loss of our basic liberties to protection from violence to issues of choice, she steadfastly avows the primacy of constitutional rights. Supporting the authorization of use of military force following the September 11 terrorist attack, Baldwin cautions the president and his administration to use this power wisely. "We will demonstrate our greatness by the way we seek justice and the way we promote freedom," she suggests (Baldwin, "Statement by Congresswoman . . . on H.J.R. 64"). "Our Constitutional liberties stand as an example to the world of what freedom means," she observes. "We must never forget that we pursue justice in order to secure liberty ("Statement by Congresswoman . . . on H.J.R. 64"). Following the invasion of Iraq and the passage of the USA Patriot Act, Baldwin tells Attorney General Ashcroft that "the threat of terrorism must not be used to justify police and prosecutorial powers that undermine our fundamental Constitutional freedoms" (Baldwin, "Statement at Attorney"). She remarks that "as the United States government works to prevent acts of terrorism, it is critical to understand that this is about protecting American lives while protecting the American way of life. In the United States," she exhorts, "we cherish our freedom of speech, we respect the right to due process, and we have expectations of privacy" ("Statement at Attorney"). Baldwin accuses the administration of "undermin[ing] the carefully designed system of checks and balances," a system that is "essential to our liberty. Checks and balances create a system of accountability to protect us from tyranny," she avers. "Checks and balances ensure our freedom" ("Statement at Attorney"). She concludes the speech, noting that "as the threat [of terrorism] grows and the pressure on government to cut corners increases, the checks and balances of due process rights are more important, not less" ("Statement at Attorney").

Baldwin often invokes the theme of *freedom* in her advocacy of social causes, particularly those involving marginalized populations. Countering the attacks on the judicial system raised with the Marriage Protection Act, for example, Baldwin confronts the supporters of the legislation. "It is a terrible mistake to try to strip one branch of the government from its involvement in evaluating particular laws," she contends. "This is particularly true when considering the Courts, whose Constitutional and historic role is to defend our liberties" (Baldwin, "House Floor Statement"). She closes her statement with a quotation from Republican Senator Barry Goldwater: "Frontal assault on the independence of the Federal courts is a dangerous blow to the foundations of a free society" (qtd. in Baldwin, "House Floor Statement"). In testifying against the Unborn Victims of Violence Act, Baldwin once again calls on the House to avoid undermining individual freedoms. "This bill," she argues, "is nothing more than an attack on a woman's right to choose" (Baldwin, "Floor Remarks"). Reiterating her position, she submits that "this bill establishes a legal framework to attack a woman's right to choose as guaranteed by the Supreme Court in the *Roe v. Wade* decision" ("Floor Remarks"). Supporting the Local Law Enforcement Hate Crimes Prevention Act, which she cosponsored, Baldwin attempts to afford citizens of marginalized groups protection from fear based on their membership in those communities. She appeals to her colleagues to adopt the act "because this country was founded on the premise that people should be free to be who they are, without fear of violence" (Baldwin, "Press").

Through her use of the three ideographs, *cooperation not confrontation, transparency not secrecy,* and *freedom,* Representative Tammy Baldwin creates a political discourse that addresses issues traditionally of concern to women and simultaneously embodies a gender-neutral rhetorical strategy. While the ideograph is not exclusively feminine, women often are discredited for seeking cooperation rather than confrontation as an emotional response and a means of avoiding difficult decision making. Baldwin, however, clearly places cooperation within the context of international diplomacy. As she couples the ideograph with the themes of builders and destroyers as well as construction versus destruction, she blends the more feminine notion of cooperation with the masculine ideas of engineering within a public sphere context. In a similar manner, Baldwin's use of the *transparency not secrecy* ideograph illustrates a concern for the empowerment of others, a concept often associated with a feminine rhetorical style. Yet, she grounds this theme, as well as the ideograph *freedom,* in the checks and balances guaranteed in the U.S. Constitution, the pillar of Second Space political rhetoric. In creating these tensions between conventional feminine and masculine ideas, between Second and Third Space interpretations, Baldwin composes an androgynous discourse of the in-between space.

Virginia Brown-Waite

"I promise never to fall in love with the place you sent me to work. I'll always be back home" (Brown-Waite, qtd. in Squires, "Brown-Waite Chats"). Congresswoman Virginia Brown-Waite's comment to Greater Dade City Chamber of Commerce members illustrates her commitment to her constituents. Representing Florida's Fifth Congressional District, she has remained true to her campaign promise: she returns home "every weekend and on all extended breaks from Congress's normal legislative session" (Brown-Waite, "Biography"). Described as having a "hands-on approach to solving problems" (Hawkings and Nutting 228), Brown-Waite has "built a reputation as a strong, tenacious leader with the ability and authority to get things done for the people she represents" (Brown-Waite, "Biography"). Although she thinks "bills are important," Brown-Waite believes "being responsive to the people back home is the most important thing" (qtd. in Solochek, "Lawmaker"). Reiterating this idea, the pragmatic Brown-Waite explains: "I learned a long time ago that the worst things an elected official can do are, A: not read your mail; B: nor respond in a timely fashion; and C: no matter what goes out of your office, it doesn't go out until you read it yourself" (Squires, "Brown-Waite Says"). "During her campaign, Brown-Waite promised she would be a visible, activist lawmaker, seeking the spotlight, fighting for issues important to Florida's 5th Congressional District" (Solochek, "Lawmaker"). By most accounts, she has done just that.

A native New Yorker, Virginia "Ginny" Brown-Waite earned a bachelor of science degree from the State University of New York, Albany, in 1976. Almost a decade later in 1984, she completed a master of arts degree in public administration at Russell Sage College (Hawkings and Nutting 228; Barone and Cohen 400). She then obtained a labor studies program certification from Cornell University (Brown-Waite, "Biography"). Before moving to Spring Hill, Florida, in 1987, Brown-Waite served for almost two decades as a Republican policy aide and legislative director in the New York Senate (Brown-Waite, "Biography"; Barone and Cohen 400; Hawkings and Nutting 228). Upon her arrival in Florida, she gained employment as a health care consultant and became involved in local politics. Brown-Waite's other career endeavors have included owning a Mr. Donut franchise and teaching college part time (Hawkings and Nutting 228).

Virginia Brown-Waite's journey in electoral politics began when she won election to the Hernando County Board of Commissioners in 1990. She served in

that capacity from 1991 to 1993 (Hawkings and Nutting 228; Barone and Cohen 400). Voters elected Brown-Waite to the Florida Senate in 1992, after she led
a successful campaign to keep a local mining company from burning hazardous
waste (Barone and Cohen 400). A self-proclaimed conservative, she also enjoys an
independent streak and doesn't restrain from crossing party lines if she believes
such action will better serve her constituents. "Her 10-year career in the Florida
Senate was notable for her ability to rise within the Republican ranks while bucking party orthodoxy on some issues" (Hawkings and Nutting 228). Brown-Waite
served as majority whip in the state senate, and her colleagues elected her president pro tempore for the 2001–2002 legislative session. As a Florida senator, she
supported the state's lawsuit against the tobacco industry, often backed environmental protection legislation, and helped provide oversight of the state's HMOs
while chairing the senate's Health Committee (Barone and Cohen 400; Hawkings
and Nutting 228).

With the support of Florida Republican leaders, Virginia Brown-Waite ran for
the U.S. House of Representatives in the 2002 election. A newly reshaped district
that favored Republican candidates encouraged the party's attempts to oust the incumbent, Democrat Karen L. Thurman, a five-term member of Congress. In the
Republican primary, Brown-Waite defeated her opponent, winning 58 percent of
the vote (Barone and Cohen 399). In one of the most competitive races in the nation, both candidates "focused on matters important to the senior citizen-heavy
district" (Solochek, "Brown-Waite Prevails"). According to reporter Jeffrey
Solochek, "The election was watched as one of only a handful of competitive
House races nationwide. The national Republican and Democratic parties poured
huge sums of money into the campaigns, as each aimed to claim control of the
108th Congress" ("Brown-Waite Prevails"). In a contest "marred by harsh negative advertisements" (Solochek, "Brown-Waite Ousts"), one voter, Melissa Russell, complained that "it's been really nasty" and that "makes it harder for people
to understand what they're really voting for" (qtd. in Solochek, "Brown-Waite Prevails"). Brown-Waite, who was one of only four House candidates in the country
to defeat an incumbent (Barone and Cohen 401), eked out a narrow victory, winning 47.9 percent of the vote while Thurman gleaned 46.2 percent of the district's
support (Hawkings and Nutting 228).

Representing a district in which 25 percent of the population is over sixty-five
(Barone and Cohen 400), Congresswoman Brown-Waite has focused much of her
attention during her first term in the House on issues affecting seniors. She has
cosponsored Medicare reform legislation and "served as vice-chair of the
Speaker's Prescription Drug Action Team" (Brown-Waite, "Biography"). Veterans,
many of whom are retired, compose an equally important element of her constituency. Two of the counties in the Fifth District boast a higher percentage of

military veterans than all but one other Florida county (Barone and Cohen 400), and Brown-Waite describes her district as "an area with the nation's third largest concentration of veterans" (Brown-Waite, "At Last"). She has "championed veterans' issues and healthcare in Washington as vigorously as she did in Tallahassee" (Brown-Waite, "Biography"). She serves on three committees: Budget, Financial Services, and Veteran's Affairs. Subcommittee assignments on the Veteran's Affairs Committee include Benefits and Health. In the 108th Congress, Brown-Waite also co-chairs the bipartisan Congressional Caucus for Women's Issues. She argues that her positions on matters before Congress "track with the 5th District's desires" (Solochek, "Freshman's"). "I spend time with the constituents," she proclaims. "My voting record reflects their views" (qtd. in Solochek, "Freshman's").

Congresswoman Brown-Waite's political discourse features two themes that reflect her conservative fiscal philosophy and her concerns for her constituents, especially veterans. Taking a variety of forms, the ideograph *spending discipline* finds its way into much of Brown-Waite's rhetoric. In the House debate on the Spending Control Act of 2004, she tells her colleagues that "spending discipline is needed and it is needed now" (Brown-Waite, "House Floor Statement on Spending"). Likewise, she expends much of her energy fighting to "protect those who protect us," as she champions veterans' causes. "Protecting those who protect us certainly is a bipartisan priority," she suggests in a statement to members of the House (Brown-Waite, "House Floor Remarks on Unscrupulous"). Using variations of this theme, Brown-Waite advocates for veterans in an assortment of contexts. In her discourse *protecting* may mean taking care of, providing for, or paying back those who have served the country in the military. And, for Brown-Waite the achievement of this protection requires fiscal responsibility.

"It's like I want to hold up a big sign that says, 'It's the spending, stupid,'" exclaims Representative Brown-Waite in a discussion of a budget enforcement bill (qtd. in Solochek, "Lawmaker"). "The time for talk is over," she scolds. "We have to focus on a basic budget problem, and that is spending. America cannot spend its way out of our deficit" (Brown-Waite, "House Floor Statement on Spending"). Continuing her argument in the floor debate on spending control, Brown-Waite contends that the legislation "reinstates spending controls with the force of law and ensures that Congress will stay the course in promoting a fiscally responsible budget" ("House Floor Statement on Spending"). Jeffrey Solochek reports that "without abandoning her zeal for tax cuts, the freshman lawmaker also has stood firmly with a minority of colleagues pushing for spending restraint. Otherwise, she suggested, all the positive effects of keeping money in taxpayers' hands will disappear under a cloud of uncontrolled appropriations" ("Lawmaker"). Advocating action that would bring spending discipline to the House, in 2003, Brown-Waite "co-sponsored legislation that would nullify the recent raise members of Congress received and eliminate automatic pay adjustments . . . saying it's just not proper to take more money 'when the economy is at a standstill'" (qtd. in "Lawmaker"). And, in legislative discussions she "regularly supports amendments that would trim the expense of a bill by 1 percent, though such measures rarely pass" (Solochek, "Freshman's").

In one of her columns, Brown-Waite outlines the budget issues for her constituents. "When crafting a budget the biggest challenge we will face is controlling spending while meeting all of the country's needs," she explains. "My job there [on the House Budget Committee] is to protect social security and Medicare and to revive the economy while at the same time making the tough decisions needed to eventually restore a balanced budget" ("FY 2003 Budget"). Representative Brown-Waite responds to the president's January 2004 State of the Union message in another column. "Like many of you," she writes, "I am a bit wary of the President's proposals to spend billions on marriage promotion and space exploration. Both are noble causes and ambitious goals but fiscal responsibility must again be a priority of this Congress" ("State of the Union"). Discussing the fiscal year 2004 budget with voters, she suggests that "somehow, a balance must be struck between sufficiently funding our nation's many worthwhile programs while 'tightening our belts' as we cut into our sizable, but manageable deficit" (Brown-Waite, "Upcoming Budget"). And in a similar discussion of the 2005 fiscal year budget, Brown-Waite assures readers that "my colleagues on the House Committee on the Budget and I have been working to rout out waste, fraud, and abuse throughout the 108th Congress. . . . As a member of the 'Washington Waste Watchers,'" she states, "I will continue to fight for bureaucratic efficiency, and work hard to trim and ultimately eliminate the current budget deficit" (Brown-Waite, "FY 2005 Budget").

Although she argues for "spending discipline," Representative Brown-Waite also wrangles for funding for those endeavors that affect the voters in her district. Veterans and those currently serving in the military appear to hold the top position on her priority list. Using a variety of phrases, Brown-Waite often promotes causes and legislation that "protect those who protect us." For example, in a floor debate about the VA Home Loan Guaranty Program, she proclaims "we owe our veterans the same chance at the American dream after their service as they had the day that they enlisted" (Brown-Waite, "House Floor Remarks on Increasing"). In a 2003 Memorial Day column, Brown-Waite praises fallen heroes and delineates the work Congress has accomplished on behalf of those courageous soldiers and the men and women currently serving in the military. "It is important to keep in mind the promise we've made to them as well as the sacrifices they've made for us," she tells her readers. "This week in Congress I am proud to report that my colleagues and I passed several pieces of legislation to provide the necessary resources to our Armed Services and to better the situation of our area's many veterans and their loved ones" ("Our Veterans"). Brown-Waite calls the FY 2004 budget the "most veterans-friendly budget in history" ("Our Veterans") and reminds her constituents that the "Republicans fully support our soldiers—both past and present" (Brown-Waite, "At Last").

Representative Brown-Waite frequently voices her support for legislation that promotes and protects the health of veterans. She explains to her colleagues in Congress that "the real people" back home in Florida always admonish her to "adequately fund veterans' health care" as well as the needs of those fighting the war in Iraq (Brown-Waite, "House Floor Remarks on Concurrent"). She congratulates everyone involved in approving the budget for fiscal year 2005, noting again that "taking care of the veterans and veterans' health care while meeting all of the other needs that the constituents tell me back home are important to them is something that we were able to accomplish in this budget" ("House Floor Remarks on Concurrent"). In a column for the voters in the Fifth District, she comments that "throughout my tenure in public office veterans have told me their stories of war and told me their stories of battle—to attain speedy access to the healthcare and benefits they were promised" ("Honoring"). She then reminds her readers of some of the legislation benefiting veterans that has been passed since she has been in the House. "I am proud of the work I've done thus far in office," she tells the voters, "and am proud that the accomplishments of this Congress on veterans' healthcare, wait times, and benefits have come about in this, my first, year in Washington" ("Honoring"). In another column, Brown-Waite laments the fact that "some of our nation's bravest heroes who fought the enemy overseas are now forced to fight illness at home for months at a time without the assistance of a physician" ("Ensuring"). Declaring this situation unacceptable and a problem that she "cannot ignore," she describes the Veterans' Healthcare Access Standards Act of 2003, which she introduced. "Making our veterans wait is indefensible," she asserts, "but being a Member of Congress and doing nothing about it is worse. That's why I was compelled to draft this legislation" ("Ensuring"). Later, she repeats her commitment to this segment of her constituency saying that "in 2004, I also want to continue [the] work I have done on behalf of the Fifth District's many veterans" (Brown-Waite, "State").

In her first term in Congress, Representative Brown-Waite has demonstrated her loyalty to the Republican Party and the Bush administration as well as her willingness to challenge the party line when doing so benefits the *people back home*. Without a doubt, she honors her commitment to *protect* or take care of those whom she represents. For many, her focus on this theme represents a typically feminine or Third Space approach to illustrating the interdependence of private and public issues. On the other hand, Brown-Waite's use of the ideograph *spending discipline* and the tenacity with which she battles for fiscal responsibility often create a rhetoric reminiscent of traditional Second Space discourse. Linked together, these rhetorical strategies exemplify Brown-Waite's ability to forge a political dialogue that speaks to both Second and Third Space concerns from a vantage point within the in-between space.

Amy Walter, House editor for the *Cook Political Report*, suggests that "it's hard breaking out in the House. . . . There are 434 other people who would like to see their names in lights, too" (qtd. in Solochek, "Brown-Waite Builds"). Walter's comment epitomizes the position of women in the U.S. House of Representatives. It is difficult for anyone, but especially females, to be seen and, thus, heard amid the cacophony of utterances filling the congressional halls. Yet, the six congresswomen whose rhetoric we examine in this chapter illustrate that the voices of women in the House can and do rise above the clamor. More importantly, these women embody a new reality of the in-between space: women's views of the world and the political discourse through which they express those perceptions are beginning to effect change in the public and private lives of all citizens.

Strangers No More
The Discourse of Twenty-first-Century Women in the U.S. Senate

4

> *In the ordinary course of their days, they don't constantly think of themselves as "women senators." They are just senators—individuals within a group of one hundred, doing the work of the People. While they sometimes unite behind a piece of legislation that has special implications for women, they do not have their own caucus. Indeed, their positions on most of the issues run across the spectrum, from conservative to liberal and those in between. Each senator has her own agenda for what she wants to accomplish in office. There is no singular women's agenda.*

—CATHERINE WHITNEY, IN MIKULSKI ET AL. 3

"THE POLICIES MADE in the United States Senate," suggests Senator Barbara Boxer, "affect everything about our lives: war and peace, a sound economy, clean air and water, health research and reform, the status of our children, human and civil rights, education, the right to choose, government spending priorities. Everything about our lives" (*Strangers* 242). Despite its influence, during most of the country's history this august body has remained off limits to more than half the population. One by one throughout the twentieth century women began opening the door to what was once an elite all-male political club, bringing previously unrecognized issues of importance to the Senate floor. However, as Senator Don Riegle observes, the women elected in 1992— Boxer, Feinstein, Moseley-Braun, and Murray—"took the door off its hinges forever" (qtd. in Boxer, *Strangers* 235).

The Senate wields significant decision-making authority on a wide variety of issues, as illustrated in Senator Boxer's statement. As a governmental body, the U.S.

Senate contains important policy-making and investigative committees and is responsible for advancing, or sometimes impeding, key legislation. Individual senators, therefore, must possess strong leadership qualities to accomplish their political agendas. This means not only envisioning a particular plan of action, but owning the ability to articulate it as well. Senator Barbara Mikulski explains that:

> Leadership is creating a state of mind in others. The difference between being a leader and manager, all due respect to managers, is that leaders have to create states of mind. But a leader, first of all, has to have a clear state of mind, which is usually her own vision, which energizes her, motivates others, and then creates that state of mind in others. President Kennedy's legislative accomplishments were skimpy, but he created a state of mind in this country that endures long after his death. (qtd. in Cantor and Bernay 188)

People enter politics for a variety of reasons. Some simply want to feel the rush of power and to expand their own sphere of influence (Cantor and Bernay 58). However, most women usually get involved in politics to right a perceived or experienced wrong "because they want to help" (Collins). According to Harriet Woods, former president of the National Women's Political Caucus, "most women begin [their political careers] with community concerns, not ambition" (qtd. in Collins). Generally, then, women enter politics with a specific purpose, an agenda to be advanced (Cantor and Bernay 58). "Power," states Senator Olympia Snowe, "means to me to be able to do something for others. I use the power of my office to help other people. I view this office as the potential of helping somebody else out" (qtd. in Cantor and Bernay 58).

Only a short time ago, there existed a mere "Nine and Counting"—the total number of women in the Senate chamber. That number has increased in the past few years with fifteen females serving in the Senate since the beginning of the twenty-first century. Fourteen of those individuals bore the title *Senator* in the 108th Congress, demonstrating that women can and have changed the characteristics of the club membership. The senators discussed in the following pages exemplify a commitment to a variety of causes and issues, and it is their power, both innate and earned, that allows them to bring their concerns to the floor. Their discourse, imbued with ideographs that reflect their worldviews, holds broad appeal, as the following examples illustrate.

Barbara Mikulski

"If you only talk and don't produce, you are just one more disappointment. You contribute to the cynicism" (Mikulski, qtd. in Mikulski et al. 32). Senator Barbara A. Mikulski, the senior woman senator, has a congressional career that spans nearly two decades and political philosophies for the ages. She "takes seriously her role in mentoring the women who have been elected after her" (Nutting). As mentioned in a previous chapter, Mikulski began her political career "by organizing neighbors to stop a sixteen lane highway through the historic Fells Point area of Baltimore" (Mikulski et al. 207). In praising the senator, President Bill Clinton once said, she is "the first Democratic woman to hold a Senate seat in her own right; the first Democratic woman to serve in both Houses; the first woman to win a statewide election in Maryland; the first woman to have a leadership position in the Senate for our party. . . . What I want to say to you," he continues, "is that she got to be all that—first, first, first, first—not because she was a woman but because she has the heart of a lion and because she's done good things for the people of Maryland" (W. Clinton, "Remarks Honoring"). Mikulski grew up in a working class, ethnic neighborhood in Baltimore where her parents ran a small grocery store, and she has never forgotten her humble beginnings. After receiving a BA degree in sociology and a master's degree in social work, Mikulski worked for a number of social work agencies. "It was her stint as a Baltimore welfare worker in the late 1960s that heightened her concern for the poor" (Schindehette and Podesta) and began the underpinnings of her desire to be an activist. "The assassinations of Robert F. Kennedy and Martin Luther King, Jr., not only left her angry and bewildered but inspired her to 'completely change [her] life'" ("Mikulski"). She eventually decided that political activism provided a solution, for as she explained in the *New York Post*, "politics is social work with power" (qtd. in "Mikulski").

Mikulski lives her public and private life as a "proud blue collar liberal" (Nutting) and holds several important committee assignments in Congress. She works tirelessly on behalf of her Maryland constituents, particularly on the issues of housing and women's health concerns. She also "does what she can for the steel industry, pushing for protections against subsidized imports of foreign steel" (Nutting). *Planning* magazine named her one of two "Legislators of the Year" in 2004, in part because she played such an "important role in securing federal funding and support for programs that help revitalize community housing and quality of life" (J. Jordan 24). Her political ideology focuses on *community* and *opportunity*, as she illustrates in the following statement: "Making sure every American has access to safe, affordable housing is the first step toward building communities and ensuring hope and opportunity for all Americans" (qtd. in J. Jordan 24). When mentoring the women who arrived in the Senate after her, she shows them her "secret weapon"—key ideas written down on a three-by-five card. These principles govern how she lives her life as a U.S. senator. Two are particularly instructive, for they illustrate her link to the people, the community, which put her in office. For instance, she states, "I am not only the senator from Maryland, but also the senator for Maryland" (Mikulski et al. 121). This statement illustrates that she is both of and for the people. Knowing that the language of politics is often confusing and divisive, Mikulski once observed, "The language of Washington is a foreign language. We need to talk about people in terms they understand" (Mikulski et al. 122), implying that a commonality exists between herself and her constituents, a community as it were, of concerned individuals.

Her interest in *community* spans both the concrete and abstract and provides an interesting ideograph to explore. Whether she discusses the local community of Baltimore, the community of the United States, or the world community of foreign policy, Mikulski frequently invokes the term to provide justification for a position or a proposed bill, as the following examples illustrate.

At the local level, Mikulski concerns herself with constituent needs. "Since my days on the city council in Baltimore," she states, "I have fought to build livable communities, places where families can live, play, work, shop, and pray" (qtd. in J. Jordan 24). She manages to secure significant federal funds to help low and middle income families obtain affordable housing. As Mikulski says of her effort to win these community grants and loans, "I'm happy to be a partner in the rebuilding of these important Maryland communities. This money is not just about building housing units. It's about creating new hope, new opportunity, new ways to empower people and new community growth" (qtd. in J. Jordan 24). One aspect of her community revitalization project is her commitment to ensuring that everyone has access to technology. She has championed the idea of putting computer centers in public housing projects so that residents can learn computer skills (J. Jordan 24). Mikulski worries that some people are not developing necessary technological skills. "There is a digital divide in America," she observes. "Those who have access to technology and know how to use it will be ready for the new digital economy. Those who don't will be left out. . . . We can avoid the social chasm that came out of the first industrial revolution, which set up a system of haves and have-nots (Mikulski et al. 159). Stratification of those with technological skills and those who lack them is clearly antithetical to the importance Mikulski places on the notion of community. Essentially, in her view everyone should belong to the community of knowledge.

Senator Mikulski directly uses the ideograph of *community* in debating a number of bills. For instance, in her lengthy speech advocating increased funding for domestic programs such as AmeriCorps, she says, "These kids [who] are trying to earn a voucher to pay for the high cost of tuition, give practical experience to America. They help our communities, and then in turn the communities have a great impact on them. It is a modest public investment" ("Urgent"). In arguing for a ban on assault weapons and an increase in funding for local crime prevention programs, Mikulski invokes the ideograph of *community* again when she argues, "Our communities are living a fragile existence. We cannot tolerate a proliferation of violence" (Mikulski, "The Crime Bill"). In this particular speech, Mikulski advocates putting more police on the streets instead of behind desks doing paperwork. "That is what community policing does," she states. "It brings the high tech of the 1990's into the community to be high touch. And it is going on in Maryland" ("The Crime Bill"). She believes the citizens must do their part too, "Get people involved in their community," she exhorts, "and encourage them to speak up about where the thugs hang out" ("The Crime Bill"). America as a country also exists as a community, linked by common values and experiences. Mikulski's floor speech in response to the World Trade Center attacks illustrates this concept of community, even though she does not explicitly use the term. "The direct victims were passengers on domestic flights, civilians and members of our Armed Forces working at the Pentagon, people working at or visiting the World Trade Center, and rescue workers," she insists. "But all Americans share the pain of those who lost loved ones. We feel this as an attack on each and every one of us, and on our way of life" (Mikulski, "Should Congress"). In the conclusion of these remarks, Mikulski reemphasizes the principles that hold the United States together as a community. "We will not sacrifice our ideals in pursuit of the monsters who carried out these attacks," she declares. "We will not compromise the principles for which so many Americans have fought and died. But we will root out those who committed these atrocities. We will have justice. And we will move forward, a stronger Nation than before" ("Should Congress").

The ideograph of *community* does not exist just at the local or national level. Senator Mikulski sees the world as an international community, particularly when the issue is the war on terror. In 1996, for instance, when supporting increased aid to Israel, she argues, "Israel has defended itself in five wars for survival. But in this war against terrorism, all ordinary citizens are on the front lines. The international community must stand with Israel. We must ensure that fanatics do not prevail" (Mikulski, "Terrorists"). Mikulski continues her use of the ideograph *community* when discussing supplemental appropriations for the Iraq War. She specifically believes that the world should be in the war together. "Last year when we debated about the war, I said if it is important enough to the world to go, the world should go with us. I voted to go to the U.N. to have international legitimacy and international burden sharing, to share the dangers along with our troops as well as to share the cost of rebuilding Iraq. We had a coalition of the willing," she continues. "Now we need a coalition of the wallet" (Mikulski, "Iraq"). Two months later, Senator Mikulski reiterates her belief in the international community when the topic of supplemental appropriations for Afghanistan and Iraq once again reaches the floor. "There must be international burden sharing," she opines. "With international burden sharing, if the stability of Iraq is in the world's interest, then the world should help pay for the reconstruction" (Mikulski, "Should a Portion").

Through the use of the ideograph of *community,* Senator Barbara A. Mikulski illustrates a belief that everyone and everything is linked together in some way. Community is not a masculine or feminine concept; on the contrary, the notion bridges the gap between the two and causes distinct entities to blend into one whole. To see the world, the nation, the city as "one" gives her approach a distinctly unified vision. This operates consistently with her philosophy that all politics and policy are local (Mikulski et al. 208).

Barbara Boxer

"My political style is to be extremely candid and straight from the shoulders, and not to be mealy-mouthed or waffle. When I believe in something, I believe in it strongly" (Boxer, qtd. in Koszczuk). Few argue with California Senator Barbara Boxer's apt description of her approach to politics. Elaborating on this trait, Boxer explains: "I'm very consistent on the issues. I'm not the type of person that changes views based on polls or . . . the way the wind is blowing" (qtd. in Koszczuk). A zealous feminist, who some political observers consider "the personification of the feminist left" (Barone and Cohen 167), Boxer continues as the Senate's leading advocate for women's rights. Her unrelenting and sometimes aggressive pursuit of the ideal often "brings her to the Senate floor for impassioned speeches and legislative efforts that can be more symbolic than effective" (Koszczuk). In the U.S. House, Boxer had proven "herself capable of working cooperatively with her opponents to achieve results when the need [arose]" in spite of "the strength of her views on any given issue" ("Boxer" 65). And in the 2002 edition of *The Almanac of American Politics,* the authors suggest that "for all her partisanship, on some issues Boxer has worked with Republicans" in the Senate (Barone, Cohen, and Cook 157). According to some of her colleagues and other congressional observers, however, the term *compromise* seldom finds its way into Boxer's senatorial vocabulary, even though on occasion she alludes to the need for bipartisan approaches to the issues affecting the country. "While some politicians pride themselves on their ability to horse-trade and compromise in pursuit of legislation, Boxer," Jackie Koszczuk suggests, "usually operates as an unremitting activist, offering proposals that have no chance of adoption just to make a point about how things ought to be" ("Sen. Barbara Boxer"). Once called "the most partisan senator I've ever known" by Bob Dole (qtd. in Hawkings and Nutting 66–67), her voting record labels her as one of the most liberal members of the Senate. Despite such commentary, she remains "unapologetic about her liberal stances" (Foerstel, "Sen. Barbara"). "In the 20 years of elected life," she declares, "no one has ever come up to me and said, 'Barbara, you've got to do something, there's too much clean water'" (qtd. in Foerstel, "Sen. Barbara").

On the surface, Barbara Boxer's early years portended a life imbued with tradition. "I was a child of the '50s," she recalls, "the time of 'Happy Days' and Doris Day movies—the Debbie Reynolds days when pert women with personalities that glowed danced their way through what was the 'perfect' life and right into the arms of Eddie Fisher guys who would sing to them 'til their dying days" (Boxer, *Strangers* 62–63). Barbara Boxer's world, however, evolved into a vastly different version of the American dream. Just as the 1960s turned the society of the fifties on its head, various incidents in her life summoned forth the independent and activist personality lurking in her spirit. Born Barbara Levy to immigrant parents in Brooklyn, New York, in 1940, Boxer attended the local public schools. In her own words, she "did what was expected of a middle-class first-generation American" (*Strangers* 63). As early as high school, however, Boxer began to push against the boundaries defining a "woman's place." She and one of her friends became the first female coaches of the "boys-only" baseball team, circumventing the ban on women's participation in sports (Boxer, *Strangers* 63; "Boxer" 63). After high-school graduation, Boxer attended Brooklyn College where she cheered for the men's basketball team and in 1962 earned a BA in economics with a minor in political science. At the time, of course, finding females on the cheerleader squad was not uncommon, but few women pursued course work in those fields. In 1962, Boxer also married, engaged in her first "fight against 'injustice'" by gathering petitions to force her landlord to upgrade the apartment building's lobby, and endured an incident of sexual harassment from a college professor (Boxer, *Strangers* 64; "Boxer" 63).

Following her college graduation, Barbara Boxer worked for three years while her husband attended Fordham Law School ("Boxer" 63). She had hoped to find employment as a stockbroker on Wall Street. She soon learned, however, that the stock exchange was not open to her. "Women aren't stockbrokers," she heard each time she knocked on a firm's door (Boxer, *Strangers* 65). So, she worked as a secretary and studied for the stockbroker's exam on her own. When she passed the exam, she naively thought that the men she worked for would welcome her expertise and newly earned stamp of credibility. They explained, however, that because she was a woman, she could not earn commission in their company. Boxer left and "found a firm that figured out that [her] commission meant dollars for them" (Boxer, *Strangers* 66; "Boxer" 63). In 1965, Boxer and her husband moved to the San Francisco Bay area and in 1968 moved to the suburb of Greenbrae in Marin County. There she watched as Robert Kennedy was assassinated on live television. "I was stunned beyond belief," she recalled, "and I was frightened. . . . How could I sit back and do nothing to change the violent America of the 60s?" she asked herself. "Looking back on it," she said, "I had two choices: I could either psychologically withdraw into a 1950s-type bomb shelter and put the family into it, protected from the pain, or reach out and try to change things. I reached and I guess I haven't stopped reaching since" (Boxer, *Strangers* 69).

Like so many of the women we discuss in this book, Boxer began her public-sphere involvement in her own neighborhood. There she established a program to help curb the high school dropout rate through the Education Corps of Marin County, created an after-school child care center, formed Woman's Way, an early women's support group, and founded Marin Alternative, a grassroots political organization (Boxer, *Strangers* 70; "Boxer" 64). Speaking of these endeavors, Boxer noted that she "was a catalyst and had no problems passing off the reins of the projects [she] helped to begin. If a project is worthy," she continued, "it will transcend the personalities of its founders" (Boxer, *Strangers* 70). In 1971, Boxer initiated her first foray into electoral politics; she ran for the Marin County Board of Supervisors. Throughout the campaign, Barbara Boxer "was actively discouraged by men and women alike who thought it was improper for a woman with two young children to seek public office" ("Boxer" 64). One of her male primary opponents even visited her at home to convince her to drop out of the race because she was a weak candidate and because her "candidacy and possible victory would be harmful for women" (Boxer, *Strangers* 71). Although she won the primary, she lost the general election and remains convinced that she was defeated for no reason other than the fact she was a woman ("Boxer" 64). After the election, Boxer pursued a two-year career in journalism at the *Pacific Sun*, where she earned an award for investigative reporting, and then joined the district staff of Democratic Representative John Burton ("Boxer" 64; Earnshaw 2). She decided once again to seek a seat on the Marin County Board of Supervisors in 1976. This time, she won. She served on the board for six years and in 1980 was elected president, the first female to fill that role in the board's 131-year history ("Boxer" 64).

When Burton retired from the Congress in 1982, Barbara Boxer ventured into the wider political arena. She ran for and easily won a seat in the U.S. House (Barone, Cohen, and Cook 156). During the decade she served as a representative, Boxer fought for the rights of women in Congress as well as for all of her constituents. For example, irritated by Speaker O'Neill's references to "the men in Congress," during her freshman year in the House, Boxer "sent him a letter politely asking him to say 'men and women' of the House. He replied with a promise not to repeat his 'mistake'" ("Boxer" 64). Outraged when one of her voters presented her with evidence of opprobrious wastefulness in the military's procurement office, Boxer decided to bring the matter to the attention of her colleagues and the people of the country. "Even though I was just a freshman member of Congress," she explained, "I knew no one else was doing anything about publicizing this scandal. I also knew that if you want to be effective on an issue, you have to take it to the people, so I did" (Boxer, *Strangers* 169). Her experiences in this matter led to a position as cochair of the Military Reform Caucus. During her tenure in the House, she also served on the Armed Services, Budget, and Government Operations committees as well as the Select Committee on Children, Youth, and Families ("Boxer" 65). Throughout her years in the House, she was a staunch advocate for human rights and environmental protection (Boxer, "Senator")

Boxer's focus on women's issues, especially a woman's right to choose, continued in the House as well. She cosponsored a bill with Republican Henry Hyde of Illinois to "punish brokers who set up surrogate motherhood arrangements" to prevent what she saw as the emergence of "paid breeders" ("Boxer" 65). She also supported legislation to provide federal funding for "abortions for poor women whose pregnancies were caused by rape or incest" (65). Following the introduction in the Senate of the Violence Against Women Act, Boxer authored the House version of the legislation in 1991 (65). In that same year, she climbed the steps to the Senate chamber with six of her colleagues to protest the nomination of Clarence Thomas to the Supreme Court and the lack of credence given the issue of sexual harassment.

After almost ten years in the U.S. House, Barbara Boxer set her sights on yet another political challenge in 1992. Alan Cranston, the venerable Democratic senator from California, decided not to seek reelection. Following discussions with Barbara Mikulski and with the blessing of her family, Boxer entered the race. Not unexpectedly, other Democrats also sought this Senate seat creating a merciless primary contest. As she detailed the gruesome campaign in her book, *Strangers in the Senate*, Boxer suggested that in this country voters want candidates to "go through campaign hell" to ensure "they don't crack under the pressure that they'll encounter in office" (124). Boxer discovered that running as a woman in a senatorial election proved far more difficult than campaigning as a woman in a smaller district in a House race. "Well-entrenched stereotypes about women in public life persisted" ("Boxer" 65) despite Boxer's successful tenure in the House. For example, with her two male opponents Boxer participated in a call-in radio show. "Despite her membership on the House Budget and Armed Services committees, Boxer was asked only about health and education, while her male counterparts were queried on their positions on crime and national security" (65). With three months left in the primary campaign, Boxer decided to drop out of the race. Following a Democratic party dinner where she watched a *60 Minutes* story about EMILY's List with a group of women, and a discussion with her children in which they made her read out loud Dr. Seuss's book, *Oh, The Places You'll Go!*, Boxer changed her mind and remained in the contest (Boxer, *Strangers* 124–45). In a come-from-behind victory, she won the primary with 44 percent of the vote. Her opponents, Lieutenant Governor Leo McCarthy and Congressman Mel Levin, garnered 31 percent and 22 percent of the vote respectively (Barone, Cohen, and Cook 156; "Boxer" 65). Explaining Boxer's success, Gloria Molina, the first woman and the first Hispanic member of the Los Angeles County Board of Supervisors, claimed "she touched people and she talked to them. She had a concise, direct, common sense message, which won the hearts of California voters" (qtd. in "Boxer" 65). Boxer went on to win in an equally heated and negative general election, securing 48 percent of the vote to her challenger's 43 percent. *The Almanac of American Politics* described the campaign as "a battle of opposites, the far left versus the far right of the American electoral spectrum" (Barone, Cook, and Cohen 156). Boxer's success mirrored that of Dianne Feinstein, Carol Moseley-Braun, and Patty Murray. In the historic 1992 Year of the Woman, constituents elected four female senators, tripling the number of women serving in the Senate in 1993 as these four joined Barbara Mikulski and Nancy Kassebaum in the Senate chamber. And, for the first time in history, the voters in a state sent two women to the U.S. Senate at the same time when Californians endorsed the candidacies of both Feinstein and Boxer.

During her first term in the Senate, Boxer served on several committees and subcommittees: Banking, Housing and Urban Affairs, Environment and Public Works, Budget, and the Joint Economic Committee as well as the Senate Health Care Task Force, among others. She served as the western deputy whip and established the California Unity Working Group to "encourage bipartisan cooperation in dealing with issues important to California's future" ("Boxer" 66). Despite her focus on issues affecting the people of California, Boxer's job ratings were among the lowest in the Senate in the first half of her term. By 1997, however, her ratings were up to 50 percent, and she decided to pursue reelection (Barone, Cohen, and Cook 157). She faced several Republican opponents in the all-party primary, which she won with 41 percent of the vote (157, 162). In the general election she opposed State Treasurer Matt Fong, a moderate Republican. Drawing on the public's negative reaction to the Monica Lewinsky scandal, Fong "sought to paint [Boxer] as a liberal extremist with ties to President Bill Clinton" (Koszczuk). Although the race was close throughout the campaign, Fong's unconvincing sound bites and Boxer's negative television advertising campaign that depicted him as "a right-wing zealot" contributed to her victory (Barone, Cohen, and Cook 157; Koszczuk). She won by ten points with 53 percent of the vote to Fong's 43 percent (Barone and Cohen 166). According to political pundits, this race exemplified the gender gap concept. Men voted equally with 48 percent supporting each candidate. Women, on the other hand, overwhelmingly cast their ballots for Boxer with a 57 to 39 percent margin (167).

Mirroring her agenda in the U.S. House, Senator Boxer has fought for human rights, especially for women and children, for environmental protection, and for fiscal responsibility. Within these contexts, she supports numerous causes. First and foremost, she advocates for abortion rights and women's health issues in this country and around the globe. She cosponsored the Freedom of Choice Act to safeguard the constitutional rights guaranteed by *Roe v. Wade* in the early 1990s and again most recently in January 2004. She advocated successfully for the passage of the Freedom of Access to Abortion Clinic Entrances Act in 1994 ("Boxer" 66). She has introduced legislation promoting breast-cancer prevention and research and has supported legalization of RU 486, known as the abortion drug (66). On behalf of children, Boxer has drafted bills that included funding for programs such as prenatal care, immunization, child care, Head Start, teenage pregnancy prevention, vocational training, and housing assistance for young and low-income parents (66) and has supported the Violence Against Children Act. Early in her senatorial career, Boxer initiated discussion of a "conversion clearinghouse" to assist communities in which military bases targeted for closing were located (66), to retrain workers, and to provide for environmental cleanup of the bases. She supported and added provisions to the 1994 Crimes Bill. Gun control adherents always find Boxer a willing partner for their cause. Among the first to do so, Boxer sponsored legislation requiring all handguns to incorporate childproof safety locks (Barone and Cohen 167). In 2001, she promoted protection of 401(k) plans "by capping concentrations of company stocks in each employee's investment portfolio" (Hawkings and Nutting 67). From her vantage point on the Environment Committee, Boxer led the 2001 efforts to clean up brownfields. And she continues as a strident critic of President Bush's policies and record on the environment (67).

An ardent champion of the middle class, Boxer asserts that "you can't hand anybody anything; it doesn't work that way. But you can give them a chance" (qtd. in Koszczuk). Protecting that chance, in its various incarnations, emerges as one of the major themes in her political discourse. From defending basic freedoms like reproductive choice, to safeguarding fundamental rights such as education, health care, employment opportunity, and personal and national security, to preserving the environment, Boxer employs the ideograph *protection* in her rhetoric. She utilizes this theme to express her advocacy for ordinary Americans and to win support from her colleagues and the public for those issues affecting her constituents as well as other citizens of the country.

Within her use of the ideograph *protection,* Senator Boxer espouses the theme "it is time to think about our people and our workers" (Boxer, "Floor Speech on Economic"). Boxer never shies away from expressing the need to protect the workers in this country. In a speech delivered on the Senate floor on March 31, 2004, Senator Boxer decries the fact that "today the unemployment insurance extension runs out" because the Senate has refused to act. Because of this inaction, she asserts that

"314,344 [California] workers will lose benefits in the first 6 months of the year" ("Floor Speech on Economic"). Minutes later, she lambastes the Bush Administration for giving to non-U.S. firms contracts to rebuild Iraq and to feed the Iraqi people. "I could not even believe it," she exclaims, "I went into farm country and the rice farmers there who are sending their sons and daughters off to war—the contracts for rice are for the people of Iraq; they went out of the country" ("Floor Speech on Economic"). She then warns her colleagues that "there is something brewing in the countryside. People are angry about the fact that they seem to be last in line" ("Floor Speech on Economic"). In presenting the Corzine Amendment in the discussion of the fiscal year 2005 congressional budget, Boxer tells her colleagues that when asked "what is on their minds" the people in this country will "say it is the economy; it is jobs; it is their security. In this particular budget," she suggests, "we should do much more to ensure that jobs are created and that our families are protected" (Boxer, "Floor Speech on Congressional Budget"). She explains that "nearly 8,000 jobs are lost per month in my State. That is about 8,000 family members coming home to tell their families they are in big trouble. We ought to do something about it," she concludes. "The good news is we can do something about it with this amendment" designed to "protect America's jobs" ("Floor Speech on Congressional Budget"). In a March 2004 debate on the JOBS Act Boxer incredulously states that "it is a stunning situation that we find ourselves re-fighting the issue of overtime in the 21st century" (Boxer, "Floor Statement on Jumpstart . . . Continued"). Describing a visit from California police officers, she relates her comments to the group. "Well, look," she tells them, "I am going to do everything I can to protect you" ("Floor Statement on Jumpstart . . . Continued"). Although some of her colleagues argue that police officers and firefighters would not be hurt by the legislation, Boxer notes that "the clout of independent police associations varies widely. Some would be able to protect their contract-required overtime, others would not" ("Floor Statement on Jumpstart . . . Continued"). These discourse samples illustrate the conviction with which Senator Boxer endeavors to protect middle-class workers.

The metamorphosis of the ideograph *protection* into *security* figures prominently in Barbara Boxer's discussion of national and international issues in which domestic concerns often trump international matters. "It is time to get our priorities in order, and it is time to do the business of the American people," she suggests in a statement responding to the 9/11 Commission Report. "If we can spend $200 billion in Iraq then we can spend $15 billion to protect American lives at home" ("Statement on the 9/11"). She calls for increased funding to implement the 2002 Maritime Transportation Security Law, arguing that while the bill included "many good provisions," it contained "no guaranteed funding mechanism" (Boxer, "Floor Statement on a Bill"). Boxer testifies that "with over 40 percent of the nation's goods imported through California's ports, freight rail is extremely important to the nation's commerce. A terrorist attack at a California port," she avers, "would not only be tragic but would be devastating for our nation's economy" ("Floor Statement on a Bill"). She then introduces a bill creating a Port Security Grant Program in the Department of Homeland Security to "provide $800 million per year for five years in grant funding" to finance projects to ensure port security ("Floor Statement on a Bill").

Questioning the viability of the ground-based midcourse missile defense system, Boxer introduces an amendment to the 2005 National Defense Authorization Act to withhold money for deployment of the system until it has been adequately tested. "Frankly, when it comes to defending our country, my goodness," she declares, "how much more important can it be before we tell our people they are protected that we actually know they are protected and that the tests which have been done have been signed off on by the very office that has been created for that purpose?" (Boxer, "Floor Statement on National Defense"). Without such tests, Boxer argues, "we have no way of knowing that these interceptor missiles will actually be able to protect us from an incoming ballistic missile attack" ("Floor Statement on National Defense"). She reiterates that she "want[s] a missile defense system. I am worried. I am just as worried, however," she concedes, "that if we tell our people they are defended and we do not have objective testing behind it, it will be a very hard blow to people and a waste of money that God knows, we need in other areas of the military and in other ways to defend our people from the suitcase bomb or an attack on a nuclear power plant, which we know the terrorists are looking at" ("Floor Statement on National Defense"). Boxer affirms the "need to spend more in high-tech equipment to better protect our people from terrorists crossing the border. . . . We know the customs and border protection is the front line in protecting the American public against terrorism" ("Floor Statement on National Defense"). She then outlines the appropriations for the various agencies involved in homeland security, noting that in many cases these institutions receive less funding than the Act authorizes for the unproven missile defense system. "Would it not be better at the moment now," she asks, "not to waste $3.7 billion on this initial deployment, if we have that extra funding, but to put it into the fight on terrorism?" ("Floor Statement on National Defense"). Noting the potential for terrorists to get their hands on a "nuclear capable intercontinental missile," Boxer emphasizes that she "want[s] to protect our country against the potential of this kind of a strike. However, I do not want a make-believe system. I do not want a Wizard of Oz system" ("Floor Statement on National Defense").

Boxer's concern for security manifests itself at an individual level as well as in the national arena, as evidenced in her rhetoric about gun control and gun safety.

Nowhere is this more obvious than in her attempts to protect children from gun violence. Participating in the floor debate on the Protection of Lawful Commerce in Arms Act, Boxer offers an amendment that "will protect our children from violence" (Boxer, "Floor Statement on Protection"). "What could be more important to us as we gather here every day," she queries her colleagues, "than to protect our children?" ("Floor Statement on Protection"). Boxer's amendment would require child safety devices on every handgun sold in the United States as well as standards established by the Consumer Product Safety Commission to ensure the effectiveness of the apparatuses. Boxer reminds her colleagues that the Senate passed a similar amendment in 1999, with bipartisan support. The House failed to support the legislation at that time. She states: "I believe we should again agree that we need to protect our children from accidental gun shootings" ("Floor Statement on Protection"). She iterates the many ways in which "we do so much to protect our children" ("Floor Statement on Protection"). She then argues that "in this day and age when we are losing a child or a youth to an accidental shooting every 48 hours, we ought to be absolutely united in doing something about it" ("Floor Statement on Protection"). After all, "we are here to protect the children. That is part of our job" ("Floor Statement on Protection"). In closing her remarks, Boxer implores her colleagues to "let us protect our kids. Let us do it in a smart way. It is the right thing to do for the families of America" ("Floor Statement on Protection").

Protecting people by safeguarding the environment also ranks high on Senator Boxer's agenda. "If we take our position seriously, what could be more fundamental than protecting our people?" she asks her fellow senators in a speech honoring Earth Day (Boxer, "Floor Remarks on Earth Day"). She then asserts that "protecting the environment is protecting our people. It is what we must do. It is the moral thing to do" ("Floor Remarks on Earth Day"). Boxer expands this argument in the following passage:

> When we hear protection of the environment, some people think of wildlife, which is true, and fisheries, which is true, and forests. It is all true. It is all about preserving these things—first of all, because they are God's gift to us and that is our moral obligation, but it also protects the people of our country because we know when species get endangered, we know when oceans get polluted, we know when we lose the wetlands, we know when the air is smoggy, it hurts the people we represent—particularly the children, who are the most vulnerable, the people who are ill, and the elderly. ("Floor Remarks on Earth Day")

Throughout her statement, Boxer criticizes the Bush Administration for its anti-environmental stance. "I hope I am wrong in what I am about to say," she tells her colleagues, "but given the history of this administration I am very worried we will not hear much from the President about steps he is going to take with us to invest in our environment, to make sure America is the model for the world when it comes to protecting its natural resources" ("Floor Remarks on Earth Day"). At this point in her remarks, Boxer proceeded to unroll a thirty-foot scroll listing more than "350 laws and regulations that have been rolled back unilaterally by this administration" ("Floor Remarks on Earth Day"). She concludes that "Earth Day would be a perfect day for him [President Bush] to say he has seen the light and he is going to reverse all of the environmental rollbacks he is perpetrating on the American people" ("Floor Remarks on Earth Day"). Declaring the president has gone around Congress in these matters, Boxer infers that "the only way the people have been protected from some of these things is the courts. We are winning some of these battles in the courts" ("Floor Remarks on Earth Day").

Boxer's concern for environmental issues prompted her to cosponsor legislation, the Boxer-Collins Bill, to elevate the Environmental Protection Agency to a cabinet-level department. In testimony before the Senate Committee on Governmental Affairs, Boxer suggests that "it is now time for the EPA to be a permanent part of the cabinet. Protection of public health and the environment," she contends, "must have a seat at the President's table, along side those cabinet members who are fighting for education, commerce, transportation, agriculture, energy, and defense. The EPA," she continues, "must no longer be an agency on the outside looking in. It must be on the inside with a permanent seat at the table" (Boxer, "Testimony"). Again demonstrating the connection between protecting the environment and protecting people, Boxer explains that the California Wild Heritage Act of 2003 "will protect many animal and plant species from the threat of development and protect the drinking water of millions of Californians" (Boxer, "The California"). She also notes that the "bill does allow activity which is necessary to protect public health and safety, such as firefighting" ("The California"). Speaking against the Department of Defense's Readiness and Range Preservation Initiative in 2002, Boxer argues that "it is not legitimate, in my view, to use the war against terrorism as an excuse to run roughshod over our environmental laws" (Boxer, "Statement of Senator"). Boxer extends her arguments, attesting that:

> Our military exists to protect the health and well-being of our homeland and our citizens. Yet ironically, the effect of DOD's far-reaching and audacious proposal is that its domestic activities would lead to the degradation of our homeland. And in the case of the air quality and hazardous waste exemptions that DOD is seeking, it would create a significant public menace. ("Statement of Senator")

She reproves the initiative, declaring it "a direct threat to the civilian population" ("Statement of Senator"). "I can think of no reason that DOD should be allowed to leave behind munitions, ordnance, and toxic waste," she affirms. "If that isn't a threat to 'homeland security,' I don't know what is" ("Statement of Senator").

Senator Boxer's commitment to protecting people finds its greatest focus in her advocacy for women's rights, health, and reproductive freedom. As she speaks about these issues, Boxer juxtaposes the theme of *protection* with that of *respect*. In this new modality, protecting women's rights becomes synonymous with respecting women. Introducing her Freedom of Choice Act in 2004, Boxer testifies that "with just a one-vote margin protecting Roe in the Supreme Court, we cannot afford to take these fundamental rights for granted. The threats we face to our right to choose are real and dangerous" (Boxer, "Floor Statement on Freedom"). Passage of this legislation "means that we respect a woman's ability to make her own decision. . . . We need to take steps to secure our right to choose," she claims. "Anti-choice is anti-woman and anti-equality, and it demonstrates a lack of respect for the intelligence and compassion that women possess" ("Floor Statement on Freedom"). On the thirtieth anniversary of *Roe v. Wade*, Boxer argues that "right now, we're in a tremendous fight to preserve Roe and to preserve the spirit of Roe and to preserve the respect that women were given after Roe. And our fight, as I see it now, is to stand up for the health and the life of a woman" ("Senator Barbara Boxer"). Clearly for Boxer, Roe symbolizes the nation's commitment to "the respect that women deserve and the trust that women deserve" ("Senator Barbara Boxer").

In a discussion about allowing Department of Defense funds to be used to abort pregnancies in cases of the rape of women in the military, Boxer scolds her colleagues for allowing these women to be treated so despicably. "There are 200,000 women in uniform," she announces, "yet while they are protecting our Nation, our Nation is failing to protect them from rape and sexual assault. It is an even greater insult," she admonishes, "that we are telling our service women that the Department of Defense will not pay if they choose to terminate a pregnancy that is the result of rape" (Boxer, "Floor Statement on S.2166"). Citing a study by the Iowa Veterans Affairs Medical Center, she informs her colleagues that "30 percent of female U.S. military veterans report having been raped or having been the victim of an attempted rape during their military service. This legislation," she contends, "will provide help for our female troops in cases of such horrific crimes" ("Floor Statement on S.2166").

Senator Boxer led the charge against the inevitable passage of the misnamed "partial-birth" abortion ban in 2003. In the debate, she urges her colleagues to reject this legislation. "I stand before you to tell you this is a very sad day for the women of America, a very sad day for the families of America, because what is about to happen here is this Senate is about to pass a piece of legislation that for the first time in history bans a medical procedure without making any exception for the health of a woman. This is a radical thing that is about to happen" (Boxer, "Floor Statement on Partial-Birth Abortion"). She implores the Senate not to "send a confusing signal to the women of this country that their health no longer matters" ("Floor Statement on Partial-Birth Abortion"). Boxer reminds senators that they have heard evidence from doctors and nurses that "this procedure is often essential to protect the life and health of a woman" ("Floor Statement on Partial-Birth Abortion"). Almost in disbelief, Boxer states that "I don't know where the compassion is on the other side. My friend talked about a civilized society. I want a civilized society. That means you care about the women of this country. That means you care about their pregnancies. That means you want to help them through the most difficult times. That means you don't play doctor here because you are not a doctor. We are about to play doctor in a big way" ("Floor Statement on Partial-Birth Abortion"). In concluding her remarks, Boxer relentlessly assails the proponents of the bill:

> I don't think it is compassionate to take away the choice of a woman . . . who is grappling with her religion, ethics, and making a decision with her family to do what is right for her family and for this unborn child. I think it is such a statement that there is no respect for the people of this country, there is no value given to their values, their souls, their religion, to their way of dealing with tragedy. I don't understand how my friends from the other side of the aisle, who always talk about Big Brother interfering, could move into this area and turn their backs on the American families. ("Floor Statement on Partial-Birth Abortion").

Even in the face of defeat, Boxer refuses to abandon the principle of *protection*, and thus *respect*, for the women of this country.

Senator Barbara Boxer's use of the theme *protection* in various manifestations throughout her rhetoric embraces a traditional feminine ethics of care. And, at times, as the preceding discourse samples evidence, she relies on emotional appeals to bolster her arguments. Clearly, she advances a woman's agenda. Alternatively, however, she expands that platform to reflect a post-9/11 masculine rhetoric of militarization as illustrated in her discussion of national and international *security* issues. In this context, she engages more gender-neutral discourse strategies. Boxer, thus, exemplifies the ability of contemporary political women to forge a discourse of the in-between space by navigating between masculine and feminine rhetorical strategies.

Kay Bailey Hutchison

"There was always the feeling, particularly among men, that because I was a woman, maybe I wouldn't be tough enough. . . . Overcoming that kind of undercurrent was one of my greatest challenges" (Hutchison, qtd. in Mikulski et al. 51).

Like many women before her, Senator Kay Bailey Hutchison of Texas faced the gendered double bind of politics. Yet, she has overcome the obstacles by being tough, uncompromising, and knowledgeable in a variety of issues that reach the Senate floor. Senator Hutchison grew up in the town of La Marque, Texas, where she had a "busy childhood, replete with Girl Scout meetings, ballet lessons, among other activities" ("Hutchison, Kay Bailey"). She attended the local high school, was elected homecoming queen, queen of her senior class, and participated in cheerleading ("Hutchison, Kay Bailey"). "We weren't encouraged to do anything other than be good citizens and raise families," she recalls (Jerome). She later attended the University of Texas Law School, earning her LLB degree in 1967.

Hutchison encountered gender-based obstacles when seeking her first position as an attorney. No law firm would hire her, because she was a woman. "She can still recite their rejections: 'We like you, but if we hire a woman and she gets married and moves away, the huge investment we've made in training you is gone'" (Jerome). However, Hutchison remained undaunted, and while disappointed, recalls those rejections as some of the most important of her life's lessons. "When I look back on it now," she remembers, "I can see that those rejections from law firms were the beginning of my future, even though at the time I thought they were the end. That crisis," she continues, "and being able to overcome it, gave me a new strength and maturity. When I speak to groups of young people, I always tell them, 'Never give up. If a door closes, open a window'" (qtd. in Mikulski et al. 23).

Unable to land a job in a Texas law firm, Hutchison worked as a television reporter in Austin. Her "big break was an assignment to interview Anne Armstrong, who had been made cochair of the Republican National Committee in 1971. Armstrong became Hutchison's patron, hiring her as her press secretary in Washington" (Weisberg). That provided the impetus for Hutchison's political career. In 1972, she successfully ran for a seat in the Texas legislature, the first Republican woman to do so (Barone and Cohen 1516). While serving in the legislature, Kay Bailey became acquainted with attorney Ray Hutchison, whom she later married. After two terms in the legislature, President Gerald R. Ford appointed her to a "patronage seat on the National Transportation Safety Board" although she had no experience in the field" (Weisberg).

After leaving the state legislature, Senator Hutchison embarked on a busy and eclectic career. "She held executive positions at two Texas banks, then in 1982 ran unsuccessfully for Congress. Hutchison spent the next eight years operating a decorating showroom and a candy company" (Weisberg). She returned to politics in January 1993, when Lloyd Bentsen resigned his Senate seat in order to become secretary of the treasury (Barone and Cohen 1516). Hutchison won the temporary seat in a special election. She mainly focused on the political unpopularity of

President Bill Clinton, who held a 73 percent negative job rating in the state. She successfully sought the Senate seat for a full term in 1994 and was reelected by a landslide in 2000. According to *Texas Monthly*, "she is by far the most popular politician in Texas history. No one else—not George W. Bush, not Ann Richards, not Phil Gramm, not Lyndon Johnson—has ever gotten more than four million votes in an election" as she did in 2000 (Hollandsworth).

Hutchison has a fairly conservative voting record, siding with President Bush in virtually every issue (Barone and Cohen 1516). However, she does not support outlawing abortion, saying that "the choice should be with a woman, her doctor, and her family until the baby is viable" (Jerome). She has sought to repeal the so-called marriage penalty, supported tax cuts, drilling in the Arctic National Wildlife Refuge, and has cosponsored national transportation security bills with Dianne Feinstein (Barone and Cohen 1515–17). Democrats have tried to portray her as "Phil Gramm in a skirt," referring to her conservatism, but she is careful to distinguish her brand of conservatism from his (Weisberg). And "although she does indeed look, as *Newsweek* once wrote, like Senator Barbie Doll, the impeccably dressed girl next door with the perfect smile and the teased honeyed hair on top of her head, she is also regarded as one of the toughest and most demanding bosses in the Senate" (Hollandsworth).

During the Clinton presidency, Hutchison frequently criticized his administration's foreign policy. "She was wary of U.S. involvement in the former Yugoslavia, called for an eventual pullout from Bosnia, and decried the Clinton administration policy in Kosovo" (Barone and Cohen 1517). Her attacks on Clinton's foreign policy provide an interesting frame for her support of President George Bush's policy regarding Iraq, for she said of Clinton's actions, "We have seen the United States stumble into a series of regional crises—dispatching local powers that share our objectives and are otherwise able to act on their own. This has led to strategic missteps—a hallmark of Clinton administration foreign policy" (qtd. in Barone and Cohen 1517). Despite these earlier views about U.S. involvement abroad, Senator Hutchison now fiercely supports President Bush's agenda in Iraq, as the following analysis demonstrates.

Kay Bailey Hutchison relies on ideographs to present her views regarding both domestic and foreign policy. As a Republican and a Texan, Hutchison is fiercely loyal to and protective of President George W. Bush. After the attack on the World Trade Center in 2001, a significant portion of Hutchison's speeches focused on U.S. economic affairs in relation to the war on terror, and, specifically, the war in Iraq that Bush launched in March 2003. Her main ideograph of choice is *freedom*, for the United States, for the Iraqi people, and for the entire Middle East. Her messages appear in two venues, her *Capitol Comments* published on her web page and in her floor speeches in the Senate.

Soon after the 9/11 attacks, Hutchison published in her *Capitol Comments*, "America Reacts." In it she attempted to build unity among the American people and praised the rescue workers as true heroes. Toward the end of her comment she issues her call for all Americans to fight for freedom. She says, "to those who did this and to those who support them, we will never back down. We will never flinch in the surety of our response. Protecting freedom transcends all other of our duties" ("America Reacts" 1). After praising America as the greatest democracy on earth, Hutchison concludes her remarks, saying "We will keep burning bright the torch of freedom that was passed to us by our ancestors, and we will pass it on with a firm hand to those who come after us" (1).

Hutchison uses the *freedom* ideograph both diachronically and synchronically; that is, she shows that freedom has held importance over time and is directly and specifically related to the current war on terror. For instance, in her November 9, 2001, *Capitol Comments* she declares that "it is our responsibility to make sure all of those who have died these past months and in the 200 plus years before that to maintain the freedom of this country, will never, ever have died in vain" ("America's Campaign" 1). Invoking America's war for independence, she elaborates: "From the very beginning of our history, we have faced the challenges presented to us with courage and integrity—and we have defended freedom no matter the crisis" (1). In a later *Comments*, used in part to justify the impending attack on Iraq, Hutchison's use of *freedom* intersects both the past and present time frames. She intones: "Each generation of Americans has been called to defend our freedom. Each time our forefathers and mothers have answered the call" ("Confronting" 1). After listing a series of terrorist attacks against American embassies and military installations, she provides the contemporary importance of the *freedom* ideograph: "Our nation finally was awakened and put the pattern together, to see the threat to the very freedom we cherish" (2).

Once the Bush administration announced its intention to invade Iraq, with the stated mission of deposing an evil dictator and finding weapons of mass destruction, Hutchison's use of the *freedom* ideograph expands. In her *Capitol Comments* as well as her floor speeches, she justifies the military action as well as increased defense spending on the premise that we are fighting for Iraq's freedom as well as America's. This approach certainly meshes tightly with the title of the military campaign, Operation Iraqi Freedom. In defending President Bush's decision to use military force in the war on terror, Hutchison argues in a floor speech to the Senate that his actions reflect a desire to make the world safe and free. "He is taking on a massive war on terrorism," she states, "to make sure that freedom reigns in the world, to make sure that our way of life—democracy, freedom, free enterprise, self reliance—lasts in the world" (Hutchison, "The Presidential Burden" 3). When talking about the military effort in Iraq, she states, "The Iraqi people are

beginning to experience freedom and rebuild their lives after a generation of oppression" (Hutchison, "A New Day" 1). To bolster her claim, Hutchison uses a
quotation from an Iraqi, because, she says, "no words can convey the appropriate
emotion better than those of the liberated people themselves" (1). The Iraqi, Raja
Habib al-Khaza'i, the director of a maternity hospital and a member of the Governing Council, states, "I helped deliver thousands of Iraqi babies, and now I am
taking part in the birth of a new country and a new rule based on women's rights,
humanity, unity, and freedom" (2).

To demonstrate the joint Iraqi-U.S. commitment to freedom, Hutchison presents a passage of the Transitional Administrative Law for Iraq in her March 19,
2004, *Capitol Comments*, "Into Baghdad." She posits that "the document sets in
place a framework for the future and provides essential freedoms and civil rights
for all Iraqis. . . . It states in part, 'everyone has the right to life, liberty, and the
security of his person'" ("Into Baghdad" 1). Since it bears close resemblance to the
U.S. Declaration of Independence, Hutchison has once again used the concept of
freedom both diachronically and synchronically. Hutchison continues to link the
concepts of *freedom* and *time* in her floor speech of April 2, 2003. "We know the
end is very near," she states, "and we know the people of Iraq now understand that
they are going to have the taste of freedom" ("Honoring Our Armed Forces [con-
tinued]" 1). She later speculates, "I think we are at the beginning of the end or at
the end of the beginning. We are seeing the light at the end of the tunnel, which
is freedom for the Iraqi people" (1).

Hutchison believes that freedom will prove so attractive and beneficial to the
Iraqis that it will spread further. She argues in a floor speech on October 15,
2003, that "what we are doing in Iraq is going to change the Middle East. It is
going to give people in this country a taste of freedom, and others will see it. It
will be a message bigger than anything we could say would happen. . . . That is
why we are debating a supplemental appropriation that would bring freedom to
this country and begin to spread it throughout the Middle East" ("Schools" 2).
Once Iraqis achieve and experience freedom, Hutchison posits, the way of life will
"catch on" and improve the Middle East: "If we can bring a quality of life and of
freedom to the people of Iraq, then we do hope this will also stabilize the rest of
the Middle East so we can bring a peace between the Palestinians and Israel"
(Hutchison, "The Good News" 2). Freedom in Iraq, she suggests, "will also send
a signal to the people of Iran that they can have freedom once again. It will send
a signal to the people of Syria and throughout the Middle East that they, too, do
not have to live under dictatorial regimes that allow them no freedom" (2). "We
want the people of the Middle East to know what freedom is," she concludes (2).

In order to support President Bush and his use of military action, Hutchison
primarily relies on the ideograph of *freedom*. This ideograph operates in the minds

of the American people and of her colleagues as one of the most deep-seated principles in America. She possesses the ability to demonstrate the importance of this ideograph historically and contemporaneously. The time period in which she locates freedom does not change and does not matter. Its relevance spans the ages. It is important to note, however, that Hutchison speaks and writes on a variety of topics. One of those topics is, quite literally, much closer to home for Hutchison. A significant portion of her *Capitol Comments* and even some of her floor speeches detail the importance of Texas, her home state, to the country, and to the world. It is her use of *Texas* as an ideograph that we turn to next.

Senator Hutchison portrays Texas as composed of proud, strong, independent *people*. The use of *the people*, according to McGee, resonates with publics because of its unifying nature. What makes Hutchison's *Texas* ideograph so effective, however, lies in her ability to portray it both historically and contemporaneously, much like she crafts her *freedom* ideograph. "Very few states," she points out, "enjoy such a rich history. We are the only state to enter the United States as a sovereign nation" (Hutchison, "Celebrate Texas" 1). Each year, Hutchison tells her constituents, she reads to her Senate colleagues Colonel William Barret Travis's letter calling for reinforcements at the Alamo. She quotes: "I shall never surrender or retreat. . . . I call on you in the name of liberty, of patriotism and of everything dear to the American character, to come to our aid with all dispatch" (Travis, qtd. in Hutchison, "Lone Star Shining" 1). Hutchison concludes this edition of her *Capitol Comments* by stating that "it is important for Texans to revel in our history and celebrate the strength and valor of our forefathers. Our independence was born out of a great battle and must never be taken for granted. . . . It is my hope that all Texans learn the wonderful and rich history of our state, and continue to pass on the tales of our past through the generations" (1).

One of Hutchison's more interesting historical anecdotes is her discussion of the trail known as "El Camino Real de Los Tejas." She explains that "winding some 2,580 miles from the Rio Grande River near Eagle Pass through San Antonio, Bastrop, and Nacogdoches to Natchitoches, Louisiana, El Camino Real opened America to Texas and Texas to the world" (Hutchison, "A Trail" 1). While the trail was "used early on for exploration, missionary work, and colonization," it later served as a "strategic corridor" during the Texas Revolution ("A Trail" 1). Finally, Hutchison suggests, the Trail "opened pathways to trade and cultural exchange. . . . El Camino Real de Los Tejas forged the way for the early development of Texas into a Spanish colony, an independent Republic, and finally our nation's 28th state. This corridor is not just a highway with a historical foundation," she concludes. "It is a road that has been the foundation of an inspirational past and will continue to pave the way for Texas academically, economically, and historically for years to come" (1). This specific aspect of Texas, a historically preserved trail, serves to define and link people of the state to the rest of the country.

In several of her *Capitol Comments*, Senator Hutchison carefully defines herself as one of *the people* by describing her heritage as a native Texan. "I have always loved Texas history in large part because of my family heritage," she writes. "My great-great-grandfather, Charles S. Taylor, was an "Alcalde" or chief magistrate under the Mexican government. He was later elected as a delegate from Nacogdoches to the Convention, where he signed the Texas Declaration of Independence in 1836" (Hutchison, "Celebrate" 1). Hutchison links herself to "the people" of both the past and the present when she adds, "He, along with 58 other delegates, declared our independence from Mexico, setting Texas on course to be an independent republic for 10 years before joining the United States. One of his fellow delegates was Thomas Rusk, who would later hold a seat in the United States Senate—the same seat I proudly hold today" (1).

Hutchison capitalizes on her ability to link the historic Texas to the present Texas several times. An example of this occurs when she discusses her experience christening the Navy ship the USS *San Antonio*. According to Hutchison, "It is the most high-tech, advanced amphibious ship ever built and appropriately named for the city of the battle of the Alamo" (Hutchison, "USS *San Antonio*" 1). The people of the Texas of the past are joined with current Texans in her statement that, "San Antonio boasts an undeniably strong military tradition. It is home to more major defense installations than any other metropolitan city in our country and more than 65,000 military retirees" (1). In at least two of her *Capitol Comments*, "Celebrate Texas" and "Lone Star Shining," she again links the Texas of the past to the Texas of the present with this same quotation: "In the nearly two centuries since the Battle of the Alamo, Texas has forged a distinct path, growing into a prosperous and vital state. We are the second most populous state, we contribute more than $750 billion to our nation's gross state product, and we have nurtured some of this country's greatest leaders" ("Celebrate"; "Lone Star Shining" 1). Linking both the historical to the contemporary allows Hutchison to make a transition to discuss the current nature of Texas as well.

In her remarks about contemporary Texas, Hutchison again focuses on the qualities the people of Texas possess. As she describes them, Texans are big-hearted, kind-hearted, generous people who are capable of many kind acts and accomplishments. For instance, in a *Capitol Comments* memorializing the crew of the space shuttle Columbia, she talks about the effect the tragedy had on the people of Texas. "Texans were profoundly affected by the tragedy," she states, "because the shuttle disintegrated in our wide-open skies, scattering wreckage throughout the northeast part of our state" ("Remembering Columbia" 1). But Texans rallied bravely, she reports. "When Texans learned of the disaster, they didn't stop and ask, 'why us?' They said, 'How can we help?'" (I). To illustrate the spirit of the Texas people, she offers the following information:

> More than 600 volunteers descended upon the east Texas community from around the state to begin the monumental task. Game wardens, fire fighters, sheriffs and forest service employees arrived at their own expense to help. The local National Guard unit canceled its scheduled training that first weekend and lent a hand. Restaurants and grocery stores provided free meals to volunteers. Business, schools, and community organizations solicited donations and rounded up food, water and supplies to keep the command center running. Churches offered the homes of their members to relief workers seeking a warm bed after grueling 24 hour shifts. Local hotels and bed and breakfasts donated lodging for the out-of-town workers. VFW and Ladies Auxiliary members volunteered countless hours. ("Remembering Columbia" I)

Ultimately, she states, "the outpouring of generosity comes as no surprise. Texans are known for their big hearts and welcoming hearts. When tragedy literally rained down upon us, it was instinctive to respond with charity, generosity, and kindness" (I).

The nature of the people can often be embodied in specific individuals. For instance, in one *Capitol Comments* Hutchison discusses the impact Lady Bird Johnson had on the state of Texas and on the country, noting that her legacy will live on forever in the wildflower fields throughout Texas. But it is the bicycle star Lance Armstrong who illustrates *the people* of and to contemporary Texas. After Lance Armstrong won his fourth consecutive Tour de France bike race, Hutchison dedicated a *Capitol Comments* to discuss his victory. "Lance Armstrong is more than a hometown hero," she states. "He's a Texas legend" ("A Texan Triumphs" I). Because he overcame testicular cancer, Hutchison exclaims, "Lance exudes the spirit of American triumph and Texas determination. This year as the race came to a close along the Champs-Elysees, more than 100,000 onlookers cheered and feverishly waved both Texas and American flags to welcome back the champion" (I). Hutchison's words imply that Texas and its people are a source of pride and strength.

Contemporary Texas symbolizes initiatives in education, science, and technology. From kindergarten through high school, "Texas is encouraging its schools to innovate and reach out to our children. Across the board, the education reforms will continue to expand public school opportunities and try to prepare the next generation to lead our nation to the future," Hutchison states in one *Capitol Comments* ("School's Out" 2). She praises higher education by saying "in the great state of Texas you will . . . discover tearless onions, search and rescue dogs, and artificial heart pumps—just a few of the unique research specialties developed at 'centers of excellence' at universities across our state" ("Higher Education" 1). Texas embodies more than historic battles. It represents the cutting edge of science. "Knowing the immense depth and breadth of our state's scientific talent and the immeasurable benefits of such expertise," Hutchison posits, "I have made it one of my top priorities in the United States Senate to elevate the profile of Texas research institutions" (Hutchison, "Texas" 1). By attracting more federal research dollars, Hutchison concludes, she can "shine a spotlight on the cutting edge discoveries that are made daily on campuses across the Lone Star State" (2).

In addition to symbolizing scientific advances, Texas also represents strong economic and trade policies. According to Hutchison, "Texas ranks third among all 50 states in exports, with an estimated $3.3 billion in sales to foreign markets in 2000. We are the leading exporters of beef, poultry, feed grains, and wheats," she concludes (Hutchison, "Promoting" 1). Perhaps most significantly, though, *Texas* as ideograph represents the national defense. "The Lone Star State," reports Senator Hutchison, "has the largest number of active-duty service members in the military. More than 114,000 are based here. We are home to the most soldiers (64,000) and Air Force members (43,000) in the United States. The Navy has 6,000 personnel here and there are 1,700 Marines. In all," she concludes, "one in ten active duty personnel calls Texas home" (Hutchison, "Visiting" 1). In this *Capitol Comments*, Hutchison recounts her experience touring Texas military bases. She states:

> At each stop on the tour I was reminded how vital a role these Texas installations play in protecting our national defense. The bases and their communities made extraordinary contributions to the operations in Iraq and Afghanistan and showed the world America's steely resolve and determination in the face of those who would destroy us. Our overwhelming victories affirm the critical role they play in preparing our troops for battle, and I could not be more proud to call Texas home. ("Visiting" 1–2)

The two main ideographs Hutchison uses, *freedom* and *Texas,* are not particularly masculine or feminine in nature. In addition, neither term exists solely in the public or private sphere. By using these two terms she has planted her discourse solidly into the rhetorical in-between space. She has managed to morph the lines between disparate styles of discourse to appeal to a vast audience. Further, her reliance on ideographs demonstrates her understanding, albeit subconsciously, of the words that resonate most strongly with her constituents. Not only do these terms provide an intersection between the previously separate masculine and feminine styles, they operate both over and with time.

Olympia Snowe

"When you think about it, maybe women are particularly well suited to the Senate, where collaboration is an essential ingredient in getting things done" (Snowe, in Mikulski et al. 130). In this brief statement, Senator Olympia Snowe articulates the raison d'etre for her involvement in public service: politicians need to make government work for the people by getting things done that affect them positively. They can accomplish that work only through bipartisan, collaborative endeavors involving, at times, compromise from all involved in the decision-making process. And, women can participate in this endeavor. The senior senator from Maine has made "finding the middle ground a hallmark of her more than two decades in Congress" (Hawkings and Nutting 447). In doing so she "has carved out a reputation as a leading moderate, focusing her attention on efforts to build bipartisan consensus on key issues" (Snowe, "About Senator Snowe: Biography"). Viewed in a slightly different light, Snowe's penchant for compromise prompts some to suggest that she "symbolize[s] the strains in her party between moderates and conservatives, deficit hawks and tax cutters" (Toner). Contending that "we live in a time when the campaigning never stops, and the governing all too frequently never begins," she views her centrist efforts as an absolutely necessary ingredient in successful public service (Snowe, "Speech"). As she began her political career, Snowe reports she believed "public service was a high calling. It was, and is," she suggests, "my deepest conviction that no pursuit is as valuable or worthy of, [sic] than the simple idea of helping others. Of enabling individuals to improve their lives. Of softening the hardest days and brightening the darkest. Put simply," she continues, "I felt that as a public servant, my job was to solve problems" ("Speech"). This conviction continues to guide Olympia Snowe's work in the U.S. Senate.

Snowe's parents were not politicians, but they both "worked in a job that had close and easy access to the politicians of the day" in Augusta, Maine, "a town where politics was passion" (Snowe, "Up" 59). Olympia Bouchles was born in Augusta in 1947 and spent the early years of her life in that city, where the "happenings at Maine's statehouse were a focus of the day" (59). From her father's State Street diner, she remembers "playfully spy[ing] on the Maine politicos" (59). Snowe's father was a Greek immigrant and her mother the daughter of Greeks who immigrated to the United States from Sparta ("Snowe, Olympia J." 544). Her happy childhood was turned upside down when she was eight years old; her mother, then thirty-nine, died of breast cancer (Snowe, "Up" 59). "Years later," she reflected, "I can look back and understand the extent to which my mother's death from breast cancer—and the indelible mark that this dreaded disease left on my life—would shape the nature of the work I would eventually pursue in the United States Congress to improve women's health" (60). Struggling as a single parent, Snowe's father sent her to St. Basil's Academy, a Greek boarding school in Garrison, New York (Snowe, "Up" 59; "Snowe, Olympia J." 544). Then, only a year after her mother's death, her father died from heart disease ("Snowe, Olympia J." 544). Snowe moved to Auburn, Maine, where she lived with her mother's brother, a barber, and his wife, who worked in a textile mill (Snowe, "Up" 60; "Snowe, Olympia J." 544). Shortly after the move, her uncle also died, leaving her aunt to raise her five children and her niece by herself. "I guess that was when I began to realize the difficulties a woman faces," noted Snowe, "the difficulties of raising a family on your own, as a single woman having lost her husband" (qtd. in "Snowe, Olympia J." 544). Snowe attended Edward Little High School in Auburn and then the University of Maine at Orono. Her childhood fascination with politics lingered throughout her collegiate career, influencing Snowe's choice of majors. She earned a BA degree in political science in 1969, after completing a summer internship in the governor's office ("Snowe, Olympia J." 544).

In *Nine and Counting*, Snowe reveals she "found conflicting choices" in her life following her college graduation. Engaged to be married, she also wanted an opportunity to fulfill her "own aspirations as an individual" and was concerned that saying "I do" would destroy her "goals and dreams" (Mikulski et al. 24). Although electoral politics seemed out of reach for women in 1969, Snowe knew she "wanted to be involved in some form of public service" and that she "wanted to be relevant to the world around [her]" (24). She did say, "I do," and less than a decade later found herself in the Maine House of Representatives. In 1969, Snowe married Republican Peter Snowe, who in 1967 had become the youngest member of the state legislature ("Snowe, Olympia J." 544). She worked on the Auburn Board of Registration from 1971 through 1973 and worked as a legislative staffer for U.S. Congressman William Cohen ("Snowe, Olympia J." 544; Barone, Cohen, and Cook 692). In 1973, Snowe's husband was killed in an automobile accident, and she was elected to fill his vacant state house seat. "I certainly had not contemplated ever running for public office," she confided. "I like behind-the-scenes work. I enjoyed what I was doing. The only reason why I decided I should probably do it was that I had such a strong passion for politics" (qtd. in "Snowe, Olympia J." 544). Voters reelected Snowe to the state house in 1974 and to the state senate in 1976, where she became only the second woman to serve in that body ("Snowe, Olympia J." 544; Stineman 143). During her short tenure as a state senator, she chaired the Joint Standing Committee on Health and Institutional Services ("Snowe, Olympia J." 544). In conjunction with that work, she gained "recognition for her sponsorship of health-care legislation" (544), which included work on "child abuse, clarification of professional and practical nursing credentials, and mental health care facilities" (Stineman 143).

Just two years later, when her former employer, Congressman Cohen, decided to campaign for the U.S. Senate in 1978 rather than seek another term in the House, Snowe concluded the time was right for a run for the U.S. House. She was unopposed in the Republican primary for the Second District House seat. In the general election she faced Maine's Secretary of State Markham Gartley, "who had gained public notice for being the first prisoner of war released by North Vietnam" ("Snowe, Olympia J." 544). During the campaign, Snowe reached out to the constituents in her district, which geographically is the largest east of the Mississippi, by taking her message directly to them. Using strategies she learned while working for Cohen, she "walked across her district" and "attend[ed] town meetings and traditional bean suppers to discuss politics with voters" (544). Drawing both Republican and crossover Democratic electors to her views, Snowe won the race by ten percentage points with 51 percent of the vote (545). With this triumph, the Maine electorate sent the youngest Republican woman and the first Greek American woman to the U.S. Congress (Snowe, "About Senator Snowe: Biography"). Maine voters returned Congresswoman Snowe to office for seven additional terms. "Embodying the character traits that Maine natives are known for—rugged individualism and seeming indifference to national political trends," Snowe garnered two-thirds to three-quarters of the vote in her next five reelection campaigns ("Snowe, Olympia J." 545). Snowe's independent streak and willingness to buck the Republican Party line when her conscience and constituents' welfare were at stake contributed to her overwhelming campaign success in the 1980s. In her 1990 reelection bid, however, Snowe encountered a more difficult task. Her district's industries had encountered the negative effects of the recession, losing "forty thousand jobs during the late 1980s" (546). Tax increases and budget cuts implemented by the state's Republican governor and Snowe's husband, John McKernan, Jr., further complicated her efforts (546). Her opponent, State Representative Patrick McGowan, accused Snowe of "spending too much time on foreign affairs at the expense of home-front issues" (546). Although she won the election, she did so with only 51 percent of the vote to McGowan's 49 percent. McGowan challenged Snowe again in the 1992 election. This time she won by an even wider margin. Snowe garnered 49 percent of the votes cast while McGowan received only 42 percent of the voters' support. Green Party candidate Jonathan Carter won the remaining 9 percent of the ballots (546).

During her sixteen-year tenure in the U.S. House, Snowe labored to effect change in a variety of contexts. During her first term, she joined the Congressional Caucus for Women's Issues, a bipartisan group dedicated to advancing legislation deemed important by the women in the House of Representatives (Snowe, "Up" 61). She later cochaired this group with Democrat Patricia Schroeder. She also served as deputy whip, becoming at the time the only woman with a House leadership position in the Republican Party ("Snowe, Olympia J." 545). Snowe supported changes in federal aid formulas that would allow states with smaller populations, like Maine, a more equitable share in federal subsidies (545). She "fought against the Reagan administration in backing the Equal Rights Amendment" (J. Abrams). She sought recognition of women's health issues and adequate funding for programs and research addressing those concerns. She advocated for the Economic Equity Act that sought to provide equality for women in "insurance and pension laws" and "tax breaks for housewives and for parents who use day care" ("Snowe, Olympia J." 545). Because of the tenuousness of the textile, shoe, timber, and fishing industries in Maine, Snowe lobbied for trade protection, often voting against Republican-sponsored free-trade agreements (546). In 1988, she introduced child-care legislation that would have augmented the federal government's contributions to these services by providing employer tax credits and various subsidies (546). She cosponsored a bill with Patricia Schroeder in 1989 to establish centers to research innovative treatments for infertility and new birth control methods (546). In the early 1990s, Representative Snowe endorsed a constitutional amendment requiring a balanced federal budget and opposed cuts in foreign aid. "After trying unsuccessfully in 1999 to forge a compromise over President Clinton's impeachment, [she] was one of five Republicans to vote to acquit Clinton on both articles of impeachment" (J. Abrams). Despite her disagreements with the more conservative Republican members of the House, Snowe's "loyalty on key issues and willingness to compromise had earned her the respect and support of the party faithful at the highest levels of government" ("Snowe, Olympia J." 546).

When Maine Democrat and Senate Majority Leader George Mitchell announced his retirement in early 1994, Olympia Snowe immediately announced her candidacy for the Senate seat. She ran unopposed in the Republican primary and faced Democratic Representative Thomas Andrews in the general election. Throughout the campaign, Snowe characterized Andrews as a tax-and-spend liberal and challenged his congressional record, including his advocacy of the bill that closed northern Maine's Loring Air Force Base, his opposition to the balanced budget amendment, and his support for gun control ("Snowe, Olympia J." 547; Barone, Cohen, and Cook 692–93). Amid the GOP victories of 1994, Snowe won the election, receiving 60 percent of the vote while Andrews secured only 36 percent of the ballots. She carried every county but lost in the cities of Portland and Lewiston (Barone, Cohen, and Cook 693). With high job approval ratings, Snowe sought reelection in 2000. Although she encountered staunch opposition from the Democratic challenger, state senate President Mark Lawrence, Snowe managed a landslide victory. Receiving 69 percent of the vote, Snowe carried Portland and Lewiston and lagged behind Lawrence in only a few small communities (693). With her election in 1994, Olympia Snowe became the second female from Maine to serve in the U.S. Senate, the fourth woman in history elected to both the U.S. House of Representatives and the Senate, and the first woman to serve in both houses of a state legislature and both houses of Congress (Snowe, "About Senator Snowe: Biography"). She has now recorded victories in more federal elections in Maine than any other person since World War II ("About Senator Snowe: Biography"). When voters elected Susan Collins in 1996, Maine joined California as the second state to elect two women to the Senate concurrently.

The least conservative of the Republicans elected to the Senate in 1994 (Barone, Cohen, and Cook 693), Snowe has maintained her reputation as a "leading moderate, focusing her attention on efforts to build bipartisan consensus on key issues" (Snowe, "About Senator Snowe: Biography"). With Louisiana Democrat John Breaux, she cochaired the Senate Centrist Coalition, which includes about thirty-five senators from both parties who try to find common ground on tax policy, campaign finance reform, and other divisive issues (Snowe, "About Senator Snowe: Biography"; Barone, Cohen, and Cook 693; Hawkings and Nutting 447; "ME: Snowe's Clout"). *Congressional Quarterly* recognized Snowe for her centrist leadership in 1999. Barbara O'Connor, director of the Institute for the Study of Politics and Media, describes Snowe as "a moderating influence [who] will work to get bipartisan agreement in a fractious environment" (qtd. in "ME: Snowe's Clout"). John Porter of the Portland *Press Herald* suggests that "in a world where advancing ideological agendas matters more than solving problems, Snowe still wants to craft legislation that actually addresses needs. There aren't many people like that left in Washington" ("Americans").

During her first term in the Senate, the Republican leadership appointed Snowe deputy whip and then in 1997, assigned her to the position of counsel to the assistant majority leader (Snowe, "About Senator Snowe: Biography"). Senator Snowe served on the Senate Armed Services Committee from 1997 to 2001, only the fourth woman ever to join this body. She became the "first woman Senator to chair the Subcommittee on Seapower, which oversees the Navy and Marine Corps" ("About Senator Snowe: Biography"). Snowe gained membership on the Senate Committee on Foreign Relations during her first term in office and chaired the Subcommittee on International Operations ("Snowe, Olympia J." 547). In 2004, she sat on the Senate Select Committee on Intelligence; the Senate Committee on Commerce, Science, and Transportation, where she chairs the Subcommittee on Oceans, Fisheries and Coast Guard; the Committee on Small Business and Entrepreneurship, which she chairs; and the Committee on Finance. There she serves on the Subcommittee on Health Care (Snowe, "About Senator Snowe: Committee"). When she joined the Finance Committee in 2001, Snowe became the first Republican woman to secure a full-term seat on the panel and only the third woman in history to gain membership on this powerful committee (Snowe, "About Senator Snowe: Biography").

Olympia Snowe's work in the Senate mirrors and expands her endeavors in the House of Representatives. For example, during her first year in the Senate, she again advocated for a constitutional amendment to balance the federal budget. "The people of Maine," she explained, "have sent clear and unequivocal signals that we must have the courage and the will to balance the federal budget" (qtd. in "Snowe, Olympia J." 547). She cosponsored legislation in 1998 to require insurance companies to pay for women's prescription contraceptives. In 2000, she "sponsored a $200 million appropriation for women's health research" and a "bill to extend osteoperosis [sic] screening to all Medicare recipients" (Barone, Cohen, and Cook 693). On the Armed Services Committee, she opposed the recommendation to segregate housing for men and women during basic training (Barone and Cook 728). She "strongly supports abortion rights, opposes oil drilling in the Arctic National Wildlife Refuge in Alaska, and backs a higher minimum wage" (J. Abrams). According to her Senate web site, Snowe's endeavors in the Senate include a focus on oceans and fisheries issues; campaign finance reform; education, including financial aid for students and technology; national security; budget and fiscal responsibility; health care; and women's issues. As expected, she also advocates for programs of specific importance to her Maine constituents, like reauthorization of the Northeast Dairy Compact and support for the state's lobster fishery. In addition, Snowe provides leadership for issues related to shipbuilding and women in the military (Snowe, "About Senator Snowe: Biography").

Making government work heads the list of phrases in Senator Snowe's political mantra. To accomplish this public service goal to which she genuinely dedicates her life, she talks about the need for *getting things done* to help the people in her state, the country, and when possible, the world. Reflecting the urgency she often feels when debating the issues confronting the government, this phrase often shares billing with the word *now* or the phrase *it is time.* As indicated throughout this discussion, Snowe believes the work of the people can be accomplished only when politicians work together. Thus, the ideograph *bipartisan cooperation* centers not only her rhetoric but her actions as well. For many, on both sides of the aisle, Senator Snowe simply embodies the concept of bipartisanship. Finally, throughout her political career, Snowe has focused attention on women's issues. Her use of the term *women* embraces those issues specific to women's rights and needs. However, in addition, Snowe uses this symbol to represent the concerns of children, families, and by extension, the public good. Throughout her political discourse, Snowe interweaves these three ideographs, *getting things done, bipartisan cooperation,* and *women,* to create a fabric of successful advocacy on behalf of her constituents.

"My aunt used to say to me, 'Olympia, don't ever wait for me to ask you. Look around and see if there's something that needs to be done and do it,'" recounts Senator Snowe. "So guess what?" she asks. "Now I can't sit still. As soon as I sit down, I find myself thinking, 'What needs to be done?' And then I start doing it. I can't help myself" (Mikulski et al. 160). Is it any wonder, then, that the theme *getting things done* lies at the heart of Snowe's political endeavors? When she first arrived in Congress, Snowe remembers finding all the pomp and circumstance humorous and thinking just "give me the work" (183). Speaking of Snowe's work with John Breaux on behalf of the Centrist Coalition, her spokesman Dave Lackey notes that for Snowe "it's all about getting things done. Both [Snowe and Breaux] at the end of the day want to see achievements instead of gridlock" (qtd. in "ME: Snowe's Clout"). In addition to her own proclivities for action, Snowe argues that the "mandate from the electorate is to get things done" (qtd. in Milligan). And, as the following discourse samples illustrate, Snowe believes this instruction from the voters applies to all issues. For example, attempting to move legislation forward to accelerate development of broadband infrastructure to facilitate high-speed Internet service, Snowe contends that "there are times when it makes sense to help the market deploy technology more quickly, and this is one of those times. Why?" she asks. "Because . . . the Government can help ensure that all our citizens have access to basic infrastructure so all Americans . . . will have the chance to participate in—and succeed under—the tremendous benefits of new technologies" (Snowe, "Floor Statement on Jumpstart"). Adding a note of urgency she suggests to her colleagues that "it is critical we act quickly in this area" so that the United States does not "fall further behind in this crucial area" ("Floor Statement on Jumpstart"). In closing she reiterates the idea that "we must engage on this issue and we must do it now" ("Floor Statement on Jumpstart").

Continuing her focus on getting things done in her introduction of the Community College Teacher Preparation Enhancement Act of 2004, Snowe contends that the legislation is needed now to help address "two of the Nation's most pressing education needs: first, the projected demand for roughly 2.4 million new 'highly qualified' teachers over the next decade . . . and second, the requirement under the No Child Left Behind Act that all teachers be 'highly qualified' by 2006" (Snowe, "Floor Statement on Community"). Emphasizing the need for immediate action on this bill, she affirms that "this legislation addresses a pressing issue. School districts across the nation are struggling to meet the requirements of No Child Left Behind and delaying assistance would only compound the problem. . . . It is time to act," she asserts, "and this legislation offers us a tremendous opportunity to send a clear and overdue signal to states that we intend to be true to this landmark legislation's title" ("Floor Statement on Community"). In one of her weekly updates, Snowe tells her constituents that "the time has come for more affordable prescription drugs" as she provides them with details of the Pharmaceutical Market Access and Drug Safety Act ("The Time"). "This bill is a recognition that after five years it's long past the time that we provide Americans access to more affordable pharmaceuticals through the safe importation of prescription drugs," she suggests. Snowe then claims that the "legislation comprehensively addresses the various concerns that have been raised over the months and years about drug importation—so we can get something done *now*" ("The Time"). In her July 2004 statement regarding the release of the Intelligence Committee Report on Pre-War Intelligence Assessments, Snowe concludes that "our enemies aren't waiting to overcome bureaucratic hurdles and inertia to strike us again—we can't wait in replacing our outmoded Intelligence Community structure and rebuilding an intelligence apparatus equipped not to respond to 21st century threats, but to prevent them" (Snowe, "Snowe Statement on Release"). The theme of *immediacy* permeates Snowe's discussion of security for the maritime transportation system. "The fact is we cannot wait any longer than necessary to acquire the necessary Coast Guard vessels, aircraft and information technology," she warns. "We can't afford to wait until dangerous cargo is already in our ports" (qtd. in "Sen. Snowe: 'First Priority'"). Emphasizing her concerns, she affirms that "confronting our homeland security challenges requires a 'must-do attitude.' I recognize that some of the mandates in MTSA are very ambitious, and rightly so," she adds. "Simply put, we can't afford to take any chances, and we can't afford to assume that time is on our side" (qtd. in "Sen. Snowe: 'First Priority'").

For Senator Snowe, the obvious way to *get things done* is to form bipartisan coalitions that place citizens' needs above ideological agendas. But even the indomitable senator from Maine grows weary at times in the heat of partisan battles. "If you want to get something done, and get away from the 'all or nothing, my way or no way,' proposition, it is a very difficult environment, to say the least," she laments (qtd. in Toner). Yet, not to be side-tracked, she perseveres, stating: "I try to bridge the difference on issues that are important to the country" even though "it's not an easy process, particularly given the ferocity of partisanship within the institution itself" (qtd. in Eilperin).

Snowe provides a blueprint of the importance of bridging the differences and strategies for embracing a spirit of bipartisan cooperation in a 1997 commencement address to the John F. Kennedy School of Government. "I want to speak with you today about the great tasks facing our nation's political leaders," she tells the graduates. "And that is, making government work. It's a task made more daunting by the mounting chorus of partisanship that has engulfed our nation's politics." She proclaims: "I come here today not to praise partisanship but to bury it" ("Speech"). Describing the tactics her audience should embrace for a successful public service career, she declares that "our great success in the 21st century will require cooperation, not confrontation. Civility not hostility. Vision not division. In short," she continues, "it will require the restoration of confidence in our nation's leaders and our political institutions. And that confidence, I believe, will only be secured by evidence of a new and lasting bipartisanship among our leaders" ("Speech"). Snowe lambastes the current political climate, arguing that "the political dynamic confronting the American political system is the ongoing erosion of bipartisanship, civility and cooperation. In many instances," she asserts, "political leaders have failed to seek compromise, and instead approach politics as an all or nothing proposition, where there are only two outcomes, a scorched earthy victory for one side, or political stagnation" ("Speech"). Suggesting that bipartisan cooperation is necessary for the government to function, she contends that although "this may sound simplistic and obvious, but democratic, that's with a small 'd,' democratic government works well only when political leaders work together. And when they don't," she proceeds, "the dissension is palpable, painful, and it grinds down the gears of effective government" ("Speech"). As the "leaders of tomorrow," Snowe describes the journey upon which her audience members are about to embark. "It begins with resoluteness, it involves cooperation, it understands bipartisanship, and it ends with leadership" ("Speech"). According to Snowe, the twenty-first century requires such a visionary leadership. "There are plenty of us in Congress who are willing to work together across the sometimes clear, and sometimes vague political party lines, that separate us. What we need, however, is a leadership to bring the spirit to life. . . . Simply put," she concludes, "it's time for our leaders to lead. . . . We need to devote less energy to judging and criticizing each other, and more to forging consensus and understanding" ("Speech").

The efforts of Olympia Snowe and John Breaux in 1999 to revive the Centrist Coalition underscore the senator's commitment to bipartisan cooperation. Addressing the need for such a group, Snowe indicated "everything up here is very separate, very divided. There's no instrument to break down those wall of separateness. It is degrading the Senate. I hear it at home. It has not gone unnoticed by the public" (qtd. in Barone, Cohen, and Cook 693). But, "if you want to be a successful, governing party, you need 60 votes," Snowe observes. "Centrists and moderates are going to play a pivotal role, without question" (qtd. in Milligan). Snowe also brings the language of bipartisanship to her discussion of issues on the Senate floor as the following example demonstrates. Speaking in favor of an amendment to the Personal Responsibility and Individual Development for Everyone Act, she acknowledges that her Republican colleagues "were willing to compromise in order to advance this benchmark legislation" (Snowe, "Floor Statement on Personal"). She states that her own support of the legislation, despite her preference for "significantly greater funding for child care," emerged from "the spirit of that compromise. . . . so that we could have the opportunity to bridge these gaps on the floor of the Senate and to move this legislation forward" ("Floor Statement on Personal"). Snowe offers her amendment, which "will provide $6 billion in new mandatory child care funding," in hopes "it will set a bipartisan tone for the debate to come" ("Floor Statement on Personal").

Although Snowe focuses on many issues in her senatorial endeavors, her concentration on matters affecting women and their families remains the benchmark for her agenda. She observes that when she first came to Congress in 1979, "it became clear to me rather quickly that Congress was practically oblivious to a critical set of issues: those of particular importance to our nation's women" (Snowe, "Speech"). Snowe charges that despite the fact women have asked the Congress to act on their behalf regarding numerous concerns throughout the history of the country, all too often their requests encountered routine dismissal. "For too long, women in America were the great 'silent majority,'" she concedes, "we were the majority of voters, yet our calls for action on the women's health agenda were too often met with silence" (Snowe, "Up" 60). Snowe asserts that "only when women ascended to take their place in the halls of Congress" did women's issues find their voice. "Early on in my tenure in Congress," she admits, "I recognized, as one of the few women representatives, that I had a major obligation—in fact, a responsibility—to raise these issues to the top of our national legislative agenda" (60). She has remained true to that responsibility. Snowe argues that quantity does make a difference when it comes to women's clout in the Congress. "As more and more women play a role in our legislative system," she avers, "legislators have an opportunity to work together on a bipartisan basis to take the next crucial steps toward achieving equity. Improving the health of American women," she persists, "requires a far greater understanding of women's health needs and conditions, and ongoing evaluation in the areas of research, education, prevention, treatment, and the delivery of services" (63). In the phrase, *women's health*, we hear the echoes of Snowe's past and the ferocious passion of her continuing commitment to getting things done in the government to improve women's health. Undoubtedly, her mother's untimely death from breast cancer informs her efforts on behalf of the country's women. Recently, she submits, "I have focused my work on women's health in several key areas—most notably, breast cancer. I am working to ensure that one day, no young girl or boy will ever have to lose a mother to this dreaded disease" (63). Summarizing her vision for women's health care in this country, Snowe states:

> I look forward to a future where the health care community will *accommodate* women's biological differences, not ignore them; where we will be treated as equals in medical research, not as an afterthought; and where our daughters and granddaughters will be able to expect the very best in health care research, funding, and treatment and not have to settle for second best. But one vision is

certain: never again will women be a missing page from America's medical textbook. ("Up" 67)

Snowe remains convinced that women can lead the way toward bipartisan cooperation in the Congress because they tend to be "more relationship-oriented and more collaborative" (Mikulski et al. 129). She provides an illustration of this concept in her description of the work of the bipartisan Congressional Caucus for Women's Issues and its support for her legislation to create an Office of Women's Health Research at the National Institutes of Health. "This was a case study of legislatures reaching across party lines to research, consider, negotiate, and then pass legislation addressing a critical policy issue. Those of us who led the charge for these women's issues," she explains, "did not agree on everything, but we shared a common vision in the needs of women. And we did not allow our differing views on abortion, or our partisan affiliations, to stand in our way" (Snowe, "Speech").

As she morphs the ideograph *women* into a symbol representing children, families, and the public good, Snowe frequently intimates that the passage of legislation that benefits women ultimately provides a win-win situation for both women and society at large; that is, the public good. Returning to Snowe's floor remarks on the PRIDE Act, we see her make this argument. "Without good child care," she asserts, "a parent is left with only two choices: to leave a child in an unsafe and often unsupervised situation, or not to work, both of which are lose-lose situations. If the aim of welfare reform is to move people off the welfare rolls and on to the payrolls," she continues, "providing support in the form of quality affordable child care is a prerequisite to realizing that goal" (Snowe, "Floor Statement on Personal"). In concluding her remarks, Snowe declares, "We have no rhyme or reason to put people who care about their own children in untenable situations where they are compelled to make these unpalatable choices. This amendment will help ensure we can prevent these types of circumstances so many families face in the real world today" ("Floor Statement on Personal"). Although she does not use the word *women* in this passage, it is obvious that many of the parents who find themselves in the position she describes are women. Thus, Snowe argues for support for women within the context of children and the family.

In a similar vein, Snowe offers support for the Child Care Access Means Parents in School Act of 2004, a bill to provide campus-based childcare for low-income parents. She reminds her colleagues in the Senate that "higher education is becoming ever more crucial to getting a job in today's global job market" and that "the majority of new jobs require education beyond high school. . . . For many low-income students who are parents," she claims, "the availability of campus-based child care is key to their ability to receive a higher education and thus achieve the American dream" (Snowe, "Floor Statement on Child"). Furthermore, she argues, "children placed in campus-based child care also reap numerous benefits, given its high quality. In fact," she attests, "children in high-quality child care exhibit higher earning as adults, higher rates of secondary school graduations, lower rates of teen pregnancy, and a reduced need for special education or costly social services" ("Floor Statement on Child"). The unstated assumption, of course, is that these benefits for children and their parents also contribute to the greater public good.

The authenticity with which Senator Snowe embraces the concept of *bipartisan cooperation* forms a vivid thread throughout the fabric of her political discourse. The fibers of this tightly woven rhetorical cloth reflect the synergistic relationship created through her use of the ideographic filaments *getting things done, women,* and *bipartisan cooperation.* Many, including Olympia Snowe, may argue these ideas represent a feminine perspective in political discourse and action. We agree. Yet, her transformation of these themes into a variegated fabric advocating for and representing the public good illustrates her ability to create a feminine-infused, gender-neutral strategy befitting the discourse of the in-between space.

Maria Cantwell

"I have concerns over the new administration's approach to family planning, women's health, and women's rights. . . . Several new senators were elected last year, and we did not come to Washington to take the party line on controversial issues. It is my hope that the Senate can get some things accomplished—like campaign finance reform, a prescription drug benefit for seniors, meaningful patients' rights protections, and real environmental protection. We run as Democrats and Republicans, but we need to govern as Americans" (Cantwell qtd. in Rasmusson 21). Senator Maria Cantwell's comments express the candor with which she approaches her work in the Senate. The junior senator from Washington state often doesn't mince words when she's focused on doing the job of the people. A moderate Democrat who is "both pro-business and pro-choice" (Schultz and van Assendelft 29), she doesn't hesitate to reach across the aisle to achieve positive results for the American people. She contends she "gained experience building consensus" in her term in the U.S. House (Rebecca Cook, "High-tech"). Announcing her senatorial campaign in the spring of 2000, Cantwell declared: "I want to represent people in Washington state because I want to be their voice . . . and not a tool of special interests" (qtd. in "High-tech"). Further, she suggested, "we need a U.S. senator who has a vision of what the 21st century will be and can play a leadership role in making sure we invest in people" (qtd. in "High-tech"). Reflecting on her decision to reenter the world of politics after working in the high-tech industry for five years, Cantwell noted that "the experience of RealNetworks, like, crystallized it. The rest of the world is moving so much faster. Was government going to be this anchor that just dragged behind? Or was it going to reinvent itself and get more in touch with people and their decision-making?" (qtd. in Galvin). In its endorsement of Cantwell's candidacy, the *Seattle Times* noted that "former congresswoman Maria Cantwell has much work to do to win a Senate seat and become a senator of stature. But she has the demonstrated guts, determination and ability to begin the task. . . . Cantwell wants to shake things up. She is a strong advocate for campaign-finance reform and reduced reliance on backroom lawmaking" ("Maria"). Reporter Kevin Galvin concluded that "admirers see Cantwell as a fresh face for Washington state: a woman succeeding in the male-dominated realm of politics; someone who 'gets tech' and considers herself a 'defender of the environment'; a diehard Mariners fan who at 43 is one of the youngest members of the Senate" (Galvin 16).

Maria Cantwell remains "true to the values and tradition of public service she learned from her family" (Cantwell, "About Maria"). She grew up in a modest home in a working class Irish neighborhood of Indianapolis ("About Maria") The Cantwell household hummed with political activity. Her father, a construction worker, entered politics as a county commissioner and city councilman and then successfully ran for a seat in the state legislature. He also served as chief of staff for U.S. Representative Andrew Jacobs (Rasmusson 21; Barone, Cohen, and Cook 1598; Hawkings and Nutting 1065). Her mother engaged actively in Democratic politics as well. As a child, Cantwell accompanied her father "to rallies and meetings, and helped him knock on doors to turn out the vote on election day" (Galvin). She recalls those adventures, noting: "I just realized that it was about effort. It was about taking something you believe in and pushing it. And if you kept that belief, then you would be successful" (qtd. in Galvin). She acknowledges that her "parents instilled in [her] that if you work hard and you care about something, but particularly the work hard part, if you work hard you can accomplish things" (qtd. in Galvin). Her mother says that she "recognized early on that she [Cantwell] was a high achiever. . . . If there's a problem, she always thinks she can fix it" (qtd. in Galvin). Cantwell attended public schools in Indianapolis and was the first young woman elected president of the citywide Catholic Youth Organization (Galvin). Following high school, Cantwell studied at Miami University of Ohio where she received a BA degree in public policy (Hawkings and Nutting 1064). There she served as president of the college Democrats. She raised money to support Democrats "by selling tickets for movie screenings to the mostly Republican student body" (Galvin). Cantwell, who worked to pay for her education, was the first in her family to earn a college degree (Cantwell, "About Maria").

Maria Cantwell's involvement in politics began soon after she graduated from the university. She volunteered for the gubernatorial campaign of Cincinnati mayor Jerry Springer and later worked as a scheduler for a Senate candidate in Delaware (Barone and Cohen 1681; Galvin). In 1983 Tom Pazzi, Senator Allan Cranston's presidential campaign manager, hired Cantwell to run Cranston's regional office in Washington, Idaho, and Alaska. Pazzi recalled: "It was obvious to me from the beginning that she had terrific political skills and an appetite for work" (qtd. in Galvin). Although Cranston dropped out of the race long before the primaries in these states, Cantwell loved the Pacific Northwest and decided to stay in the area. She moved to Mountlake Terrace, a Seattle suburb, where she organized a successful effort to build a new library (Barone, Cohen, and Cook 1598). In 1986, Cantwell ran for office, becoming at age twenty-eight the youngest woman ever elected to the Washington House of Representatives. In the state legislature, Cantwell gained a reputation as a person who could engender action by building consensus and "earned a high degree of respect among her peers of both parties" (Cantwell, "About Maria"). During her six years in the state House, Cantwell supported a state Family and Medical Leave Law and crafted the state's Growth Management Act, which she managed during a marathon sixty-five-day session (Barone, Cohen, and Cook 1598; Cantwell, "About Maria").

In 1992, Cantwell successfully campaigned for the U.S. House of Representatives from the First District located north of Seattle. She won with 55 percent of the votes compared to her opponent's 42 percent (Barone and Cohen 1682). Mirroring her work in the state legislature, Congresswoman Cantwell championed the Family and Medical Leave Act. She endorsed the 1993 deficit reduction plan, supported positions taken by environmental advocacy and pro-choice groups, backed gun-control legislation, fought against export restrictions on software encryption products, worked to defeat the "clipper chip" proposal, and opposed the Clinton health care plan (Barone, Cohen, and Cook 1598; Cantwell, "About Maria"). Cantwell ran unsuccessfully for a second term in the House. In the 1994 election, she lost to Republican Rick White by four percentage points. Following her defeat, Cantwell returned to Seattle where in 1995, she joined a startup firm, Progressive Networks, which later became RealNetworks, a leader in Internet-based software (Barone and Cohen 1682). As one of the company's first ten employees and as senior vice-president of consumer products, she helped create more than one thousand jobs in the state and became a multimillionaire in the process (Rasmusson 20; Barone and Cohen 1682; Cantwell, "About Maria").

Encouraged by Democratic Party officials, Cantwell formed an exploratory committee in 1999 to investigate a return to politics, and in January 2000, she decided to enter the U.S. Senate race against three-term incumbent Republican Senator Slade Gorton ("Encyclopedia"). In the all-party primary, she faced Democrat

Deborah Senn, the state's insurance commissioner, whom party officials considered too liberal to defeat Gorton. Cantwell secured 37 percent of the primary votes while Senn received support from only 13 percent of the voters. Electors cast only 44 percent of their ballots for Gorton. In the general election, Cantwell campaigned as a "champion of the new economy . . . . cast[ing] herself as a product of the new century economy who could move Washington well beyond its old roots in the natural resource-based economy" (Egan). Asked in a 2001 interview for *Working Woman* why she chose politics over business at that time, Cantwell replied: "While I was very excited to be part of an Internet startup, right now I think the U.S. Senate could use someone who understands the New Economy. As it emerges, government needs to think about the implications for campaign finance reform, education, and flexibility in infrastructure investments" (qtd. in Rasmusson 21). Focusing on her experience in the "high-tech private sector" and adopting the slogan "your voice for a change," Cantwell "claimed Gorton supported '19th century solutions to 21st century problems'" (Barone and Cohen 1682; "Encyclopedia"). "I've just spent the past five years in the private sector learning how to do things on the outside," she told voters. "Senator Gorton's been in office for 41 years. He seems to like government a lot" (qtd. in Barone, Cohen, and Cook 1598–99). With this strategy in a state "support[ive] of women in the political process" (Palchikoff), Cantwell employed a gender-neutral discourse in her campaign. Liz Perini, president of the Washington State League of Women Voters, claimed "the people of Washington are looking at women candidates the way they are looking at any men candidates. Gender is becoming less and less an important factor" (qtd. in Palchikoff).

A supporter of "McCain-Feingold-type campaign finance regulation," Cantwell refused to accept "political action committee contributions or any unregulated money from the Democratic Party" (Palchikoff). Instead, she dipped into her own fortune. Overall, she spent approximately $11.5 million in the race with her own contributions and loans to the campaign totaling about $10.3 million (Barone and Cohen 1682; "Maria"). In what was generally considered the closest and most scrutinized Senate contest in the country, Cantwell ultimately defeated Gorton. She was not declared the winner, however, until the absentee ballots were counted and then an automatically mandated recount completed. Almost a month after the election, Cantwell declared victory with a margin of 2,229 votes, less than one-tenth of one percent of the ballots cast, winning only five of the state's thirty-nine counties (Hawkings and Nutting 1065). Ron Sims, the executive of King County who lost the previous Senate race against Gorton, commented that "Slade Gorton lost because he was not a moderate and not green enough." On the other hand, he noted that "Maria came across as moderate, nonpartisan and environmentalist—and that's what people want in this state" (qtd. in Egan).

Cantwell's success generated praise from around the country, especially from women who applauded her "ability to compete financially with her Republican opponent and for her determination to take on a longtime incumbent" (Palchikoff). Mary Hawkesworth, director of the Center for American Women and Politics, suggested Cantwell's triumph was a "major step for women in politics. This is an example for women around the country," she continued (qtd. in Palchikoff). Her accomplishment contributed at least two entries to the Senate history books as well: Washington became the third state to send two elected females to the Senate concurrently. And, in a time of bitter division in the country and the Congress, Cantwell's success created a tie in the Senate with Democrats and Republicans each holding fifty seats until "James Jeffords became an independent in May 2001 and gave Democrats a razor-thin majority" (Barone and Cohen 1682).

Senator Maria Cantwell promised voters during the campaign that she would visit each of the state's thirty-nine counties annually. She travels the state in her car eager to meet her constituents in person rather than their self-appointed representatives back in the capital. "You just get the human face of it," she says. "You realize you need to consider other things" (qtd. in Galvin). In the 108th Congress, Cantwell served on the Commerce, Science, and Transportation Committee with subcommittee appointments to Communications, Competition, Commerce and Infrastructure, and Oceans, Fisheries, and Coast Guard; Energy and National Resources; Indian Affairs; and Small Business and Entrepreneurship (Barone and Cohen 1681). The issues Cantwell targets in the Senate reflect her previous public service efforts, her high-tech business background, and her commitment to protecting the voters of Washington state. She remains a stalwart champion of pro-choice and other women's rights concerns. She has endeavored to "boost Washington's economy and create jobs by supporting longtime state industries such as aerospace, trade, and agriculture, and by cultivating new ones, such as software and biotechnology" (Cantwell, "About Maria"). Honoring promises she made during the Senate race, she has continued her efforts on behalf of campaign finance reform. She has supported small businesses and high-tech initiatives. Cantwell has carved a unique niche in the Senate using her expertise with new technology. "She has earned the respect of her colleagues," suggests her Senate cohort Patty Murray. "She knows the issues well and is a voice that is listened to, particularly on issues affecting high-tech" (qtd. in Galvin). Cantwell has fought for the extension of unemployment benefits and for retraining programs for employees who have lost jobs in the recession. Cantwell added amendments to the Patriot Act that tripled the number of guards on the Canadian border and that required the development of a type of biometric identification to aid Homeland Security protections (Barone and Cohen 1682). She has sponsored legislation to assist victims and law enforcement agencies battle identity theft. In terms of national energy policy, a hallmark of her work has been her endeavors to "ban market manipulation tactics like those used by Enron to defraud both ratepayers and businesses of billions of dollars" (Cantwell, "About Maria"). Unlike many of her Western colleagues, Cantwell continues to advocate for gun-control legislation. Although she concentrates much of her legislative efforts on those issues that affect her Washington state constituents, Cantwell argues on behalf of all U.S. citizens, especially the worker.

Throughout her political discourse, Cantwell offers a theme with variations focusing on the *American people* and the *American worker*. Her commitment to public service finds its voice in her frequent reminders that legislators should be *doing our job* to represent and protect constituents. When she senses that partisanship and hesitancy to embrace new ideas block effective leadership and legislation for the people, she employs a *hold hostage* ideograph to describe the impasse and harangues her colleagues about their political impotence. Grounding her political agenda in the needs of a newer and greener twenty-first-century economy that sustains the American people, Cantwell concentrates her rhetorical strategies on holding the collective feet of the Senate to the fire of progress.

The ideograph *the American worker*, and its variations, *the American people, the American family,* and *the consumer,* permeate Cantwell's remarks on the floor of the Senate and elsewhere as she battles for economic protections for her constituents. Undoubtedly, her concerns for Washington state workers hit hard by layoffs in the recession drive her insistence on providing sufficient benefits for the unemployed. In November 2002, the House adjourned without passing legislation approved by the Senate to extend unemployment benefits. Responding to President Bush's radio address on December 7, 2002, Cantwell argued that "sending laid-off workers into the holiday season without unemployment insurance is like playing Scrooge at Christmas time, giving American workers a lump of coal in their stocking instead of the economic security they deserve" (Cantwell, "Democratic"). Cantwell explains that everyone prefers a paycheck to an unemployment check, "but in these slow times, temporary unemployment benefits help workers who have lost their job through no fault of their own" ("Democratic"). Recalling previous difficult economic times, she reminds her listeners that "in the 1990s, Presidents Bush and Clinton extended unemployment benefits five times, helping working families make mortgage payments, pay health care bills, and put food on the table" ("Democratic"). She describes the bipartisan extension plan authored by Senator Hillary Clinton and passed by the full Senate. This bill "would not only have protected 820,000 American workers from being cut off from benefits, it would have also helped 1.2 million newly unemployment [sic] Americans receive benefits," she claims. "Yet the Republican-controlled House failed to pass the legislation, leaving American workers out in the cold. I ask my fellow Americans," she continues, "is it fair to bail out American corporations while leaving American workers in the lurch?" ("Democratic"). She also indicts the White House for not exhibiting the "leadership or concern for American workers necessary to get this needed benefit passed" ("Democratic").

Fourteen months later, in February 2004, Cantwell once again argues for unemployment compensation in a Senate floor debate as she contends that "a more important question for this body to be debating is the liability we are leaving the American workers with when, in fact, this body refuses to pass unemployment benefit extensions at a time when our economy is not recovering at the speed it takes to create new jobs" (Cantwell, "Floor Remarks on Extension of the Temporary"). She reiterates her message from the 2002 radio address that American workers prefer a paycheck to federal or state assistance. But when the jobs are not there, other avenues are needed to assist these people. "The American worker is not a rounding error on a statistician's desk" she states. "They are real people who are not getting the economic assistance they deserve" ("Floor Remarks on Extension of the Temporary"). Furthermore, she argues that with a slow-moving economy "we should not leave people out in the cold" ("Floor Remarks on Extension of the Temporary"). Cantwell decries President Bush's refusal to support extension of the federal unemployment benefit program. "Basically," she asserts, "we have left the American workers out in the cold as it relates to this opportunity to sustain themselves and sustain our economy in great economically challenging times" ("Floor Remarks on Extension of the Temporary"). Noting the inevitable vote, Senator Cantwell urges her colleagues to "stand up for the American worker" ("Floor Remarks on Extension of the Temporary").

A month later in a similar debate Cantwell suggests that the Senate continues "to ignore the plight of the American workers who have lost their jobs through no fault of their own" (Cantwell, "Floor Statement on Extension of Unemployment"). She then asks her "colleagues on the other side of the aisle to not make this a partisan issue. I am asking them to make this about the American worker who needs our help utilizing a Federal program designed to help out in times just like this" ("Floor Statement on Extension of Unemployment"). Cantwell acknowledges the country has seen "an increase in productivity" but also notes that, "consequently there have been fewer new hires. While corporate CEOs have made more money and the stock market has benefited from the efficiencies of business, the person who has not benefited is the American worker who has not found a job" ("Floor Statement on Extension of Unemployment"). Returning to the legislation to extend unemployment benefits in a floor discussion of the JOBS Act, Cantwell submits that "the question is whether we want to give the American worker who is unemployed an opportunity to receive the

Federal benefit this program was created for, what they paid into through their employer so there could be assistance in tough economic times" (Cantwell, "Floor Statement on Jumpstart"). She returns to this theme later in her speech when she declares, "The question is whether this body is going to stand up and do the right thing and come up with a program to expand unemployment benefits for the next several months so unemployed workers in America can have some certainty they are going to have a future where they can stay in their home" ("Floor Statement on Jumpstart"). Frustrated by the Senate's inaction on the unemployment benefits matter, Cantwell returns to the topic at regular intervals. In April 2004, she once again reminds senators that the administration is not living up to its promise to create 2.6 millions jobs during the year. "And because of that empty promise," she contends, "the American people want to know when this body will take up and pass legislation to reinstate the unemployment compensation program" (Cantwell, "Floor Statement on Electricity Grid").

Infuriated by the Enron scandal and the harmful effects of market manipulation "that have gouged [her] constituents for millions of dollars," Cantwell prods the Senate to take a stand on this issue to protect the American people from unfair business practices. "The question," she declares, "is whether this body and this administration are going to do anything about market manipulation, whether they are going to stand up and say that the Enrons of the world have taken the consumer to the cleaners" (Cantwell, "Sen. Cantwell's Floor Statement on Enron"). Rather than energy policies that benefit corporations, Cantwell makes it clear that she "would like to have an energy bill that protects consumers" ("Sen. Cantwell's Floor Statement on Enron"). She argues that "electricity rates resulting from manipulative practices are simply not lawful. . . . When companies are known to have gouged consumers—in some cases, even admitting as much—those same consumers should not be stuck with the inflated energy bills that result" (Cantwell, "Floor Statement on Electric").

On a related issue, Maria Cantwell admonishes the Senate to adopt reliability standards for the nation's electricity grid for the protection of both consumers and the economy. "There is no doubt," she asserts, "that this nation's consumers and businesses cannot afford further delay in improving the reliability of the electricity grid. Last August's Northeast/Midwest blackout, which affected 50 million consumers from New York to Michigan, again sounded the wake up call for federal electric reliability legislation" (Cantwell, "Floor Remarks on Stand-Alone"). Cantwell has been instrumental in placing stand-alone electric reliability legislation on the Senate calendar, suggesting that "American consumers have waited long enough for Congress to take this simple step" ("Floor Remarks on Stand-Alone"). She reminds the senators that "while consumers may think there are standards by which supply needs to be on the grid and reliability [are] maintained, there are actually no mandatory rules" (Cantwell, "Floor Statement on Energy"). Therefore, when demands are high and transmission availability is limited consumers quite literally are "caught in the dark" ("Floor Statement on Energy").

As Cantwell exhorts her colleagues to protect the American worker and consumer through legislation to provide unemployment benefits and reliable electricity, she disparages the Senate by calling its inaction *hostage taking*. "Good energy policy must not be held hostage to the bad," she avers. "I am of the firm belief that we cannot allow these crucial reliability provisions to be held hostage to a flawed comprehensive energy bill" (Cantwell, "Floor Remarks on Stand-Alone"). Concluding that energy reliability standards can be enacted apart from a larger energy bill, Cantwell argues that "we cannot continue to hold hostage good energy reliability legislation for a comprehensive bill when consumers are at risk" (Cantwell, "Floor Statement on Energy"). She claims the standards legislation "is just being used as bait and being held hostage" for partisan concerns (Cantwell, "Floor Statement on Electricity Grid"). Insistence on considering the standards only as part of an entire package "means holding reliability hostage," Cantwell testifies as she hammers home her message ("Floor Statement on Electricity Grid"). Continuing her harangue, Cantwell states:

> Why are we going to continue to hold hostage legislation on reliability standards that would protect consumers across America from future blackouts, just to getting a big, fat, energy bill for which there is never enough support? My colleagues know how bad that legislation is.
>
> My colleagues want to continue to use the reliability standards, which all the blackout commissions and various organizations across America have said consumers deserve as protection, as the train driving the energy bill. My colleagues are going to say, no, we are going to keep holding reliability hostage. We want to see if Congress blinks and maybe will go ahead and pass that big energy bill. ("Floor Statement on Electricity Grid")

Imploring her colleagues to take action, Cantwell contends that "rather than holding good energy policy hostage for the bad . . . I believe this body can and must make necessary progress in upgrading our electricity grid and protecting our nation's consumers" (Cantwell, "Floor Statement on Electric"). Cantwell also uses this ideograph in her discussions of unemployment compensation. Discussing the legislation to extend benefits, she affirms that "it is time to get past the obstructionists who are holding this up" (Cantwell, "Floor Statement on Extension of Unemployment"). She contends the Senate is "being irresponsible, not allowing Americans to participate in a Federal program that was designed to create opportunity for people" ("Floor Statement on Extension of Unemployment"). In April 2004, Cantwell acknowledges the directness with which she has confronted her colleagues on the issues of unemployment benefits and job creation as well as electric reliability standards. "I am being pointed in my remarks today," she suggests, "because I believe these are two issues this body has the responsibility to deal with. These are two issues we can't get done and we are holding the American people hostage by not addressing our basic domestic economic security needs by giving people jobs and the reliable security of electricity grids" (Cantwell, "Floor Statement on Electricity Grid").

Maria Cantwell came to the Senate to act on behalf of her constituents. Throughout her statements quoted above, her words echo her impatience with partisan politics when the result is inaction. She believes the Senate has an obligation to *do its job* on behalf of the American people. Turning her attention to the matter of cleanup at the Hanford nuclear reservation, Cantwell argues that "now it is our turn to do our job and clean this up" (Cantwell, "Sen. Cantwell's Floor Statement on Proposed Reclassification"). She asserts, "It is a Federal responsibility to clean up nuclear waste" and declares that "we spend budget money on this issue, and we need to get the job done" ("Sen. Cantwell's Floor Statement on Proposed Reclassification"). As the following statement focusing on energy reliability standards and unemployment compensation indicates, Cantwell doesn't hesitate to remind her colleagues of their responsibility to the citizens.

> I rise to discuss with my colleagues two bills that I believe we are being negligent as a body in not taking up and passing. I am sure many of my colleagues are heading to the airport feeling like this week we accomplished a lot, or maybe they feel they gave a lot of speeches. The world is obviously a very dangerous and threatening place right now, and maybe my colleagues think if we get up and we communicate about that, we have done our job in Washington, DC. Well, the discussion is good, but action is even better when it comes to the American people. And there are two critical issues—two issues we have bipartisan support on, two critical issues both the House and the Senate have passed legislation in the past to deal with and on which we could pass legislation today—that we cannot put on the priority list to take up and take action to help the American people. (Cantwell, "Floor Statement on Electricity Grid")

Later in this same speech, Cantwell proclaims, "Congress needs to get about our business in passing legislation to make these rules mandatory" ("Floor Statement on Electricity Grid"). Asking "why hasn't Congress operated and gotten this done?" she declares the "voters should be demanding that we do our job" ("Floor Statement on Electricity Grid"). In yet another speech, Cantwell reminds the senators that "we must do our job in continuing to protect consumers from this market manipulation. . . . Congress needs to do its job" (Cantwell, "Floor Statement on Energy"). Again, discussing the energy reliability standards Cantwell rather bluntly tells her colleagues "this is about us doing our job. . . . We should do our job" (Cantwell, "Floor Statement on Electricity Grid").

As these samples from her discourse illustrate, Senator Maria Cantwell is not afraid to push the ideas in which she believes. In addition, she has a dogged determination to actually pass legislation that benefits constituents rather than her fellow politicians. This ideological agenda drives her focus on a discourse of *doing our job* rather than holding legislation, and consequently people, *hostage*. Her orchestration of the theme and variations of the ideograph *the American worker* signifies her belief in the ideals of the primacy of the people, hard work, progress, expansion of new frontiers, and ultimately, the American dream. Although she uses the language of *protection*, which some may view as a more feminine construct, Senator Cantwell employs a directness in her discourse that illustrates a gender-neutral rhetorical strategy in support of an androgynous political agenda.

Hillary Rodham Clinton

"Being first lady is a very different position than I've ever had before. . . . I've always had jobs and worked for a living. I'm here, as everyone else in the White House is here, because of one person, the president. It was bewildering to me and has taken a while to get used to" (H. Clinton, qtd. in Marton 306). Hillary Rodham Clinton's role as first lady proved bewildering to the American public as well. Accustomed to a traditional model of first ladies, one where the women presided over teas and other social functions and performed primarily behind the scenes, Americans found Clinton an enigma and a lightning rod for controversy. She sought a public role as a policy maker, specifically in health care reform and, according to her memoirs, had great private influence on her husband's decisions as well. From the moment she entered the White House she generated controversy. As White House correspondent Ann Blackman recalls, "Right away she would go by Hillary Rodham Clinton . . . when all during the campaign she was Hillary Clinton. She was making a statement: take me seriously. Then she took an office in the West Wing. Another statement. She was often on the Hill, and outspoken at meetings. She could have changed the way the first lady operates," Blackman continues, "if she had been very traditional. They've all had their own personalities and have emerged gradually. She offended people by moving so fast" (qtd. in Marton 319).

Certainly, as Blackman hints, Hillary Clinton must take some of the blame for creating such a stir. However, she also found herself caught in a public/private duality many women in politics face. The "position" of first lady, however, brings with it added gendered expectations that women such as Clinton find difficult to overcome. "Conflicting expectations of wife and citizen are at the core of the first lady role itself . . . [d]ual expectations for contemporary first ladies—that they be both public wife and citizen—puts a woman who tries to do both roles in the position of gender outlaw" (Brown and Gardetto 22). This position functions as "damned if you do, damned if you don't," for if "she speaks as a citizen, she is speaking from a masculine position and therefore violates her role as a public wife (first lady)" (22). Yet, the very nature of the role of first lady forces women to operate in both the public and private spheres and at the same time often criticizes them for doing so. "As a wife the first lady serves as a 'crucial signifier' for the family and thus, symbolically, for the private sphere of social life. But as a post-suffrage woman and because of her elite position as wife of the president," suggest D. E. Brown and C. M. Gardetto, "she is allowed a speaking position in the news. Thus, first ladies, as public wives, are located symbolically in both the private and public spheres and are caught between conflicting definitions of the news and femininity, just as they are caught between conflicting definitions of citizen and woman" (42). Hillary Rodham Clinton, however, faced the added pressure from her friends and colleagues who wanted a woman to change the face of the first lady, so to speak. As President Clinton's first press secretary, George Stephanopolous suggests:

> She was fulfilling her generation's goal. There was this sense among her core support that we want a woman to break this barrier. Her institutional, formal success would be of political benefit to the community which was her base. Just like the gay community wanted gays in the military, a lot of Hillary's friends and colleagues wanted her to be co-president, since Hillary would have deserved a job in a Democratic administration. There was the feeling that if she did it the traditional first-lady way, it would be a surrender. She would be accepting that she was just serving her husband, that all her power was derivative. Whereas, if she had an office in the West Wing and her own policies, it was not derivative. She was being recognized in her own right. (qtd. in Marton 313)

In addition to the controversy Hillary Rodham Clinton generated, the Clinton administration found itself embroiled in numerous issues of contention. The Whitewater deal, Vince Foster's death, the failed health care plan, Bill Clinton's impeachment hearing, and of course, the Monica Lewinsky scandal all served to draw negative publicity to both of the Clintons and to the administration. However, Hillary Clinton's handling of the press eventually evolved into one of her most significant rhetorical attributes. Colleen Kelley observes that "Mrs. Clinton's chief rhetorical strategy was to take advantage of the press by joining with them in creating good stories about herself and her role as first lady, wife, mother, and woman that were more interesting to—and so more attended to by—the press, and therefore the public, than were the narratives about her husband" (239). Kelley later adds that the Clinton's partnership "became the primary rhetorical strategy throughout the Clintons' terms as First Couple. The co-presidency empowered Hillary Clinton to deflect attention away from her husband to herself and pull particularly negative media attention—and the public eye as well—to herself" (240).

As Bill Clinton's term and the impeachment hearings were drawing to a close, speculation ran rampant in Washington, D.C., that Hillary Rodham Clinton would run for New York Senator Patrick Moynihan's newly vacated seat. Initially, she had "no interest in running for Senator Moynihan's seat, but by the beginning of 1999 the Democratic leadership was in a full court press" to change her mind (H. Clinton, *Living* 495). In her autobiography, *Living History*, Clinton recounts that many people worked to encourage her to run, and others "worked feverishly" to discourage her (498). She consulted her closest political and personal ally, her husband, who offered his advice. She recalls that "Bill patiently talked over each of my concerns and carefully evaluated the odds I faced. The tables were now turned, as he played for me the role I had always performed for him. Once he had given his advice," she adds, "it was my decision to make" (501). In the end, neither a politician nor a political advisor provided the impetus for Clinton to run. Instead, Clinton recounts, it was the captain of a high school girl's basketball team. When Sofia Totti introduced Clinton at an event promoting an HBO special on female athletes, she leaned over and whispered, "Dare to compete, Mrs. Clinton. Dare to compete" (qtd. in H. Clinton, *Living* 501).

Clinton had just spent eight years as a "political spouse" and had "no idea," she says, whether she could "step from the sidelines into the political arena," but she began to think she might "enjoy an independent role in politics" (H. Clinton, *Living* 501). As she recounts in her autobiography, "All over the United States, and in scores of countries, I had spoken out about the importance of women participating in politics and government, seeking elective office and using the power of their own voices to shape public policy and chart their nations' futures. How could I," she concludes, "pass up an opportunity to do the same" (502). On July 7, 2000, Hillary Clinton held a press conference, with Senator Moynihan at her side, to announce that she was forming a campaign committee. More than two hundred reporters showed up at the event (506).

Clinton and her associates knew she would not have an easy time with the media, either in New York or nationally. "Given the historic nature of a First Lady running for the Senate, I could also expect more than the usual New York press contingent scrutinizing my campaign. Just the prospect of my running," she reflects, "prompted national and international media outlets to flood my White House press office with interview requests" (H. Clinton, *Living* 499). The treatment Clinton received from the press proved less than flattering. As she became more politically active, reports Erica Scharrer, the newspaper coverage adopted "a more scrutinizing and negative tone" (403). In comparison to the coverage afforded her opponents, Rudolph Giuliani and later Rick Lazio, the focus of stories about Clinton "contained both a greater number of negative statements, and, overall, a more negative tone" (Scharrer 403). What was truly unprecedented, however, was that the articles consistently attacked the Clinton campaign itself. "These critiques of political foibles and strategic missteps serve[d] to delegitimize her candidacy" (404). In the final analysis, the news media placed the same gendered double binds upon Clinton that she had experienced as first lady. In fact, it is probably because of her position as first lady that these added barriers arose. In the news coverage of her campaign, Clinton was being "held to narrow definitions of gender roles and receiving unfavorable coverage due to her failure to comply with those roles. A resistance to first ladies taking on politically active roles," suggests Scharrer, "is possible in either journalists' own views or their perceptions of the views of their audience members" (403).

Yet, Clinton was able to prevail because of her tireless campaigning and her capacity to listen to the voters. Her approach was quite human. As she remembers in her memoirs, "I stopped at diners and cafes along the road, just as Bill and I had done during his campaigns. Even if only a handful of people were inside, I'd sit down, have a cup of coffee and talk about whatever topics were on their minds. Campaign professionals call this 'retail politics,'" she explains, "but to me it was the best way to stay in touch with people's everyday concerns" (H. Clinton, *Living* 511). Eventually, Clinton began to recognize that her campaign was going well. "I finally felt," she states, "that I was starting to connect to voters. Gradually, I could sense the mood of the electorate shifting my way. . . . After two or three visits to many towns and cities, I became a more familiar presence, and my prospective constituents seemed generally comfortable sharing their stories and worries with me. We had real conversations about the issues that mattered to them," she adds, "and people began to care less about where I was from than what I was for" (511).

On November 7, 2000, Hillary Rodham Clinton defeated Rick Lazio by a margin of 55 to 43 percent. At her victory party, Clinton stood at the podium to thank her supporters and declared, "sixty-two counties, sixteen months, three debates, two opponents and six black pantsuits later, because of you, we are here" (H. Clinton, *Living* 524). "After eight years with a title but no portfolio," she was now "Senator-elect" (514).

While many people both inside and outside the beltway may have been skeptical about Hillary Clinton's ability to serve as a U.S. senator, her performance has showcased her political acumen. Essentially, by "spending most of her first two years in office quietly tending to parochial concerns, working assiduously on policy, and showing deference and charm to fellow senators, Clinton appears to have won over most of her colleagues" (Vandettei 14). At the end of her first two years, however, Clinton became a key player in politics. Senator Clinton, after "lying low" for her first two years, "is emerging as one of the Senate's most prominent and influential democrats, moving aggressively on fundraising and policy matters and fueling speculation that she plans to run for president in 2008" (14).

Scholars and journalists have written reams about the press coverage Hillary Clinton received, her rhetorical strategies as first lady, her marriage with Bill Clinton, and even her changing hairdos. Since she has been serving in office, however, little attention has been paid to her rhetorical strategies as a senator. This section seeks to examine Hillary Rodham Clinton's discourse while serving as the junior senator from New York and specifically focuses on her prominent use of two ideographs, *bilateralism* and *bipartisan*.

The first ideograph, *bilateralism*, crosses both international and national boundaries, so to speak. Clinton promotes cooperation within the world, and within Congress. What is perhaps most notable about this ideological bent is that it is strikingly absent prior to the events of September 11, 2001, when terrorists hijacked planes and crashed them into the World Trade Center and the Pentagon. She uses the issue of bilateral foreign policy—the need to work with allies as opposed to isolation—as a key thrust of criticizing President George Bush's administration. In a speech to the Center for American Progress, for instance, Clinton states that "in our dealings abroad, we more often than not have promoted, not the principles of international cooperation, but the propensity for an aggressive unilateralism that alienates our allies and undermines our tenets. It deeply saddens me," she continues, "as I speak with friends and colleagues around the world, that the friends of America from my generation tell me painfully that for the first time in their lives they are on the defensive when it comes to explaining to their own children that America truly is a good and benign nation" (H. Clinton, "New"). In this same speech, Clinton uses specific examples of America's flouting of international laws and treaties since Bush came to power. "In our dealings abroad," she argues, "we claim to champion the rule of law, yet we too often have turned our backs on international agreements." She then enumerates the list of accords the president has disregarded. "The Kyoto Treaty, which represents an attempt by the international community to meaningfully address the global problem of climate change and global warming. The biological weapons enforcement protocol. The Comprehensive Test Ban Treaty. This unwillingness to engage the international community on problems that will require international cooperation," she adds, "sends a clear signal to other nations that we believe in the rule of law—if it is our law as we interpret it" ("New").

This speech also provides the opportunity for Clinton to criticize the Bush administration's handling of the Iraq War. The United States invaded Iraq in the spring of 2003 on the basis of the administration's claim that Saddam Hussein had links to the al-Qaeda terrorists who attacked the United States and that Iraq had weapons of mass destruction. Neither claim has proven to be true. So in 2004, Congress set out to investigate the "faulty intelligence" that provided the rationale for the invasion. Clinton frames her criticism around the assertion that Congress and the Bush administration are acting in a partisan manner that harms the democratic process and the American people. "Anybody who follows what is going on Capitol Hill is aware that we are locked in a partisan conflict as to how far to go in analyzing the intelligence with respect to Iraq," she insists, "with the other side complaining that we can look to the intelligence community, but we cannot look at the decision makers. We can't look at the uses to which the intelligence was put and we can't look at the particular viewpoint that was brought to the analysis. I think that is a profound error," she concludes, "and undermining to our democratic institutions" (H. Clinton, "New"). Isolationism, going it alone, will not be conducive to building a new Iraq. The United States, Clinton believes, must work with others. "We must abide by those basic principles that we hold dear and demonstrate that we are willing to be open and have partnerships and build coalitions that are more than just in name" ("New").

Hillary Clinton launched some of her strongest attacks against the Bush administration's unilateral policies in her February 25, 2004, speech, "Addressing the National Security Challenges of Our Time: Fighting Terror and the Spread of Weapons of Mass Destruction." The Bush administration essentially invaded Iraq without approval or help from the United Nations or many of its usually staunchest allies. This unilateral act, according to Clinton, has cost the United States friends and credibility, and she extensively outlines the problems with unilateralism and the benefits of collaboration. She first indicates that bilateralism is a historically honored approach to government and foreign policy when she asks, "has the Administration come to understand that the 50-year bipartisan consensus supporting multilateralism was not an excuse for weakness, but an exercise of strength" (H. Clinton, "Addressing"). She further contends that the tension between the concepts of unilateral vs. bilateral approaches to foreign policy have always been resolved in favor of bilateralism. "Critical to fighting this new 21st century war [on terror]," she posits, "is a fundamental re-orientation away from a unilateral posture to a multilateral strategy that strengthens all who participate. Such a change," she continues, "would bring us back in line with more than half a century of bipartisan consensus on foreign policy. . . . If we do that, I believe that we can build a world with more friends and fewer terrorists and create a climate in which we can move from fear to hope" ("Addressing").

According to Clinton, America's loss of credibility around the world borders on staggering. She points out that although the United States was "dismissive of broader international support before the war, it is now seeking NATO and U.N.

involvement in Iraq" (H. Clinton, "Addressing"). But, as she explains, "we already have a profound problem with how we are perceived in the world, with many viewing the United States as arrogant and unilateralist. Recent international polls confirm what many of us sense and feel," she points out, "which is that respect and admiration for the United States has plummeted in many places around the world" ("Addressing"). As she did in her speech to the Center for American Progress, Clinton outlines all of the treaties that the United States has abandoned or broken during the Bush administration. "That sequence of diplomatic retrenchments sent a clear message," she warns. "We're going it alone, whether you like it or not. In fact, we hope you don't like it, because that will make us feel even stronger as we pursue our objectives around the world" ("Addressing"). The Bush administration ignores decades of collaborative problem solving, according to Clinton. Under Bush's leadership, "we do not trust international efforts to deal with common problems. We are better served by freedom of action, rather than collective action," she sarcastically states ("Addressing"). Again, Clinton returns to the historic importance of bilateralism when she intones, "and that gets to the heart of such a big difference between this Administration and the bipartisan consensus of the 20th century about foreign policy. Indeed," she elucidates, "the benefit of international support has been apparent during the 20th century, most obviously in the defeat of fascism in World War II and the defeat of communism during the Cold War" ("Addressing").

Pursuing a unilateral foreign policy proves harmful, both abroad and at home. There is a growing potential for other nations to unite against us. "The more we throw our weight around, the more we encourage other nations to join with each other as counterweight," Clinton warns ("Addressing"). In addition, Americans suffer from a unilateral policy as well. "One more thing," she states, "a go-it-alone strategy necessarily builds domestic support on a bedrock of fear" ("Addressing"). Clinton concludes her attack on unilateralism by invoking the words of President Dwight Eisenhower. "More than 40 years ago, warning against arrogance, President Eisenhower said that the people of the world, and I quote, 'must avoid becoming a community of dreadful fear and hate and be, instead, a proud confederation of mutual trust and respect.' . . . We have many reasons to work more closely together with the peoples and nations of the world," she adds. And so doing, "we help create a more hopeful future for our people and those who look to us for example and support" ("Addressing").

While the issue of bilateral foreign policy occupies a number of Clinton's speeches, the bipartisan approach she champions appears in a variety of topics, from health care and prescription drug benefits to support for AmeriCorps. In one of her floor statements on the Medicare Prescription Drug Proposal, for instance, she applauds "the bipartisan effort to work toward a goal many of [the

Senators] share—providing prescription drug coverage to more than 40 million seniors, including 2.7 million in New York—1 million who are living without any coverage today" (H. Clinton, "Floor Statement . . . on Medicare Drug Proposal"). In criticizing the Bush Administration's prescription drug plan that passed in November 2003, Clinton argues that "New York deserves a better bipartisan alternative than the one that passed today, and I will continue fighting this year, as well as in years to come, to correct the deficiencies" (H. Clinton, "Floor Statement . . . on Medicare/Prescription Drug Legislation").

Other issues, according to Clinton, need a bipartisan approach to solving problems. The lack of funding for a very popular program, AmeriCorps, requires a cooperative solution. "Mr. President," she argues, "this is not a partisan issue. When I organized a letter of support of providing $3 million for Teach for America in April, nine Republicans and ten Democrats signed on. This program has strong bipartisan support" (H. Clinton, "Statement . . . on AmeriCorps"). When discussing America's budget problem with the American Society of Newspaper Editors, Clinton remarks: "The kinds of priorities I speak of today, many of which I have been fighting for during most of my life, are not only bipartisan, they are genuinely American. American concerns: Child care, child abuse prevention, safe food in our schools, police on our streets. We don't stop to ask: Are you for it or against that based on party?" She concludes, "We say, isn't this something we should do together in America?" (H. Clinton, "Remarks of Senator Hillary Rodham Clinton to the American Society"). Clinton often criticizes the partisan nature of the Bush administration's budget priorities, as exemplified in her floor remarks on the 2002 federal budget. "Will President Bush try to push through his one-sided and lop-sided proposals with the votes of his own party? If he does, I will respectfully have to dissent" (H. Clinton, "Floor Remarks of Senator Hillary Rodham Clinton on the 2002 Federal Budget"). In keeping with the bipartisan theme, Clinton elaborates:

> Bipartisanship is a two way street—it is not about Democrats supporting Republican proposals or even Republicans supporting Democratic proposals. It's about Republicans and Democrats working together to do what is right for the country. And the true test of leadership is not appealing to the people under the guise of bipartisanships, but actually hammering out a bipartisan compromise bill that merits the support of both sides of the aisle. ("Floor Remarks of Senator Hillary Rodham Clinton on the 2002 Federal Budget")

Senator Hillary Rodham Clinton relies primarily on two key ideographs, *bilateralism* and *bipartisan*, in her speeches to get her message across. It is not enough, however, for a critic to merely identify the ideographs; instead, one must be able to locate society's ideographs in a historical context and describe the clashes and tensions in usage (Dana Cloud 387). Clinton demonstrates the benefits of a just and credible foreign policy that is bilateral by contrasting it with the unpopular and dangerous unilateral policy currently in place. She asserts with success the notion that prior to the Bush administration the country historically reaped the benefits of policies that were inclusive of others rather than isolationist. Similarly, her continued use of the term *bipartisan,* in particular when discussing domestic policy, again taps into the apparent need for both parties to work together to solve the nation's problems.

Clinton's use of these ideographs should prove to serve her well. While the theme of *cooperation* has traditionally been viewed as "feminine" in nature, Clinton masculinizes it by putting the concept into the traditionally male forum and topic of foreign policy. Clinton shows that, historically, a cooperative approach to solving problems has been the most effective way to accomplish the country's goals. By using these ideographs she has essentially made both foreign policy and domestic affairs gender neutral. She has created and operated in the rhetorical in-between space.

These two ideographs also allow Clinton to position herself effectively for the future. By constantly using the ideograph of *bipartisan* she is reinforcing the notion that she can work with everyone—something definitely needed should she decide to run for the presidency, as many suspect, in 2008 or 2012. At the same time, her focus on bilateral foreign policy demonstrates that she knows about more than just New York or domestic issues. Therefore, she is tapping into an audience of the future, and doing so on gender neutral grounds.

Following her successful bid for the Senate in 2000, Debbie Stabenow commented: "I think what's important is that in a democracy that everyone is represented. And, if slightly over half the population are women, it's incredibly important that women are at the table. Every table. Not only the kitchen table, but every decision-making table" (qtd. in Alvarez). Despite their paucity, Catherine Whitney observes that "individually and collectively, the women serving in the Senate have created a legacy through legislation that will significantly improve the lives of Americans for the next hundred years and beyond" (Mikulski et al. 179–80). The six senators whose political discourse we interrogate in this chapter certainly contribute to that legacy. More importantly, they now demand that a more inclusive view permeate the discussions of all legislation and governance issues and that the discourse of the in-between space be heard. Their numbers may be small, but the voices of the women in the Senate resound loudly and clearly within and without the chamber walls. In 2000, Mississippi Senator Thad Cochran, who began his Senate service in 1978, concluded that "the good old boy days in the Senate are over" (qtd. in Alvarez). We agree.

Voices from All Directions
Women's Discourse in the
Twenty-first-Century State House

5

> *In the absence of role models and expectations that they should be leaders, and defying odds that they could make a difference, these women [political pioneers] across two centuries claimed their authority. At the present time, a trio of women governors elected in 2002 have broadened that reach by laying claim to issues normally reserved for men, bridging the gap in style and substance, successfully assuring voters they could be both tough and caring.*
>
> —MARIE WILSON 46

THE DISCOURSE OF GOVERNORS HOLDS GREAT POTENTIAL for rhetorical scholarship. As the head of her state, the governor finds herself in a leadership position that resonates at the local and state levels as well as on the national playing field. Specifically, contemporary governors bear responsibility for setting the state's agenda and for formulating key policies. Thus, the governor should be the most recognizable and proactive figure in state government. As Terry Sanford suggests in his book, *Storm Over the States:*

> The governor by his very office embodies his state. He stands alone at his inauguration as the spokesman for all the people. . . . He must, like the President of the United States, energize his administration, search out the experts, formulate the programs, mobilize support and carry out new ideas into action. . . . Few major undertakings ever get off the ground without his support and leadership. The governor sets the agenda for public debate; frames the issues; decides the timing; and can blanket the state with good ideas by using his access to the mass media. . . . The governor is the most potent political power in the state. (185–88)

To accomplish the myriad tasks a governor encounters, he or she must possess effective managerial and leadership skills. Governors must operate proactively and both possess and articulate a clear vision for their state. Thad Beyle and Lynn Muchmore explain that:

> The governor is looked to as an active and superior force who imposes on the far-flung bureaucracy a coherent fabric of goals and objectives and then guides the executive machinery towards them. He is more than a problem solver concerned that government functions smoothly and without corruption; he is a policy maker who sets the agenda for executive action and shapes priorities that affect decision making at every level. (82)

While the analyses offered by Beyle and Muchmore as well as Sanford accurately reflect many of the functions governors perform, they fail to take into account a new factor: women can be governors, and vice versa. Furthermore, as the forthcoming discussion demonstrates, these contemporary heads of state have rejected the traditional liberal-conservative paradigm and instead embrace a new "political paradigm that envisions an active public role that aims to promote economic development and reshape the economic marketplace" (Hedge 96). Many contemporary women governors see themselves as the CEO and their state as a corporation. While they still engage in governing, they work in and promote a collaborative approach, between public and private sectors as well as across party lines. Women governors of the twenty-first century thus restructure the political landscape. As the new millennium dawned, three women occupied the highest electoral position in their states. New Jersey's Christine Todd Whitman, Arizona's Jane Dee Hull, and New Hampshire's Jeanne Shaheen were each completing terms of office to which they had been elected in the late 1990s. In the 2000 elections voters chose two additional women for governorships. Ruth Minner won election in Delaware and Judy Martz of Montana moved from the office of lieutenant governor to that of governor. Thus, the year 2001 began with five women serving as state governors, then the largest number of women ever to serve simultaneously as the chief political officers of their states.

With ten women running for the office of governor in 2002, political observers called the period the "Year of the Woman Governor" (Polman). Each of the "women candidates [was] either favored to win, or [had] a very good shot" at conducting successful campaigns (Kohut qtd. in Polman). While not all succeeded in their gubernatorial quest, the sheer number of women running signaled a significant change in the ability of women to alter the perceptions of who can govern. Because women have served in a variety of governmental positions, such as attorney general, state treasurer, and mayor, "voters have gotten used to seeing women as executive decision makers" (Kohut qtd. in Polman). Many of these women made strong candidates because they previously "demonstrated on the job that they can handle state finances and law enforcement" (Polman).

In the first five years of the twenty-first century, fourteen women have served as state governors and one as governor of the Commonwealth of Puerto Rico. In view of the fact that only seventeen women occupied this position during the entire twentieth century, we have some indication that voters increasingly recognize the leadership potential of women in their states. In 2004, nine women occupied governorships, the largest number of women serving simultaneously in this position in the history of the country. They included Judy Martz of Montana, Ruth Ann Minner from Delaware, Michigan's Jennifer M. Granholm, Linda Lingle from Hawaii, Janet Napolitano of Arizona, Kathleen Sebelius from Kansas, Utah's Olene Walker, Kathleen Blanco from Louisiana, and M. Jodi Rell of Connecticut. In addition, Silda Calderon served as the first woman governor of Puerto Rico. Given the diversity of their viewpoints, geographic location, and expanding rhetorical strategies, we have elected to interrogate the political discourse of six of these women, Jeanne Shaheen, Judy Martz, Linda Lingle, Jennifer Granholm, Janet Napolitano, and Kathleen Blanco, to discover the ways in which both individually and collectively they have contributed to the reframing of the gubernatorial discursive space.

Jeanne Shaheen

With her election in 2000 and subsequent completion of that two-year term of office, Jeanne Shaheen became the only woman in the United States to serve a full term as governor in both the twentieth and twenty-first centuries. New Hampshire voters sent Shaheen, the state's first elected female governor and "only its fourth Democratic governor in 100 years" (Robinson 499) to Concord three times beginning with the 1996 election. During her first campaign and term in office, critics and supporters alike often compared the moderate Shaheen to President Bill Clinton, who also won favor with New Hampshire voters in 1996. For example, Scott Baldauf, a staff writer for the *Christian Science Monitor,* suggests that "New Hampshire's new governor may offer a clearer definition of what it means to be a 'New Democrat' than the president himself" (Baldauf). President Clinton described her as "a diamond waiting to be discovered" (qtd. in Robinson 498). Certainly, her centrist approach propelled Shaheen to victory in a staunch Republican state known traditionally for its own unique brand of Yankee conservatism and independence. "There are those who said, when Shaheen decided to run, that the joke was on her," quips Sally Jacobs of the *Boston Globe.* "A woman running for governor in the conservative bastion of New Hampshire? A Democrat running in one of the most Republican states in the nation, where antitax fever runs deeper than the unyielding granite bedrock? Couldn't be done" (Jacobs). But win, she did.

Jeanne Bowers Shaheen's journey to the New Hampshire statehouse began in an unlikely place, St. Charles, Missouri, where she was born in 1947. In high school she was a prom queen and a basketball star (Jacobs; "Sketches"). After graduating from high school, Shaheen attended Shippensburg University in Pennsylvania where she received a degree in English in 1969 (Shaheen, "Jeanne"). Honoring her family's deep-rooted Republican tradition, Shaheen "cast her first presidential vote for Richard Nixon in 1968" (Jacobs). While at Shippensburg she participated in her first political battle, successfully challenging a campus curfew that allowed men later hours than women (Baldauf; Jacobs). Disenchanted by the war in Vietnam, "stunned by Watergate and the bombing of Cambodia, [and] swept up by unrest at Shippensburg . . . Shaheen registered as a Democrat" (Jacobs). In the summer of 1969, she "made one of the most unpragmatic, and possibly wisest, choices of her lifetime" when she met and agreed to marry Bill Shaheen (Jacobs). The couple attended the University of Mississippi where he completed a law degree and she graduated in 1973 with a master's degree in political science (Shaheen, "Jeanne"; Robinson 498; Jacobs). Shaheen pursued high-school teaching in Mississippi and New Hampshire in the early 1970s and owned and managed a small business with her husband in New Hampshire (Robinson 498; Shaheen, "Jeanne").

Jeanne Shaheen's first endeavors in formal politics occurred in 1975 when she and her husband worked on Jimmy Carter's primary campaign (Robinson 498; Jacobs). She later "managed victorious New Hampshire primary campaigns for President Carter in 1980 and Democratic presidential hopeful Gary Hart in 1984" (Robinson 498) as well as several gubernatorial campaigns. In the late 1980s, Shaheen decided to turn from managing political campaigns for others to running one of her own. Many questioned "whether the skills of a campaigner could be transferred to those of a candidate" (Jacobs). Obviously, they could. Voters elected Shaheen to the first of three terms in the state senate in 1990. Some credited her win to her ability to listen, a "political skill that many men did not" possess (Jacobs). "Jeanne listens," proclaims Susan McLane, a long-term Republican state legislator. "She studies the issues. She doesn't just hold forth as though she knew. Men, and particularly men of late in the Republican Party, tell you what to think" (qtd. in Jacobs). During her senate career, Shaheen "focused on lowering electric rates, making health care more accessible and affordable, developing New Hampshire's economy, and improving public education" (Shaheen, "Jeanne"). She "sponsored legislation to curb abuses by health-insurance providers and worked on increasing funding for higher education and industrial research" (Robinson 498). Given her success in the state senate, in 1995 Shaheen announced her intention to run for governor of New Hampshire.

Previous scholarship regarding women's political discourse has focused on the candidates' tendencies to campaign by promoting themselves as women for women. Senator Patty Murray, for instance, packaged herself as a "mom in tennis shoes" and promised to bring women's issues to the Senate floor. While Jeanne Shaheen did not overtly play the "woman" or "mom" card in her first campaign for governor as Murray did in her run for the U.S. Senate, she cleverly did not spurn the "volleyball mom" moniker others attributed to her. "She did not talk much about balancing work and family, or the missed volleyball games and the many nights of pizza dinners," writes one reporter. "She just showed up. And a lot of times she took her family with her" (Jacobs). Others also suggest that Shaheen "shun[s] playing the gender card. And that, precisely, is what some New Hampshire women find appealing" (Shea). Kelly Myers, a pollster from the University of New Hampshire, concludes that Shaheen has "been extremely effective in using gender without talking about it. That's key. She's been able to capitalize on it without having to talk about it" (qtd. in Shea). Speaking of this phenomenon, Shaheen comments that "being a woman was not one of those things I needed to talk about. It's clear," she continues. "All I have to do is walk into a room with my opponent and it's clear that I'm a woman" (qtd. in Jacobs). Shaheen attributes her success to a focus on "issues that make a difference for the average family—improving the schools, lowering electric rates, affordable health care" (Baldauf). She also concedes that "talking about the kind of pocketbook issues I made the focus of my campaign also helped because those are things women care about" (qtd. in Jacobs).

In her 1996 and 1998 campaigns, Jeanne Shaheen took the famous New Hampshire "Pledge"; she promised voters she would not support a broad-based, statewide tax. Traditionally, candidates who refuse to take this stand, as many Democrats do, find winning an election in New Hampshire virtually impossible. Taking a more modest, "pro-business approach to economic issues and a more traditionally Democratic, liberal approach to social ones" (Robinson 498) proved successful for Shaheen. She won her first term as governor with 57 percent of the vote to her Republican challenger's 40 percent (Barone, Cohen, and Cook 959). Two years later, campaigning on her record and focusing on the need for continued progress on the issues she had supported since her days in the state Senate, Shaheen won reelection with 66 percent of the vote (959). In 2000, analysts deemed Shaheen a strong potential running mate for Al Gore. "Mindful, however, of the ambitious and important projects she had started but not yet finished as governor" (Robinson 498) and especially with state funding for education still unresolved, Jeanne Shaheen decided to remain in New Hampshire and seek a third term as governor. But, unlike her stance in previous campaigns, this time she refused to take the pledge. "This year I can't make that promise," she said. "Because my first priority is to make sure that all children, wherever they live, get the education they deserve, I will not rule out any potential solution" (qtd. in Barone, Cohen, and Cook 959). Despite the odds, Shaheen again won reelection but by a much smaller margin—49 to 44 percent with 6 percent of the vote going to the Independent candidate. Her triumph marked the first time in thirty years that a candidate who refused to take the pledge had won an election (Barone, Cohen, and Cook 960). In August of 2001, Shaheen announced her 2002 candidacy for the U.S. Senate. In a hotly contested race, Shaheen narrowly lost to Republican candidate John Sununu. Although she currently holds no elected position, Shaheen has not left politics behind. In September 2003, Senator John Kerry named her national chair of his presidential campaign (G. Johnson).

During her tenure as governor, Shaheen "pursued an agenda of reform focused on education, health care, and privatization of the state's electric utilities" (Robinson 498). She focused on expanding high-tech business to bring stability to the state's bruised economy. She fought to provide public kindergarten for all of New Hampshire's children and to provide them with low-cost health insurance. Shaheen supported higher education—both the state university system and community colleges—and endeavored to create a state-sponsored industrial research center ("Governor Jeanne"). She also focused on civil rights and equality issues as illustrated by her support for an official Martin Luther King Jr. Day as well as antidiscrimination legislation to protect gays and lesbians. Shaheen reminded her audience of New Hampshire's "heritage of fighting against tyranny and for justice" ("New Hampshire Governor") as she signed the bill adding King's name to the state's Civil Rights Day. And, in signing the antidiscrimination legislation she argued that "if we are to be true to our belief that all people are created equal, we must insure that all of our people enjoy the same basic rights under the law" (qtd. in "New Hampshire Chief").

As illustrated above, Jeanne Shaheen's discourse as governor of New Hampshire honors the priorities she established in her campaigns and in her administration and reflects a desire to find common ground among all of her constituents in order to solve the state's serious economic and social problems. Two major ideographs emanate from Shaheen's 1997 inaugural address and, consequently, appear in her discourse throughout her three gubernatorial terms. Although she does not use this specific phrase, Shaheen focuses on the necessity for *responsible change* that preserves the traditions of the state and simultaneously moves New Hampshire forward. To accomplish this balanced or responsible change, Shaheen calls for a new commitment to collaboration or a government based on the tenet of *togetherness*. Through the use of the ideograph, *togetherness*, she solicits cooperation from the state's citizens and from the legislature to effect a *responsible change* to improve the quality of life for New Hampshire's residents.

Despite her role as the state's first elected woman governor, Shaheen continually tells her constituents that she "did not seek this office to make history but rather to make a difference in the lives of every New Hampshire family" (Shaheen, "Inaugural 1997"). She promises the people of her state to "work to bring people together to solve the problems we face" and tells them that "together we will make our government work better" ("Inaugural 1997"). She challenges New Hampshire citizens to work together. "If we are to succeed, she argues, "we must write these new chapters in New Hampshire history together" ("Inaugural 1997"). She sustains this theme as she seeks to mold her relationship with her constituents and members of the state legislature. "We must work together to make our dreams real," she notes. "Instead of allowing fear to divide us, we must let hope bring us together. Above all," she continues, "we must never forget this simple truth: New Hampshire belongs to all of us" ("Inaugural 1997"). To facilitate this togetherness Shaheen pledges to maintain an open-door policy for the state's citizens and its legislators. "The door to my office will be open to the people of New Hampshire," and it "stands open to you [state employees] and your ideas," she assures her audience ("Inaugural 1997"). She invites "every New Hampshire citizen to become a part of our history and a part of our future" by sharing his or her ideas with her. "If you have an idea about how to improve the quality of life in our state, I want to hear it," she tells her listeners. "If you know a way to help our state government work better, I want you to share it with me" ("Inaugural 1997"). Promising to listen to and learn from her constituents, she vows that with their help "we will take action to meet the challenges we face" ("Inaugural 1997").

Speaking directly to the members of the legislature, Shaheen cautions her mostly Republican colleagues that "the people of New Hampshire are not looking to us for partisanship; they want leadership. So let us provide it" (Shaheen, "Inaugural 1997"). Returning to this theme near the end of the speech, she reminds them that "we are here to serve the people of New Hampshire. They are not interested in whether we are Republicans or Democrats, liberals or conservatives, men or women," she argues. "What they expect from us is results, or at least an honest effort to achieve them. That is our responsibility to the people of our great state" ("Inaugural 1997"). She establishes the tone of her administration and the nature of her leadership style as she concludes the address. "For now, join me in celebrating this moment. And tomorrow let us begin the quiet, steady work of the people," she urges. "Let us do it without acrimony or bitterness. Let us do it without petty partisanship. And let us do it together. Then, we will truly make history" ("Inaugural 1997").

While her first inaugural address understandably focuses on a call for *togetherness,* Governor Shaheen carefully weaves the threads of her agenda for *responsible change* throughout the speech. She articulates the challenges facing the state: "improving our schools; lowering electric rates; protecting health care; creating jobs, and building our economy" (Shaheen, "Inaugural 1997"). As she admonishes the legislature to provide the leadership necessary to solve these problems, Shaheen introduces the concept of *responsible change.* "Leadership," she remarks, "requires us to recognize the difference between what makes New Hampshire special and what threatens its future, between what must be protected and what can no longer be tolerated as status quo" ("Inaugural 1997"). Reiterating her campaign pledge, Shaheen promises to preserve the New Hampshire tradition of rejecting a broad-based sales or income tax. "But," she admonishes, "there are others [traditions] we must change" ("Inaugural 1997"). She makes it clear that education is at the top of her list of issues requiring a new and responsible strategy. Noting that "our future depends on the quality of education we provide our children," she declares that "to compete successfully in the 21st century, New Hampshire must have citizens who are better prepared and better educated" ("Inaugural 1997"). Confirming her commitment to education, she vows to "make education a priority—in my budget, in my appointments, and in the full weight and visibility granted by this office" ("Inaugural 1997"). She chastises the legislators for previous failed efforts to reform educational financing and promises a transformation, if not of results at least of effort. "For too long the vital issue of education has been sidetracked into arguments about ideology and politics," she proclaims. "Let me assure every citizen of New Hampshire—those days are over" ("Inaugural 1997"). Ever mindful of the state's fiercely independent streak, however, Shaheen carefully echoes her theme of responsible change that balances tradition and new vision as she acknowledges that "without intruding upon the tradition of local control, the state has a vital role to play in education. It must provide leadership" ("Inaugural 1997").

In her second inaugural address, delivered on January 7, 1999, Governor Shaheen recapitulates the themes of her first inaugural speech. Yet, while the threads retain the same hues, the weaving together of the ideas creates a discourse tapestry with a distinctly new focus. Acknowledging the momentous occasion of New Hampshire's final gubernatorial inauguration of the 1900s and the significance of her term as governor that spans the twentieth and twenty-first centuries, Shaheen brings the ideograph of *responsible change* to the foreground in this text. She describes the event as "an appropriate moment to look back and reflect on our history and traditions and to look ahead to build on those traditions as New Hampshire moves into the next century" (Shaheen, "Inaugural 1999"). She continues, noting "throughout our history, we have been careful to preserve the traditions that make New Hampshire special, and we have been willing to change the things that need to be changed. That is the New Hampshire way" ("Inaugural 1999"). The governor presents a notable list of historic citizens who embodied the "New Hampshire way" and then proceeds to inventory the challenges New Hampshirites face at the beginning of the twenty-first century. These issues, for the most part, are the issues she addressed in her 1997 inaugural. She delineates the changes that have taken place in each of these areas during her first term as governor and then outlines modifications still needed to create a prosperous state. "We must meet the challenges of these changing times and determine what kind of state we want New Hampshire to be," she argues. "It is up to us to create the kind of future we want" ("Inaugural 1999").

As she did in her first inaugural speech, Shaheen shifts much of the focus to education. Shortly after her election in 1997, the New Hampshire Supreme Court ruled that the "state's extreme reliance on local property taxes" for financing schools was "unconstitutional because it led to large disparities of funding among school districts" (Robinson 499). While the court's ruling augmented her personal concern for educational reform, it also obligated her, as governor, to implement changes. Despite Shaheen's call for responsible change created through a cooperative endeavor, by the end of her first term the legislature had refused to endorse Shaheen's ABC plan for educational reform and had failed to find a long-term solution to the problem. Responding to the state supreme court's deadline of April 1999 for implementation of the Claremont decision, Shaheen appeals to her audience to work together for the sake of the state's children. "Most of all," she says, "our top priority must be educating our children. Quite simply," she continues, "the excellence of the education we provide our children will determine New Hampshire's future—the strength of our economy, the quality of our lives, and the vibrancy of our democracy" (Shaheen, "Inaugural 1999"). Arguing that "nothing else is as important" and that "nothing else that we do now will have a greater impact on the future of this state," Shaheen still advocates a responsible change that will honor tradition and embrace a visionary transformation of the system. "Our challenge," she suggests, "is to change the way we fund public education, without losing what is special about our schools and our state. Our tradition of local decision-making has served us well, and we must preserve that local control," she assures the audience. "Our solution must serve our school children, our taxpayers and our economy" ("Inaugural 1999").

To envision and enact change in the education system, Jeanne Shaheen once again returns to the ideology of *togetherness*. She reminds her constituents that "for the last several months I have been meeting with the legislative leadership of both parties, and with many of you individually, to explore a variety of options" ("Inaugural 1999"). Turning her attention to the members of the legislature, she declares,

"The people want us to put partisan politics aside, to use our common sense and apply our collective creativity to find a solution. We can do it," she admonishes. "We must do it. To do it right, we must do it together" ("Inaugural 1999"). She admits that "we do not always immediately agree" and "sometimes we test each other's patience. Often, each of us is called upon to compromise a little bit. But, in the end," she observes, "what progress we make is always made together" because "working together is a New Hampshire story with a long tradition" ("Inaugural 1999"). In the conclusion of her speech, Shaheen employs the ideograph of the *New Hampshire story* to encompass both *togetherness* and *responsible change*. "Working together—that is what the people who elected us expect" she argues. "When we work together, we can accomplish anything. That is the New Hampshire story. It is now our turn to write our own chapter in that story. Let us make it a story that is remembered far into the next century. Let us make it a story worth celebrating. Let us write it together" ("Inaugural 1999").

On January 3, 2001, Governor Jeanne Shaheen delivered her third inaugural address to the citizens of New Hampshire. In her attempt to move the state's senators and representatives toward resolution of long-standing issues, she orchestrated themes and variations of her previous inaugurals in this appeal. Yet, the tone is decisively different. The ideograph of *responsible change* carries with it more urgency; the theme of *togetherness* becomes more nonnegotiable. Addressing the speaker of the house and the senate president in the introduction of her speech, Governor Shaheen notes: "We have much to do and I look forward to working with you" (Shaheen, "Inaugural 2001"). She then commemorates New Hampshire's "first inauguration of the 21st century," just as she celebrated the final one of the twentieth century in her second inaugural, and uses the opportunity to focus on the importance and urgency of change. "More than ever," she suggests, "we see ourselves at the dawning of new times—new challenges and new opportunities. More than ever, we look to the future . . . marveling that the world seems to be changing at a faster and faster pace" ("Inaugural 2001"). Shaheen implies, and at times explicitly states, that New Hampshire must maintain a significant place in this race. Quoting words uttered at the turn of the twentieth century by former governor Chester Jordan, Shaheen acknowledges that the state "stand[s] on the threshold of a century that promises beyond what we can think or ask" (qtd. in Shaheen, "Inaugural 2001"). "New Hampshire," she concludes, "must keep adapting to a fast-changing and increasingly global economy, or we will fall behind" ("Inaugural 2001").

Touting the turnaround of the state's economy, Governor Shaheen reminds her audience that it is an economy "run on brainpower, not horsepower," and that the "foundation for this new economy is education" (Shaheen, "Inaugural 2001"). With this, she turns her focus to the necessity for responsible change in education reform, just as she did in her earlier inaugurals. "If New Hampshire's future is to be bright and secure—then we must recognize that improving education is the single most important issue we face," she asserts. "Nothing else that we do here will have a greater impact on New Hampshire's success or failure in this new century" ("Inaugural 2001"). Reiterating this idea, she suggests that "the equation is really quite simple: how well we educate our students will determine New Hampshire's future" ("Inaugural 2001"). Shaheen admits that education reform has "come a long way" during her tenure as governor. "But," she attests, "our greatest challenge—a permanent school funding law—is still before us; and we must meet that challenge this year" ("Inaugural 2001"). Revealing her impatience with the lack of progress on this issue, Shaheen reminds her audience that "the State must pay for the cost of an adequate education for every child in New Hampshire. It's that simple and that difficult. We must face up to this obligation," she continues, "and we must acknowledge that we cannot meet it without change" ("Inaugural 2001"). She recognizes the difficult task of funding education reform without alterations in the state tax structure and the seemingly ineluctable deadlock discussions of this issue engender. Shaheen bluntly tells the legislature and the citizens of New Hampshire that "'None of the above' is not an option. Putting off the hard choices until next year or a future legislature will not make this challenge go away or make it any easier to resolve. It will only make it more difficult" ("Inaugural 2001"). Shaheen continues to emphasize the immediacy with which education reform needs to occur. "Without a permanent solution this year," she explains to the legislators, "the state's bond ratings and strong fiscal position will be jeopardized. But even more important, without a permanent solution, New Hampshire's public schools—and therefore our prosperity—will be threatened" ("Inaugural 2001"). She warns her legislative colleagues that the people of New Hampshire "want this issue solved. They are tired of the old debates driven by slogans and unyielding ideology," she cautions. "They want results, and they expect all of us to keep an open mind as we seek to do what's best for our state" ("Inaugural 2001").

As Governor Shaheen hammers away at this issue in her speech, she also insists that finding a solution to the problem requires a cooperative effort. "I am ready to meet this challenge," she tells her audience. "I will propose a solution, but it will require all of us—in the Senate, in the House, and in the Executive—in the business community and education community—Democrats, Republicans, and Independents working together and putting aside partisanship to get this job done" (Shaheen, "Inaugural 2001"). Again, she implores her colleagues to work together to solve the education crisis. "Let us pledge today that we will not let the people of New Hampshire down. Let us agree that in the coming months we will turn our greatest challenge—our greatest responsibility—into our greatest opportunity"

("Inaugural 2001"). Shaheen closes her speech with a harmonic coupling of the two ideographs. Referring to the kindergarten students who have participated in the inaugural ceremonies, she urges the audience to "remember that the 21st century is their century, a century sure to be filled with astounding changes—changes we cannot even imagine; changes far more profound and breathtaking than the changes of the last 100 years. It will be their century," she continues, "but it is up to us, in the decisions we will soon be called upon to make, to prepare them—and New Hampshire for the future they deserve" ("Inaugural 2001"). In one final appeal to the legislature to work together to effect responsible change, Shaheen closes her speech by asking her colleagues to "proceed with the work we have been elected to do" ("Inaugural 2001").

As the first woman elected to the governorship in New Hampshire and as a Democrat in a state with an overwhelming Republican majority as well as a fierce sense of Yankee independence, Jeanne Shaheen knew she had to bring the legislators and the citizens together to achieve any meaningful change. In a similar vein, she understood that significant alterations were needed for New Hampshire to recover from the recession of the early 1990s and to position itself successfully in a twenty-first-century economy. Given the state's deep-rooted traditions, especially its antitax stance, Shaheen also realized that alterations to the "normal way of doing things" would require recognition of those traditions and that they would not occur easily. Accordingly, she artfully interspersed the themes of *togetherness* and *responsible change* throughout her gubernatorial discourse in an effort to build consensus and a vision of change the legislature and citizens could endorse. While a feminine style incorporates the concepts of cooperation and reaching out to empower others, exemplified in Shaheen's *togetherness* ideograph, the governor does not overtly play the gender card in her discourse. Rather, as she did in her first campaign, Shaheen allows her feminine perspective to permeate her understanding of the challenges facing the state without focusing on or denying her womanhood and moves forward to meet those challenges with a seemingly gender-neutral approach. Although under her leadership New Hampshire did not create a permanent solution for the school funding issue, the revitalization of the state's economy, the institution of both health care and education reform, and the realization of many of Governor Shaheen's programs attest to the success of this rhetorical strategy.

Judy Martz

Montana, the first state to send a woman to the U.S. Congress in the early twentieth century, did not elect a woman to its own governorship until the initial election of the twenty-first century. The people of the "Big Sky" state chose Republican

Judy Martz, "an unabashed conservative and strong champion of family values" (Gizzi, "Politics 2000") to serve as their governor on November 7, 2000. Martz campaigned on a gender-neutral, pro-business platform declaring Montana *open for business*. Martz did not bring a feminist stance to her campaign and often received criticism for her nonfeminist agenda from the League of Women Voters and other women's groups ("Politics 2000"). Governor Martz's priorities clearly place her role as wife and mother first. As she noted in her 2001 "State of the State Address," "I am proud to be a small businesswoman. I'm proud to serve as your governor. But I'll always be most proud to be 'Mom' and 'Mrs. Harry Martz.' Those are the titles that will endure" (Martz, "State").

Judy Morstein Martz's early life did not portend her political career. A native Montanan, Martz was born in Big Timber to parents who were ranchers (Martz, "Biography"). She graduated from Butte High School and attended Eastern Montana College ("Biography"). Athletics captured Martz's attention during her youth. A member of the 1963 U.S. World Speed Skating Team, she represented the United States as a speed skater at the 1964 Olympic Winter Games (Martz, "Biography"; Barone and Cohen 951). In 1965, she married Harry Martz and together they created a commercial solid-waste business in Butte, which they have operated for almost forty years (Martz, "Biography").

Governor Martz's civic engagement planted the seeds for her political involvement. An active citizen in her hometown, she served as president of the Butte Chamber of Commerce in the 1990s and worked for the St. James Hospital Board of Directors as its vice chair (Martz, "Biography"; Barone and Cohen 951). Her ownership of a small business propelled her into local and statewide economic development issues (Martz, "Biography"). Martz "worked to clean up mining tailings and build baseball fields on the site" and "helped build a high altitude speed skating center in Butte" (Barone and Cohen 951). She entered the world of electoral politics through her support of Republican candidates as early as the 1960s (951). Later, from 1989 to 1995, she worked as a field representative for U.S. Senator Conrad Burns (Martz, "Biography").

In 1995, Lieutenant Governor Dennis Rehberg decided to run for the Senate; therefore, Republican incumbent Governor Marc Racicot needed a new running mate. Following the advice in one of her favorite quotations, "Martz stuck out her neck and called him [Governor Racicot] up and asked him for the job. After two extensive interviews, he chose her" (Barone and Cohen 951). At the ballot box, constituents favored the Racicot-Martz ticket with 79 percent of the vote (952) electing the state's first female lieutenant governor.

In 1999 with Governor Racicot term-limited, Martz announced her decision to run for governor. Despite her term as lieutenant governor, many saw her as an unlikely candidate. In support of her *open for business* platform, Martz campaigned to eliminate a 3 percent business equipment tax, supported five-year tax credits for high-tech companies, promoted a "21-point JOBS program to encourage public-private partnerships," and favored "Racicot's Vision 2005 program to double agricultural output" (Barone and Cohen 952). Just one week before the election, her opponent, State Auditor Mark O'Keefe, had raised nearly three million dollars, with more than 70 percent of the funds coming from his own fortune, while Martz had garnered only $838,000 ("Governor of Montana"). Although "handicappers rated the race as too close to call through election day" and late-October polls gave O'Keefe "a 2 to 3 point lead" ("Governor of Montana"), Martz won the election with 51 percent of the vote to O'Keefe's 47 percent. George W. Bush's receipt of 58 percent of Montanans' votes in the presidential election, according to some, helped push Martz over the edge ("Governor of Montana").

During her term in office, Governor Martz encountered numerous difficulties. In August 2001, the state house majority leader was killed in an automobile accident. The driver, Martz's chief policy adviser, denied being at the wheel but was later found guilty of felony negligent homicide. The night of the accident, Martz took her adviser home from the hospital and washed his bloody clothes, which were later sought as evidence in the case (Barone and Cohen 952; Gizzi, "Politics 2003"). When the incident was made public in January 2002, Martz admitted her actions were wrong (Barone and Cohen 952). Accused of violating state ethics laws in a 1999 land purchase from Arco, Martz faced a hearing before the political practices commissioner in 2002. The commissioner ruled that Martz did not violate the law, but in the meantime, she "endure[d] months of unfavorable publicity" (952). Not unexpectedly, Martz's pro-business agenda raised the ire of Montana's environmentalists. Martz argues that officials of the logging industry "are the true environmentalists" and that protesters who call themselves environmentalists and who disrupt logging activities should "get a job" (qtd. in Barone and Cohen 952).

With approval ratings hovering around 20 percent ("MT: Martz Won't"), Judy Martz announced in August 2003 that she would not seek reelection. In her announcement, Martz enumerates the achievements her administration has accomplished with the help of the legislature and the citizens of Montana. She reminds the audience of her straightforward approach to leadership. "In very difficult times, that demanded true leadership, I have done what I said I would. I think everyone would agree that I have always been upfront and honest with my neighbors. Maybe even too honest and frank," she concedes, "but I have resisted political temptations and done what is right" (Martz, "Governor Judy"). She acknowledges that she has made difficult decisions "without a regard for public opinion polls" ("Governor Judy"). Arguing that she has "accomplished what [she] set out to do" and that she has enacted [her] vision" ("Governor Judy"), Martz tells her constituents that her decision is best for Montana and for her family. "As you know," she says, "I have been away from home for nearly eight years. That has been very difficult" ("Governor Judy"). Martz identifies the tough balancing act many women in politics face. "When I am on the job, it's the greatest job in the world," she says. "But when you go home at night and it's a quiet house and no one's there, there's a tugging at your heart" (qtd. in "MT: Martz Won't").

Governor Martz's pro-business agenda and commitment to traditional family values grounded her political ideology. She entwines three major ideographs throughout her discourse to create a rhetorical vision for Montana. Declaring the state open for business, she unabashedly seeks to create a more favorable business climate to facilitate "a journey to build a new Montana that will keep our young people living, working and raising their own families here at home" (Martz, "Inaugural"). The governor's new economic culture promises the hope of prosperity for the *Montana family*, the second major ideograph she interweaves with the *open for business* thread to facilitate a statewide discussion of a *new Montana*, the third filament in her Montana tapestry. This *Montana family* encompasses both nuclear families and the extended family that includes all citizens of the state. The "greatness of Montana," Martz argues, is found "in the generations of families who have always worked with civility and respect for one another to make Montana the last best place" ("Inaugural"). Projecting the focus of her administration, she tells her inaugural audience that "we will build new jobs, new futures, and a new Montana" ("Inaugural").

Turning our attention to the *open for business* ideograph, we find Martz declaring "it's all about jobs, jobs, and more jobs" (Martz, "Martz Announces") as she vows to "make government more responsive to the people who create high paying jobs in this state" (Martz, "Governor-Elect Martz Announces Another"). In her first "State of the State Address," she pledges to "not rest until Montana's economy reflects the diversity and capacity of the people within it. The Martz Administration's primary goal," she persists, "is to diversify our economy, expand our job market with higher paying jobs, actively supporting and recruiting businesses that can thrive within our current environmental standards" ("State"). In no uncertain terms she places the legislature on notice that the "government can no longer be a barrier to business development" as she promises "not [to] leave this office until we've made it business friendly" ("State").

To move her business agenda forward, Martz created the Governor's Office of Economic Opportunity, housed in the state capitol. "Its function," she notes, "is to promote and attract business expansion and to develop our workforce for better paying jobs" (Martz, "Remarks"). Martz reiterates her pledge to make "Montana a more business friendly place" in a June 2001 address to the Montana

Economic Development Summit. "That's why I've implemented a new marketing campaign for 'Business Montana,'" she continues. "We will put Montana 'on the business map,' and turn the state's image as a vacation destination into an equally recognized business location" ("Remarks"). Understanding the competitive business environment in which the state hopes to restructure its economy, Martz acknowledges that "we would all agree that Montana is a great place to live. Now," she reminds the audience, "our challenge is to prove that Montana is also a great place to do business" ("Remarks"). Creating this new perception requires the "courage to embrace change, not run from it" and the willingness to "be aggressive," Martz argues. "And collectively we must send a message loud and clear, far and wide, that Montana is open for business" ("Remarks").

In January 2002, the Office of Economic Opportunity unveiled "A Framework for Economic Development" in which Martz asserts that "we have learned that as we move down the road to ensuring that Montana is 'open for business,' we must focus first on our existing businesses and their ability to stay and expand in Montana" (Martz, "Montana Framework" 1). This commitment reflects her earlier statement in June 2001: "Our fundamental principle is that the people who are already in business here employing Montanans, paying taxes and contributing to their communities deserve a government that will remove barriers to business growth and expansion" (Martz, "Remarks"). The cornerstone of this strategy, according to Martz, is to "provide our students with educations that match the needs of new economy job creators" ("Remarks"). Attaining this goal requires a more responsive educational system that "must craft curriculums at all levels to match the needs of job creators in the 21st century" ("Remarks"). In January 2004, Martz recounts the progress her administration has made in recasting Montana's business image. "Let's look at the record," she suggests. "Because of our relationship with many of you in Montana's business community, we've been successful in passing the most significant tax reform legislation in three decades, recruiting two new agriculture facilities to Montana, [and] re-opening the Montana Resources mine" (Martz, "Progress"). These accomplishments, according to Martz, signify that her administration has been "true to our word [and] that Montana is 'open for business'" ("Progress").

In her 2002 report to the citizens of Montana, Martz expresses the synergism inherent in the themes of her rhetorical vision. "Because we're delivering a business friendly environment," she claims, "Montana families are better off today" ("A Bolder"). In many ways the governor's commitment to families and traditional family values becomes the raison d'etre of her call for cooperative action and adoption of her economic plan. "And while we come with different ideas and different views," she explains, "I have faith that we will find the common ground and build a better future for our Montana" that is "worth fighting for" with a "shared belief that families are the foundation upon which Montana is built" ("A Bolder"). And, it is our families, Martz avers, that "make life worth living" (Martz, "Progress"). She evidences her concern for the extended Montana family as she discusses the diverse citizenship of the state, and in particular, Montana's Native American population. "Our pursuit of economic growth must include Native Americans," she tells legislators in her first state of the state speech. "For the first Montanans, I am committed to improving the quality of life on our reservations" (Martz, "State"). Again in 2002, Martz pledges her commitment to the Native American segment of the state's family, as she guarantees "we will not leave any Montanan behind" (Martz, "A Bolder"). The governor argues that "we cannot move Montana forward without working with every citizen of this state" (Martz, "Governor Judy"). And in this endeavor, "everyone has a role to play because everyone is a member of our Montana family" (Martz, "2003").

The invocation of the *Montana family* ideograph permeates Martz's discussion of health care policy. She tells the attendees at a Health Care Summit in 2002 that they have been asked to participate in the conference "because, quite simply, our Montana families need you" (Martz, "Governor's Health 2002"). She also describes her "Strong Families/Healthy Families Initiative," a plan "to encourage Montanans to develop healthy lifestyles through exercise and diet that will prevent future health problems" ("Governor's Health 2002"). And in her "2003 State of the State Address," Martz asks for cooperation from the legislature because "the safety and health of our Montana families is too important for partisanship" ("2003"). Describing "A Bolder, Better Future for Montana Families," Martz iterates the accomplishments of her administration in the area of healthcare policy. "We pledged to work for quality, affordable healthcare for every Montana family," she says. "And we ARE delivering." For example, she notes, "We successfully gained federal approval to provide better healthcare for our rural families" and, "We're partnering with the healthcare community to provide quality healthcare for all Montana families" (Martz, "A Bolder"). Showing her appreciation for their work, Martz commends the participants in the 2003 Health Care Summit for their "participation and input in a constructive manner [that] truly shows that we can work together for the health of our families, and for the future of our great state" (Martz, "Governor's Health 2003"). For Martz, the *Montana family* is significant because it is the foundation of a *new Montana*, which "will be built neighbor by neighbor—FAMILY BY FAMILY" (Martz, "A Bolder").

As indicated throughout this discussion, Judy Martz consistently weaves three ideographs, *open for business, Montana family,* and *new Montana,* together in her political discourse. As she traveled the state during her campaign for governor, Martz "told Montanans that by working together we would build new jobs—new futures— a new Montana" (Martz, "Remarks"). Clearly, once in office, she attempted to honor her campaign promises. Speaking to the Montana Economic Development Summit, she declares, "Our vision for a new Montana is one that celebrates our rich and proud heritage, but that also recognizes the need for new industries, new markets and new opportunities" ("Remarks"). She characterizes her Jobs and Opportunities Initiative as "a comprehensive strategy for applying our traditional values to build a new Montana" ("Remarks"). Martz predicates her new Montana tapestry on the idea of balancing change and tradition. "Our vision is to make our new Montana a better Montana by building on the traditional values that have always made us great" ("Remarks"). Concluding her first state of the state speech, Martz delivers an impassioned plea for others to join in the realization of her vision. "Montana is the Big Sky State, but it is also a state for big dreams," she reminds her audience. "Determination to succeed and a blessing from above will make great new things happen. New jobs. New futures. A new Montana" ("State").

Although her tenure as governor of Montana was plagued by controversy and record-breaking low ratings, Judy Martz honored her pledge to "call it the way it is" (Martz, "State"). Through her rhetoric she consistently wove a Montana tapestry that honored her campaign pledges and celebrated her vision of a twenty-first-century state—a *new Montana open for business* to create a quality life for *Montana families*. Martz's use of the *Montana family* ideograph and her description of her own priorities in life lend a decidedly feminine perspective to her rhetoric. On the other hand, by her very performance of the gubernatorial role and her focus on a pro-business theme, the governor brought a masculine sensitivity to her work. However history may judge her stewardship of the state, Judy Martz's political discourse reveals that she steadfastly governed "with a vision that [was] crystal clear and a determination that [was] unshakable" (Martz, "Inaugural").

Linda Lingle

One of the most recently elected governors, Hawaii's Linda Lingle, provides a salient example of how a woman's gubernatorial discourse has evolved from an exercise in feminine style to a rhetorical approach that blends gender boundaries and addresses all constituents. An examination of her key speeches reveals that she uses few personal examples or anecdotes, for instance, and her tone is impersonal and businesslike, despite the sprinkling of Hawaiian terms throughout her discourse. Instead, she apparently sees the governorship as the CEO of a corporation, or state. Lingle campaigned primarily on three issues—"restoring trust and integrity in government, improving public education, and strengthening the economy" (Lingle, "Lingle Announces"). She titled her platform "A New Beginning" and laid out several plans for a vast number of government services, from education to the economy to the environment. She stuck with the Republican Party mantra of "no more taxes" and argued for more efficiency in government. These positions were consistent with her previous political activity.

Prior to her governmental experience, Lingle received a degree in journalism from California State University—Northridge. She moved to Hawaii in 1975 with her father and uncle. There, Lingle edited press releases and newsletters for Hawaii Teamsters' labor union. She then moved from Honolulu to Molokai and began her own newspaper, the *Molokai Free Press*, reporting on community issues ("Linda Lingle"). As a journalist she discovered what she believed to be corruption in the way the Democratic Party was running the government. Convinced she could do better, she ran for and won a seat on the Maui County Council in 1980. She served five two-year terms and then successfully ran for mayor of Maui in 1990 ("Linda Lingle"). Her victory made her Maui County's first female mayor and the youngest mayor in Maui's history ("Linda Lingle"). In 1998, she ran un-successfully for governor, but lost by less than 1 percent of the vote. She used her notoriety in that election to become Hawaii's Republican Party chairwoman and while serving in that capacity is credited with increasing the party's membership by four thousand and helping the Republicans gain seven seats in the legislature ("Linda Lingle"). In her 2003 gubernatorial bid, she ran against the incumbent Lieutenant Governor Mazie Hirono in what turned out to be the most expensive campaign for the governorship in Hawaii's history ("Linda Lingle"). Lingle garnered 52 percent of the vote and became the state's sixth governor. Knowing she would have to work with a Democratic controlled legislature, upon hearing the news of her election victory Lingle stated: "We have a very big responsibility to deliver for the people of Hawaii. The most important message is our commitment to work with all the people of Hawaii. We face some very tough challenges in the year ahead" (Lingle, "Lingle Defeats").

While campaigning for governor, Lingle lobbed sharply worded criticisms toward the Democratic controlled legislature. In 2002, for instance, she stated that the recently concluded legislative session should be labeled "Back to the Future—Stuck in the Past" for its failure to accomplish any meaningful reforms (Lingle, "Back"). Lingle sounds quite forward thinking in her speeches, as the themes of *the future* and subsequently *progress* comprise her most oft-used ideographs. These themes provide a timeline for the state to work toward as well as to demonstrate how well the state operates under her guidance. The idea of *future* provides the hope and optimism for Hawaii's citizens and contrasts with the failures of the past administration. Conversely, Lingle's use of the ideograph *progress* anchors her in the present and allows her to argue she has provided concrete results.

In her inaugural address Lingle outlines her plan for Hawaii's New Beginning. She lists a number of challenges Hawaii faces, and then says, "It is time for everyone in our state to participate fully in planning Hawaii's future" ("New"). This statement gives her audience a stake in the outcome of their government. She brings up the future again in the speech, this time by linking herself with a very important figure of the past. "As I stand here today talking about our future," she states, "I can't help but think about Hawaii's past. More specifically, I am thinking about the last woman to lead these islands. Queen Liliuokalani gave us a model for leadership that is needed in today's Hawaii" ("New"). In the conclusion of this speech, Lingle successfully unites the people of Hawaii by imbuing them with a sense of optimism and necessity. She says that working together, the people of Hawaii can "restore integrity to government, expand and diversify [the] economy, and improve public education" ("New"). They must do this, she implores, for "we owe it to those who have gone before us, we owe it to ourselves, and we owe it to future generations" ("New"). She ends her speech by saying that "the challenges are great, but the opportunities are even greater. Working together, our future is bright and anything is possible" ("New"). In addition to optimism, the future also signifies responsibility. As Lingle muses in a speech designed to explain the state's budget condition to the citizens, "It is hard to say no to some of these worthwhile programs but it is my responsibility to put our financial house in order and to make certain we don't leave unpaid bills for future generations to pay" (Lingle, "Governor"). She does conclude the speech, however, on a positive note, once again linking the future to optimism. "By working together," she intones, "I know the future will be bright for all of us, especially for the children of our great state. I won't let you down" ("Governor"). In the final speech available for analysis, her "State of the State Address," Lingle again uses the ideograph of *future* to provide a spirit of optimism as well as to unite the citizens of Hawaii. She observes that her policies have Hawaii's "residents feeling good about the future for the first time in a long time" ("State"). She concludes the address by stating, "I truly believe the brightest days lie ahead for the Great State of Hawaii. By working together for Hawaii's future we can turn that shining promise into a reality" ("State").

After serving as governor of Hawaii for one year, Lingle gave her state of the state speech on January 26, 2004. In it she lists several of her administration's accomplishments. This allows her to shift from the forward thinking ideograph of *future* to one of the recent past, *progress*. By grounding her points this way, Governor Lingle demonstrates that she is working successfully on behalf of the Hawaiian people, and thus, gives them a reason to trust her. She begins by defining progress by what it is not. "Progress," she says, "is not limited by our ability to get a new law passed. Sometimes we make progress by rewriting administrative rules, as we did when we modernized and simplified the animal quarantine laws" ("State"). Lingle then touts her initiative in medical care as an example of progress. "Sometimes progress is achieved in the form of public-private partnerships, such as Hawaii Prescription Care, which is helping thousands of low-income people obtain medications at no cost to taxpayers" ("State"). Lingle also believes she has succeeded in improving the tourism industry which suffered a loss after the World Trade Center attacks. "Progress," she states, "means bringing a comprehensive focus to an important issue, as we did by appointing our state's first tourism liaison" ("State"). This has enabled Lingle and her cabinet to make sure that "state parks, airports, harbors and other infrastructure is in place to sustain a healthy visitor industry" ("State").

Lingle also highlights her acumen in working with diverse groups and organizations. For instance, she informs the audience that her administration makes "progress through a more creative and aggressive use of federal funds" (Lingle, "State"). She provides the information that under her leadership the "state took the necessary steps to begin receiving more than $10 million each year in new federal dollars without spending additional funds" ("State"), specifically claiming millions of federal Medicaid dollars. Even an intangible, nonpolitical gesture can signify success. "Progress," Lingle asserts, "comes about through appropriate expressions of gratitude and respect for our friends, as we have shown our nation's military leaders stationed in Hawaii" ("State").

As a new governor, the first woman governor of Hawaii, and the first Republican governor of that state in several decades, Linda Lingle found herself in a situation where she had much to prove. By using two common ideographs, *future* and *progress*, she formed a link to the audience and gave them reason to trust her. The terms resonate with the audience, giving them both something to hope for and something to assess. While Lingle does not sound particularly flashy or eloquent, she "gets the rhetorical job done" by tapping into the audience's expectations and by providing them with examples of her accomplishments.

Jennifer Granholm

Elected in 2002 as the first female governor of the state of Michigan, Jennifer Granholm eschewed the traditional "feminized" approach to campaigning. She recognized that a feminine discourse strategy fails when running for governor "because the qualities that voters typically covet in a chief executive—decisiveness, a commanding presence, even an ability to intimidate—are not ones they associate with traditional femininity" (Cohn). Unlike representing a state, "the chief executive is . . . getting people to a new idea of what women are—as the final decision-maker, as the person where the buck stops" (Cohn). Rather than focus on her qualities as a woman, Granholm campaigned on issues of environment, health care, and her career as a prosecutor. Jonathan Cohn suggests that "Granholm's decision to emphasize her career as a crusading attorney is in some ways most interesting for what it means she's not emphasizing—namely, her roles as wife and mother" (Cohn). Instead, her basic platform demonstrated that "she is a hard-nosed, decisive leader capable of steering the state through hard times. Her campaign, in other words, is exactly the kind she would be running if she were a man. And that's not the sort of campaign women have traditionally run. At least not until now" (Cohn). Reporter Laura Berman, writing for the *Detroit News*, points out the difficulty in maintaining an effective balance. She states that Granholm "figured out a way to campaign as a contemporary woman, without stridency and gender stereotyping. And without alienating her own sex" (Berman). As Granholm herself suggests, "I don't think I want anybody to vote for me because of my gender. I think that we all live in a society, and in a world, where there are expectations about men and women. You've either got to live up to them or be higher than them" (qtd. in "Speaking With").

Jennifer Granholm had early aspirations of becoming an actress. Born in Vancouver, B.C., in 1959, she moved with her family to San Francisco in 1962. After graduating from high school in 1977, she moved to Los Angeles in hopes of pursuing a movie career. She once appeared on the television show *The Dating Game*. Granholm paid her own way through the University of California at Berkeley ("Granholm"), graduating with honors, and attended Harvard University Law School where she earned her JD degree in 1987. She then moved to Detroit, Michigan, to work as a clerk for Judge Damon Keith of the U.S. Court of Appeals. Granholm served as a federal prosecutor for the U.S. Department of Justice from 1990 to 1994, achieving a 98 percent conviction rate in the cases she prosecuted ("Granholm"). From 1998 to 2002, Granholm served as Michigan's attorney general. She ran a modern and successful campaign for governor, beating out two well-known Democrats in the primary and then defeating her Republican opponent, Dick Posthumus, by capturing 51 percent of the votes ("Granholm"). She enjoys broad-based support and is considered a "rising star" in the Democratic Party. "Granholm's appeal is so widespread that conservative commentator George Will proposed changing the Constitution to allow foreign-born American citizens to become president" (Clift, "Jennifer").

Reporters covering the Michigan gubernatorial campaign noted Jennifer Granholm's collaborative approach in solving problems ("The Times Require"); she frequently argued that the state should be "One Michigan" (Berman). It is to Granholm's concept of collaboration that we now turn, to her use of the ideograph *partnership* that is liberally injected throughout her public speeches. Whether she actually uses the term *partnership* or substitutes concepts like *working together*, or even the metaphoric *family*, Governor Granholm makes it clear in her speeches that she believes in and promotes collaboration to meet the state's challenges, as the following examples illustrate.

In a speech to the Oakland Democrats, for instance, Granholm criticizes the previous administration's unilateral, closed way of getting things done. Granholm promises to do things differently, shifting "some paradigms about how we serve. I want to forge unusual partnerships between public and private sectors, between the faith communities, between the education communities. I want to do things in a way that we have not done them before," she states (Granholm, "Speech"). She attacks the self-centered, myopic approach that people sometimes have, saying "it is not my problem, those are not my kids, it is not my backyard" ("Speech"). She encourages her constituents to have a collective view, to work together to solve the state's problems. She chides: "My my my—it's not about MY it's about US. It's about engaging people to connect with one another across the street and meet the new neighbor and getting out of this box we were taught to be in" ("Speech"). Later in the campaign she addresses the Michigan Education Association, an organization that endorsed her candidacy. She acknowledges the financial hardships that the state faces and praises the teachers for their fine work in the midst of funding problems. She tells them that they will work together to make Michigan's schools among the best in the nation. "With this partnership," she promises, "we will not lower our expectations; we will increase our efforts. . . . Thank you for not being merely a spectator, but for having the courage to join me in the arena" (Granholm, "MEA"). And at the Democratic State Convention in August 2002, she underscored her belief that an individualistic approach to governing should end, when she announces, "In essence, my friends, we believe—no, we know—that we are more than just a collection of individuals. We are a family—and in a family, no one loses" (Granholm, "State").

Granholm continues this theme in her inaugural address. She begins by thanking those she believes helped her succeed in life, implying that nothing is accomplished alone. "As I walk through this door . . . I must stop and honor all of those who made it possible for me to even reach this door. I give thanks to my parents and my incredible family, my utterly selfless husband Dan, my great teachers, and the activists, and workers, and citizens who cared and who voted" (Granholm, "Text"). Later in the speech she admits that government cannot do everything, "that it will take much more than government to enhance our quality of life. . . . It will take all of us working together as a family" ("Text"). At the end of the speech, Granholm exhorts the citizens of Michigan to get involved in their state. "Walk with me, talk with me, work with me," she implores, "to light anew the flame of engagement, of action, and of service to our Michigan family" ("Text").

Like many governors at the turn of this century, Granholm inherited a state budget deficit and funding problems resultant from an economic recession. In February and March 2003, Granholm chose to address the state, explaining budget cuts and other methods for rectifying the state's fiscal problems. She continues to promote her idea that working together benefits everyone. For instance, in the February speech she states, "nowhere does our spirit soar higher than when hard work is united with innovation—to build stronger bonds of community" (Granholm, "Michigan"). She tells her audience that "together, we will have to work hard. We will have to innovate, and we will have to act as one community—especially right here in this building" ("Michigan"). After listing some problems that all states face, such as inadequate school funding and crime, she says that "they are all problems we share—and we will either tackle them together or suffer the collective consequences" ("Michigan"). When making her budget presentation to the state legislature, Governor Granholm once again underscores her belief in collaboration. "To make this budget work for the people of Michigan," she suggests, "we also need to develop a new kind of partnership in state government, one that can bridge the differences that too often divide us. When I traveled across Michigan on my budget tour over the last month," she continues, "I was struck by how rarely partisanship came up as we discussed our budget crisis and how to solve it. The citizens of Michigan don't want us to resolve this crisis as members of two bickering parties," she concludes. "They want us to find common ground as leaders of one Michigan" (Granholm, "Fiscal Year '04").

A state of the state address provides leaders with an opportunity to present their vision of the state and to set the tone for their administration. It allows the executive to review the year's accomplishments. Granholm is no exception. She uses her speech to promote the ideas of partnership and of working together. She lets the audience know that they will play a part in making decisions about Michigan. "My fellow citizens," Granholm states, "I will continue to engage you—as I have for the last 13 months—in this discussion about shared priorities and scarce funds" (Granholm, "Our Determination"). In order to work within the budget constraints, "local governments should be compelled to consider new partnerships with one another: pooling resources, sharing services, technology, office space, and even employees" ("Our Determination"). According to Granholm, working with a Republican state legislature could have led to partisan bickering. She and the members of the legislature could have merely allowed their egos and party politics to prevent them from solving the state's problems. "But we did not," she offers. "We worked together to get good things done for the people of this state" ("Our Determination"). She ends her address by inviting all citizens of Michigan to join her in working for a better state:

> Tonight let us set out together, knowing that the road to educational excellence expands the road to good jobs. The road to a healthy people in a healthy land merges with the road to good jobs. And the roads to a stronger business climate widen the highway to high quality jobs. . . . Let it be said of us that we have moved

with focus and determination on those roads our citizens most need—the roads to quality jobs and quality life. And let it be said, my colleagues, that we did it together. ("Our Determination")

While the concept of "collaboration" has been traditionally viewed as feminine, Governor Jennifer Granholm essentially has made it gender neutral, showing that all benefit from partnerships. She campaigned, not as a woman candidate, but as a candidate who happened to be a woman, and worked to demonstrate that she could govern successfully. Her use of the terms *partnership* and *family* may seem feminine in nature, but they have evolved into concepts that hold relevance for all, male or female. In a state that is highly diverse politically, ethnically, and socio-economically, Granholm recognized the importance of uniting all interested parties. Truly, the state could not survive with too many competing plans and intransigent members of the governing body.

Janet Napolitano

Like Linda Lingle and Jennifer Granholm, in 2003 Janet Napolitano carved her niche in history. She became not the first but rather the third woman to be sworn in as governor of Arizona, the first state to send three women to the capitol. Furthermore, Napolitano succeeded a woman governor, Jane Dee Hull, catapulting Arizona to yet another electoral first. While Napolitano's platform for "Moving Arizona Forward" included issues traditionally associated with the private sphere, she did not campaign as a "woman." Instead, employing a more gender-neutral strategy, Napolitano exuded a businesslike personae and "stressed her experience" (Barone and Cohen 99) focusing on her record as attorney general, which in October 2001 "had earned her a 55% positive job rating" (99). Given Arizona's history of sustaining women in leadership positions, gender was not a major factor in the race. For example, a 1999 article in *Time* reported that "to Arizonans, having women run things is no big deal" (Barovick and Laughlin). That does not mean, however, that gender issues were ignored totally in the campaign. As noted in a *Philadelphia Inquirer* article, the Republican candidate "constantly tout[ed]s his family in TV ads, as a way of pointing out that Napolitano is single and childless" (Polman). Bruce Merrill, an Arizona political analyst, argued that Napolitano's opponent "knows exactly what he's doing when he runs those (family) ads. She's being attacked on everything, and, as a woman, this has actually benefited her. Culturally, this is still the Old West, and we tend to rally around women when they're getting beaten up" (qtd. in Polman).

Campaigning as a "conservative Democrat," the moderate Napolitano focused much of her attention on the state budget deficit and on education, vowing to place education at the top of her agenda as governor. Stating "there is no more important issue than the education of our children" (Napolitano, "Achieving" 1), she promised that "we will become a state with an education system that enhances economic development, produces a quality, innovative workforce, and gives all Arizona children the opportunity to reach their full potential" (20). Other areas of concern exemplified in Napolitano's plan for "Moving Arizona Forward" included health care (especially for children and seniors), economic development, the environment, protection of the state's children, creation of a viable tax structure, and security.

Although she did not focus her campaign on gender or women's issues, Napolitano refused to abdicate her avid support for women's rights and human rights in general. For example, in the gubernatorial debates she denied support to some of the state's legislators in their attempt to impose a twenty-four-hour waiting period for abortions. She viewed "this legislation and similar restrictions on abortions as thinly disguised efforts to throw roadblocks in the path of women seeking to exercise their constitutional right to an abortion" ("AZ: Napolitano Opposes"). A late October survey indicated that Napolitano held a "30-point lead among women" ("AZ: Napolitano Opposes"). In what newspapers proclaimed the "tightest and ugliest race for governor in memory" (Squitieri), Janet Napolitano defeated her Republican challenger Matt Salmon with 46 percent of the vote to his 45 percent; Independent candidate Richard Maloney won endorsement from 7 percent of the voters (Barone and Cohen 99). Most pundits agree that women, political moderates, and crossover voters made the difference in this election (Davenport, "Candidate's"; "AZ: Moderates"). For example, results from a poll of 768 registered voters with a sampling error of plus or minus 3.5 percentage points conducted by KAET-TV and Arizona State University concluded that 65 percent of participants identified as political moderates voted for Napolitano while only 27 percent voted for her opponent. Likewise, 56 percent of the women voted for Napolitano while only 39 percent cast their vote for Salmon. Finally, according to the poll, 20 percent of the Republicans surveyed indicated they voted for Napolitano, while only 10 percent of Democrats proclaimed they voted for the Republican contender ("AZ: Moderates"). In this upset of Republican politics as usual, Arizona voters sent the "first elected Democratic governor in 20 years" (Davenport, "Candidate's") to Arizona's statehouse.

Janet Napolitano's path to the governorship included several visible and high-level positions, both within and without Arizona politics. Like many of her constituents, Napolitano is not a native Arizonan. Born in New York City, she lived for a short while in Pittsburgh and then in Albuquerque where her father helped establish the medical school at the University of New Mexico (Tarullo 50; Barone and Cohen 99). Following her graduation from Sandia High in 1975,

Napolitano attended Santa Clara University in California where she majored in political science, won a Truman Scholarship, and graduated *summa cum laude* (Tarullo 50). Upon completion of her undergraduate degree, she studied law at the University of Virginia from which she graduated in 1983 (Napolitano, "Governor's Biography").

Napolitano began her professional career with a move to Phoenix in 1983 to clerk for U.S. Appeals Court Judge Mary Schroeder. Arizona has been her home since that time. Following her work for Judge Schroeder, Napolitano joined the Phoenix law firm, Lewis and Roca, where she became partner in 1989, specializing in appellate and commercial litigation (Napolitano, "Governor's Biography"; Brock; Tarullo 51). In the fall of 1991, Napolitano found herself in the limelight as a member of the team of attorneys representing Anita Hill at the confirmation hearings of Clarence Thomas (Barone and Cohen 99). And, she successfully argued the Sanctuary case before the 9th Circuit Court of Appeals (Napolitano, "Governor's Biography"). Before holding public office, she served as a volunteer lawyer for the Arizona state Democratic Party, managed various state Senate races, and worked on Bill Clinton's campaign in Arizona (Brock). In 1993 amid a storm of controversy over her participation in the Anita Hill case, President Clinton appointed Napolitano U.S. attorney for Arizona, a position she held until she ran for state attorney general in 1998 (Barone and Cohen 99; "Senate Confirms"). In that historic election, she became not only the state's first female attorney general but also a member of the "Fab Five" when Arizona voters elected the first all-female state administration in the country. The roster included Napolitano, the only Democrat, Governor Jane Dee Hull, Secretary of State Betsey Bayless, Treasurer Carol Springer, and Superintendent of Public Instruction Lisa Graham Keegan (Barovick and Laughlin).

As attorney general, Napolitano pursued Qwest for consumer fraud, "negotiated a $217 million settlement with Arthur Andersen on behalf of investors," and "sued Ford for explosions in Crown Victoria police cars" (Barone and Cohen 99). She also reduced the backlog of child abuse and neglect cases from almost six thousand to seven hundred, created the first Office for Women within the Attorney General's Office, and "distinguished herself as a fierce protector of children and a tireless advocate for women, senior citizens and the environment" (Napolitano, "Governor's Biography"; Barone and Cohen 99; Tarullo 53). The respect and popularity Napolitano garnered during her tenure as Arizona's attorney general undoubtedly helped propel her into the governorship.

Janet Napolitano's gubernatorial rhetoric extends her campaign slogan, "Moving Arizona Forward," through the use of three interconnected ideographs: *cultural mosaic, culture of cooperation,* and *a new Arizona.* Honoring her commitment to speak honestly and openly with her constituents, within each of these ideographs

Napolitano artfully weaves an image of obstacles the citizens of Arizona face in the twenty-first century juxtaposed with complex, yet achievable, illustrations of solutions to those problems. The governor articulates the synergistic nature of these three concepts in the motto, "Many Lands, Many People, Many Faiths—One Arizona," gracing her official website (*Arizona Governor*). Many lands, many people, and many faiths certainly create a *cultural mosaic* that requires unity, fashioned from diversity and equality and achieved through a *culture of cooperation* emphasizing partnership, to forge *one Arizona*—a new Arizona for the twenty-first century that embraces change and innovation grounded in the traditions of the past. Napolitano interprets her win as a mandate for change. "I think in this election voters sent a message for fundamental change in the way Arizona is governed," she submits. "I promise you this," she continues, "I won't let you [the voters] down." Furthermore, the voters "wanted a no-nonsense leadership. They wanted nonpartisan leadership," she argues. "They didn't want all slogans from the 1980s merely repeated. They wanted somebody who was going to talk honestly with them about the problems we confront" (qtd. in Davenport, "Napolitano Launches"). In short, just a few days after the election Napolitano promised to deliver on her campaign pledges.

Napolitano speaks of "the American ideal of a true cultural mosaic of equality and diversity" in her commencement address, "Law Is a Public Service," delivered to the Arizona State University College of Law on May 16, 2003 (3). She posits that demographic transformations including "the rapid growth of our Latino population will change our culture, our language and our perspectives" creating that mosaic (3). Napolitano also weaves together the threads of this theme and the other ideographs in her first speech as a new governor. She states in her Inaugural Address, delivered on January 6, 2003, that "our [Arizona's] strength lies in our diversity and it lies in our heritage. . . . Our diversity gives us a rich mix of cultures, faiths and traditions from across Arizona's communities and around the world" ("Inaugural"). The state's diversity and heritage "define the vital Arizona" Napolitano "saw throughout [her] journey" to the inaugural stage ("Inaugural"). A portrait of "young Navaho children learning to use the Internet" ("Inaugural") exemplifies this new vitality. She acknowledges that while she has seen the positive results of the state's diversity she has also witnessed the intolerance of uniqueness and erosion of indifference. Napolitano depicts this facet of Arizona "that we simply cannot wish away. I saw it through the eyes of the Sikh community after the murder of Balbir Sinngh Sodhi, the victim of a hate crime," she laments. "I saw it through the eyes of parents going to a food bank to get food for their children. I still see it through the eyes of a homeless World War II veteran I pass each morning on my way to the Capitol" ("Inaugural").

To overcome these obstacles to a healthy new Arizona, Napolitano introduces a second motif, a *culture of cooperation*. She argues that to create a new Arizona "we must come back together as one, united in the knowledge that we need each other, and bound by our commitment to each other. My friends," she implores, "we are all in this together" (Napolitano, "Inaugural"). Noting the budget crisis facing the state, she contends the solution requires a change in "the political culture at this Capitol" ("Inaugural"), a modification she pledges to begin at that moment. "With this inaugural, I declare an end to government where winners take all to the exclusion of everyone else. There is no room for this brand of politics in the new Arizona, and it will not be practiced in my office" ("Inaugural"). Recognizing that her constituents desire tangible evidence of this commitment, Napolitano details action she has taken to facilitate her vision. "As a testament to my firm belief that we need a new culture of cooperation, I have appointed a bipartisan administration. My team members reflect the diversity of our culture, and they represent the best thinking of all Arizonans" ("Inaugural"). This undertaking also honors the promise she made shortly after the announcement of her success at the polls. "My cabinet will look and think like all of Arizona," she pledged. "It will be bipartisan and diverse" (Davenport, "Napolitano Celebrates"). Her transition team appointments had reflected this undertaking as well. One of her cochairs had served as chief of staff to two Democratic governors and the second had held the same position in a Republican administration (Davenport, "Napolitano Launches").

Conceding the dismal situation haunting the state, Napolitano tells her audience that "to emerge from this quagmire, we need patience, discipline and a long-term vision of a new Arizona . . . . We must," she continues, "sacrifice short-term rewards and agendas, and keep our eyes on a larger prize, a new Arizona where hope and opportunity abound" (Napolitano, "Inaugural"). This new Arizona will find its origins in "our heritage [that] gives us its strength of character and its stubborn optimism" and that "thrives in our modern-day values of rugged independence and a can-do spirit" ("Inaugural"). Reaching the conclusion of the address, Napolitano tells her audience that "we are building a new Arizona, and in so doing we are creating our own proud legacy of an Arizona that offers the best public education in America, leads the world in research and product development, and boasts of prosperous and growing communities" ("Inaugural"). Thanking her constituents for their confidence and trust, she requests their "support and understanding as [she] embark[s] on the task ahead." And, returning to her call for a culture of cooperation, she asks for their "hand[s] in partnership" ("Inaugural"). Thus, in her first official speech as governor, Napolitano clearly establishes the interrelated themes of her administration: *a new Arizona* crafted from the state's *cultural mosaic* through a *culture of cooperation*.

These themes persist in Governor Napolitano's subsequent discourse. In her first state of the state address delivered only one week after her inauguration, Napolitano minces no words with her colleagues in the legislature. "Today the state of our state is grim" (Napolitano, "State 2003" 1), she bluntly tells them. She follows this statement with a note of optimism about the possibility of a new Arizona. "But this condition is tempered by the opportunity for us to build the most vibrant Arizona we have ever known" (1). Using a metaphor drawn from the geology of the state and her own love for hiking and the outdoors, Napolitano vividly describes the situation. "Yes, we find ourselves deep in a valley. But we have a good view of the summit, and we are ready to start the long journey back up the mountain" (1). She suggests that the new leaders the voters have just sent to the capitol embody the state's can-do spirit and "are filled with that Arizona brand of stubborn optimism to roll up our sleeves and build the new Arizona we envision" (1).

In order to realize this dream of a new Arizona, throughout this address Napolitano asserts the need for a culture of cooperation. She notes that the speaker of the house and the president of the Senate "extended their hands of partnership on your [the state legislature's] behalf" at her inaugural and that she "look[s] forward to working with [the legislature]" (Napolitano, "State 2003" 2). She continues, "My friends, we are all in this together" (2). As the legislature and her administration look to the future she exhorts everyone to ground every decision "in its impact on the next generation and beyond. This," she contends, "is how we will create the new Arizona of the 21st Century" (2). Again, she characterizes the current circumstances of Arizona: "We have been handed the reins of a state that ranks at or near the bottom of nearly every measure of quality," and she calls for a new approach to governing. "It is up to us to put this great state on a path of renewal, by fixing our short-term problems and focusing on our long-term vision of a new Arizona" (2). The governor then presents her plan to "build the new Arizona of the 21st Century" by restoring "fiscal sanity to state government" to meet the current crisis and "building a long-term strategy for a stronger, more vibrant Arizona of the future (2–3). Spearheading the quest for these long-term strategies and calling for a spirit of cooperation, Napolitano mentions she has requested "Efficiency Reviews" for all state departments to identify budget savings. Through this effort "we will create a new spirit of efficiency in state government, where everyone understands that saving resources in large and small ways helps to contribute to the greater good," she remarks. "I want state employees to take pride in knowing that by finding savings they are helping to free up resources to renew our schools, support our health care services and strengthen our communities" (3). Leading by example, Napolitano notes that she e-mailed copies of her speech to each legislator rather than "delivering printed versions with fancy covers" and consequently, "saved nearly two thousand dollars in printing expenses" (3–4).

Governor Napolitano next maintains that "a solid education system is vital if we are to strengthen our economy and provide hope and opportunity to the next generation" in a new Arizona (Napolitano, "State 2003" 4). "Improving public education," she proclaims as she did throughout her campaign, "is my top priority as Governor" (4). She envisions yet another culture of cooperation created by "private-public partnerships" to help fund various educational initiatives such as all-day kindergarten for every child in Arizona. (5). She advocates the "coordination of technology transfer from universities to the commercial sector" to invigorate both higher education and the economy in a new Arizona where "our public and private sectors must speak with one economic voice" (6). Acknowledging the many serious tasks ahead of them, Napolitano appeals to her colleagues to work collaboratively. And, in so doing, "together, we will solve the problems of today," she suggests, "so that we can get on with the business of building the new Arizona of tomorrow" (10).

Napolitano once again emphasizes the importance of a culture of cooperation for a new Arizona in her June 2003 speech announcing the creation of Arizona's Fire Service Mutual Aid Plan. In the face of the devastating wildfires that plague Arizona virtually every year, Napolitano salutes those who have worked together to develop a system to better manage responses to wildfires. "If there is a positive outcome to last year's tragic events [the Rodeo-Chediski fire]," she asserts, "it is that we emerged from it united in our determination to find new and better ways to manage our forests and reduce the threat of megafires" (Napolitano, "Announcement" 1). Discussing the Blue Ridge Demonstration Project, she notes that "people from across the ideological spectrum have come together to restore healthy forests to this community's urban-wildland interface. It was an impressive display of unity and smart forest management" (1). The Fire Service Mutual Aid Plan, "a product of thousands of hours of collaborative, grassroots effort" and the "first of its kind in the nation" (2–3), allows for regional cooperation among fire departments by setting "up a regional structure for fire service agencies in local jurisdictions, allowing them to reach far beyond their boundaries and limitations" (1). "When catastrophe strikes," Napolitano continues, "this plan provides for the immediate and coordinated response and operation of fire service resources to assist our neighbors in times of need" (2). For the governor, this cooperative plan contributes yet another piece to the vision of a new Arizona. "By working together toward this common goal," she says, "we will develop a system that better protects our wildlands and forest communities both now and in the future" (3).

In her second state of the state address delivered on January 12, 2004, Janet Napolitano accentuates the themes developed in her inaugural address. She speaks of the need for partnership and cooperation in the efforts to build a new Arizona, which must be grounded in a quality education for all children who are part of the cultural mosaic that is the diverse face of Arizona. Napolitano begins the address, as one would expect in a second state of the state speech, by outlining the accomplishments of the past year. In doing so, she focuses on the cooperative efforts that underlie those successes:

> Looking back, we balanced our budgets while protecting our schools, investing in our universities, and without raising taxes. Together, we passed important legislation on university research funding and technology transfer. . . . And in a special session that ended on a remarkable note of bipartisanship we made significant progress in addressing child protection and prison overcrowding. (Napolitano, "State 2004" 1)

She continues the recitation of achievements, noting that "along the way, we have reawakened that trademark can-do spirit of Arizona, as citizens from across the state have come forward to help tackle many other challenges that we must address" (Napolitano, "State 2004" 1). Napolitano continues to list the cooperative endeavors involved in meeting these demands. "We have partnered with the private sector to create a free prescription drug discount card," she notes. And, "businesses and educators alike share our enthusiasm to invest in fundamental school reform" (1). Referring again to the efforts to restore forests and contain wildfires, the governor states that "we have found an eagerness among all interested parties— including many who have not seen eye to eye for years—to sit down together and forge a consensus approach to restoring Arizona's forests" (1). She applauds the help offered by volunteer citizens from throughout the state who have recommended solutions for a myriad of challenges, and she salutes state workers who have "helped to generate more than $843 million in efficiency savings over the next five years" (1–2). Concluding this section of her address, Napolitano asserts that "this is how government gets it right in the new Arizona—by partnering with businesses and empowering individuals to make a personal commitment to the state they choose to call home" (2). She adds that "there is an increasing sense of excitement about the future of the new Arizona" (2).

Next, Napolitano turns to the work that still must be done to continue the construction of the new Arizona. She elaborates on the state's efforts on behalf of seniors, who constitute 13 percent (Barone and Cohen 94) of the state's diverse population, and she announces plans for a Benefits Check Up Plan to "quickly ascertain eligibility for hundreds of government and private programs" ("State 2004" 3). Stating "Arizona must be more than a great state to grow old in. It must also be a great state to grow up in" (3), Napolitano returns to her number one priority, education for the state's children who represent the many faces of Arizona's cultural mosaic. "To build the new Arizona of our highest aspirations," she continues, "we must enhance our commitment to Arizona's children and their education" (3). A new Arizona demands that "every child must start first grade safe, healthy and ready to learn" and that "as children advance through school, they must obtain the skills they will need to succeed in the 21st Century" (3). Finally, in a new Arizona high school graduates "must have access to technical and vocational training, to community colleges and to universities" (3). Turning to her focus on reading literacy as one facet of educational reform, the governor thanks "the Arizona businesses that provided all financial support" in backing her effort to provide every first-grade child in Arizona with a book (6). Once again, she acknowledges the contributions of private/public partnership. Recognizing that "higher education is the economic engine of the knowledge-based economy we are seeking to build in the new Arizona," Napolitano pledges to "work in partnership with Arizona's universities and community colleges to enhance access to a higher education, intensify university research efforts, and increase graduation rates" (7). In the remainder of the address, Napolitano discusses the new Arizona economy, homeland security, the preservation of Arizona's environment, and the 2005 budget. Within each of these topics she stresses the importance of cooperative efforts to build a new Arizona that respects tradition and honors the diversity of the state's citizens. She concludes her remarks by telling the legislators that she looks forward to working with them "to continue to build the new Arizona" (12).

Like Jennifer Granholm and others in the gubernatorial ranks, Janet Napolitano inherited the reins of a state ravaged by budget deficits threatening to decimate state services as well as the morale and quality of life of its citizens. In a state where the electorate appears to be less concerned about the sex of its state officials, Janet Napolitano creatively weaves the themes of partnership and empowerment, often considered feminine ideals, into a gender-*neutral culture of cooperation* characterized by a can-do spirit required to meet the challenges of today and create the *new Arizona* of tomorrow. She is adamant that this new Arizona must exemplify both the diversity and the unity that typify the *cultural mosaic* that depicts the true image of Arizona's citizens. Not quite halfway through her first term, Napolitano's diligent effort to bring her constituents together through a discourse peppered with gender-neutral ideographs and supported by concrete actions does indeed appear to be leading the state toward a new Arizona.

Kathleen Blanco

On January 12, 2004, Kathleen Babineaux Blanco became the first woman to serve as governor of Louisiana ("Kathleen"). Prior to this election, the state elected Blanco as lieutenant governor in 1995 and overwhelmingly reelected her to a second term of that office in 1999. While lieutenant governor she supervised the Department of Culture, Recreation, and Tourism ("Kathleen") and is credited with significantly increasing the state's tourism revenue. She began her political career in 1984, when she became the first woman ever elected to represent Lafayette in the state legislature ("Kathleen"). Her public service career is made up of "firsts," as she was also the first woman to hold a position as public service commissioner, and subsequently, the first woman to chair that commission as well. Before entering politics, she taught high school in southwest Louisiana, not far from where she was born. She received a BS degree in business education from the University of Louisiana at Lafayette ("Kathleen").

The race for the governorship appeared tight, with her opponent, Republican Bobby Jindal, polling well and leading two days prior to the election. A strong turnout in the black community, coupled with a series of seven different attack ads against Jindal's record as head of the state's Health and Hospitals Department, provided the margin Blanco needed for victory (Gizzi, "Democrat"). Considered an upset victory, Blanco won the election by a 52 percent to 48 percent margin (C. Cook). She did not run as a "traditional woman" candidate, nor did she run as a true Democrat. Instead, "Blanco ran dramatically to the right of her party on social issues, opposing gun control, abortion, affirmative action, and benefits for gay couples" (Gizzi, "Democrat"). This conservative bent forms the basis of the main thrust of the majority of Blanco's speeches. Rather than argue for the social good or the benefits of government, Blanco casts her discourse in the language of a conservative CEO. Like Montana's Governor Martz, Blanco markets Louisiana as a state open to new business ventures. Specifically, she consistently uses the ideographs of *business* and *efficiency* as the main themes of her political discourse.

In her commencement address to Xavier University, for instance, Blanco details the achievements of her brief tenure as governor. She states, "We are working hard to stabilize the state budgeting process, and to give Louisiana a more honest, efficient, and accountable government. We are making it easier to do business in Louisiana" ("Xavier"). *Efficiency* as a rallying term again appears, this time in a speech to the Public Affairs Research Council of the Louisiana Health Care Conference. She focuses specifically on health care, which she acknowledges does not reach all who are in need. However, she does not believe that new programs are required. Instead, she says, "It is clear to me that we don't need to spend more. Our problem is not a lack of money. Our problem is that we haven't been spending our money wisely and we have poor results to show for our investments" (Blanco, "Speech"). Although she does not say the word, her belief in *efficiency* is clearly implied in the above statement. In her "State of the State Address," however, she is much more blatant, promising that "in this time of economic challenge, we will give the people a more efficient government—one that increases the value of government services, not our taxes" ("State").

Blanco portrays the state of Louisiana as a giant corporation. In her "Inaugural Address," for example, she enthusiastically announces, "Louisiana is ready to do business" ("Inaugural "). She later repeats the same mantra to the Greater New Orleans Inc. Luncheon, when she states, "Louisiana is ready to do business. Big business and small business; large public corporations and small entrepreneurs; in our cities and our rural areas. You are a treasured asset to this state" (Blanco, "Governor Blanco Remarks"). In discussing her plans for a new beginning in the state, Blanco argues that the legislative session is "our chance to show the world that in Louisiana there is a new way of doing business" (Blanco, "State"). She praises the members of the legislature for sending a strong message that "Louisiana is open for business" (Blanco, "Inaugural"). She vests her audience members with a sense of responsibility when she intones, "Building a new economy is everyone's business" ("Inaugural"). Blanco carries that theme into her speech to the Louisiana Center for Women and Government, when she informs her audience, "I am proud to report to you that we are fundamentally changing the way that our state does business. In fact, I think I can safely declare today that . . . Louisiana is open for business" (Blanco, "Governor Blanco Addresses"). She again attempts to reach out to her female audience by describing their role in government and in the state—they are essentially domestic and government CEOs. "Women are more likely to be the head of the household in Louisiana. Women manage healthcare, budgets, education, and nutrition" ("Governor Blanco Addresses").

Finally, Blanco offers her last fiscally conservative approach to state government. After describing the somewhat bleak economic picture Louisiana faces, Blanco informs her audience that "we have far more demand on government services than we can afford. Despite these profound challenges, I am proud to report to you that my executive budget for the coming fiscal year is balanced. A first principle of good government is that we must live within our means" (Blanco, "State"). She later reiterates that principle in her state of the state address, when she argues, "Government should live within its means—that when times are tough, our government should tighten its belt, just like the average family. We are living within our means and not raising new taxes. And we will work to serve the people by working harder and more creatively on their behalf" (Blanco, "State").

Democratic Senator Zell Miller from Georgia argued in his recently published book, *A National Party No More*, that the Democratic Party has lost relevance in the South because it is too far left on many issues. Blanco, with her politically conservative approach to both social and economic issues, has seemingly overcome that barrier to become Louisiana's first woman governor. By focusing on *business*

and *efficiency* as her guiding ideographs, Blanco provides her constituents with a political approach that firmly anchors her in a gender-neutral realm. She has eschewed traditionally "feminine" discourse and adopted issues and rhetoric that
have broad appeal in these economically troubled times.

The six women we discuss in this chapter exemplify a new persona of the
woman governor. They bring governmental experience to their campaigns and to
their leadership. As discussed throughout this book, previous scholarship has suggested that women in politics operate within a "feminine" rhetorical paradigm.
This theoretical perspective, in turn, has grounded much of the research in this
area. However, the scholarship, much like the political campaigns and terms of office it studies, must change to represent and reflect a more contemporary approach
to seeking, gaining, and maintaining office, particularly where the governorship is
concerned. While the Patty Murray strategy can be successful in some circumstances, it is constraining in others. These women governors have not denied their
womanhood, but they have not relied on it for their campaigns nor in their governing strategies. They have focused on issues traditionally associated with women,
but they have transformed them into "the people's" issues. Further, they have illustrated that women do understand state economies and the business of business.
Although many politicians focus their agendas on change and progress, these
women governors endeavor to make progress using a collaborative approach involving constituents and political opponents alike. The ideographs in their discourse clearly illustrate these conscious rhetorical strategies. Neither totally
masculine nor completely feminine in nature, these themes form a discourse that
morphs the boundaries of the public and the private spheres, creating a new in-
between rhetorical space.

Conclusion

Progress isn't inevitable. If you want to have power over your life, then you must make sure that more women have power to make public policy. . . . You too can be a candidate. . . . Have great expectations.

—HARRIET WOODS 195

WE BEGAN THIS PROJECT with the belief that women's political discourse had changed since communication scholars first began studying the phenomenon. While at first women seemingly packaged themselves "as women, for women," focusing primarily on women's issues and using what scholars term a "feminine style," we have discovered that women's political discourse is now far more complex. Past studies have focused on individual women, "without comparison across women in similar positions at one time period" (Thomas, "Impact" 90). Our study has taken a more inclusive approach that allows us to draw conclusions based on the rhetoric of several women in similar positions, irrespective of party affiliation and geographic location.

In our examination of the discourse of twenty-first-century representatives, senators, and governors, we reveal that women have created and now operate in a rhetorical in-between space that values issues and perspectives traditionally seen as women's issues. Moreover, as evidenced in their overwhelming use of ideographs, these women not only understand but also bring expertise to discussions of issues historically relegated to the public sphere and often considered beyond their intellectual capacity. In this newly recognized role, women in contemporary politics have blurred the boundaries between the public and private spheres and have crafted a discourse style that can only be termed androgynous in nature. Concurrently, what was once seen as "feminine style" has become virtually mainstream and many of the so-called "women's issues" now carry the label, "the people's is-sues." And with only minor exceptions, such as comments sometimes found in the discourse of Senators Kay Bailey Hutchison and Barbara Boxer, as well as Repre-sentative Nancy Pelosi, the rhetoric illustrates that these women understand the need for cooperation across party lines. "Certainly, women can be confrontational, but their capacity for cooperative political bargaining is largely responsible for their many successful projects" (Dabrowski 146). Many women in contemporary politics adopt the strategy Senator Dianne Feinstein describes:

> I learned that when you live in a diverse society, you run terrible risks of polarization—because the smallest thing can disrupt everything. I determined a long time ago that my kind of politics was to concentrate on bringing people together—working out practical solutions. I wasn't going to be the ideologue who didn't enable people to solve problems. (qtd. in Mikulski et al. 173)

Contrary to the media's almost exclusive focus on partisanship and the deep di-vide, evidenced in the 2004 election, that permeates our political and social insti-tutions, an examination of the daily discourse in the House, the Senate, and the state houses indicates the dawning of a more collaborative approach to decision making. Thus, a significant development within the rhetorical in-between space is a new culture of cooperation.

This shifting or changing of cultural discourse provides an important justifi-cation for the expansion of studies addressing women's political communication. As Cindy Rosenthal suggests, "If cultural change leads to institutional change, then perhaps the transformation of gender roles and social relations will produce a consequent redefinition of politics and institutional life in the future" (452). This redefinition will allow for increased participation in the democratic process and should provide a more complete picture of not only how the political process functions, but also how women and other inhabitants of the Third Space function within it. Therefore, as Martha Ackelsberg posits, "Attention to a broader concept of women's participation has much to contribute to a rethinking of the meanings and practice of citizenship and participation for everyone as we prepare to meet the challenges of the twenty-first century" (215). A culture of cooperation is ad-vantageous for our nation, for "if we are ever to have a truly pluralistic society, where people's differences are freely expressed, celebrated—and utilized for every-one's benefit, it must begin with a partnership between women and men" (Riane Eisler, qtd. in Aburdene and Naisbitt xxiii).

As we have seen, despite the waltz of "gain two seats, lose one race" danced from election to election, the number of women involved in electoral politics con-tinues to increase. Many, like Senator Barbara Mikulski, successfully run several times for reelection. The increasing ranks of women, their rise in seniority, and the gaining legitimacy of their voices bode well for the eventual election of a woman as president of the United States. For at the very least, as more women enter the political fray as senators, representatives, and governors, and increasingly voice their opinions, they provide role models for women of the future. "As men have studied presidents and generals as models of leadership from which to build their own Leadership Equation, women now have and can study a growing cadre of models of the ways women lead. These women can show the way for all leaders, men or women, who want to lead in the new," more collaborative style of contemporary politics (Cantor and Bernay 285). Clearly, as the examples in this study indicate, the political women of the twenty-first century have changed the rules for participation. Although not universal, many of their ideographs suggest the emergence of a gender-neutral discourse of the in-between space that bridges the gap between Second and Third Space rhetorics and experiences.

While we would like to argue otherwise, we must admit that our study of women's political discourse is not exhaustive. We have attempted to piece together bits of glass in the broad mosaic of political discourse. One of the key factors limiting our study was the availability of discourse samples themselves. With only a few exceptions, the speeches of women, even those in high-profile positions, seldom find their way into mainstream publications. Some of the women, like Hillary Rodham Clinton, Kay Bailey Hutchison, Tammy Baldwin, and Judy Biggert from Congress, and Governors Kathleen Blanco and Janet Napolitano, post floor speeches and other documents on their web pages. Unfortunately, others have no such collections, and we were left examining fragmented samples from diverse and often obscure places. There exists no clearinghouse for women's political discourse. Dale Spender argues in her book, *Women of Ideas and What Men Have Done with Them,* that women's viewpoints are often suppressed or trivialized by men. Women, themselves, have contributed to this situation, because they have not always recognized the importance of recording their thoughts for posterity. Thus, women's key contributions to literature, politics, and society frequently are overlooked. We implore the twenty-first-century women politicians to help create an infrastructure for archiving the political discourse of women and then to take the time to make their own words more accessible to their successors. Society cannot assess the impact of their participation, nor can future generations benefit from their wisdom, if their words are not available. Not only does this accessibility allow a culture of mentoring, it provides a new avenue for a transparent government indicative of an in-between space worldview.

In her book, *The Boundaries of Her Body,* Debran Rowland recalls that "as the 'gentler sex,' women were urged 'not to wrinkle their foreheads' with politics. Women should be 'content' instead to 'soothe and calm the minds of their husbands returning ruffled from political debates'" (24). Thankfully, twenty-first-century women need not content themselves with serving merely as nurturers or cheerleaders. Because of the hard-fought battles of the nineteenth and twentieth centuries, women can and do successfully participate in the twenty-first-century political process. Society increasingly hears women's voices on a variety of issues and recognizes that these matters belong to everyone. As such, these women reorchestrate the discordant strains of politics as usual to create an anthem of cooperation and equality. It is a composition from the in-between space whose chorus echoes the melodies of the past and bears witness to the harmonies of the future. It is time for all of us to listen.

Afterword

I think we have turned a corner and we will never go back. It's never going to be the way it was. This is just the prologue.

—MARJORIE MARGOLIES-MEZVINSKY 213

A S THIS BOOK GOES TO PRESS, we have just witnessed the elections of 2004. In this political arena, women experienced what has now become the traditional electoral dance amassing both wins and losses as record numbers of women participated in some areas of the process while fewer women ventured into the contest in other contexts. For instance, a record 141 women won "major-party nominations" for seats in the U.S. House of Representatives ("Record Number"). Fifty-seven of these women were officeholders who successfully retained their seats while sixty-five of the candidates faced incumbents. Sixty-five women from twenty-six states serve in the U.S. House of Representatives in the 109th Congress occupying 14.9 percent of the 435 available seats ("Women in Elected Office 2005") and setting a new benchmark for the number of women simultaneously holding office in this legislative body. Three women still serve as delegates from Guam, the Virgin Islands, and Washington, D.C. ("Women in Elected Office 2005"). Ten women sought seats in the U.S. Senate. This was one less than the record number of eleven women running for the Senate in 1992 and again in 2002 ("Record Number"). Five, who were serving in the Senate, retained their seats; three unsuccessfully sought open seats, and two challenged incumbents, but lost. The fourteen women who served in the 108th Congress have returned to their work in 2005. Three women entered the race for the governorship. One, Ruth Minner, an incumbent, successfully retained her position. In the two races for open seats, Claire McCaskill of Missouri lost her bid for the statehouse while

Christine Gregoire of Washington claimed the governorship with a narrow victory in a hotly contested campaign. In 2005, eight women now lead their states.

The results of the 2004 election showcase the political waltz that women find themselves dancing. As noted above, it is often an exercise of two steps forward, one step back, where losses sometimes offset gains. While the increased number of women vying for U.S. House seats in 2004 was an anomaly and many were not successful, their participation in the process signals a change in the political arena. As we have seen in the preceding chapters, in many cases women are entering politics, not as wives or widows or concerned soccer moms, but as savvy politicians in their own right. As Peter Slevin reports, contemporary candidates represent what has been called "the third wave. The first, notable through the 1970s, often involved women who reached office because they were wives or widows of prominent politicians. The second featured women emerging from volunteer work in civic groups or single issue fights with city hall. The third is defined by women who earned their spurs in elective political office" (Slevin A6). Although the "number of women candidates seems stuck" (Debbie Walsh, qtd. in "Record Number"), as we illustrate throughout this book, women's voices have entered public-sphere discussions at the local, state, and national levels. Because of their increasing political presence, our twenty-first-century society can no longer view women in politics as aberrations, abnormalities, or accidents. Rather, they must be seen as key participants in the electoral process.

While the path to change remains long and arduous, politics in the United States has turned a corner. The voices from the in-between space will be heard.

Appendix A
Women in the U.S. House of Representatives

The Twentieth Century

Representative and Party	State	Years of Service
Jeannette Rankin (R)	MT	03/04/1917–03/03/1919
		01/03/1941–01/03/1943
Alice Mary Robertson (R)	OK	03/04/1921–03/03/1923
Winnifred Sprague Mason Huck (R)	IL	11/07/1922–03/03/1923
Mae Ella Nolan (R)	CA	01/23/1923–03/03/1925
Florence Prag Kahn (R)	CA	03/04/1925–01/03/1937
Mary Teresa Norton (D)	NJ	03/04/1925–01/03/1951
Edith Nourse Rogers (R)	MA	06/30/1925–09/10/1960
Katherine Gudger Langley (R)	KY	03/04/1927–03/03/1937
Pearl Peden Oldfield (D)	AR	01/11/1929–03/03/1931
Ruth Hanna McCormick (R)	IL	03/04/1929–03/03/1931
Ruth Bryan Owen (D)	FL	03/04/1929–03/03/1933
Ruth Sears Baker Pratt (R)	NY	03/04/1929–03/03/1933
Effiegene Locke Wingo (D)	AR	11/04/1930–03/03/1933
Willa McCord Blake Eslick (D)	TN	08/04/1932–03/03/1933
Virginia Ellis Jenckes (D)	IN	03/04/1933–01/03/1939
Kathryn Ellen O'Loughlin (McCarthy) (D)	KS	03/04/1933–01/03/1935
Isabella Selmes Greenway (D)	AZ	10/03/1933–01/03/1937
Marian Williams Clarke (R)	NY	12/28/1933–01/03/1935
Caroline Love Goodwin O'Day (D)	NY	01/03/1935–01/03/1943
Nan Wood Honeyman (D)	OR	01/03/1937–01/03/1939
Elizabeth Hawley Gasque (D)	SC	09/13/1938–01/03/1939
Jessie Sumner (R)	IL	01/03/1939–01/03/1947
Clara Gooding McMillan (D)	SC	11/07/1939–01/03/1941
Frances Payne Bolton (R)	OH	02/27/1940–01/03/1969
Margaret Chase Smith (R)	ME	06/03/1940–01/03/1949
Florence Reville Gibbs (D)	GA	10/01/1940–01/03/1941
Katharine Edgar Byron (D)	MD	05/27/1941–01/03/1943
Veronica Grace Boland (D)	PA	11/03/1942–01/03/1943

(continued)

The Twentieth Century   (*continued*)

Representative and Party	State	Years of Service
Clare Boothe Luce (R)	CT	01/03/1943–01/03/1947
Winifred Claire Stanley (R)	NY	01/03/1943–01/03/1945
Willa Lybrand Fulmer (D)	SC	11/07/1944–01/03/1945
Emily Taft Douglas (D)	IL	01/03/1945–01/03/1947
Helen Gahagan Douglas (D)	CA	01/03/1945–01/03/1951
Chase Going Woodhouse (D)	CT	01/03/1945–01/03/1947
		01/03/1949–01/03/1951
Helen Douglas Mankin (D)	GA	02/12/1946–01/03/1947
Eliza Jane Pratt (D)	NC	05/25/1946–01/03/1947
Georgia Lee Lusk (D)	NM	01/03/1947–01/03/1949
Katharine Price Collier St. George (R)	NY	01/03/1947–01/03/1965
Reva Zilpha Beck Bosone (D)	UT	01/03/1949–01/03/1953
Cecil Murray Harden (R)	IN	01/03/1949–01/03/1959
Edna Flannery Kelly (D)	NY	11/08/1949–01/03/1969
Marguerite Stitt Church (R)	IL	01/03/1951–01/03/1963
Ruth Thompson (R)	MI	01/03/1951–01/03/1957
Maude Elizabeth Kee (D)	WV	07/17/1951–01/03/1965
Vera Daerr Buchanan (D)	PA	07/24/1951–11/26/1955
Gracis Bowers Pfost (D)	ID	01/03/1953–01/03/1963
Leonor Kretzer Sullivan (D)	MO	01/03/1953–01/03/1977
Mary Elizabeth Pruett Farrington (R)*	HI	07/31/1954–01/03/1957
Iris Faircloth Blitch (D)	GA	01/03/1955–01/03/1963
Edith Starrett Green (D)	OR	01/03/1955–12/31/1974
Martha Wright Griffiths (D)	MI	01/03/1955–12/31/1974
Coya Gjesdal Knutson (D)	MN	01/03/1955–01/03/1959
Kathryn Elizabeth Granahan (D)	PA	11/06/1956–01/03/1963
Florence Price Dwyer (R)	NJ	01/03/1957–01/03/1973
Catherine Dean May (R)	WA	01/03/1959–01/03/1971
Edna Oakes Simpson (R)	IL	01/03/1959–01/03/1961
Jessica McCullough Weis (R)	NY	01/03/1959–01/03/1963
Julia Butler Hansen (D)	WA	11/08/1960–12/31/1974
Catherine Dorris Norrell (D)	AR	04/18/1961–01/03/1963
Louise Goff Reece (R)	TN	05/16/1961–01/03/1963
Corinne Boyd Riley (D)	SC	04/10/1962–01/03/1963
Charlotte Thompson Reid (R)	IL	01/03/1963–10/07/1971
Irene Bailey Baker (R)	TN	03/10/1964–01/03/1965
Patsy Takemoto Mink (D)	HI	01/03/1965–01/03/1977
		09/22/1990–09/28/2002
Lera Millard Thomas (D)	TX	03/26/1966–01/03/1967
Margaret M. Heckler (R)	MA	01/03/1967–01/03/1983
Shirley Anita Chisholm (D)	NY	01/03/1969–01/03/1983
Bella Savitzky Abzug (D)	NY	01/03/1971–01/03/1977
Ella Tambussi Grasso (D)	CT	01/03/1971–01/03/1975
Louise Day Hicks (D)	MA	01/03/1971–01/03/1973
Elizabeth Andrews (D)	AL	04/04/1972–01/03/1973
Yvonne Brathwaite Burke (D)	CA	01/03/1973–01/03/1979
Marjorie Sewell Holt (R)	MD	01/03/1973–01/03/1987
Elizabeth Holtzman (D)	NY	01/03/1973–01/03/1981

The Twentieth Century   (*continued*)

Representative and Party	State	Years of Service
Barbara Charline Jordan (D)	TX	01/03/1973–01/03/1979
Patricia Scott Schroeder (D)	CO	01/03/1973–01/03/1997
Corinne Claiborne (Lindy) Boggs (D)	LA	03/20/1973–01/03/1991
Cardiss Collins (D)	IL	06/05/1973–01/03/1997
Millicent Hammond Fenwick (R)	NJ	01/03/1975–01/03/1983
Martha Elizabeth Keys (D)	KS	01/03/1975–01/03/1979
Marilyn Laird Lloyd (D)	TN	01/03/1975–01/03/1995
Helen Stevenson Meyner (D)	NJ	01/03/1975–01/03/1979
Virginia Dodd Smith (R)	NE	01/03/1975–01/03/1991
Gladys Noon Spellman (D)	MD	01/03/1975–02/24/1981
Shirley Neil Pettis (R)	CA	04/29/1975–01/03/1979
Barbara Ann Mikulski (D)	MD	01/03/1977–01/03/1987
Mary Rose Oakar (D)	OH	01/03/1977–01/03/1993
Beverly Barton Butcher Byron (D)	MD	01/03/1979–01/03/1993
Geraldine Ann Ferraro (D)	NY	01/03/1979–01/03/1985
Olympia Jean Snowe (R)	ME	01/03/1979–01/03/1995
Bobbi Fiedler (R)	CA	01/03/1981–01/03/1987
Lynn Morley Martin (R)	IL	01/03/1981–01/03/1991
Margaret Scafati Roukema (R)	NJ	01/03/1981–01/03/2003
Claudine Schneider (R)	RI	01/03/1981–01/03/1991
Barbara Bailey Kennelly (D)	CT	01/12/1982–01/03/1999
Jean Spencer Ashbrook (R)	OH	06/29/1982–01/03/1983
Katie Beatrice Hall (D)	IN	11/02/1982–01/03/1985
Barbara Boxer (D)	CA	01/03/1983–01/03/1993
Nancy Lee Johnson (R)	CT	01/03/1983–
Marcia Carolyn (Marcy) Kaptur (D)	OH	01/03/1983–
Barbara Farrell Vucanovich (R)	NV	01/03/1983–01/03/1997
Sala Burton (D)	CA	06/21/1983–02/01/1987
Helen Delich Bentley (R)	MD	01/03/1985–01/03/1995
Jan Meyers (R)	KS	01/03/1985–01/03/1997
Catherine S. Long (D)	LA	03/30/1985–01/03/1987
Constance A. Morella (R)	MD	01/03/1987–01/03/2003
Elizabeth J. Patterson (D)	SC	01/03/1987–01/03/1993
Patricia Fukuda Saiki (R)	HI	01/03/1987–01/03/1991
Louise McIntosh Slaughter (D)	NY	01/03/1987–
Nancy Pelosi (D)	CA	06/02/1987–
Nita M. Lowey (D)	NY	01/03/1989–
Jolene Unsoeld (D)	WA	01/03/1989–01/03/1995
Jill Long (D)	IN	03/28/1989–01/03/1995
Ileana Ros-Lehtinen (R)	FL	08/29/1989–
Susan Molinari (R)	NY	03/20/1990–08/01/1997
Barbara-Rose Collins (D)	MI	01/03/1991–01/03/1997
Rosa L. DeLauro (D)	CT	01/03/1991–
Joan Kelly Horn (D)	MO	01/03/1991–01/03/1993
Eleanor Holmes Norton (D)*	DC	01/03/1991–
Maxine Waters (D)	CA	01/03/1991–

(*continued*)

The Twentieth Century (*continued*)

Representative and Party	State	Years of Service
Eva Clayton (D)	NC	11/03/1992–01/03/2003
Corrine Brown (D)	FL	01/03/1993–
Leslie Byrne (D)	VA	01/03/1993–01/03/1995
Maria Cantwell (D)	WA	01/03/1993–01/03/1995
Pat Danner (D)	MO	01/03/1993–01/03/2001
Jennifer Dunn (R)	WA	01/03/1993–01/03/2005
Karan English (D)	AZ	01/03/1993–01/03/1995
Anna G. Eshoo (D)	CA	01/03/1993–
Tillie Fowler (R)	FL	01/03/1993–01/02/2001
Elizabeth Furse (D)	OR	01/03/1993–01/03/1999
Jane Harman (D)	CA	01/03/1993–01/03/1999
Eddie Bernice Johnson (D)	TX	01/03/1993–
Blanche Lambert Lincoln (D)	AR	01/03/1993–01/03/1997
Carolyn B. Maloney (D)	NY	01/03/1993–
Marjorie Margolies-Mezvinsky (D)	PA	01/03/1993–01/03/1995
Cynthia McKinney (D)	GA	01/03/1993–01/03/2003
Carrie P. Meek (D)	FL	01/03/1993–01/03/2003
Deborah Pryce (R)	OH	01/03/1993–
Lucille Roybal-Allard (D)	CA	01/03/1993–
Lynn Schenk (D)	CA	01/03/1993–01/03/1995
Karen Shepherd (D)	UT	01/03/1993–01/03/1995
Karen Thurman (D)	FL	01/03/1993–01/03/2003
Nydia M. Velazquez (D)	NY	01/03/1993–
Lynn Woolsey (D)	CA	01/03/1993–
Helen Chenoweth-Hage (R)	ID	01/03/1995–01/02/2001
Barbara Cubin (R)	WY	01/03/1995–
Enid Greene (Waldholtz) (R)	UT	01/03/1995–01/03/1997
Sheila Jackson-Lee (D)	TX	01/03/1995–
Sue Kelly (R)	NY	01/03/1995–
Zoe Lofgren (D)	CA	01/03/1995–
Karen McCarthy (D)	MO	01/03/1995–01/03/2005
Sue Myrick (R)	NC	01/03/1995–
Lynn Rivers (D)	MI	01/03/1995–01/03/2003
Andrea Seastrand (R)	CA	01/03/1995–01/03/1997
Linda Smith (R)	WA	01/03/1995–01/03/1999
Juanita Millender-McDonald (D)	CA	03/26/1996–
JoAnn Emerson (R)	MO	11/05/1996–
Julia Carson (D)	IN	01/03/1997–
Donna MC Christensen (D)*	VI	01/03/1997–
Diana DeGette (D)	CO	01/03/1997–
Kay Granger (R)	TX	01/03/1997–
Darlene Hooley (D)	OR	01/03/1997–
Carolyn Cheeks Kilpatrick (D)	MI	01/03/1997–
Carolyn McCarthy (D)	NY	01/03/1997–
Anne Northup (R)	KY	01/03/1997–
Loretta Sanchez (D)	CA	01/03/1997–
Debbie Stabenow (D)	MI	01/03/1997–01/02/2001
Ellen Tauscher (D)	CA	01/03/1997–

The Twentieth Century   (*continued*)

Representative and Party	State	Years of Service
Lois Capps (D)	CA	03/10/1998–
Mary Bono (R)	CA	04/07/1998–
Barbara Lee (D)	CA	04/07/1998–
Heather Wilson (R)	NM	06/23/1998–
Tammy Baldwin (D)	WI	01/03/1999–
Shelley Berkley (D)	NV	01/03/1999–
Judith Borg Biggert (R)	IL	01/03/1999–
Stephanie Tubbs Jones (D)	OH	01/03/1999–
Grace Napolitano (D)	CA	01/03/1999–
Janice Schakowsky (D)	IL	01/03/1999–

* Delegate
Data from "Women in Congress." United States Congress. House of Representatives.

Appendix B
Women in the U.S. House of Representatives

The Twenty-first Century

Representative and Party	State	Years of Service
Margaret Scafati Roukema (R)	NJ	01/03/1981–01/03/2003
Nancy Lee Johnson (R)	CT	01/03/1983–
Marcia Carolyn (Marcy) Kaptur (D)	OH	01/03/1983–
Louise McIntosh Slaughter (D)	NY	01/03/1987–
Constance A. Morella (R)	MD	01/03/1987–01/03/2003
Nancy Pelosi (D)	CA	06/02/1987–
Nita M. Lowey (D)	NY	01/03/1989–
Ileana Ros-Lehtinen (R)	FL	08/29/1989–
Patsy Takemoto Mink (D)	HI	01/03/1965–01/03/1977
		09/22/1990–09/28/2002
Rosa L. DeLauro (D)	CT	01/03/1991–
Eleanor Holmes Norton (D)*	DC	01/03/1991–
Maxine Waters (D)	CA	01/03/1991–
Eva Clayton (D)	NC	11/03/1992–01/03/2003
Corrine Brown (D)	FL	01/03/1993–
Pat Danner (D)	MO	01/03/1993–01/03/2001
Jennifer Dunn (R)	WA	01/03/1993–01/03/2005
Anna G. Eshoo (D)	CA	01/03/1993–
Tillie Fowler (R))	FL	01/03/1993–01/02/2001
Eddie Bernice Johnson (D)	TX	01/03/1993–
Carolyn B. Maloney (D)	NY	01/03/1993–
Cynthia McKinney (D)	GA	01/03/1993–01/03/2003
		01/03/2005–
Carrie P. Meek (D)	FL	01/03/1993–01/03/2003
Deborah Pryce (R)	OH	01/03/1993–
Lucille Roybal-Allard (D)	CA	01/03/1993–
Karen Thurman (D)	FL	01/03/1993–01/03/2003
Nydia M. Velazquez (D)	NY	01/03/1993–
Lynn Woolsey (D)	CA	01/03/1993–

(*continued*)

The Twenty-first Century   (*continued*)

Representative and Party	State	Years of Service
Helen Chenoweth-Hage (R)	ID	01/03/1995–01/02/2001
Barbara Cubin (R)	WY	01/03/1995–
Sheila Jackson-Lee (D)	TX	01/03/1995–
Sue Kelly (R)	NY	01/03/1995–
Zoe Lofgren (D)	CA	01/03/1995–
Karen McCarthy (D)	MO	01/03/1995–01/03/2005
Sue Myrick (R)	NC	01/03/1995–
Lynn Rivers (D)	MI	01/03/1995–01/03/2003
Juanita Millender-McDonald (D)	CA	03/26/1996–
JoAnn Emerson (R)	MO	11/05/1996–
Julia Carson (D)	IN	01/03/1997–
Donna McChristensen (D)*	VI	01/03/1997–
Diana DeGette (D)	CO	01/03/1997–
Kay Granger (R)	TX	01/03/1997–
Darlene Hooley (D)	OR	01/03/1997–
Carolyn Cheeks Kilpatrick (D)	MI	01/03/1997–
Carolyn McCarthy (D)	NY	01/03/1997–
Anne Northup (R)	KY	01/03/1997–
Loretta Sanchez (D)	CA	01/03/1997–
Debbie Stabenow (D)	MI	01/03/1997–01/02/2001
Ellen Tauscher (D)	CA	01/03/1997–
Lois Capps (D)	CA	03/10/1998–
Mary Bono (R)	CA	04/07/1998–
Barbara Lee (D)	CA	04/07/1998–
Heather Wilson (R)	NM	06/23/1998–
Tammy Baldwin (D)	WI	01/03/1999–
Shelley Berkley (D)	NV	01/03/1999–
Judith Borg Biggert (R)	IL	01/03/1999–
Stephanie Tubbs Jones (D)	OH	01/03/1999–
Grace Napolitano (D)	CA	01/03/1999–
Janice Schakowsky (D)	IL	01/03/1999–
Shelly Capito (R)	WV	01/03/2001–
Jo Ann Davis (R)	VA	01/03/2001–
Susan Davis (D)	CA	01/03/2001–
Jane Harman (D)	CA	01/03/1993–01/03/1999
		01/03/2001–
Melissa Hart (R)	PA	01/03/2001–
Betty McCollum (D)	MN	01/03/2001–
Hilda Solis (D)	CA	01/03/2001–
Diane E. Watson (D)	CA	06/05/2001–
Marsha Blackburn (R)	TN	01/03/2003–
Madeleine Bordallo (D)*	GU	01/03/2003–
Virginia Brown-Waite (R)	FL	01/03/2003–
Katherine Harris (R)	FL	01/03/2003–
Denise Majette (D)	GA	01/03/2003–01/03/2005
Candice Miller (R)	MI	01/03/2003–
Marilyn Musgrave (R)	CO	01/03/2003–
Linda T. Sánchez (D)	CA	01/03/2003–

The Twenty-first Century   (*continued*)

Representative and Party	State	Years of Service
Stephanie Herseth (D)	SD	06/01/2004–
Melissa Bean (D)	IL	01/03/2005
Thelma Drake (R)	VA	01/03/2005–
Virginia Foxx (R)	NC	01/03/2005–
Kathy McMorris (R)	WA	01/03/2005–
Gwen Moore (D)	WI	01/03/2005–
Allison Schwartz (D)	PA	01/03/2005–
Debbie Wasserman-Schultz (D)	FL	01/03/2005–

* Delegate
Data from "Women in Congress." United States Congress. House of Representatives.

Appendix C
Women in the U.S. Senate

The Twentieth Century

Senator and Party	State	Years of Service
Rebecca Latimer Felton (D)	GA	11/21/1922–11/22/1922
Hattie Wyatt Caraway (D)	AR	12/08/1931–01/02/1945
Rose McConnell Long (D)	LA	02/10/1936–01/02/1937
Dixie Bibb Graves (D)	AL	08/20/1937–01/10/1938
Gladys Pyle (R)	SD	11/09/1938–01/03/1939
Vera Cahalan Bushfield (R)	SD	10/06/1948–12/27/1948
Margaret Chase Smith (R)	ME	01/03/1949–01/03/1973
Eva Kelly Bowring (R)	NE	04/26/1954–11/07/1954
Hazel Hempel Abel (R)	NE	11/08/1954–12/31/1954
Maurine Brown Neuberger (D)	OR	11/08/1960–01/03/1967
Elaine Schwartzenburg Edwards (D)	LA	08/07/1972–11/13/1972
Muriel Buck Humphrey (D)	MN	02/06/1978–11/07/1978
Maryon Pittman Allen (D)	AL	06/12/1978–11/07/1978
Nancy Landon Kassebaum (R)	KS	12/23/1978–01/07/1997
Paula Hawkins (R)	FL	01/01/1981–01/03/1987
Barbara Ann Mikulski (D)	MD	01/03/1987–
Jocelyn Birch Burdick (D)	ND	09/16/1992–12/14/1992
Dianne Feinstein (D)	CA	11/10/1992–
Barbara Boxer (D)	CA	01/05/1993–
Carol Mosley-Braun (D)	IL	01/05/1993–01/06/1999
Patty Murray (D)	WA	01/05/1993–
Kay Bailey Hutchison (R)	TX	06/14/1993–
Olympia Snowe (R)	ME	01/04/1995–
Sheila Frahm (R)	KS	06/11/1996–11/08/1996
Susan Collins (R)	ME	01/07/1997–
Mary Landrieu (D)	LA	01/07/1997–
Blanche Lincoln (D)	AR	01/06/1999–

Data from "Women in the United States Senate." Center for American Women and Politics.

Appendix D
Women in the U.S. Senate

The Twenty-first Century

Senator and Party	State	Years of Service
Barbara Ann Mikulski (D)	MD	01/03/1987–
Dianne Feinstein (D)	CA	11/10/1992–
Barbara Boxer (D)	CA	01/05/1993–
Patty Murray (D)	WA	01/05/1993–
Kay Bailey Hutchison (R)	TX	06/14/1993–
Olympia Snowe (R)	ME	01/04/1995–
Susan Collins (R)	ME	01/07/1997–
Mary Landrieu (D)	LA	01/07/1997–
Blanche Lincoln (D)	AR	01/06/1999–
Maria Cantwell (D)	WA	01/03/2001–
Jean Carnahan (D)	MO	01/03/2001–11/23/2002
Hillary Rodham Clinton (D)	NY	01/03/2001–
Debbie Stabenow (D)	MI	01/03/2001–
Lisa Murkowski (R)	AK	12/20/2002–
Elizabeth Dole (R)	NC	01/07/2003–

Data from "Women in the United States Senate." Center for American Women and Politics.

Appendix E
Women Governors

The Twentieth Century

Governor and Party	State	Years of Service
Nellie Tayloe Ross (D)	WY	1925–1927
Miriam "Ma" Ferguson (D)	TX	1925–1927
		1933–1935
Lurleen Wallace (D)	AL	1967–1968
Ella Grasso (D)	CT	1975–1980
Dixie Lee Ray (D)	WA	1977–1981
Vesta Roy (R)	NH	1982–1983
Martha Layne Collins (D)	KY	1984–1987
Madeleine Kunin (D)	VT	1985–1991
Kay Orr (R)	NE	1987–1991
Rose Mofford (D)	AZ	1988–1991
Joan Finney (D)	KS	1991–1995
Ann Richards (D)	TX	1991–1995
Barbara Roberts (D)	OR	1991–1995
Christine Todd Whitman (R)	NJ	1994–2001
Jeanne Shaheen (D)	NH	1993–2003
Jane Dee Hull (R)	AZ	1997–2003
Nancy Hollister (R)	OH	1998–1999

Data from "History of Women Governors." Center for American Women and Politics.

Appendix F
Women Governors

The Twenty-first Century

Governor and Party	State	Years of Service
Christine Todd Whitman (R)	NJ	1994–2001
Jeanne Shaheen (D)	NH	1993–2003
Jane Dee Hull (R)	AZ	1997–2003
Jane Swift (R)	MA	2001–2003
Judy Martz (R)	MT	2001–2005
Ruth Ann Minner (D)	DE	2001–
Jennifer M. Granholm (D)	MI	2003–
Linda Lingle (R)	HI	2003–
Janet Napolitano (D)	AZ	2003–
Kathleen Sebelius (D)	KS	2003–
Olene Walker (R)	UT	2003–2005
Kathleen Blanco (D)	LA	2004–
M. Jodi Rell (R)	CT	2004–
Christine Gregoire (D)	WA	2005–
Sila Calderon (Pop. Dem.-PR)	Puerto Rico	2001–

Data from "History of Women Governors," Center for American Women and Politics, and "Statewide Elective Executive Women 2005," Center for American Women and Politics.

References

Abrams, Jim. "Maine Senator Has History of Being in the Middle of Things." *Associated Press State and Local Wire.* 11 Apr. 2003. *LexisNexis.* Linfield College Lib. 11 Aug. 2004. web.lexis-nexis.com/universe/.

Abrams, Lynn. *The Making of Modern Woman: Europe 1789–1918.* London: Pearson-Longman, 2002.

Aburdene, Patricia, and John Naisbitt. *Megatrends for Women.* New York: Villard, 1992.

Ackelsberg, Martha A. "Broadening the Study of Women's Participation." *Women and American Politics: New Questions, New Directions.* Ed. Susan J. Carroll. Oxford: Oxford University Press, 2003.

Addams, Jane. "Why Women Should Vote." *Ladies Home Journal.* 1909. Rpt. in *Jane Addams: A Centennial Reader.* New York: Macmillan, 1960.

Albright, Madeleine. *Madam Secretary: A Memoir.* New York: Miramax, 2003.

Allen, Jonathon. "How House Democrats Got Their Groove Back." *CQ Weekly* 14 June 2003. 22 May 2004. web5.epnet.com.

Alvarez, Lizette. "Feminine Mystique Grows in Senate." *New York Times* 7 Dec. 2000, late ed., sec. A: 30. *LexisNexis.* Linfield College Lib. 26 Oct. 2004. web.lexis-nexis.com/universe/.

American Women: Report of the President's Commission on the Status of Women. Washington, D.C.: U.S. Government Printing Office, 1963.

"And the Ferraro Phenomenon." *Washington Post* 20 July 1984, editorial: A20.

Anderson, Kathryn. "Steps to Political Equality: Woman Suffrage and Electoral Politics in the Lives of Emily Newell Blair, Anne Henrietta Martin, and Jeannette Rankin." *Frontiers* 18.1 (1997): 101–21.

"Arizona Gov. Wants to Open State Lobbying Office in Washington." *CongressDaily* 24 Feb. 2003. *Academic Search Premier.* Linfield College Lib. 11 Aug. 2004. web7.epnet.com/.

Arizona Governor Janet Napolitano. Office of Governor Napolitano. 2003. 14 Jan. 2003. www.governor.state.az.us/.

"Arizona Governor Vetoes Bill to Impose Waiting Period on Abortions." *Health & Medicine Week* 22 Mar. 2004. *NewsRX. Academic Search Premier.* Linfield College Lib. 11 Aug. 2004. web7.epnet.com/.

"Arizona's Drift to the Left." *Economist* 15 May 2004: 28. *Academic Search Elite.* Linfield College Lib. 11 Aug. 2004. web5.epnet.com/.

Aslakson, Barbara Jean. "Nellie Tayloe Ross: First Woman Governor." MA thesis, University of Wyoming, 1960.

"AZ: Debate Focuses on Taxes, Abortion." *Bulletin's Frontrunner.* Bulletin Broadfaxing Network. 23 Oct. 2002. *LexisNexis.* Linfield College Lib. 20 Jan. 2003. web.lexis-nexis .com/.

"AZ: Moderates, Women Credited with Napolitano Win." *Bulletin's Frontrunner.* Bulletin Broadfaxing Network. 20 Nov. 2002. *LexisNexis.* Linfield College Lib. 20 Jan. 2003. web.lexis-nexis.com/.

"AZ: Napolitano Opposes 24-Hour Waiting Period for Abortions." *Bulletin's Frontrunner.* Bulletin Broadfaxing Network. 24 Oct. 2002. *LexisNexis.* Linfield College Lib. 20 Jan. 2003. web.lexis-nexis.com/.

"AZ: Napolitano's Team Beginning to Take Shape." *Bulletin's Frontrunner.* Bulletin Broadfaxing Network. 13 Nov. 2002. *LexisNexis.* Linfield College Lib. 20 Jan. 2003. web .lexis-nexis.com/.

"Baldacci, Lee, and Pelosi are APHA's Legislators of the Year." *Nation's Health* 33.8 (n.d.). 17 Aug. 2004. web14.epnet.com/.

Baldauf, Scott. "'Volleyball Mom' Redefines N.H. Politics." *Christian Science Monitor* 24 Apr. 1997: 4. *LexisNexis.* Linfield College Lib. 26 Sept. 1999. web.lexis-nexis.com.

Baldwin, Tammy. "About Tammy." *Congresswoman Tammy Baldwin.* n.d. 13 Apr. 2004. tammybaldwin.house.gov/.

———. "Address to the 2004 National Democratic Convention." *2004 National Convention Official Site.* 26 July 2004. 27 July 2004. www.dems2004.org.

———. "Australian Free Trade Agreement." *Congresswoman Tammy Baldwin.* 14 July 2004. 27 July 2004. tammybaldwin.house.gov/.

———. "Baldwin Cosponsors Bipartisan Hate Crimes Legislation." Press Release. *Congresswoman Tammy Baldwin.* 27 Mar. 2001. 27 July 2004. tammybaldwin.house.gov/.

———. "Budget Special Order: Medicare and Medicaid Cuts." *Congresswoman Tammy Baldwin.* 7 Apr. 2003. 27 July 2004. tammybaldwin.house.gov/.

———. "Floor Remarks on Unborn Victims of Violence Act of 2003." *Cong. Rec.* 26 Feb. 2004. *Thomas.* Library of Congress. 27 July 2004. thomas.loc.gov.

———. "Harvey Milk and Tammy Baldwin." *Advocate* 15 Aug. 2000: 32. *Academic Search Premier.* Linfield College Lib. 15 Apr. 2004. web13.epnet.com.

———. "House Debate on Energy Legislation." *Congresswoman Tammy Baldwin.* 15 June 2004. 27 July 2004. tammybaldwin.house.gov/.

———. "House Floor Statement on H.R. 3313, the 'Marriage Protection Act.'" *Congresswoman Tammy Baldwin.* 22 July 2004. 27 July 2004. tammybaldwin.house.gov/.

———. "H.R. 4250, The American Jobs Creation Act of 2004." *Congresswoman Tammy Baldwin.* 17 June 2004. 27 July 2004. tammybaldwin.house.gov/.

———. "Iraq Special Order." *Congresswoman Tammy Baldwin*. 6 March 2003. 27 July 2004. tammybaldwin.house.gov/.

———. "Judiciary Committee Statement on H.R. 3313, the 'Marriage Protection Act.'" *Congresswoman Tammy Baldwin*. 14 July 2004. 27 July 2004. tammybaldwin.house.gov/.

———. "Press Conference on the Hate Crimes Provisions in the Senate Defense Authorization Bill." Press Release. *Congresswoman Tammy Baldwin*. 12 Sept. 2000. 27 July 2004. tammybaldwin.house.gov/.

———. "Remarks of Rep. Tammy Baldwin (D-WI) Entered into the Congressional Record in Honor of Memorial Day." *Congresswoman Tammy Baldwin*. 20 May 2004. 27 July 2004. tammybaldwin.house.gov/.

———. "Rep. Baldwin Receives Perfect Score from NAACP Legislative Report Card." Press Release. *Congresswoman Tammy Baldwin*. 9 Aug. 2002. 27 July 2004. tammybaldwin.house.gov/.

———. "Statement at Attorney General Ashcroft Hearing." *Congresswoman Tammy Baldwin*. 5 June 2003. 27 July 2004. tammybaldwin.house.gov/.

———. "Statement by Congresswoman Tammy Baldwin on Dairy Compacts." *Congresswoman Tammy Baldwin*. 4 Oct. 2001. 27 July 2004. tammybaldwin.house.gov/.

———. "Statement by Congresswoman Tammy Baldwin on H.J.R. 64, Authorization for the Use of Military Force." *Congresswoman Tammy Baldwin*. 14 Sept. 2001. 27 July 2004. tammybaldwin.house.gov/.

———. "Statement by Congresswoman Tammy Baldwin on HR 2586, Defense Authorization." *Congresswoman Tammy Baldwin*. 25 Sept. 2001. 27 July 2004. tammybaldwin.house.gov/.

———. "Statement by Congresswoman Tammy Baldwin on Special Order on H.R. 1343." *Congresswoman Tammy Baldwin*. 5 Dec. 2001. 10 Mar. 2004. tammybaldwin.house.gov/.

———. "Statement of Congresswoman Baldwin: 'Extend Unemployment Benefits Now.'" *Congresswoman Tammy Baldwin*. 8 Dec. 2003. 27 July 2004. tammybaldwin.house.gov/.

———. "Statement on Iraq Supplemental Appropriations Bill." *Congresswoman Tammy Baldwin*. 16 Oct. 2003. 27 July 2004. tammybaldwin.house.gov/.

———. "Statement on Supplemental Appropriations Bill." *Congresswoman Tammy Baldwin*. 3 Apr. 2003. 27 July 2004. tammybaldwin.house.gov/.

———. "Statement on Support for the Troops Resolution." *Congresswoman Tammy Baldwin*. 26 Mar. 2003. 27 July 2004. tammybaldwin.house.gov/.

———. "Statement on Use of Force Against Iraq for Congressional Record." *Congresswoman Tammy Baldwin*. 8 Oct. 2002. 27 July 2004. tammybaldwin.house.gov/.

"Barbara Boxer." *Congressional Quarterly Weekly Report* 16 Jan. 1993: 18. *Academic Search Premier*. Linfield College Lib. 10 Oct. 2004. web5.epnet.com/.

Barber, James David, and Barbara Kellerman, eds. *Women Leaders in American Politics*. Englewood Cliffs, NJ: Prentice-Hall, 1986.

Barone, Michael, and Richard E. Cohen, eds. *The Almanac of American Politics 2004*. Washington, D.C.: National Journal, 2003.

Barone, Michael, Richard E. Cohen, and Charles E. Cook, Jr., eds. *The Almanac of American Politics 2002*. Washington, D.C.: National Journal, 2001.

Barovick, Harriet, and Laura Laughlin. "Party of Five." *Time* 18 Jan. 1999: 35. *Academic Search Elite*. Linfield College Lib. 11 Aug. 2004. web7.epnet.com/.

Barron, James. "Shirley Chisholm, 80, Is Dead; 'Unbossed' Pioneer in Congress." *New York Times* 3 Jan. 2005: B5.

Beard, Patricia. *Growing Up Republican: Christie Whitman: The Politics of Character*. New York: HarperCollins, 1996.

Berman, Laura. "In Posthumus' Attempt to Appeal to Everyman, He's Neglected Women." *Detroit News*. 27 Oct. 2002. 4 Nov. 2002. www.detnews.com.2002/metro/0210/ 27/b01-623297.htm.

Beyle, Thad, and Lynn Muchmore. *Being Governor*. Durham, NC: Duke University Press, 1983.

Bhabha, Homi K. *The Location of Culture*. London: Routledge, 1994.

Biesecker, Barbara. "Coming to Terms with Recent Attempts to Write Women into the History of Rhetoric." *Philosophy and Rhetoric* 25.2 (1992): 140–61.

Biggert, Judy. "Biggert Opposes Court-Stripping Legislation." *Office of the Congresswoman*. 22 July 2004. 18 Aug. 2004. judyBiggert.house.gov/News.asp?FormMode=detail& ID=439.

———. "Floor Statement on the House Resolution Commending Afghan Women." *Office of the Congresswoman*. 24 Nov. 2003. 17 Aug. 2004. judybiggert.house.gov/News.asp ?FormMode=Detail&ID=390.

———. "Judy's Latest Statement Concerning Iraq." *Office of the Congresswoman*. 24 Mar. 2003. 17 Aug. 2004. judybiggert.house.gov/.

———. "Judy's Remarks at the Bolingbrook Citizen Police Academy Commencement Ceremony." *Office of the Congresswoman*. 11 May 2004. 17 Aug. 2004. judybiggert.house .gov/News.asp?FormMode=Detail&ID=422.

———. "Judy's Remarks to the Hinsdale Rotary Club." Office of the Congresswoman. 3 June 2004. 17 Aug. 2004. judybiggert.house.gov/.

———. "Meet Judy: U.S. Representative Judy Biggert." *Office of the Congresswoman*. n.d. 17 Aug. 2004. judybiggert.house.gov/bio.asp.

———. "War on Terrorism and Homeland Security." *Office of the Congresswoman*. 5 May 2002. 17 Aug. 2004. judybiggert.house.gov/.

Billings, Erin P. "Female Firsts Mark Inauguration." *Independent Record* [Helena, MT] 3 Jan. 2001: 10A.

Bingham, Clara. *Women on the Hill: Changing the Culture of Congress*. New York: Times Books– Random House, 1997.

Blanco, Kathleen Babineaux. "Address to the Louisiana Economic Development Confer- ence." *Office of the Governor*. 24 Mar. 2003. 2 July 2004. www.gov.louisiana.gov/ speeches_detail.asp?id=67.

———. "Governor Blanco Addresses the LA Center for Women and Government." *Office of the Governor*. 13 Mar. 2004. 2 July 2004. www.gov.Louisiana.gov/speeches_detail .asp?id=59.

———. "Governor Blanco Remarks to Greater Orleans Inc. Luncheon." *Office of the Gover- nor*. 21 Jan. 2004. 2 July 2004. www.gov.louisiana.gov/speeches_detail.asp?id=54.

———."Governor Blanco's Address to the First Extraordinary Session of the 2004 Legislature." *Office of the Governor.* 7 Mar. 2004. 2 July 2004. www.gov.louisiana.gov/ speeches_detail.asp?id=57.

———. "Inaugural Address." *Office of the Governor.* 12 Jan. 2004. 2 July 2004. www.gov .louisiana.gov/speeches_detail.asp?id=53.

———. "Kathleen Babineaux Blanco." *Office of the Governor.* n.d. 2 July 2004. www.gov .state.la.us/biography.asp.

———. "Speech to Public Affairs Research Council of Louisiana Health Care Conference." *Office of the Governor.* 23 Apr. 2004. 2 July 2004. http:/www.gov.louisiana.gov/ speechesdetail.asp?id=72.

———. "State of the State Address." *Office of the Governor.* 29 Mar. 2004. 2 July 2004. www.gov.louisiana/speeches_detail.asp?id=68.

———. "Xavier University Address." *Office of the Governor.* 8 May 2004. 2 July 2004. www.gov.louisiana/gov/speeches_detail.asp?id=76.

Blankenship, Jane. "Geraldine Ann Ferraro." *Women Public Speakers in the United States, 1925–1993: A Bio-Critical Sourcebook.* Ed. Karlyn Kohrs Campbell. Westport, CT: Greenwood, 1994.

Blankenship, Jane, and Deborah C. Robson. "A 'Feminine Style' in Women's Political Discourse: An Exploratory Essay." *Communication Quarterly* 43.2 (1995): 353–66.

Bookmen, Ann, and Sandra Morgen. *Women and the Politics of Empowerment.* Philadelphia: Temple University Press, 1988.

Bowman, Darcia Harris. "Arizona Governor Unveils Early-Education Fund." *Education Week* 7 Apr. 2004. *Academic Search Elite.* Linfield College Lib. 11 Aug. 2004. web13 .epnet.com/.

Boxer, Barbara. "The California Wild Heritage Act of 2003 (S.1555)." *Official Website of U.S. Senator Barbara Boxer.* n.d. 12 Aug. 2004. boxer.senate.gov/senate/b_1555.cfm.

———. "Floor Remarks on Earth Day." *Cong. Rec.* 21 Apr. 2004. *Thomas.* Library of Congress. 10 Oct. 2004. thomas.loc.gov/.

———. "Floor Remarks on FEDEX Corporation and Hybrid Vehicles." *Cong. Rec.* 23 May 2003. *Thomas.* Library of Congress. 12 Aug. 2004. thomas.loc.gov/.

———. "Floor Remarks on National Day to Prevent Teen Pregnancy 2004." *Cong. Rec.* 4 May 2004. *Thomas.* Library of Congress. 12 Aug. 2004. thomas.loc.gov/.

———. "Floor Speech on Congressional Budget for the United States Government for Fiscal Year 2005." *Cong. Rec.* 11 Mar. 2004. *Thomas.* Library of Congress. 10 Oct. 2004. thomas.loc.gov/.

———. "Floor Speech on Economic Reality." *Cong. Rec.* 31 Mar. 2004. *Thomas.* Library of Congress. 18 Aug. 2004. thomas.loc.gov/.

———. "Floor Statement on a Bill to Improve Seaport Security: S.2240." *Cong. Rec.* 25 Mar. 2004. *Thomas.* Library of Congress. 18 Aug. 2004. thomas.loc.gov/.

———. "Floor Statement on Freedom of Choice Act." *Cong. Rec.* 22 Jan. 2004. *Thomas.* Library of Congress. 10 Oct. 2004. thomas.loc.gov/.

———. "Floor Statement on Jumpstart Our Business Strength (JOBS) Act." *Cong. Rec.* 5 May 2004. *Thomas.* Library of Congress. 18 Aug. 2004. thomas.loc.gov/.

———. "Floor Statement on Jumpstart Our Business Strength (JOBS) Act—Continued." *Cong. Rec.* 23 Mar. 2004. *Thomas.* Library of Congress. 10 Oct. 2004. thomas.loc.gov/.

———. "Floor Statement on National Defense Authorization Act for Fiscal Year 2005." *Cong. Rec.* 17 June 2004. *Thomas.* Library of Congress. 10 Oct. 2004. thomas.loc.gov/.

———. "Floor Statement on Partial-Birth Abortion Ban Act of 2003—Conference Report." *Cong. Rec.* 21 Oct. 2003. *Thomas.* Library of Congress. 12 Aug. 2004. thomas.loc.gov/.

———. "Floor Statement on Protection of Lawful Commerce in Arms Act—Motion to Proceed." *Cong. Rec.* 26 Feb. 2004. *Thomas.* Library of Congress. 18 Aug. 2004. thomas.loc.gov/.

———. "Floor Statement on S.2032." *Cong. Rec.* 27 Jan. 2004. *Thomas.* Library of Congress. 10 Oct. 2004. thomas.loc.gov/.

———. "Floor Statement on S.2166." *Cong. Rec.* 4 Mar. 2004. *Thomas.* Library of Congress. 18 Aug. 2004. thomas.loc.gov/.

———. "Floor Statement on Unborn Victims of Violence Act of 2004." *Cong. Rec.* 25 Mar. 2004. *Thomas.* Library of Congress. 13 Aug. 2004. thomas.loc.gov/.

———. "Senator Boxer's Biography." *Official Website of U.S. Senator Barbara Boxer.* n.d. 4 Aug. 2004. boxer.senate.gov/about/index/cfm.

———. "Speech Given to the California Legislative Symposium of the Planning and Conservation League, January 10, 1992." *California Women Speak: Speeches of California Women in Public Office.* Ed. Doris Earnshaw. Davis, CA: Alta Vista, 1994.

———. "Statement by U.S. Senator Barbara Boxer on the U.S. Commission on Ocean Policy Report." *Official Website of U.S. Senator Barbara Boxer.* 20 Sept. 2004. 10 Oct. 2004. boxer.senate.gov/news/.

———. "Statement of Senator Barbara Boxer: EPW Committee Hearing on DOD's Readiness and Range Preservation Initiative." 9 July 2002. 12 Oct. 2004. epw.senate.gov/107th/box_070902.htm.

———. "Statement on the 9/11 Commission Report." *Official Website of U.S. Senator Barbara Boxer.* 22 July 2004. 10 Oct. 2004. boxer.senate.gov/news/.

———. "Testimony before the Senate Committee on Governmental Affairs on the Boxer-Collins Bill: Elevation of the Environmental Protection Agency to a Cabinet-Level Department." Committee on Governmental Affairs. The United States Senate. 24 July 2001. 12 Aug. 2004. www.senate.gov/~gov_affairs/072401_boxer.htm.

"Boxer, Barbara." *Current Biography Yearbook.* Ed. Judith Graham. New York: H. W. Wilson, 1994. 63–66.

Boxer, Barbara, with Nicole Boxer. *Strangers in the Senate: Politics and the New Revolution of Women in America.* Washington, D.C.: National Press, 1994.

Braden, Waldo, ed. *Representative American Speeches: 1971–1972.* New York: H. W. Wilson, 1972.

———, ed. *Representative American Speeches: 1972–1973.* New York: H. W. Wilson, 1973.

"Braun for Senate—with Big Reservations." *Crain's Chicago Business* 19 Oct. 1992, Opinion: 14. *LexisNexis.* Linfield College Lib. 13 Nov. 2004. calvin.linfield.edu:2092/universe/.

Brehm, Sharon S., ed. *Seeing Female: Social Roles and Personal Lives*. Contributions in Women's Studies Ser. New York: Greenwood, 1988.

Brill, Alida, ed. *A Rising Public Voice: Women in Politics Worldwide*. New York: Feminist Press, 1995.

Brock, David. "Who Is Janet Napolitano?" *American Spectator* Oct. 1993: 20–26. *Academic Search Elite*. Linfield College Lib. 11 Aug. 2004. web7.epnet.com/.

Broder, David S. "New Hampshire's Year of the Woman." *Washington Post* 8 Jan. 1997, final ed., Op-ed sec.: A25. *LexisNexis*. Linfield College Lib. 26 Sept. 1999. web.lexis-nexis.com.

Brown, D. E., and C. M. Gardetto. "Representing Hillary Rodham Clinton: Gender, Meaning, and News Media." *Gender, Politics, and Communication*. Ed. Annabelle Sreberney and Lisbet van Zoonen. Creskill, NY: Hampton, 1996.

Brown-Waite, Ginny. "At Last, Concurrent Receipt Is a Reality." Column 27. *Congresswoman Ginny Brown-Waite*. 17 Oct. 2003. 24 Sept. 2004. www.house.gov/.

———. "August Recess: A Time to Hear from You." Column 22. *Congresswoman Ginny Brown-Waite*. 5 Sept. 2003. 24 Sept. 2004. www.house.gov/.

———. "Biography." *Congresswoman Ginny Brown-Waite*. n.d. 2 Oct. 2004. www.house.gov/brown-waite/biography.htm.

———. "Ensuring Timely Access to VA Healthcare." Column 15. *Congresswoman Ginny Brown-Waite*. 6 June 2003. 24 Sept. 2004. www.house.gov/.

———. "Fighting for America's Veterans." *Cong. Rec.* 4 Mar. 2004. *Thomas*. Library of Congress. 24 Sept. 2004. thomas.loc.gov/.

———. "The FY 2003 Budget." Column 2. *Congresswoman Ginny Brown-Waite*. 6 Feb. 2003. 24 Sept. 2004. www.house.gov/.

———. "The FY 2005 Budget: Fulfilling Our Needs while Restoring Fiscal Discipline." Column 34. *Congresswoman Ginny Brown-Waite*. 26 Mar. 2004. 4 Sept. 2004. www.house.gov/.

———. "Honoring Our Veterans." Column 30. *Congresswoman Ginny Brown-Waite*. 7 Nov. 2003. 24 Sept. 2004. www.house.gov/.

———. "House Floor Remarks on Changing Medicare." *Cong. Rec.* 4 May 2004. *Thomas*. Library of Congress. 24 Sept. 2004. thomas.loc.gov/.

———. "House Floor Remarks on Concurrent Resolution on the Budget for Fiscal Year 2005." *Cong. Rec.* 24 Mar. 2004. *Thomas*. Library of Congress. 24 Sept. 2004. thomas.loc.gov/.

———. "House Floor Remarks on Conference Report on S. Con. Res. 95, Concurrent Resolution on the Budget for Fiscal Year 2005." *Cong. Rec.* 19 May 2004. *Thomas*. Library of Congress. 24 Sept. 2004. thomas.loc.gov/.

———. "House Floor Remarks on Increasing Maximum Amount of Loan Guaranty Affairs Under Home Loan Guaranty Program of the Department of Veterans Affairs." *Cong. Rec.* 23 June 2004. *Thomas*. Library of Congress. 24 Sept. 2004. thomas.loc.gov/.

———. "House Floor Remarks on Unborn Victims of Violence Act of 2003." *Cong. Rec.* 26 Feb. 2004. *Thomas*. Library of Congress. 24 Sept. 2004. thomas.loc.gov/.

———. "House Floor Remarks on Unscrupulous Tactics on Military Bases." *Cong. Rec.* 21 Sept. 2004. *Thomas.* Library of Congress. 24 Sept. 2004. thomas.loc.gov/.

———. "House Floor Statement on Spending Control Act of 2004." *Cong. Rec.* 24 June 2004. *Thomas.* Library of Congress. 24 Sept. 2004. thomas.loc.gov/.

———. "My Goals as Your Representative." Column 1. *Congresswoman Ginny Brown-Waite.* 31 Jan. 2003. 4 Sept. 2004. www.house.gov/.

———. "Our Veterans, Our Troops, Our Promise." Column 14. *Congresswoman Ginny Brown-Waite.* 23 May 2003. 4 Sept. 2004. www.house.gov/.

———. "Praise for the President's Jobs and Growth Tax Relief Package." *Cong. Rec.* 22 June 2004. *Thomas.* Library of Congress. 24 Sept. 2004. thomas.loc.gov/.

———. "Righting a Wrong for Wounded Servicemen." Column 24. *Congresswoman Ginny Brown-Waite.* 26 Sept. 2003. 24 Sept. 2004. www.house.gov/.

———. "State of the Union: Outlining the Agenda for a Safe and Prosperous 2004." Column 32. *Congresswoman Ginny Brown-Waite.* 23 Jan. 2004. 24 Sept. 2004. www.house.gov/.

———. "Supporting Our Troops: America's Top Priority." Column 9. *Congresswoman Ginny Brown-Waite.* 4 Apr. 2003. 4 Sept. 2004. www.house.gov/.

———. "The Upcoming Budget and a Call for Sound Immigration Reform." Column 33. *Congresswoman Ginny Brown-Waite.* 30 Jan. 2004. 24 Sept. 2004. www.house.gov/.

———. "Wrangling in the Federal Bureaucracy." Column 28. *Congresswoman Ginny Brown-Waite.* 24 Oct. 2003. 24 Sept. 2004. www.house.gov/.

Buker, Eloise A. *Talking Feminist Politics: Conversations on Law, Science, and the Postmodern.* Lanham, MD: Rowman & Littlefield, 1999.

Bull, Chilis. "The View from the Hill." *Advocate* 30 Apr. 2000: 13–15. *Academic Search Premier.* 15 Apr. 2004. web13.epnet.com.

Bunch, Charlotte. "A Broom of One's Own: Views on the Women's Liberation Program." *The New Women.* Ed. Joanne Cooke, Charlotte Bunch-Weeks, and Robin Morgan. Indianapolis: Bobbs-Merrill, 1970. Rpt. in Charlotte Bunch, *Passionate Politics.* New York: St. Martin's, 1987. 27–45.

———. *Passionate Politics.* New York: St. Martin's, 1987.

Burrell, Barbara. *Public Opinion, the First Ladyship, and Hillary Rodham Clinton.* Rev. ed. New York: Routledge, 2001.

Burrell, Barabara C. *A Woman's Place Is in the House: Campaigning for Congress in the Feminist Era.* Ann Arbor, MI: University of Michigan Press, 1997.

Butler, Judith, and Joan W. Scott, eds. *Feminists Theorize the Political.* New York: Routledge, 1992.

Bysiewicz, Susan. *Ella: A Biography of Governor Ella Grasso.* Old Saybrook, CT: Peregrine, 1984.

Cahn, Richard. "Senator from Oregon." *Saturday Evening Post* 7 Jan. 1961: 24–25.

Calhoun, Craig, ed. *Habermas and the Public Sphere.* Cambridge, MA: MIT Press, 1992.

Campbell, Karlyn Kohrs. Introduction. *Women Public Speakers in the United States, 1800–1925: A Bio-critical Sourcebook.* Ed. Karlyn Kohrs Campbell. Westport, CT: Greenwood, 1993.

———. *Man Cannot Speak for Her: A Critical Study of Early Feminist Rhetoric.* Vol. 1. New York: Greenwood, 1989.

——, ed. *Women Public Speakers in the United States, 1800–1925: A Bio-critical Sourcebook*. Westport, CT: Greenwood, 1994.

——, ed. *Women Public Speakers in the United States, 1925–1993: A Bio-critical Sourcebook*. Westport, CT: Greenwood, 1994.

Campbell, Karlyn Kohrs, and E. Claire Jerry. "Woman and Speaker: A Conflict in Roles." *Seeing Female: Social Roles and Personal Lives*. Ed. Sharon S. Brehm. Contributions in Women's Studies Ser. New York: Greenwood, 1988.

Canon, David. T., and Paul S. Herrnson. "First Things First." *Campaigns and Elections* 20.4 (1999): 50–53. *Academic Search Premier*. 15 Apr. 2004. web19.epnet.com/.

Cantor, Dorothy, and Toni Bernay. *Women in Power: The Secrets of Leadership*. Boston: Houghton Mifflin, 1992.

Cantwell, Maria. "About Maria." *Senator Maria Cantwell Website*. n.d. 19 April 2004. cantwell.senate.gov/about/index.html.

——. "Bush Administration Declares Support for Cantwell's Upper White Salmon and Scenic Rivers Act." News Release. *Senator Maria Cantwell Website*. 21 July 2004. 13 Aug. 2004. cantwell.senate.gov/news/releases/.

——. "Cantwell Introduces Legislation to Address Critical Shortage of Health Care Professionals." News Release. *Senator Maria Cantwell Website*. 18 June 2004. 13 Aug. 2004. cantwell.senate.gov/news/releases/.

——. "Cantwell to Senate Committee Today: End Mail Order Bride Abuse." Testimony before Foreign Relations Committee. News Release. *Senator Maria Cantwell Website*. 13 July 2004. 13 Aug. 2004. cantwell.senate.gov/news/releases/.

——. "Democratic Response to the President's Radio Address." 7 Dec. 2002. *FDCH Political Transcripts*. FDCH e-Media. 26 Oct. 2004. web.lexis-nexis.com/universe/.

——. "Floor Remarks on 9/11 Commission Report." *Cong. Rec.* 22 July 2004. *Thomas*. Library of Congress. 18 Aug. 2004. thomas.loc.gov/.

——. "Floor Remarks on a Bill to Amend the Internal Revenue Code of 1986: S.2972." *Cong. Rec.* 9 Oct. 2004. *Thomas*. Library of Congress. 26 Oct. 2004. thomas.loc.gov/.

——. "Floor Remarks on Extension of the Temporary Extended Unemployment Compensation Act of 2002." *Cong. Rec.* 26 Feb. 2004. *Thomas*. Library of Congress. 18 Aug. 2004. thomas.loc.gov/.

——. "Floor Remarks on Sales Tax Deduction for Individual States." *Cong. Rec.* 11 Oct. 2004. *Thomas*. Library of Congress. 26 Oct. 2004. thomas.loc.gov/.

——. "Floor Remarks on Stand-Alone Reliability." *Cong. Rec.* 25 Mar. 2004. *Thomas*. Library of Congress. 18 Aug. 2004. thomas.loc.gov/.

——. "Floor Remarks on the Bunning Amendment to the Energy Employee Occupational Illness Compensation Program." *Cong. Rec.* 16 June 2004. *Thomas*. Library of Congress. 26 Oct. 2004. thomas.loc.gov/.

——. "Floor Remarks on the Confronting Methamphetamines Act of 2004." *Cong. Rec.* 7 Oct. 2004. *Thomas*. Library of Congress. 26 Oct. 2004. thomas.loc.gov/.

——. "Floor Statement on Electric Reliability Act of 2004: S.2015." *Cong. Rec.* 21 Jan. 2004. *Thomas*. Library of Congress. 18 Aug. 2004. thomas.loc.gov/.

——. "Floor Statement on Electricity Grid and Reliability." *Cong. Rec.* 22 Apr. 2004. *Thomas.* Library of Congress. 18 Aug. 2004. thomas.loc.gov/.

——. "Floor Statement on Energy Reliability." *Cong. Rec.* 15 July 2004. *Thomas.* Library of Congress. 18 Aug. 2004. thomas.loc.gov/.

——. "Floor Statement on Extension of Unemployment Benefits." *Cong. Rec.* 24 Mar. 2004. *Thomas.* Library of Congress. 26 Oct. 2004. thomas.loc.gov/.

——. "Floor Statement on Healthy Mothers and Healthy Babies Access to Care Act of 2003—Motion to Proceed." 24 Feb. 2004. *Thomas.* Library of Congress. 18 Aug. 2004. thomas.loc.gov/.

——. "Floor Statement on Jumpstart Our Business Strength (JOBS) Act. *Cong. Rec.* 5 May 2004. *Thomas.* Library of Congress. 18 Aug. 2004. thomas.loc.gov/.

——. "Floor Statement on Public Health Service Act: S.2491." *Cong. Rec.* 2 June 2004. *Thomas.* Library of Congress. 26 Oct. 2004. thomas.loc.gov/.

——. "Funding for Cantwell's Center of Excellence Gets Final Approval." News Release. *Senator Maria Cantwell Website.* 29 Jan. 2004. 13 Aug. 2004. cantwell.senate.gov/news/releases/.

——. "The Road to the United States Senate." *Cantwell 2000 Campaign Website.* 4 Aug. 2000. 4 Aug. 2004. www.cantwell.com/.

——. "Sen. Cantwell Statement on 9/11 Commission Report." News Release. *Senator Maria Cantwell Website.* 22 July 2004. 13 Aug. 2004. cantwell.senate.gov/news/releases/.

——. "Sen. Cantwell's Floor Statement on Enron Tapes." News Release. *Senator Maria Cantwell Website.* 2 June 2004. 13 Aug. 2004. cantwell.senate.gov/news/releases/.

——. "Sen. Cantwell's Floor Statement on Proposed Reclassification of Nuclear Waste." *Senator Maria Cantwell Website.* 20 May 2004. 13 Aug. 2004. cantwell.senate.gov/news/releases/.

Caraway, Hattie. "Floor Statement on Antilynching Bill." *Cong. Rec.* 13 Jan. 1938: 430–42.

——. "Floor Statement on Federal Aid to Public Education." *Cong. Rec.* 18 Oct. 1943: 8410–11.

——. "Floor Statement on Repeal of Poll Tax." *Cong. Rec.* May 1944: 4317.

——. "The Lend-Lease Bill." Radio Address, 1941. *From Megaphones to Microphones: Speeches of American Women, 1920–1960.* Sandra J. Sarkela, Susan Mallon Ross, and Margaret A. Lowe. Westport, CT: Praeger, 2003.

——. *Silent Hattie Speaks: The Personal Journal of Senator Hattie Caraway.* Ed. Diane D. Kincaid. Contributions to Women's Studies 9. Westport, CT: Greenwood, 1979.

Carney, Dan, and Rebecca Carr. "Diana Degette, D-Colo. (1)." *Congressional Quarterly Weekly* 54.45 (9 Nov. 1996): 27. *Academic Search Elite.* Linfield College Lib. 12 Aug. 2004. web9.epnet.com/.

Carroll, Susan J. "Women in State Government: Historical Overview and Current Trends." *The Book of the States.* Lexington, KY: The Council of State Governments, 2004.

——., ed. *The Impact of Women in Public Office.* Bloomington, IN: Indiana University Press, 2001.

——., ed. *Women and American Politics: New Questions, New Directions.* Oxford: Oxford University Press, 2003.

Carruth, Reba, and Vivian Jenkins Nelsen. "Shirley Chisholm: Woman of Complexity, Conscience, and Compassion." *Women Leaders in Contemporary U.S. Politics*. Ed. Frank P. Le Veness and Jane P. Sweeney. Boulder, CO: Lynne Rienner, 1987.

Center for American Women in Politics. Eagleton Institute of Politics. New Brunswick, NJ: Rutgers University Press, 1995–2005. www.rci.rutgers.edu/~cawp.

Chamberlin, Hope. *A Minority of Members: Women in the U.S. Congress*. New York: Praeger, 1973.

Chesler, Ellen. *Woman of Valor: Margaret Sanger and the Birth Control Movement in America*. New York: Simon and Schuster, 1992.

Chisholm, Shirley. "Economic Injustice in America Today." *Representative American Speeches*. Ed. Waldo W. Braden. New York: Wilson, 1972. 28–36.

———. "Economic Justice for Women." *The Good Fight*. Shirley Chisholm. New York: Harper and Row, 1973. 188–92.

———. "Equal Rights for Women." *Cong. Rec.* Extensions of Remarks. 21 May 1969: 13380–81.

———. "Floor Statement on the Equal Rights Amendment." *Cong. Rec.* 6 Oct. 1971: 35314–15.

———. "Floor Statement on the House Joint Resolution 264: The Equal Rights Amendment." *Cong. Rec.* 10 Aug. 1970: 28028–29.

———. *The Good Fight*. New York: Harper and Row, 1973.

———. "It Is Time to Reassess Our National Priorities." *Representative American Speeches: 1968–1969*. Ed. Lester Thonssen. New York: Wilson, 1969. 69–72.

———. "Progress through Understanding." *Cong. Rec.* Extension of Remarks. 16 June 1969: 15972–73.

———. "Statement on the Equal Rights Amendment." *Cong. Rec.* 5 Oct. 1971–13 Oct. 1971: 5314–15.

———. *Unbought and Unbossed*. New York: Avon, 1970.

———. "Women in Politics." *Representative American Speeches, 1972–1973*. Ed. Waldo Braden. New York: Wilson, 1973. 80–89.

"Christine Todd Whitman." Thomas Gale Resources. 1997. 3 Nov. 2004. www.galegroup .com/free_resources/whm/bio/whitman_c.htm.

Clift, Eleanor. "Jennifer Granholm: Brainy, Blond, and Ready to Rumble." *NewsWeek Online*. 6 Jan. 2003. 17 Jan. 2003. www.msnbc.Com/news/85073.asp?cpI=I.

Clift, Eleanor, and Tom Brazaitis. *Madam President: Women Blazing the Leadership Trail*. New York: Routledge, 2003.

Clinton, Hillary Rodham. "Addressing the National Security Challenges of Our Time: Fighting Terror and the Spread of Weapons of Mass Destruction." *Office of Senator Hillary Rodham Clinton.* 25 Feb. 2004. 24 Mar. 2004. clinton.senate.gov/~clinton/ speeches/2004302428.html.

———. "Floor Remarks of Senator Hillary Rodham Clinton on the 2002 Federal Budget." *Office of Senator Hillary Rodham Clinton*. 15 Feb. 2001. 16 June 2003. clinton .senate.gov/~clinton.speeches/010215.html.

———. "Floor Speech of Senator Hillary Rodham Clinton on S.J. Res. 45, A Resolution to Authorize the Use of United States Armed Forces Against Iraq." *Office of Senator*

Hillary Rodham Clinton. 10 Oct. 2002. 16 June 2003. clinton.senate.gov/~clinton/speeches/iraq_101002.htm.

———. "Floor Statement of Senator Hillary Rodham Clinton on Medicare/Prescription Drug Legislation." *Office of Senator Hillary Rodham Clinton.* 19 Nov. 2003. 24 Mar. 2004. clinton. senate.gov/~clinton/speeches/2003B21712.html.

———. "Floor Statement of Senator Hillary Rodham Clinton on Medicare Prescription Drug Proposal." *Office of Senator Hillary Rodham Clinton.* 20 June 2003. 24 Mar. 2004. clinton.senate.gov/~clinton/speeches/2003808703.html.

———. "Floor Statement of Senator Hillary Rodham Clinton on the Final Vote on H.R. 1." *Office of Senator Hillary Rodham Clinton.* 25 Nov. 2003. 24 Mar. 2004. clinton.senate.gov/~clinton.speeches/2003B25A30.html.

———. *Living History.* New York: Simon and Schuster, 2003.

———. "New American Strategies for Security and Peace." *Office of Senator Hillary Rodham Clinton.* 29 Oct. 2003. 24 March 2004. clinton.Senate.gov/~clinton/speeches/2003A29A31.html.

———. "Remarks of Senator Hillary Rodham Clinton: Class Day, Yale University." *Office of Senator Hillary Rodham Clinton.* 20 May 2001. 16 June 2003. clinton.senate.gov/~clinton/speeches/010520.html.

———. "Remarks of Senator Hillary Rodham Clinton to the American Society of Newspaper Editors." *Office of Senator Hillary Rodham Clinton.* 5 Apr. 2001. 16 June 2003. clinton.senate.gov/~clinton/speeches/010405.html.

———. "Remarks of Senator Hillary Rodham Clinton to the Council of Foreign Relations." *Office of Senator Hillary Rodham Clinton.* 15 Dec. 2003. 24 Mar. 2004. clinton.senate.gov/~clinton/speeches/2003C16B05.html.

———. "Statement of Hillary Rodham Clinton on AmeriCorps Funding Crisis." *Office of Senator Hillary Rodham Clinton.* 31 July 2003. 24 March 2004. clinton.senate.gov/~clinton.speeches/2003808655.htm.

———. "Statement of Senator Hillary Rodham Clinton, Schumer-Clinton Amendment to the Budget, Senate Floor." *Office of Senator Hillary Rodham Clinton.* 20 Mar. 2003. 16 June 2003. clinton.senate.gov/~clinton/speeches/2003411609.html.

Clinton, William J. "Remarks at a Reception Honoring Senator Barbara Boxer in Los Angeles." *Weekly Compilation of Presidential Documents.* 2 Nov. 1998. *Ebsco Host,* Linfield College Lib. 10 Oct. 2004. web13.epnet.com/.

———. "Remarks Honoring Barbara A. Mikulski." *Weekly Compilation of Presidential Documents.* 13 May 1998. 8 May 2004. web13.epnet.com/.

Cloud, Dana L. "The Rhetoric of Family Values: Scapegoating, Utopia, and the Privatization of Social Responsibility." *Western Journal of Communication* 62 (1998): 387–410.

Cloud, David S., and Phillip A. Davis. "Barbara Boxer, D-Calif." *Congressional Quarterly Weekly Report* 7 Nov. 1992: 14. *Academic Search Premier.* Linfield College Lib. 10 Oct. 2004. web5.epnet.com/.

Clymer, Adam. "In 2002, Woman's Place May Be the Statehouse." *New York Times* 15 Apr. 2002, politics sec.: n.pag. *New York Times on the Web.* 8 May 2002. www.nytimes.com/2002/.

Cohen, Cathy J., Kathleen B. Jones, and Joan C. Tronto, eds. *Women Transforming Politics: An Alternative Reader*. New York: New York University Press, 1997.

Cohen, Richard E. "Pelosi's Fast Start." *National Journal* 22 Feb. 2003. 22 May 2004. web1.epnet.com/.

———. "Pelosi's Fixed Path." *National Journal* 24 May 2003. 22 May 2004. web1.epnet.com/.

Cohn, Jonathan. "Jennifer Granholm and the New Woman Candidate." *New Republic* 8 Oct. 2002. 4 Nov. 2002. www.tnr.com.Mhtml?i=20021014&s=cohn101402.

Collins, Gail. "Why the Women Are Fading Away." *New York Times* 25 Oct. 1998, late ed., sec. 6: 54. *LexisNexis*. Linfield College Lib. 26 Sept. 1999. www.lexis-nexis.com.

"Colorado Senator's Food Inspection Votes Called into Question." *Denver Post* 26 July 2002: n.pag. *Academic Search Elite*. Linfield College Lib. 12 Aug. 2004. web9.epnet.com/.

Condit, Celeste M., and John Louis Lucaites. *Crafting Equality: America's Anglo-African Word*. Chicago: University of Chicago Press, 1993.

Condon, Lee. "Win Some, Lose Some." *Advocate* 19 Dec. 2000: 29–30. *Academic Search Premier*. Linfield College Lib. 15 Apr. 2004. web13.epnet.com/.

"Congressional Diabetes Caucus Supports Initiative to Lower Diabetes Risk by Monitoring A1C Levels." *PR Newswire Online* 14 Nov. 2002. *LexisNexis*. Linfield College Lib. 12 Aug. 2004. web.lexis-nexis.com/universe/.

"Congresswoman Calls for Investigation of Qwest's Audit Committee." *Denver Post* 26 Sept. 2002. *Ebsco Host*. Linfield College Lib. 12 Aug. 2004. web0.epnet.com/.

Conniff, Ruth. "Fading Passion." *Progressive* Aug. 2003:12–13. *Academic Search Premier*. 15 Apr. 2004. web13.epnet.com/.

———. "Tammy Baldwin." *Progressive* Jan. 1999: 64–68. 24 Apr. 2004. www.progressive.org/baldwin9901.htm.

"Contraceptive Coverage Edges Closer to Reality." *Nation's Health* 28.8 (Sept. 1998): 1–2. *Ebsco Host*. Linfield College Lib. 11 Aug. 2004. web3.epnet.com/.

Conway, M. Margaret, Gertrude A. Steuernagel, and David W. Ahern. *Women and Political Participation: Cultural Change in the Political Arena*. Washington, D.C.: Congressional Quarterly, 1997.

Cook, Charlie. "As Turnovers Show, It's a Lousy Time to Be Governor." *National Journal* 22 Nov. 2003. 2 July 2004. web20.epnet.com/Citation.asp?tb=1&_ug=sid60BAC0DEDF071%2D48AD%2DA2.

Cook, Elizabeth Adell, Sue Thomas, and Clyde Wilcox, eds. *The Year of the Woman: Myths and Realities*. Boulder, CO: Westview, 1994.

Cook, Jeanne F. "Winning Isn't Everything: Jeannette Rankin's Views on War." *AFFILIA* 6.4 (1991): 92–104.

Cook, Rebecca. "High-tech Millionaire Maria Cantwell Kicks Off Senate Campaign." *Associated Press State and Local Wire*. 5 May 2000. *LexisNexis*. Linfield College Lib. 26 Oct. 2004. web.lexis-nexis.com/universe/.

———. "Recount Swings Wash. Race." *Rocky Mountain News* [Denver, CO] 23 Dec. 2004: 38A.

Cook, Rhodes, and Alan Greenblatt. "Diana DeGette." *Congressional Quarterly Weekly Report* 55.1 (4 Jan. 1997): 52–53. *Academic Search Elite.* Linfield College Lib. 12 Aug. 2004. web9.com/.

Corbin, Carol, ed. *Rhetoric in Postmodern America: Conversations with Michael Calvin McGee.* New York: Guilford, 1998.

Costello, Cynthia B., Vanessa R. Wright, and Anne F. Stone, eds. *The American Woman 2003–2004: Daughters of a Revolution—Young Women Today.* New York: Palgrave-Macmillan, 2003.

Crary, David. "Five Women Will Be Governors." *Election 2000 Governor: Associated Press News Wire.* 8 Nov. 2000. 8 Nov. 2000. www,wire.ap.org/APnews/main.html?PACKAGEID =ELNgovernor.

Crossley, Nick, and John Michael Roberts, eds. *After Habermas: New Perspectives on the Public Sphere.* Oxford: Blackwell, 2004.

Crummy, Karen E. "DeGette Gets Her 3 Minutes: Colorado Congresswoman Kicks Off an Evening Focused on Health Care and Research." *Denver Post* 28 July 2004, final ed., sec. A: 13. *LexisNexis.* Linfield College Lib. 12 Aug. 2004. web.lexis-nexis.com/ universe/.

Curran, James, David Morley, and Valerie Walkerdine, eds. *Cultural Studies and Communications.* London: Arnold, 1996.

Dabrowski, Irene J. "The Unnamed Political Woman." *Women Leaders in Contemporary U.S. Politics.* Ed. Frank P. Le Veness and Jane P. Sweeney. Boulder, CO: Lynne Rienner, 1987. 137–49.

Daly, Matthew. "FEC Says Cantwell Violated Election Law." *Associated Press State and Local Wire.* 20 Feb. 2004. *LexisNexis.* Linfield College Lib. 26 Oct. 2004. web.lexis-nexis.com/ universe/.

Davenport, Paul. "Candidate's Strengths, State's Woes Help Democrat's Victory." *Associated Press State and Local Wire.* 8 Nov. 2002. *LexisNexis.* Linfield College Lib. 20 Jan. 2003. web.lexis-nexis.com/universe/.

———. "Napolitano Celebrates Win in Arizona Governor's Race as Salmon Concedes." *Associated Press State and Local Wire.* 11 Nov. 2002. *LexisNexis.* Linfield College Lib. 20 Jan. 2003. web.lexis-nexis.com/universe/.

———. "Napolitano Elected Arizona Governor." *Associated Press State and Local Wire.* 6 Nov. 2002. *LexisNexis.* Linfield College Lib. 20 Jan. 2003. web.lexis-nexis.com/universe/.

———. "Napolitano Fills Economic Posts, Keeps DES Director for Now." *Associated Press State and Local Wire.* 20 Dec. 2002. *LexisNexis.* Linfield College Lib. 20 Jan. 2003. web.lexis-nexis.com/universe/.

———. "Napolitano Launches Transition after Salmon Concedes." *Associated Press State and Local Wire.* 11 Nov. 2002. *LexisNexis.* Linfield College Lib. 20 Jan. 2003. web.lexis-nexis .com/universe/.

———. "Napolitano Wants CPS to Err on Side of Child Safety." *Associated Press State and Local Wire.* 20 Dec. 2002. *LexisNexis.* Linfield College Lib. 20 Jan. 2003. web.lexis-nexis .com/universe/.

"A Death Adds to Travails of Democrats in Hawaii." *New York Times* 30 Sept. 2003: A19.

DeGette, Diana. "About Diana: Biography." *Congresswoman Diana DeGette*. n.d. 12 Aug. 2004. www.house.gov/degette/.

———. "America's Growing International Credibility Gap." Column. *Congresswoman Diana DeGette*. 7 June 2003. 12 Aug. 2004. www.house.gov/degette/.

———. "Bush Breaks Promise to Protect America's Last Roadless Treasures." Press Release. *Congresswoman Diana DeGette*. 12 July 2004. 12 Aug. 2004. www.house.gov/degette/.

———. "Congresswoman Diana DeGette." *Congresswoman Diana DeGette*. n.d. 27 July 2004. www.house.gov/degette/BIOLAST.htm.

———. "Cuts to Social Security Would Disproportionately Harm Minorities." Column. *Congresswoman Diana DeGette*. 2 May 2003. 12 Aug. 2004. www.house.gov/degette/.

———. "The DeGette Report 1." *Congresswoman Diana DeGette*. 21 Jan. 2004. 12 Aug. 2004. www.house.gov/degette/.

———. "The DeGette Report 6." *Congresswoman Diana DeGette*. 17 June 2004. 12 Aug. 2004. www.house.gov/degette/.

———. "The DeGette Report 7." *Congresswoman Diana DeGette*. 25 June 2004. 12 Aug. 2004. www.house.gov/degette/.

———. "The DeGette Report 8." *Congresswoman Diana DeGette*. 12 July 2004. 12 Aug. 2004. www.house.gov/degette/.

———. "Diana DeGette Formally Launched Her Re-election Campaign for Congress." Press Release. *Congresswoman Diana DeGette.* 18 Mar. 2002. 27 July 2004. www.house .gov/degette/.

———. "FY 2003 Appropriations." FDCH Congressional Testimony. *Ebsco Host.* Linfield College Lib. 16 May 2002. 12 Aug. 2004. www.house.gov/degette/.

———. "House Floor Debate on H.R. 2427, the Pharmaceutical Market Access Act: July 24, 2003." *Congressional Digest* Nov. 2003: 283.

———. "House Floor Remarks: America's International Standing Is Being Damaged." *Cong. Rec.* 10 June 2003. *Thomas.* Library of Congress. 27 July 2004. thomas.loc.gov/.

———. "House Floor Remarks on Deploring Misuse of International Court of Justice by United National General Assembly for Political Purpose." *Cong. Rec.* 14 July 2004. *Thomas.* Library of Congress. 27 July 2004. thomas.loc.gov/.

———. "House Floor Remarks on Help Efficient, Accessible, Low-cost, Timely Healthcare (Health) Act of 2004." *Cong. Rec.* 12 May 2004. *Thomas.* Library of Congress. 24 Sept. 2004. thomas.loc.gov/.

———. "House Floor Remarks on Relating to the Liberation of the Iraqi People and the Valiant Service of the United States Armed Forces and Coalition Forces." *Cong. Rec.* 26 Mar. 2004. *Thomas.* Library of Congress. 27 July 2004. thomas.loc.gov/.

———. "House Floor Remarks on Unborn Victims of Violence Act of 2003." *Cong. Rec.* 26 Feb. 2004. *Thomas.* Library of Congress. 24 Sept. 2004. thomas.loc.gov/.

———. "House Floor Remarks on Youth Attitudes about Civic Education." *Cong. Rec.* 22 Nov. 2003. *Thomas.* Library of Congress. 27 July 2004. thomas.loc.gov/.

———. "House Should Put Science Over Politics, Consider Stem Cell Plan." News Release. *Congresswoman Diana DeGette*. 5 Aug. 2004. 12 Aug. 2004. www.house.gov/degette/.

———. "Issues: Health Care." *Congresswoman Diana DeGette*. n.d. 12 Aug. 2004. www.house.gov/degette/.

———. "Overturning Roe Could Soon Be Reality." Column. *Congresswoman Diana DeGette*. 15 Jan. 2003. 12 Aug. 2004. www.house.gov/degette/.

———. "U.S. Representative Diana DeGette (D-CO) Delivers Remarks at Democratic National Convention." *FDCH Political Transcripts*. FDCH e-Media. 27 July 2004. *Ebsco Host*. Linfield College Lib. 12 Aug. 2004. www.house.gov/degette/.

"DeGette, Diana." Biographical Information. *Biographical Directory of the United States Congress: 1974–Present*. n.d. 27 July 2004. bioguide.congress.gov/.

De Landtsheer, Christ'l. "Introduction to the Study of Political Discourse." *Politically Speaking: A Worldwide Examination of Language Used in the Public Sphere*. Ed. Ofer Feldman and Christ'l De Landtsheer. Westport, CT: Praeger, 1998.

De Landtsheer, Christ'l, and Ofer Feldman, eds. *Beyond Public Speech and Symbols: Explorations in the Rhetoric of Politicians and the Media*. Westport, CT: Praeger, 2000.

"Dem's Win Finally Ends Wash. Race—For Now." *Rocky Mountain News* [Denver, CO] 31 Dec. 2004: 40A.

Dodd, Chris. "Statement of Senator Chris Dodd on the 25th Anniversary of Governor Ella Grasso's Inauguration." 10 Jan. 2000. 12 August 2004. www.senate.gov/~dodd/press/Releases/00/0110b.htm.

Doherty, Diane M. "A Congresswoman Speaks: A Rhetorical Analysis of Selected Speeches of Representative Edith Green." MA thesis, University of Portland, 1967.

Dow, Bonnie J., and Mari Boor Tonn. "'Feminine Style' and Political Judgment in the Rhetoric of Ann Richards." *Quarterly Journal of Speech* 79 (1993): 286–302.

Dubois, William, and Mable Brown. "Wyoming Citizen of the Century Nominee Nellie Tayloe Ross." Ts. 24 Mar. 1998. *American Heritage Center*. University of Wyoming. 7 Mar. 2001. uwadminweb.uwyo.edu/ahc/.

Duffus, R. L. "A Woman Treads New Paths as Senator." *New York Times Magazine*. 24 Jan. 1932: 4.

Duffy, Bernard K., and Halford Ross Ryan, eds. *American Orators of the Twentieth Century: Critical Studies and Sources*. New York: Greenwood, 1987.

Duke, Lois Lovelace. *Women in Politics: Outsiders or Insiders? A Collection of Readings*. Englewood Cliffs, NJ: Prentice Hall, 1993.

Earnshaw, Doris. *California Women Speak: Speeches of California Women in Public Office*. Davis, CA: Alta Vista, 1994.

Egan, Timothy. "Cantwell Declared Washington Victor." *New York Times* 23 Nov. 2000, late ed., sec. A: 24. *LexisNexis*. Linfield College Lib. 26 Oct. 2004. web.lexis-nexis.com/universe/.

Ehrenhaus, Peter. "Cultural Narratives and the Therapeutic Motif: The Poltical Containment of Vietnam Veterans." *Narrative and Social Control*. Ed. Dennis K. Mumby. Newbury Park, CA: Sage, 1993. 77–97.

Eilperin, Juliet. "Maine's Rebel with a Moderate Cause: Senator Sides with Democrats on Tax Cut." *Washington Post* 9 Apr. 2003, final ed., sec. A: A19. *Washingtonpost.com*. 11 Aug. 2004. web.lexis-nexis.com/universe/.

"Ella Giovanna Oliva (Tambussi) Grasso." *Connecticut State Library*. 2002. 12 Aug. 2004. www.cslib.org/gov/grassoe.htm.

Ellis, David, and Jane Sims Podesta. "Woman Warrior: Once a Harassment Victim, Barbara Boxer Keeps up the Pressure on Senator Packwood." *People* 11 Sept. 1995. *Academic Search Premier*. Linfield College Lib. 10 Oct. 2004. web5.epnet.com.

Elving, Ronald D., Ines Pinto Alicea, and Jeffrey L. Katz. "Boxer and Feinstein Victorious in 'Year of the Woman.'" *Congressional Quarterly Weekly Report* 6 June 1992: 11–13. *Academic Search Premier*. Linfield College Lib. 10 Oct. 2004. web5.epnet.com.

"Encyclopedia: Maria Cantwell." *Nationmaster.com*. n.d. 25 Oct. 2004. www.nationmaster .com/encyclopedia/Maria-Cantwell.

Engelbarts, Rudolph. *Women in the United States Congress, 1917–1972*. Littleton, CO: Libraries Unlimited, 1974.

Enloe, Cynthia. *Maneuvers: The International Politics of Militarizing Women's Lives*. Berkeley, CA: University of California Press, 2000.

Ettema, James S., and Theodore L. Glasser. "Narrative and Moral Form: The Realization of Innocence and Guilt through Investigative Journalism." *Methods of Rhetorical Criticism: A Twentieth-century Perspective*. 3rd ed. Ed. Bernard L. Brock, Robert Scott, and James W. Chesebro. Detroit: Wayne State University Press, 1989. 256–71.

Evans, Sarah. *Personal Politics: The Roots of Women's Liberation in the Civil Rights Movement and the New Left*. New York: Vintage Books, 1979.

Faludi, Susan. *Backlash: The Undeclared War against American Women*. New York: Crown, 1991.

Feldman, Ofer. "Epilogue: Where Do We Stand?" *Politically Speaking: A Worldwide Examination of Language Used in the Public Sphere*. Ed. Ofer Feldman and Christ'l De Landtsheer. Westport, CT: Praeger, 1998.

Feldman, Ofer, and Christ'l De Landtsheer, eds. *Politically Speaking: A Worldwide Examination of Language Used in the Public Sphere*. Westport, CT: Praeger, 1998.

Feldman, Ofer, and Linda O. Valenty, eds. *Profiling Political Leaders: Cross-Cultural Studies of Personality and Behavior*. Westport, CT: Praeger, 2001.

Felski, Rita. *Doing Time: Feminist Theory and Postmodern Culture*. New York: New York University Press, 2000.

———. *The Gender of Modernity*. Cambridge, MA: Harvard University Press, 1995.

Fenton, Matthew McCann. "I Can't Stand Being a Worm." *Biography* 1.5 (1997): 73–76. *Academic Search Elite*. 4 October 2000. ehostvgw2.epnet.com.

Ferguson, Margaret, and Jennifer Wicke, eds. *Feminism and Postmodernism*. Durham, NC: Duke University Press, 1994.

Ferguson, Russell, Martha Gever, Trinh T. Minh-ha, and Cornel West, eds. *Out There: Marginalization and Contemporary Cultures*. Documentary Series in Contemporary Art. New York: New Museum of Contemporary Art. Cambridge, MA: MIT Press, 1990.

Ferraro, Geraldine. "Acceptance Speech to the 1984 Democratic National Convention." *Three Centuries of American Rhetorical Discourse*. Ed. Ronald Reid. Prospect Heights, IL: Waveland, 1988. 727–32.

Ferraro, Geraldine A. *Changing History: Women, Power and Politics*. Wakefield, RI: Moyer Bell, 1993.

"Ferraro, Geraldine A." *Current Biography*. New York: H. W. Wilson, 1984. 29 Apr. 2004. vnweb.hwwilsonweb.com/hww.results/results_single.jtml?nn=19.

Ferraro, Geraldine, and Linda B. Francke. *Ferraro: My Story*. New York: Bantam, 1985.

Ferrechio, Susan. "Rep. Nancy Pelosi." *CQ Weekly* 28 Dec. 2002. 22 May 2004. web5 .epnet.com/.

Fields-Meyer, Thomas, Elizabeth Velez, and Mary Boone. "From Welfare to Washington." *People* 3 Dec. 2001. 4 July 2004. web17.epnet.com/ DeliveryPrintSave.asp?tb=1&ug= sidE183EC66-7164-40C3-A551.

"Final Election Results Show Women Losing Ground." Press Release. *Center for American Women and Politics*. n.d. New Brunswick, NJ: Eagleton Institute of Politics, Rutgers University, 2001. 27 Jan. 2003. www.rci.rutgers.edu/~cawp/News/CAWPpress01-02-03 .html.

"First Woman Presides over Senate." *Historical Almanac of the U.S. Senate*. Robert J. Dole. Ed. Wendy Wolff and Richard A. Baker. Washington, D.C.: U.S. Government Printing Office, 1982. 232. *American Reference Library*. *Ebsco Host*. Linfield College Lib. 12 Aug. 2004. web9.epnet.com/.

"Firsts for Women in U.S. Politics." *Center for American Women and Politics*. n.d. New Brunswick, NJ: Eagleton Institute of Politics, Rutgers University, 5 Nov. 2004. www .rci.rutgers.edu/~cawp/Facts/Officeholders/first.html.

Fisher, Walter R. *Human Communication as Narration: Toward a Philosophy of Reason, Value, and Action*. Columbia, SC: University of South Carolina Press, 1989.

Flammang, Janet A. *Women's Political Voice: How Women Are Transforming the Practice and Study of Politics*. Philadelphia: Temple University Press, 1997.

Flanagan, James W. "Ancient Perceptions of Space/Perceptions of Ancient Space." *Semeia* 87 (1999): 15–43.

Foerstel, Karen. "Rep. Nancy Pelosi." *CQ Weekly* 5 Jan. 2002. 22 May 2004 web5 .epnet.com/.

———. "Sen. Barbara Boxer, Calif./Sen. Dianne Feinstein, Calif.: Co-Chairwomen, Democratic National Convention." *CQ Weekly* 12 Aug. 2000: 18–19. *Academic Search Premier*. Linfield College Lib. 10 Oct. 2004. web5.epnet.com/.

Foss, Karen A., Sonja K. Foss, and Cindy L. Griffin. *Feminist Rhetorical Theories*. Thousand Oaks, CA: Sage, 1999.

Fox, Geoff. "Farmworker Legislation Discussed at Gathering." *Tampa Tribune* 28 May 2004, final ed., sec. Pasco: 5. *LexisNexis* Linfield College Lib. 24 Sept. 2004. web.lexis-nexis .com.

Frazer, Elizabeth. "Feminist Political Theory." *Contemporary Feminist Theories*. Ed. Stevi Jackson and Jackie Jones. New York: New York University Press, 1998.

Freeborn, Julia. "Hon. Nellie Tayloe Ross." Personal Memoir. Ts. 1930. Nellie Tayloe Ross Papers. University of Wyoming, Cheyenne.

Freedman, Estelle B. *No Turning Back: The History of Feminism and the Future of Women*. New York: Ballantine, 2002.

Freeman, Jo. *A Room at a Time: How Women Entered Party Politics*. Lanham, MD: Rowman and Littlefield, 2000.

"From Anita Hill to Capitol Hill." *Time* 16 Nov. 1992. *Academic Search Premier*. Linfield College Lib. 10 Oct. 2004. web5.epnet.com/.

Galvin, Kevin. "A Will and a Way: Convinced that Work Can Fix Anything, Maria Cantwell Takes On the Senate." *Seattle Times* 2 Dec. 2001, fourth ed., sec. ROP Zone, Pacific Northwest: 16. *LexisNexis*. Linfield College Lib. 26 Oct. 2004. web.lexis-nexis.com/universe/.

Gerber, Robin. "Female Candidates Still Battle for Serious Attention." *USA Today* 3 Jan. 2002: 11A.

Gertzog, Irwin N. *Congressional Women: Their Recruitment, Treatment, and Behavior*. Praeger Ser. Women and Politics. New York: Praeger, 1984.

Giles, Kevin S. *Flight of the Dove: The Story of Jeannette Rankin*. Beaverton, OR: Loscha Experience-Touchstone, 1980.

Gill, LaVerne McCain. *African American Women in Congress: Forming and Transforming History*. New Brunswick, NJ: Rutgers University Press, 1997.

Gizzi, John. "Democrat Ran to Right in Louisiana." *Human Events* 24 Nov. 2003. 2 July 2004 web20.epnet.com/.

——. "Politics 2000: Cowboys and 'Alice Kramden.'" *Human Events* 15 Dec. 2000. *Academic Search Elite*. Linfield College Lib. 11 Aug. 2004. web14.epnet.com/.

——. "Politics 2003: Statehouse Update." *Human Events* 25 Aug. 2003. *Academic Search Elite*. Linfield College Lib. 11 Aug. 2004. web14.epnet.com/.

Gold, Leslie. "A Masterful Machiavellian Matriarch." *Salon* 13 July 1998. 12 Apr. 2004. dir.salon.com/mwf/feature/1998/07/13feature.html.

"Governor Jeanne Shaheen Elected Vice-Chairman of the New England Governors' Conference, Inc. for 1997." *PR Newswire* 5 Feb. 1997. *LexisNexis*. Linfield College Lib. 26 Sept. 1999. web.lexis-nexis.com.

"Governor of Montana, TV Spots." *Campaigns and Elections* 22.5 (2001): 35. *Academic Search Elite*. Linfield College Lib. 11 Aug. 2004. web14.epnet.com/.

"Governors-elect Discussion with Governors-elect Sanford and Napolitano." *This Week with George Stephanopoulos*. 29 Dec. 2002. ABC News Transcripts. American Broadcasting Companies. *LexisNexis*. Linfield College Lib. 20 Jan. 2003. web.lexis-nexis.com/universe/.

Graff, Christopher. "Governor Kunin's 1st Term Has Been a Learning Experience." *Burlington Free Press* 20 July 1986: 2B.

Granholm, Jennifer. "Fiscal Year '04 Budget Presentation." Transcript. *Office of Jennifer Granholm*. 6 Mar. 2003. 20 Mar. 2003. www.Michigan.gov/gov/.

——. "MEA Press Conference." Transcript. *Office of Jennifer Granholm*. 22 Apr. 2002. 6 Nov. 2002. www.granholmforgov.com/news/tr_4_22.htm.

——. "Michigan: Greatness through Challenge." Transcript. *Office of the Governor*. 6 Feb. 2003. 7 Feb. 2003. www.michigan.gov/gov/.

——. "Our Determination, Our Strength." Transcript. *Office of the Governor*. n.d. 9 Feb. 2004. www.michigan/gov/gov/.

——. "Speech to Oakland County Democrats." Transcript. *Office of Jennifer Granholm*. 8 Jan. 2002. 6 Nov. 2002. www.granholmforgov.com/news/album/010802oakland transcript.html.

———. "State Democratic Convention." Transcript. *Office of Jennifer Granholm.* Aug. 2002. 6 Nov. 2002. www.granholmforgov.com/News/tr_8_02.htm.

———. "Text of Jennifer Granholm's Inaugural Remarks." Transcript. *Detroit Free Press.* 2 Jan. 2003. 17 Jan. 2003. www.freep.com/news/Politics/pmx12477_20030101.htm.

"Granholm, Jennifer." *Current Biography.* New York: H. W. Wilson, 2003. 5 June 2004. vnweb.hwwilsonweb.com/hww/emailprintsave/.

Grasso, Ella. "Budget Address by Governor Ella Grasso, Joint Session of Connecticut General Assembly Hall of the House, State Capitol." *Journal of the House of Representatives of the State of Connecticut.* Hartford, CT: Connecticut General Assembly, HR, 6 Feb. 1980: 54–57.

———. "Budget Message to the Connecticut General Assembly." *Journal of the House of Representatives of the State of Connecticut.* Hartford, CT: Connecticut General Assembly, HR, 4 Feb. 1976: 34–37.

———. "Budget Message to the Connecticut General Assembly." *Journal of the House of Representatives of the State of Connecticut.* Hartford, CT: Connecticut General Assembly, HR, 10 Feb. 1978: 58–64.

———. "Inaugural Message to the Connecticut General Assembly." *Journal of the House of Representatives of the State of Connecticut.* Hartford, CT: Connecticut General Assembly, HR, 3 Jan. 1979: 72–74.

———. "State of the State Address to the Connecticut General Asssembly." *Journal of the House of Representatives of the State of Connecticut.* Hartford, CT: Connecticut General Assembly, HR, 5 Jan. 1977: 96–100.

Grasso, Ella T. "Commencement Address." Mount Holyoke College. 1 June 1975. Mount Holyoke College Archives and Special Collections. South Hadley, MA.

———. "Inaugural Message to the Connecticut General Assembly." *Journal of the House of Representatives of the State of Connecticut.* Hartford, CT: Connecticut General Assembly, HR, 8 Jan. 1975: 61–65.

"Grasso, Ella T(ambussi)." *Current Biography Yearbook.* Ed. Charles Moritz. New York: H. W. Wilson, 1982.

"Grasso, Ella Tambussi." *Current Biography Yearbook.* Ed. Charles Moritz. New York: H. W. Wilson, 1975.

Green, Edith. "Address of the Honorable Edith Green." Clark Lecture. *Scripps College Bulletin.* Claremont, CA: Scripps College, 1966.

———. "The Educational Entrepreneur—A Portrait." *Cong. Rec.* Extension of Remarks. 31 July 1972: 26145–49.

———. "Fears and Fallacies: Equal Opportunities in the 1970s." William. K. McInally Lecture. Graduate School of Business Administration. Ann Arbor, MI: University of Michigan, 1975.

———. "The Federal Role in Education." *Education and the Public Good.* The Burton Lecture. Graduate School of Education of Harvard University. Cambridge, MA: Harvard University Press, 1964.

———. "Floor Statement on Equal Employment Opportunities Enforcement Act of 1971." *Cong. Rec.* 18 Nov. 1971: 42097–101.

———. "Floor Statement on Equal Pay for Equal Work Bill." *Cong. Rec.* 26 May 1955: 7172–73.

———. "Floor Statement on Equal Rights for Men and Women." *Cong. Rec.* 12 October 1971: 35810–13.

———. "Floor Statement on Higher Education Act: Discrimination on the Basis of Sex Prohibited." *Cong. Rec.* 1 July 1971: 23248–49.

———. "Floor Statement on Higher Education Act of 1971." *Cong. Rec.* 6 April 1971: 9821–23.

———. "Floor Statement on H.R. 13915: Busing." *Cong. Rec.* 17 Aug. 1972: 28849–55, 28888–89.

"Green, Edith Starrett." *Current Biography Yearbook.* Ed. Marjorie Dent Candee. New York: H. W. Wilson, 1956.

"Green, Edith Starrett: Obituary." *Current Biography Yearbook.* Ed. Charles Moritz. New York: H. W. Wilson, 1987.

Greenblatt, Alan. "Re-election Prospects Brighten for 'Year of Woman' Senators." *Congressional Quarterly Weekly Report* 30 Aug. 1997: 20. *Academic Search Premier.* Linfield College Lib. 10 Oct. 2004. web5.epnet.com/.

Greene, R.W. "The Aesthetic Turn in the Rhetorical Perspective on Argumentation." *Argumentation and Advocacy* 35 (1998): 19–29.

"Gubernatorial History in Oregon: Governor Barbara Roberts." Oregon Historical Society. 8 Jan. 2005. www.ohs.org/education/focus_on_oregon_history/GHO-Governor-Roberts.cfm.

"Gubernatorial Vote in Wyoming." *Wyoming Secretary of State.* n.d. 7 Mar. 2001. soswy .state.wy.us/informat.gov.htm.

Gunther-Canada, Wendy. *Rebel Writer: Mary Wollstonecraft and Enlightenment Politics.* DeKalb, IL: Northern Illinois University Press, 2001.

Gutner, Toddi. "The Road to the Governor's Mansion." *BusinessWeek* 29 Apr. 2002: 120.

Habermas, Jurgen. *Communication and the Evolution of Society.* Trans. Thomas McCarthy. Boston: Beacon, 1976.

Hall, Stuart. "The Toad in the Garden: Thatcherism among Theorists." *Marxism and the Interpretation of Culture.* Ed. Cary Nelson and Lawrence Grossberg. Urbana, IL: University of Illinois Press, 1988.

Hanisch, Carol. "The Personal Is Political." *Notes from the Second Year: Major Writings of the Radical Feminists.* Ed. Shulamith Firestone and Anne Koedt. New York: Radical Feminism, 1970.

Hargrove, Thomas. "Governor Races Only Bright Spot for Women." *Albuquerque Tribune* 7 Nov. 2002, evening ed.: A1. *LexisNexis.* Linfield College Lib. 20 Jan. 2003. web.lexis-nexis.com/universe/.

Harris, John F. "In Ohio, Building a Political Echo." *Washington Post* 12 May 2004. *Washington Post* Online. 12 May 2004. www.washingtonpost.com/.

Harris, Ted Carlton. *Jeannette Rankin: Suffragist, First Woman Elected to Congress, and Pacifist.* Dissertations in American Biography Ser. New York: Arno, 1982.

Hartman, Mary S., ed. *Talking Leadership: Conversations with Powerful Women.* New Brunswick, NJ: Rutgers University Press, 1999.

Hartmann, Susan M. "Caraway, Hattie Ophelia Wyatt." *American National Biography*. Ed. John A. Garraty and Mark C. Carnes. Vol. 4. New York: Oxford University Press, 1999.

———. *From Margin to Mainstream: American Women and Politics Since 1960*. Philadelphia: Temple University Press, 1989.

Hattam, Jennifer. "Make Polluters Pay." *Sierra* Mar./Apr. 2004: 15. *Academic Search Premier*. Linfield College Lib. 10 Oct. 2004. web5.epnet.com/.

Hawkings, David, and Brian Nutting, eds. *CQ's Politics in America 2004: The 108th Congress*. Washington, D.C.: Congressional Quarterly Press, 2003.

Hayden, Sara. "Negotiating Femininity and Power in the Early Twentieth Century West: Domestic Ideology and Feminine Style in Jeannette Rankin's Suffrage Rhetoric." *Communication Studies* 50.2 (1999): 83–102.

Healy, Patrick. "Granite State's Shaheens Put Weight behind Kerry." *Boston Globe* 4 Jan. 2004. *Boston.com*. 24 Aug. 2004. www.boston.com/news/nation/.

Hedge, David M. *Governance and the Changing American States*. Boulder, CO: Westview, 1998.

Heidegger, Martin. *Poetry, Language, Thought*. Trans. Albert Hofstadter. New York: Harper and Row, 1971.

Henry, David. "Barbara Jordan: Member of Congress from Texas, Public Advocate." *American Orators of the Twentieth Century: Critical Studies and Sources*. Ed. Bernard K. Duffy and Halford R. Ryan. New York: Greenwood, 1987.

Hetherington, Kevin. *Expressions of Identity: Space, Performance, Politics*. London: Sage, 1998.

"History of Women Governors in the United States." Fact Sheet. *Center for American Women and Politics*. New Brunswick, NJ: Center for American Women and Politics, 2004. www.ric.rutgers.edu/~cawp/.

Hollandsworth, Skip. "What Does Kay Want?" *Texas Monthly* Feb. 2003. 28 Oct. 2004. vnweb.hwwilsonweb.com/hww/emailprintsave/.

hooks, bell. *Yearning: Race, Gender, and Cultural Politics*. Boston: South End, 1990.

Humm, Maggie. *The Dictionary of Feminist Theory*. Columbus, OH: Ohio State University Press, 1990.

Hutchison, Kay Bailey. "America Reacts." *Capitol Comments. Office of the Senator*. 24 Sept. 2001. 28 Oct. 2004. www.hutchison.senate.gov/ccreacts.htm.

———. "America's Campaign against Terrorism Begins." *Capitol Comments. Office of the Senator*. 6 Nov. 2001. 28 Oct. 2004. hutchison.senate.gov.ccafghan.htm.

———. "Celebrate Texas." *Capitol Comments. Office of the Senator*. 14 Mar. 2003. 28 Oct. 2004. hutchison.senate.gov/cccelebrate.htm.

———. "Confronting Saddam Hussein." *Capitol Comments. Office of the Senator*. 11 Oct. 2002. 28 Oct. 2004. hutchison.senate.gov/cciraq.htm.

———. "The Good News in Iraq." *Cong. Rec.* 24 July 2003. *Office of the Senator*. 28 Oct. 2004. hutchison.senate.gov/speec341.htm.

———. "Higher Education Initiative." *Capitol Comments. Office of the Senator*. 21 Feb. 2003. 28 Oct. 2004. hutchison.senate.gov.cchighered.htm.

———. "Honoring Our Armed Forces." *Capitol Comments. Office of the Senator*. 10 Apr. 2003. 28 Oct. 2004. www.hutchison.senate.gov/speec312.htm.

———. "Honoring Our Armed Forces (continued)." *Cong. Rec.* 2 April 2003. *Office of the Senator.* 28 Oct. 2004. www.hutchison.Senate.gov/speec308.htm.

———. "Into Baghdad." *Capitol Comments. Office of the Senator.* 19 Mar. 2004. 28 Oct. 2004. hutchison.senate.gov/ccbaghdad.htm.

———. "Lady Bird's Wildflowers." *Capitol Comments. Office of the Senator.* 24 July 2002. 28 October 2004. hutchison.senate.gov/ccladybird.htm.

———. "Lone Star Shining." *Capitol Comments. Office of the Senator.* 27 Feb. 2004. 28 Oct. 2004. hutchison.senate.gov/cclonestar.htm.

———. "A New Day Dawns." *Capitol Comments. Office of the Senator.* 17 Oct. 2003. 28 Oct. 2004. hutchison.senate.gov.ccnewday.htm.

———. "A New Look at Texas Bases." *Capitol Comments. Office of the Senator.* 6 Feb. 2004. 28 Oct. 2004. hutchison.senate.gov.ccbases3.htm.

———. "Preserving Our Historic Past." *Capitol Comments. Office of the Senator.* 15 Nov. 2003. 28 Oct. 2004. hutchison.senate.gov/cchistoric.htm.

———. "The Presidential Burden." *Cong. Rec.* 28 Jan. 2003. *Office of the Senator.* 28 Oct. 2004. www.hutchison.senate.gov/speec286.htm.

———. "Promoting Trade." *Capitol Comments. Office of the Senator.* 24 Apr. 2002. 28 Oct. 2004. hutchison.senate.gov.cctpa.htm.

———. "Remembering Columbia." *Capitol Comments. Office of the Senator.* 28 July 2003. 28 Oct. 2004. www.hutchison.gov/cccolumbia.htm.

———. "Schools for Iraq's Children." *Cong. Rec.* 15 October 2003. *Office of the Senator.* 28 Oct. 2004. hutchison.senate.gov/speec358.htm.

———. "School's Out. Reform's In." *Capitol Comments. Office of the Senator.* 20 June 2003. 28 Oct. 2004. www.hutchison.senate.gov/ccreform.htm.

———. "Supplemental Appropriations Request for Iraq." *Cong. Rec.* 30 Sept. 2003. *Office of the Senator.* 28 Oct. 2004. hutchison.senate.gov/speec355.htm.

———. "Supporting President Bush and Our Troops." *Cong. Rec.* 24 Sept. 2003. *Office of the Senator.* 28 Oct. 2004. hutchison.Senate.gov/speec353.htm.

———. "Texacopia." *Capitol Comments. Office of the Senator.* 26 Sept. 2003. 28 Oct. 2004. hutchison.senate.gov/cctexacopia.htm.

———. "A Texan Triumphs . . . Again." *Capitol Comments. Office of the Senator.* 31 July 2002. 28 Oct. 2004. hutchison.senate.gov/cclance.htm.

———. "Texas: A State of Science." *Capitol Comments. Office of the Senator.* 9 Jan. 2004. 28 Oct. 2004. hutchison.senate.gov/ccscience.htm.

———. "A Trail through History." *Capitol Comments. Office of the Senator.* 20 Feb. 2004. 28 Oct. 2004. hutchison.senate.gov/cctrail.htm.

———. "USS *San Antonio*." *Capitol Comments. Office of the Senator.* 21 July 2003. 28 Oct. 2004. www.hutchison.senate.gov/cclpd17.htm.

———. "Visiting Our Military Bases." *Capitol Comments. Office of the Senator.* 2 May 2003. 28 Oct. 2004. hutchison.senate.gov/ccbases2.htm.

"Hutchison, Kay Bailey." *Current Biography.* New York: H. W. Wilson, 1997. 28 Oct. 2004. vnweb.hwwilsonweb.com/hww/results_single.jthml?nn=5.

"In a First, Woman Takes Over Governorship of Massachusetts." *New York Times* 11 Apr. 2001: n.pag.

"In Memoriam: Congresswoman Shirley Chisholm." *Center for American Women and Politics*. n.d. New Brunswick, NJ: Center for American Women and Politics, Eagleton Institute of Politics, Rutgers University. 25 Jan. 2005. www.ric.rutgers.edu/~cawp/Chisholm.html.

"Increased Spending for People Programs Great, but . . ." *Associated Press State and Local Wire*. 20 Nov. 2003. *LexisNexis*. Linfield College Lib. 11 Aug. 2004. web.lexis-nexis.com/universe/.

"Inside Politics: New Congress More Diverse." *CNN.com*. 5 Nov. 2004. 7 Nov. 2004. www.cnn.com.

Jacobs, Sally. "Jeanne Shaheen's Journey: N. H. Governor-elect Forged Political, Personal Bonds." *Boston Globe* 14 Nov. 1996, city ed., metro/region sec.: A1. *LexisNexis*. Linfield College Lib. 26 Sept. 1999. web.lexis-nexis.com/.

Jacobson, Louis. "DeGette Prevailing, But Battles State's Political Wildfires." *CongressDaily AM* 2 Aug. 2002: 7–8. *Ebsco Host*. Linfield College Lib. 12 Aug. 2004. web0.epnet.com/.

James, Edward T., ed. *Notable American Women 1607–1950: A Biographical Dictionary*. 3 vols. Cambridge MA: Belknap-Harvard University Press, 1971.

Jamieson, Kathleen Hall. *Beyond the Double Bind: Women and Leadership*. New York: Oxford University Press, 1995.

Jamieson, Kathleen Hall, and Paul Waldman. *The Press Effect: Politicians, Journalists, and the Stories that Shape the Political World*. Oxford: Oxford University Press, 2003.

Jeansonne, Glen. "The Lone Dissenting Voice." *American History* 34.1 (1999): 46–52. *Academic Search Premier*. Linfield College Lib. 25 July 2004. web7.epnet.com/.

Jennings, Peter. "Introduction to Christine Todd Whitman," *ABC Breaking News* 24 Jan. 1995.

Jerome, Richard. "Texas Trailblazer." *People Weekly* 19 Mar. 2001. 8 Oct. 2004. vnweb.hwwilsonweb.com/hww/emailprintsave/email/printsave_results.jhyml:jsessio.

Jerry, E. Claire, and Michael Spangle. "Patricia Scott Schroeder." *Women Public Speakers in the United States, 1925–1993: A Bio-Critical Sourcebook*. Ed. Karlyn Kohrs Campbell. Westport, CT: Greenwood, 1994.

Jimenez, Ralph. "Shaheen Calls for N.H. to Get in Line on King: At Inaugural, Governor Makes Push." *Boston Globe* 8 Jan. 1999, city ed., metro/region sec.: B1. *LexisNexis*. Linfield College Lib. 26 Sept. 1999. web.lexis-nexis.com.

Jimenez, Ralph, and Jordana Hart. "Time of Fulfillment in N.H. for Veteran MLK Crusaders." *Boston Globe* 7 June 1999, city ed., metro/region sec.: A1. *LexisNexis*. Linfield College Lib. 26 Sept. 1999. web.lexis-nexis.com.

Johnson, Charles S. "Martz Inaugurated: New Chief Karla Gray Performs First Official Ceremony." *Independent Record* [Helena, MT] 3 Jan. 2001: 1A.

Johnson, Glen. "Shaheen Chairs Kerry Campaign." *Boston Globe* 24 Sept. 2003. *Boston.com*. 24 Aug. 2004. www.boston.com/news/nation/articles.

Johnson, Nan. *Gender and Rhetorical Space in American Life: 1866–1910*. Carbondale, IL: Southern Illinois University Press, 2002.

Jordan, Barbara. "Democratic Convention Keynote Address." *American Rhetoric from Roosevelt to Reagan*. Ed. Halford Ross Ryan. Prospect Heights, IL: Waveland. 1987. 225–29.

———. "Statement on the Articles of Impeachment." 25 July 1974. Top 100 American Speeches. *Online Speech Bank*. 29 Apr. 2004. www.Americanrhetoric.com/speeches/.

"Jordan, Barbara." *Current Biography*. New York: H. W. Wilson. 1993. 29 Apr. 2004. vnweb.hwwilsonweb.com/hww/results/results_single.jtml?nn=41.

Jordan, Jason. "Legislators of the Year." *Planning* April 2002: 24.

Josephson, Hannah. *Jeannette Rankin: First Lady in Congress*. Indianapolis: Bobbs-Merrill, 1974.

"Judy Biggert." *CQ Weekly* 7 Nov. 2004. 17 Aug. 2004. web9.epnet.com/.

Kahn, Kim Fridkin. *The Political Consequences of Being a Woman: How Stereotypes Influence the Conduct and Consequences of Political Campaigns*. New York: Columbia University Press, 1996.

Kaml, Shannon Skarhol. "The Fusion of Populist and Feminine Styles in the Rhetoric of Ann Richards." *Navigating Boundaries: The Rhetoric of Women Governors*. Ed. Brenda DeVore Marshall and Molly A. Mayhead. Westport, CT: Praeger, 2000.

Kaptur, Marcy. *Women of Congress: A Twentieth-Century Odyssey*. Washington, D.C.: Congressional Quarterly, 1996.

Kassebaum, Nancy Landon. "Deteriorating Human Rights Conditions in Kenya." Floor Speech. *Cong. Rec. Thomas*. Library of Congress. 2 Oct. 1990. 3 Aug. 2004. thomas.loc .gov/.

———. "The Intersection of Hope and Doubt." Landon Lecture at Kansas State University. *Gifts of Speech*. 9 September 1996. 12 August 2004. gos.sbc.edu/k/kassebaum .html.

"Kassebaum, Nancy Landon." *Current Biography Yearbook*. Ed. Charles Moritz. New York: H. W. Wilson, 1982.

"Kathleen Babineaux Blanco." *Office of the Governor*. n.d. 2 July 2004. gov.loiuisiana.gov/ biography.asp.

Keetley, Dawns, and John Pettegrew, eds. *Public Women, Public Words: A Documentary History of American Feminism*. Vol. 3. Lanham, MD: Rowman & Littlefield, 2002.

Kelley, Colleen Elizabeth. *The Rhetoric of First Lady Hillary Rodham Clinton: Crisis Management Discourse*. Praeger Ser. in Political Communication. Westport, CT: Praeger, 2001.

Kelly, Rita Mae, and Mary Boutilier. *The Making of Political Women: A Study of Socialization and Role Conflict*. Chicago: Nelson-Hall, 1978.

Kerber, Linda K. *No Constitutional Right to Be Ladies: Women and the Obligations of Citizenship*. New York: Hill and Wang, 1998.

Khan, Shahnaz. "Muslim Women: Negotiations in the Third Space." *Gender, Politics, and Islam*. Ed. Therese Saliba, Carolyn Allen, and Judith A. Howard. Chicago: University of Chicago Press, 2002.

Kiely, Kathy. "Shaheen 'Critical' to Kerry's Political Upturn." *USA Today* 26 Jan. 2004. 24 Aug. 2004. www.usatoday.com/news/politicselections.

Kincaid, Diane D. Introduction. *Silent Hattie Speaks: The Personal Journal of Senator Hattie Caraway*. Ed. Diane D. Kincaid. Contributions in Women's Studies 9. Westport, CT: Greenwood, 1979.

Kirkpatrick, Jean J. *Political Woman.* New York: Basic Books, 1974.

Klausen, Jytte, and Charles S. Maier, eds. *Has Liberalism Failed Women?* New York: Palgrave, 2001.

Knickerbocker, Brad. "Washington State Women Change Tenor of Politics." *Christian Science Monitor* 19 Oct. 1998. 4 July 2004. web17.epnet.com/.

———. "Women Grab More Governorships and US Senate Seats." *Christian Science Monitor* 9 Nov. 2000: 11.

Koszczuk, Jackie. "Sen. Barbara Boxer." *CQ Weekly* 28 Dec. 2002: 11–12. *Academic Search Premier.* Linfield College Lib. 24 Apr. 2004. calvin.linfield.edu:2281/.

Kramarae, Cheris, and Paula A. Treichler. *A Feminist Dictionary.* Boston: Pandora Press, 1985.

Krisberg, Kim. "Lawmakers Seek Guarantee for Woman's Right to Choose." *Nation's Health* Mar 2004: 6. Linfield College Lib. 10 Oct. 2004. web5.epnet.com/.

Kunin, Madeleine. *Living a Political Life.* New York: Knopf, 1994.

"Kunin, Madeleine M." Madeleine May Kunin Collection. University of Vermont. 8 Jan. 2005. bailey.uvm.edu:6336/dynaweb/findingaids/kunin/@Generic_BookTextView/125;cs=default;ts=default.

"Kunin, Madeleine (May)." *Current Biography Yearbook.* Ed. Charles Moritz. New York: H. W. Wilson, 1987.

Lamson, Peggy. *Few Are Chosen: American Women in Political Life Today.* Boston: Houghton Mifflin, 1968.

———. *In the Vanguard: Six American Women in Public Life.* Boston: Houghton Mifflin, 1979.

Landes, Joan B., ed. *Feminism: The Public and the Private.* New York: Oxford University Press, 1998.

Larson, Sylvia B. "Green, Edith." *American National Biography.* Ed. John A. Garraty and Mark C. Carnes. Vol. 9. New York: Oxford University Press, 1999.

"Late-term Abortions." Interview with Sen. Robert Smith and Sen. Barbara Boxer. Interviewer, Elizabeth Farnsworth. *Online Newshour.* MacNeil/Lehrer Productions. 7 Nov. 1995. 12 Aug. 2004. www.pbs.org/newshour.

"Lawmaker from Colorado Seeks Tax Breaks for Workers, Extended Jobless Benefits." *Denver Post* 24 Jan. 2003. *Ebsco Host.* Linfield College Lib. 12 Aug. 2004. web9.epnet.com.

Lee, Barbara. "Accepting the Challenge to Continue to Be a Long Distance Runner for Economic, Social, and Political Justice." *Cong. Rec.* 21 April 1998. *Thomas.* Library of Congress. 17 August 2004. thomas.loc.gov/.

———. "Congresswoman Barbara Lee Calls President Bush's FY '05 Budget a Tale of Misplaced Priorities." n.d. 12 Oct. 2004. www.house/gov/lee.

———. "Improving the Community Services Block Grant Act of 2003." *Cong. Rec.* 4 Feb. 2004. *Thomas.* Library of Congress. 17 Aug. 2004. thomas.loc.gov/.

———. "Investing in America's Future: Congressional Black Caucus Fiscal Year 2005 Budget Alternative." *Cong. Rec.* 25 March 2004. *Thomas.* Library of Congress. 18 Aug. 2004. thomas.loc.gov/.

———. "Jobs and the Economy." *Cong. Rec.* 28 April 2004. *Thomas.* Library of Congress. 18 Aug. 2004. thomas.loc.gov/.

———. "Presidential Mistakes." *Cong. Rec.* 21 April 2004. *Thomas.* Library of Congress. 18 Aug.2004. thomas.loc.gov/.

———. "Statement of Congresswoman Barbara Lee on Opposing the Use of Force Resolution." *Black Scholar* (2002). 18 Aug. 2004. web19.epnet.com/.

———. "Supporting World AIDS Day." *Cong. Rec.* 29 Nov. 2001. *Thomas.* Library of Congress. 17 Aug. 2004. thomas.loc.gov/.

———. "U.S. Congresswoman Barbara Lee: About Congresswoman Lee." *Congresswoman Lee's Official Web Page.* n.d. 17 Aug. 2004. www.house.gov/lee/Biography.htm.

"Lee, Barbara." *Current Biography.* Ed. Clifford Thompson. Vol. 65. New York: H. W. Wilson, 2004. 62–67.

Lee, Jennifer S. "Ex-Senator Announces for Presidency." *New York Times* 23 Sept. 2003: A27.

Lefebvre, Henri. *Key Writings.* Ed. Stuart Elden, Elizabeth Lebas, and Eleonore Kofman. New York: Continuum, 2003.

———. *The Production of Space.* Trans. Donald Nicholson-Smith. Malden, MA: Blackwell, 1991.

Le Veness, Frank P., and Jane P. Sweeney, eds. *Women Leaders in Contemporary U.S. Politics.* Boulder, CO: Lynne Rienner, 1987.

Levinthal, Dave. "Sununu Hits Shaheen on Education Funding." *Eagle-Tribune* [New Hampshire] 30 Oct. 2002. 24 Aug. 2004. www.eagletribune.com/news/.

Lingle, Linda. "Back to the Future, Stuck in the Past." Press Release. 29 May 2002. 29 September 2003. www.lindalingle.com/grid.asp?baseReleases&ID=18.

———. "Governor Linda Lingle's Address to the People of Hawaii on the State's Budget Condition." *Office of the Governor.* 25 June 2003. 29 Sept. 2003. www.hawaii.gov/gov/Members/stevb/speeches/Speech.2003-06-25.4651.

———. "Lingle Announces Her Plan for 'A New Hawaii.'" Press Release. 22 July 2002. 10 October 2002. www.lindalingle.com/grid.asp?base= Releases&ID=24.

———. "Lingle Defeats Hirono for Governor." Press Release. 6 Nov. 2002. 19 Nov. 2002. www.lindalingle.com/grid.asp?base=news& ID=441.

———. "A New Beginning for Hawaii." *Honolulu Star Bulletin.* 2 Dec. 2002. 17 Jan. 2003. starbulletin.com/2002/12/02/news/story14.html.

———. "State of the State Address." *Office of the Governor.* 26 Jan. 2004. 27 Jan. 2004. www.hawaii.gov/gov/.

"Lingle, Linda." *Current Biography.* New York: H. W. Wilson, 2003. 5 June 2004. vnweb.hwwilsonweb.com/.

Linthicum, Leslie. "Up to the Challenge." *Albuquerque Journal* 6 Jan. 2003: A1. *LexisNexis.* Linfield College Lib. 20 Jan. 2003. web.lexis-nexis.com/universe/.

Little, Danity. *How Women Executives Succeed: Lessons and Experiences from the Federal Government.* Westport, CT: Quorum Books, 1994.

Lloyd, Jillian. "A New Push for Wilderness." *Christian Science Monitor* 4 Mar. 1999: 2. *Ebsco Host.* Linfield College Lib. 12 Aug. 2004. web9.epnet.com/.

Luce, Clare. "America in the Post-War Air World." *Vital Speeches of the Day.* 15 March 1943: 331–36.

———. "A Greater and Freer America." *Vital Speeches of the Day*. 15 July 1944: 586–88.

———. "The Permanent Revolution." *Vital Speeches of the Day*. 15 August 1955: 1415–17.

———. "The Search for an American Foreign Policy." *Vital Speeches of the Day*. 1 July 2004: 550–54.

———. "Waging the Peace." *Vital Speeches of the Day*. 1 Nov. 1944: 43–47.

"Luce, Clare Booth." *Current Biography 1953*. New York: H. W. Wilson, 1954. 4 Mar. 2004. vnweb.hwwilsonweb.com/hww/results/results_single.jtml?nn=32.

"Luce, Clare Booth." *World Authors 1900–1950*. Ed. Martin Seymour-Smith and Andrew C. Kimmens. Wilson Authors Series. Vol. 3. New York: H. W. Wilson, 1996. 1617–19.

MacKinnon, Catharine A. "Feminism, Marxism, Method, and the State: An Agenda for Theory." *Signs: Journal of Women in Culture and Society* 7.3 (1982): 515–44.

Mankiller, Wilma, et al. *The Reader's Companion to U.S. Women's History*. Boston: Houghton Mifflin, 1998.

Manning, Beverly. *Index to American Women Speakers 1878–1978*. Metuchen, NJ: Scarecrow, 1980.

———. *We Shall Be Heard: An Index to Speeches by American Women, 1978 to 1985*. Metuchen, NJ: Scarecrow, 1988.

Mapes, Jeff. "Roberts Plots Stealthy-As-She-Goes Tax Fix." *Oregonian* [Portland] 28 June 1992: E1.

Margolies-Mezvinsky, Marjorie, with Barbara Feinman. *A Woman's Place . . . : The Freshman Women Who Changed the Face of Congress*. New York: Crown, 1994.

"Maria Cantwell for U.S. Senate: *Times* Endorsements." *Seattle Times* 29 Oct. 2000, second ed., sec. ROP Zone, Opinion: E2. *LexisNexis*. Linfield College Lib. 26 Oct. 2004. web.lexis-nexis.com/universe/.

Marks, Alexandra. "More Women's Places Are in the House, Senate." *Christian Science Monitor* 17 Oct. 2000: 3.

———. "The Quest of Carol Moseley-Braun." *Christian Science Monitor* 20 Nov. 2003. 12 Aug. 2004. www.csmonitor.com/2003/1120/p01s04-uspo.html.

Marshall, Brenda DeVore, and Molly Mayhead, eds. *Navigating Boundaries: The Rhetoric of Women Governors*. Praeger Ser. in Political Communication. Westport, CT: Praeger, 2000.

Martin, Janet M. *The Presidency and Women: Promise, Performance, & Illusion*. College Station, TX: Texas A&M University Press, 2003.

Martin, Mart. *The Almanac of Women and Minorities in American Politics 2002*. Boulder, CO: Westview-Perseus, 2001.

Marton, Kati. *Hidden Power: Presidential Marriages That Shaped Our History*. New York: Anchor Books, 2002.

Martz, Judy. "Biography of Governor Judy Martz." *Office of the Governor*. n.d. 11 Aug. 2004. www.discovering montana.com/gov2/.

———. "A Bolder, Better Future for Montana Families." Speech. *Office of the Governor*. 23 Jan. 2002. 11 Aug. 2004. www.discovering montana.com/gov2/.

———. "Creating the Culture of a Secure Homeland: Combating Terrorism in Montana." Speech. *Office of the Governor*. 13 May 2003. 11 Aug. 2004. www.discovering montana .com/gov2/.

———. "Governor Judy Martz Professional Announcement." Speech. *Office of the Governor.* 13 Aug. 2003. 11 Aug. 2004. www.discovering montana.com/gov2/.

———. "Governor-elect Martz Announces Another Legislative Priority." News Release. *Office of the Governor.* 29 Dec. 2000. 11 Aug. 2004. www.discovering montana.com/gov2/.

———. "Governor-elect Martz Announces Legislative Priority." News Release. *Office of the Governor.* 22 Dec. 2000. 11 Aug. 2004. www.discovering montana.com/gov2/.

———. "Governor's Health Care Summit 2002." Speech. *Office of the Governor.* 17 May 2002. 11 Aug. 2004. www.discoveringmontana.com/gov2/.

———. "Governor's Health Care Summit 2003." Speech. *Office of the Governor.* 25 Sept. 2003. 11 Aug. 2004. www.discoveringmontana.com/gov2/.

———. "Inaugural Speech." *Office of the Governor.* 2 Jan. 2001. 28 Feb. 2001. www .discoveringmontana.com/gov2/.

———. "Martz Announces Economic Development Process." News Release. *Office of the Governor.* 8 Dec. 2000. 11 Aug. 2004. www.discovering montana.com/gov2/.

———. "Micro-business Awards." Speech. *Office of the Governor.* 4 Mar. 2004. 11 Aug. 2004. www.discovering montana.com/gov2/.

———. "Montana Framework for Economic Development." Governor's Office of Economic Opportunity. *Office of the Governor.* 9 Jan. 2002. 11 Aug. 2004. www.discovering montana.com/gov2/.

———. "Progress 2004—Business Days at the Capitol." Speech. *Office of the Governor.* 7 Jan. 2004. 11 Aug. 2004. www.discovering montana.com/gov2/.

———. "Remarks of Governor Judy Martz at Montana Economic Development Summit." *Office of the Governor.* 29 June 2001. 11 Aug. 2004. www.discovering montana .com/gov2/.

———. "Speech Before the Senate Committee on Energy and Natural Resources." *Office of the Governor.* 16 July 2002. 11 Aug. 2004. www.discovering montana.com/gov2/.

———. "State of the State Address." *Office of the Governor.* 25 Jan. 2001. 11 Aug. 2004. www.discovering montana.com/gov2/.

———. "Testimony of Gov. Judy Martz at Senate Business and Labor Committee for Senate Bill 445." *Office of the Governor.* 14 Feb. 2001. 28 Feb. 2001. www.discovering montana.com/gov2/.

———. "2003 State of the State Address." *Office of the Governor.* 21 Jan. 2003. 11 Aug. 2004. www.discovering montana.com/gov2/.

Mattingly, Carol. *Appropriate[ing] Dress: Women's Rhetorical Style in Nineteenth-Century America.* Carbondale, IL: Southern Illinois University Press, 2002.

McCann, Carole R., and Seung-Kyung Kim, eds. *Feminist Theory Reader: Local and Global Perspectives.* New York: Routledge, 2003.

McGee, Michael. "The 'Ideograph:' A Link between Rhetoric and Ideology." *Quarterly Journal of Speech* 66.1 (1980): 1–16.

McGee, Michael, and J. Michael Hogan. "In Search of 'The People': A Rhetorical Alternative." *Quarterly Journal of Speech* 70 (1984): 444–59.

McGinty, Brian. "Jeannette Rankin: First Woman in Congress." *American History Illustrated* 23.3 (1988): 32–33.

McLure, Sandy. *Christine Whitman for the People: A Political Biography*. Amherst, NY: Prometheus, 1996

McNay, Lois. *Foucault and Feminism: Power, Gender and the Self*. Boston: Northeastern University Press, 1992.

"ME: Snowe's Clout Seen as Growing." *Bulletin's Frontrunner*. Bulleting Broadfaxing Network. 17 Dec. 2002. *LexisNexis*. 11 Aug. 2004. web.lexis-nexis.com/universe/.

Mead, Rebecca J. *How the Vote Was Won: Woman Suffrage in the Western United States, 1868–1914*. New York: New York University Press, 2004.

"Measure That Would Have Eliminated Ariz. Presidential Primary Vetoed." *CongressDaily* 21 Apr. 2003: 11–13. *Academic Search Premiere*. Linfield College Lib. 11 Aug. 2004. web7.epnet.com/.

Melvin, Don. "Critics Fault Gov. Kunin's Leadership Ability." *Burlington Free Press* 30 Dec. 1986: 1A.

Mikulski, Barbara. "The Crime Bill." Floor Statement. *Cong. Rec*. 10 Nov. 2003. *Thomas*. Library of Congress. 10 May 2004. thomas.loc.gov/.

———. "Iraq." Floor Statement. *Cong. Rec*. 15 Oct. 2003. *Thomas*. Library of Congress. 10 May 2004. thomas.loc.gov/.

———. "Prescription Drugs." Floor Statement. *Cong. Rec*. 10 June 2003. *Thomas*. Library of Congress. 10 May 2004. thomas.loc.gov/.

———. "Should a Portion of the President's Proposed Iraqi Construction Grant Be in the Form of a Loan?" *Congressional Digest*. Dec. 2003. 8 May 2004. web/35epnet.com/ resultslist.asp?tb=1&_ug=sid63CD.4C3%2.

———. "Should Congress Approve Emergency Funding and Military Force in Response to the Terrorists Attacks?" *Congressional Digest* 80 (2001): 274 and 276.

———. "Terrorists in Israel." *Cong. Rec*. 6 Mar. 1996. *Thomas*. Library of Congress. 10 May 2004. thomas.loc.gov/.

———. "Urgent Supplemental Appropriations." Floor Speech. *Cong. Rec*. 25 July 2003. *Thomas*. Library of Congress. 5 May 2004. thomas.loc.gov/.

"Mikulski, Barbara A." *Current Biography*. New York: H. W. Wilson, 2001–2002. 8 May 2004. vnweb/hwwilsonweb.com/hww/.

Mikulski, Barbara, et al., with Catharine Whitney. *Nine and Counting: The Women of the Senate*. New York: William Morrow–HarperCollins, 2000.

Millar, William. "Third Space, *Priesthood in Ancient Israel*, and the Jewishness of Jesus." Faculty Lecture. Ts. Linfield College, McMinnville, OR. 12 Sept. 2001.

Miller, Zell. *A National Party No More: The Conscience of a Conservative Democrat*. Macon, GA: Stroud and Hall, 2003.

Milligan, Susan. "Centrists Poised to Shape Issues in New Congress." *Boston Globe* 17 Nov. 2002, third ed., national/foreign sec.: A1. *LexisNexis*. 11 Aug. 2004. web.lexis-nexis .com/universe/.

Mink, Patsy. "English Language Empowerment Act of 1996." Senate Committee on Governmental Affairs. 7 March 1996. *Gifts of Speech*. 12 August 2004. gos.sbc.edu/m/ mink1.html.

———. "Floor Remarks Commemorating Susan B. Anthony and Congresswoman Jeannette Rankin." *Cong. Rec.* 28 February 1967: 4816.

———. "Floor Remarks on the Economic Opportunity Amendments of 1965." *Cong. Rec.* 21 July 1965: 17603–5.

———. "Floor Remarks on the National Vocational Student Loan Act of 1965." *Cong. Rec.* 21 June 1965: 14120–21.

———. "Floor Remarks on the Older Americans Amendments of 1967." *Cong. Rec.* 19 June 1967: 16208–9.

———. "Floor Remarks: President Johnson Offers Equal Opportunity to Women." *Cong. Rec.* 20 Oct. 1967: 29588–89.

———. "Statement Before the House Commerce Committee Subcommittee on Commerce, Trade, and Hazardous Materials Product Liability Reform." 21 February 1995. *Gifts of Speech.* 12 August 2004. gos.sbc.edu/m/mink2.html.

———. "Statement of U.S. Congresswoman Patsy T. Mink. Senate Committee on Governmental Affairs. 7 March 1996. Revised to Apply to H.R. 123 as Passed the House on August 1, 1996." *Gifts of Speech.* 12 August 2004. gos.sbc.edu/m/mink1.html.

———. "Statement on Behalf of the Family Stability and Work Act (H.R. 1250)." 24 March 1995. *Gifts of Speech.* 12 August 2004. gos.sbc.edu/m/mink3.html.

Mink, Patsy T. "A Change in Plans." *True to Ourselves: A Celebration of Women Making a Difference.* Ed. Nancy M. Neuman. San Francisco: Jossey-Bass, 1998. 137–41.

"Mink, Patsy T." *Current Biography Yearbook.* Ed. Clifford Thompson. New York: H. W. Wilson, 2003.

"Mink, Patsy T(akemoto)." *Current Biography Yearbook.* Ed. Charles Moritz. New York: H. W. Wilson, 1968.

"Montana Gov. Martz Will Not Seek Second Term Next Year." *CongressDaily* 13 Aug. 2003. *Academic Search Premier.* Linfield College Lib. 11 Aug. 2004. web14.epnet.com/.

Moore, Mark P. "The Rhetoric of Ideology: Confronting a Critical Dilemma." *Southern Communication Journal* 54 (1988): 74–92.

Morgan, Robin, ed. and comp. *Sisterhood Is Forever: The Women's Anthology for a New Millennium.* New York: Washington Square, 2003.

Morgan, Ryan. "Styles Clash in 1st District Race: Democratic Incumbent Faces Challenge for Denver Seat from Transplanted Leadville State Senator, DeGette Delves into the Details, Indulging Taste for Complex Issues." *Denver Post* 21 Oct. 2002, 1st ed., sec. News Desk: A-10. *LexisNexis.* Linfield College Lib. 12 Aug. 2004. lexis-nexis.com/universe/.

Morris, Celia. *Storming the Statehouse: Running for Governor with Ann Richards and Dianne Feinstein.* New York: Scribner's, 1992.

Moseley-Braun, Carol. "About Carol: Biography." *Carol Moseley-Braun for President 2004.* Carol Moseley-Braun for President. 13 Nov. 2004. www.carolforpresident.com/content.php?pagsabout.

———. "Church Burnings." *Representative American Speeches 1996–1997.* Ed. Calvin McLeod Logue and Jean DeHart. New York: H. W. Wilson, 1997. 48–50.

———. "Getting Beyond Racism." *Representative American Speeches 1993–1994*. Ed. Owen Peterson. New York: H. W. Wilson, 1994. 88–99.

———. "Standing Alone." *True to Ourselves: A Celebration of Women Making a Difference*. Ed. Nancy M. Neuman. San Francisco: Jossey-Bass, 1998. 101–9.

———. "Tribute to Thurgood Marshall." *Representative American Speeches 1992–1993*. Ed. Owen Peterson. New York: H. W. Wilson, 1993. 123–27.

"Moseley-Braun, Carol." *Current Biography*. New York: H. W. Wilson, 1994. *Biographies Plus Illustrated*. 6 November 2004. vnweb.hwwilsonweb.com/hww/results/results_single .jhtml?nn=5.

"MT: Martz Asked to Spend Part of New-found Funds on Education." *Bulletin's Frontrunner*. Bulletin Broadfaxing Network. 21 Aug. 2003. *LexisNexis*. Linfield College Lib. 11 Aug. 2004. web.lexis-nexis.com/universe/.

"MT: Martz Cites Cigarette Tax Increase as One of Legislature's 'Biggest Disappointments.'" *Bulletin's Frontrunner*. Bulletin Broadfaxing Network. 15 May. 2003. *LexisNexis*. Linfield College Lib. 11 Aug. 2004. web.lexis-nexis.com/universe/.

"MT: Martz Ranks Poorly in State Poll." *Bulletin's Frontrunner*. Bulletin Broadfaxing Network. 15 Dec. 2003. *LexisNexis*. Linfield College Lib. 11 Aug. 2004. web.lexis-nexis .com/universe/.

"MT: Martz Says No Child Left Behind Put Undue Burden on State." *Bulletin's Frontrunner*. Bulletin Broadfaxing Network. 9 Oct. 2003. *LexisNexis*. Linfield College Lib. 11 Aug. 2004. web.lexis-nexis.com/universe/.

"MT: Martz Signs Bill Overturning State's Strict Indoor Smoking Ban." *Bulletin's Frontrunner*. Bulletin Broadfaxing Network. 24 Apr. 2003. *LexisNexis*. Linfield College Lib. 11 Aug. 2004. web.lexis-nexis.com/universe/.

"MT: Martz Won't Seek Reelection." *Bulletin's Frontrunner*. Bulletin Broadfaxing Network. 14 Aug. 2003. *LexisNexis*. Linfield College Lib. 11 Aug. 2004. web.lexis-nexis.com/ universe/.

Mullaney, Marie Marmo. *Biographical Dictionary of the Governors of the United States, 1988–1994*. Westport, CT: Greenwood, 1994.

Murdock, Maggi. "Ross, Nellie Tayloe." *American National Biography*. Ed. John A. Garraty and Mark C. Carnes. Vol. 18. New York: Oxford University Press, 1999.

Murray, Judith Sargent. "On the Equality of the Sexes." *Massachusetts Magazine* March 1790: 132–35, April 1790: 223–26. Rpt. in Sheila L. Skemp, *Judith Sargent Murray: A Brief Biography with Documents*. Bedford Ser. in History and Culture. Boston: Bedford, 1998. 176–82.

Murray, Patty. "State of Education." *Cong. Rec.* 19 May 2004. *Thomas*. Library of Congress. 4 July 2004. thomas.loc.gov/.

———. "World Health Day." *Cong. Rec.* 7 April 2004. *Thomas*. Library of Congress. 4 July 2004. thomas.loc.gov/.

"Murray, Patty." *Current Biography*. New York: H. W. Wilson, 1994. 4 July 2004. vnweb .hwwilsonweb.com/hww/.

"Nancy Landon Kassebaum." *Women of Congress: A Twentieth-Century Odyssey*. Marcy Kaptur. Washington, D.C.: Congressional Quarterly, 1996.

Napolitano, Janet. "Achieving Educational Excellence in Arizona: The Napolitano Plan for Improving K-12 Education." *Janet Napolitano for Governor.* 26 August 2002. 2 Nov. 2002. www.gojanet.org/issues/.

———. "Announcement of America's First Mutual Aid Plan for Emergency Services." Speech. *Arizona Governor Janet Napolitano.* 21 June 2003. 29 July 2004. governor.state.az.us/.

———. "*Brown v. Board of Education* 50th Anniversary." Speech. *Arizona Governor Janet Napolitano.* 1 May 2004. 29 July 2004. governor.state.az.us/.

———. "Governor's Biography." *Arizona Governor Janet Napolitano.* n.d. 22 Jan. 2003. governor.state.az.us/.

———. "Inaugural Address." *Arizona Governor Janet Napolitano.* 6 January 2003. 14 Jan. 2003. governor.state.az.us/.

———. "Introduction for Governor Janet Napolitano." *Arizona Governor Janet Napolitano.* Rev. 8 Apr. 2004. 29 July 2004. governor.state.az.us/.

———. "Kinder Morgan Pipeline Rupture News Conference." *Arizona Governor Janet Napolitano.* 19 Aug. 2003. 29 July 2004. governor.state.az.us/.

———. "Law Is a Public Service." Commencement Address: Arizona State University College of Law. *Vital Speeches of the Day.* 15 June 2003: 533–35. *Academic Search Elite.* Linfield College Lib. 11 Aug. 2004. web7.epnet.com/.

———. "A Leader—A Hero—Is Someone Who Reaches Out a Hand when Neighbors Need Help." Address to the Democratic National Convention. *Arizona Governor Janet Napolitano.* 27 July 2004. 29 July 2004. governor.state.az.us/.

———. "News Conference to Announce Response to Kinishba Fire." *Arizona Governor Janet Napolitano.* 15 July 2003. 29 July 2004. governor.state.az.us/.

———. "Remarks to Media on the Governor's Blue Ribbon Panel Preliminary Report on Events Leading to the Lewis Prison Standoff." *Arizona Governor Janet Napolitano.* 8 Mar. 2004. 29 July 2004. governor.state.az.us/.

———. "Remarks to Supporters of the National Task Force on Public Education." *Arizona Governor Janet Napolitano.* 22 Apr. 2004. 29 July 2004. governor.state.az.us/.

———. "State of the State Address 2003." *Arizona Governor Janet Napolitano.* 13 Jan. 2003. 22 Jan. 2003. governor.state.az.us/.

———. "State of the State Address 2004." *Arizona Governor Janet Napolitano.* 12 Jan. 2004. 29 July 2004. governor.state.az.us/.

———. "Women's History Luncheon." Speech. *Arizona Governor Janet Napolitano.* 5 Mar. 2003. 29 July 2004. governor.state.az.us/.

Nash, Kate. "Year of Woman Guv." *Albuquerque Tribune* 4 Nov. 2002. *LexisNexis.* Linfield College Lib. 20 Jan. 2003. web.lexis-nexis.com/universe/.

"National Association of Community Health Centers Honors Snowe as Champion in the Senate." *States News Service. LexisNexis.* 26 Mar. 2003. 11 Aug. 2004. web.lexis-nexis.com/universe/.

Neff, Lisa. "2 for Wisconsin." *Advocate* 12 Nov. 2002: 58. *Academic Search Premier.* 15 Apr. 2004. web13.epnet.com.

"Nellie Tayloe Ross." Wyoming State Archives. n.d. *Women of the West Museum.* 7 Mar. 2001. www.wowmuseum.org/.

Neuberger, Maurine. "Cigarette Smoking." *Cong. Rec.* 2 Oct.–15 Oct. 1964: 512–13.

———. Foreword. *Few Are Chosen: American Women in Political Life Today.* By Peggy Lamson. Boston: Houghton Mifflin, 1968.

———. *Smoke Screen: Tobacco and the Public Welfare.* Englewood Cliffs, NJ: Prentice Hall, 1963.

"Neuberger, Maurine Brown." *Current Biography.* New York: H. W. Wilson, 1961. 7 May 2004. mail.edu/frame.html?rtfPossible=true&lang=en.

Neuman, Nancy M., ed. *True to Ourselves: A Celebration of Women Making a Difference.* San Francisco: Jossey-Bass, 1998.

———. *A Voice of Our Own: Leading American Women Celebrate the Right to Vote.* San Francisco: Jossey-Bass, 1996.

"New Hampshire Chief Signs Gay Rights Bill." *New York Times* 8 June 1997, late ed., sec. 1: 37. *LexisNexis.* 26 Sept. 1999. web.lexis-nexis.com/universe/.

"New Hampshire Governor Shaheen Named Chairman-elect of Education Commission of the States." *PR Newswire* 7 July 1999. *LexisNexis.* 26 Sept. 1999. web.lexis-nexis .com/universe/.

"News Conference: Compromise Agreement on Child Tax Credit." *Federal News Service.* 5 June 2003. *LexisNexis.* 11 Aug. 2004. web.lexis-nexis.com/universe/.

"N.H. Governor Signs MLK Holiday into Law." *Boston Globe* 8 June 1999, city ed., metro/region sec.: B8. *LexisNexis.* 26 Sept. 1999. web.lexis-nexis.com/universe/.

Nix, S. Michelle, ed. *Women at the Podium: Memorable Speeches in History.* New York: Harper-Collins, 2000.

Norris, Pippa, ed. *Women, Media and Politics.* New York: Oxford University Press, 1997.

Norton, Eleanor Holmes. "Notes of a Feminist Long Distance Runner." *Sisterhood Is Forever: The Women's Anthology for a New Millennium.* Ed. and comp. Robin Morgan. New York: Washington Square, 2003.

Nutting, Brian. "Sen. Barbara A. Mikulski." *CQ Weekly* 28 Dec. 2002. 8 May 2004. web13.epnet.com/.

Ocamb, Karen. "How a Genuine Lesbian Liberal Made It to Congress." *Lesbian* June 1999: 26–27. *Academic Search Premier.* Linfield College Lib. 15 Apr. 2004. web19.epnet.com.

O'Connor, Lillian. *Pioneer Women Orators.* New York: Columbia University Press, 1954.

O'Donnell, Nora. "More Women Candidates in Gubernatorial Races Than in Any Previous Election." *NBC Nightly News.* 4 Nov. 2002. NBC News Transcripts. National Broadcasting Company. *LexisNexis.* Linfield College Lib. 20 Jan. 2003. web.lexis-nexis.com/ universe/.

O'Donnell, Victoria. "Dreams Can Come True for Little Girls Too: A Fantasy Theme Analysis of Geraldine Ferraro's 1984 Acceptance Speech." *Great Speeches for Criticism and Analysis.* Ed. Lloyd Rohler and Roger Cook. Greenwood, IN: Alistair, 1988. 43–54.

Oliphant, Thomas. "Shaheen's Deft Inaugural Message Plays Well in New Hampshire." *Boston Globe,* 12 Jan. 1997, city ed., op-ed sec.: E7. *LexisNexis.* 26 Sept. 1999. web .lexis-nexis.com/universe/.

Page, Susan. "Women Advance in Governor Races." *USA Today* 26 Aug. 2002: 1A.

Palchikoff, Kim. "Cantwell Makes History: 13th Woman in U.S. Senate." *Women's eNews.* 27 Nov. 2000. 4 Aug. 2004. www.womensenews.org/.

Pelosi, Nancy. "American Workers Cannot Wait Any Longer for Help." Press Release. *Office of the Representative*. 25 Feb. 2004. 21 May 2004. www.house.gov/pelosi/press/releases/Feb04.

———. "Are You Better Off?" *Cong. Rec.* 18 May 2004. *Thomas*. Library of Congress. 21 May 2004. thomas.loc.gov/.

———. "Bush Administration Has Not Even Tried to Hide Contempt for Roadless Rule." Press Release. *Office of the Representative*. 12 Jan. 2004. 21 May 2004. www.house/gov/pelosi/press/releases/Jan04/.

———. "Bush Administration Reversing More Than Three Decades of Bipartisan Progress on Environment." Press Release. *Office of the Representative*. 22 Apr. 2004. 21 May 2004. www.house.gov/pelosi/press/releases/April04/.

———. "The Democratic Response to the State of the Union." *Vital Speeches of the Day* 70 (1 Feb. 2004). 22 May 2004. web1.epnet.com/.

———. "Our Manufacturing Sector Is Critical, But after Three Years of President Bush It Is in Crisis." Press Release. *Office of the Representative*. Apr. 2004. 22 May 2004. www.house.gov/Pelosi/press/releases/April04/.

———. "Pelosi and Daschle Deliver Pre-Buttal to State of the Union Address." Press Release. *Office of the Representative*. 16 Jan. 2004. 21 May 2004. www.house.gov/pelosi/press/releases/Jan04/.

———. "Pelosi Statement on Decision to Allow Rice to Testify Before the Joint 9/11 Inquiry." *Office of the Representative*. 30 March 2004. 21 May 2004. www.house.gov/pelosi/press/releases/March03/911RiceTestify.html.

———. "Pelosi Statement on Democratic Resolution on Iraq." Press Release. *Office of the Representative*. 17 Mar. 2004. 21 May 2004. www.house/gov/Pelosi/press/releases/March03/.

———. "Pelosi Statement on the Effect of Bush Budget on Women." Press Release. *Office of the Representative*. 17 Mar. 2004. 21 May 2004. www.house.gov/pelosi/press/releases/March03/.

———. "Pelosi Statement on Military Construction Appropriations Act." 26 June 2003. *Thomas*. Library of Congress. 21 May 2004. thomas.loc.gov/.

———. "Pelosi Statement on State of the Union Address." Transcript. *Office of the Representative*. 28 Jan. 2003. 21 May 2004. www.house.gov.pelosi/prStateoftheUnion012803/htm.

———. "Pelosi Statement on 31st Anniversary of *Roe v. Wade*." Press Release. *Office of the Representative*. 22 Jan. 2004. 21 May 2004. www.house.gov/Pelosi/press/releases/Jan04/.

———. "President's Education Budget Leaves Millions of Children Behind." News Conference Statement/Press Release. *Office of the Representative*. 23 Sept. 2002. 21 May 2004. www.house.gov/pelosi/prBushEducationPlan092302.htm.

———. "President's Resolve on Iraq May Be Firm, But His Plan Remains Woefully Inadequate." Press Release. *Office of the Representative*. 14 Apr. 2004. 21 May 2004. www.house.gov/pelosi.press/releases.April04/.

———. "Republican Economic Plan Fails." *Cong. Rec.* 9 May 2003. *Thomas*. Library of Congress. 21 May 2004. thomas.loc.gov/.

———. "We Must Have a Strong Violence against Women Office." *Office of the Representative.* 1 May 2002. 21 May 2004. www.house.gov/pelosi/flDegetteMotion050102.HTM.

"Pelosi, Nancy." *Current Biography.* New York: H. W. Wilson, 2003. 22 May 2004. vnweb .hwilsonweb.com/hww.results/results_single.jhtml?nn=9.

"Pelosi to Support $50B Supplemental for Iraq Operations." *Congress Daily.* 29 Apr. 2004. 21 May 2004. webnet5.epnet.com/.

Pereira, I. Rice. *The Nature of Space: A Metaphysical and Aesthetic Inquiry.* New York: Privately published, 1956.

Perine, Keith. "Rep. Barbara Lee." *CQ Weekly* 5 Jan. 2002. 17 Aug. 2004. web14 .epnet.com/.

Pertman, Adam. "Shaheen Establishes a Tone in Landmark Inaugural." *Boston Globe* 10 Jan. 1997, city ed., metro/region sec.: A1. *LexisNexis.* 26 Sept, 1999. web.lexis-nexis.com/ universe/.

Peterson, Owen, ed. *Representative American Speeches, 1993–1994.* New York: H. W. Wilson, 1994.

Phillips, Anne, ed. *Feminism and Equality.* New York: New York University Press, 1987.

———. *Feminism and Politics.* New York: Oxford University Press, 1998.

Pierce, Jennifer. "Portrait of a 'Governor Lady': An Examination of Nellie Tayloe Ross's Autobiographical Political Advocacy." *Navigating Boundaries: The Rhetoric of Women Governors.* Ed. Brenda DeVore Marshall and Molly A. Mayhead. Westport, CT: Praeger, 2000.

Pindell, James W., and Sam Youngman. "Gov. Shaheen Named Kerry National Chair." *PoliticsNH.com.* New Hampshire's Online Political Network. 23 Sept. 2004. 24 Aug. 2004. www.politicalsnh.com/archives/.

Polman, Dick. "Ranks of Female Governors Due to Swell Rapidly." *Philadelphia Inquirer* 3 Nov. 2002, sec. national political news: n.pag. *LexisNexis.* Linfield College Lib. 20 Jan. 2003. web.lexis-nexis.com/universe/.

Pomper, Gerald M., and Marc D. Weiner, eds. *The Future of American Democratic Politics.* New Brunswick, NJ: Rutgers University Press, 2003.

Ponessa, Jeanne. "Margaret Chase Smith: A Principled Voice." *Congressional Quarterly Weekly Report.* 3 June 1995. 7 May 2004. web4.epnet.com/tb=1&ug=dbsaphsidFF864857-7EB9-4C4.

Ponnuru, Ramesh. "A Good Woman Is Hard to Find." *National Review* 48.14 (1996): 24. *Academic Search Elite.* 11 Aug. 2004. web3.epnet.com/.

Porter, John W. "Americans Now Stand Divided: The Struggle between Right and Left Has Overwhelmed Any Sense of the Common Good." *Portland Press Herald* [Maine] 30 May 2004, final ed., editorial sec.: 4C. *LexisNexis.* 11 Aug. 2004. web.lexis-nexis.com/ universe/.

Prince, Carolyn J. "Swiss Born Envoy to Talk Trade and NATO." *Christian Science Monitor.* 18 Sept. 1996. 12 Nov. 2004. web30.epnet.com/Citation.asp?tb=1&ug=sidD032B 270%2D4EAC%2.

"Profiles of the Six New Governors." *Election 2000 Governor: Associated Press News Wire.* 8 Nov. 2000. 8 Nov. 2000. www.wire.ap.org/APnews/center_package.html?FRONTID= ELECTION&PACKAGEID=.

Rankin, Jeannette. "Floor Statement: Is an American-Japanese Cooperation Possible? Or Will an American-Japanese War Follow the Russian Collapse?" *Cong. Rec.* 17 Oct. 1941: A4715–16.

———. "Floor Statement on Woman Suffrage: A Small Measure of Democracy." *Cong. Rec.* 10 Jan. 1918: 770–72.

———. *Jeannette Rankin: Activist for World Peace, Women's Rights, and Democratic Government.* Suffragist Oral History Project. Berkeley, CA: Regional Oral History Office, University of California, 1974. *Online Archive of California.* 12 Nov. 2003. ark.cdlib.org/ark:/13030/kt758005dx.

———. "Some Questions about Pearl Harbor." *Cong. Rec.* 8 Dec. 1942: 1–3.

Rasmusson, Erika. "The New Technocrat." *Working Woman* 26.4 (Apr. 2001): 20–21.

"Record Number of Women Seek Seats in U.S. House; Candidate Numbers at Other Levels Don't Match Record Highs." Press Release. *Center for American Women and Politics.* 24 Sept. 2004, rev. 4 Jan. 2005. New Brunswick, NJ: Center for American Women and Politics. 10 Jan. 2005. www.cawp.rutgers.edu.

Reid, Ronald F., ed. *Three Centuries of American Rhetorical Discourse.* Prospect Heights, IL: Waveland, 1988.

"A Return to the Campaign Trail." America Votes 2004: Presidential Primary Preview. *CNN.com.* 2003. Cable News Network. 22 September 2003. www.cnn.com/Election/2004/.

Rhode, Deborah L., ed. *The Difference "Difference" Makes: Women and Leadership.* Palo Alto, CA: Stanford Law and Politics–Stanford University Press, 2003.

Richards, Ann. "Keynote Address." Democratic National Convention, San Antonio, TX. 23 July 1988.

———. "Remarks of Governor Ann W. Richards on the Occasion of the Inauguration." Inauguration of the Governor, State of Texas, State Legislature, Austin, TX. 15 Jan. 1991.

———. "State of the State Address of Governor Ann W. Richards." State of Texas, State Legislature, Austin, TX. 6 Feb. 1991.

"Richards, Ann." *Current Biography.* Ed. Charles Moritz. New York: H. W. Wilson, 1991. 468–71.

Richter, Linda. "Nancy Landon Kassebaum: From School Board to the Senate." *Women Leaders in Contemporary U.S. Politics.* Ed. Frank P. Le Veness and Jane P. Sweeney. Boulder, CO: Lynne Rienner, 1987.

Ritchie, Joy, and Kate Ronald, eds. *Available Means: An Anthology of Women's Rhetoric(s).* Pittsburgh, PA: University of Pittsburgh Press, 2001.

Roberts, Barbara. "Governor Roberts' Statement: Association of Oregon Counties." 29 May 1992. Ts. Governor Roberts' Papers, Box 62. Oregon State Archives, Salem, OR.

———. "Oregon Employment and Training Association Conference: Remarks of Governor Barbara Roberts." 24 Feb. 1991. Ts. Governor Roberts' Papers, Box 62. Oregon State Archives, Salem, OR.

———. "Press Release." Office of the Governor, Salem, OR. 13 Nov. 1991.

———. "Remarks of Governor Barbara Roberts: Portland Metropolitan Chamber of Commerce." 20 May 1992. Ts. Governor Roberts' Papers, Box 63. Oregon State Archives, Salem, OR.

———. "State of the State Address." 23 Jan. 1992. Ts. Governor Roberts' Papers, Box 63. Oregon State Archives, Salem, OR.

Robinson, Gregory K. "Shaheen, Jeanne." *Current Biography Yearbook*. Ed. Clifford Thompson. New York: H. W. Wilson, 2001. 498–501.

Rogers, Edith Nourse. "The Berlin Crisis." *Cong. Rec.* 10 Mar. 1959: 3788–90.

———. "Does Naval Preparedness Prevent War?" *Congressional Digest* (Jan. 1929): 18–19.

"Rogers, Edith Nourse." *Current Biography*. New York: H. W. Wilson, 1942. 3 Apr. 2004. vnweb.hwwilsonweb.com/.

Rosenberg, Emily S. "Grasso, Ella Tambussi." *American National Biography*. Ed. John A. Garraty and Mark C. Carnes. Vol. 9. New York: Oxford University Press, 1999.

Rosenberg, Marie Barovic. "Women in Politics. A Comparative Study of Congresswomen Edith Green and Julia Butler Hansen." Diss., University of Washington, 1973.

Rosenthal, Cindy Simon, ed. *Women Transforming Congress*. Norman, OK: University of Oklahoma Press, 2002.

Ross, Karen, ed. *Women, Politics, and Change*. Hansard Society Ser. in Politics and Government. Oxford: Oxford University Press, 2002.

Ross, Nellie Tayloe. "Address Delivered by Governor Ross at the National Women's Democratic Club Dinner, Washington D.C., Saturday, March 7, 1925." Ts. Nellie Tayloe Ross Papers. The American Heritage Center, University of Wyoming, Cheyenne, WY.

———. "Message of Governor Nellie Tayloe Ross to the Eighteenth Wyoming Legislature." *Journal of the House of Representatives of the Eighteenth State Legislature of Wyoming*. Cheyenne, WY: *Wyoming Labor Journal*, 1925: 24–35.

———. "Women and Representative Government." Ts. n.d. Nellie Tayloe Ross Papers. The American Heritage Center, University of Wyoming, Cheyenne, WY.

Rossi, Alice S., ed. *The Feminist Papers: From Adams to de Beauvoir*. New York: Columbia University Press, 1973. Boston: Northeastern University Press, 1988.

Rowbotham, Sheila. *A Century of Women: The History of Women in Britain and the United States in the Twentieth Century*. New York: Penguin, 1997.

Rowland, Debran. *The Boundaries of Her Body: The Troubling History of Women's Rights in America*. Naperville, IL: Sphinx, 2004.

Ryan, Halford Ross, ed. *American Rhetoric from Roosevelt to Reagan*. Prospect Heights, IL: Waveland, 1987.

Sanford, Terry. *Storm Over the States*. New York: McGraw, 1967.

Sanger, Margaret. *Margaret Sanger: An Autobiography*. New York: Dover, 1971.

———. *My Fight for Birth Control*. New York: Farrar and Rinehart, 1931.

Sargent, Lydia, ed. *Women and Revolution: A Discussion of the Unhappy Marriage of Marxism and Feminism*. Boston: South End Press, 1981.

Sarkela, Sandra J., Susan Mallon Ross, and Margaret A. Lowe. *From Megaphones to Microphones: Speeches of American Women, 1920–1960*. Westport, CT: Praeger, 2003.

Scala, Dante J. "Heartbreak Hill, or Queen of the Mountain?" *PoliticsNH.com*. New Hampshire's Online Political Network. 28 Oct. 2002. 24 Aug. 2004. www.politicalsnh.com/.

Schakowsky, Jan. "Progressives Shape Up for the New Millennium." *Nation* 270.5 (2000): 22. *Academic Search Premier*. Linfield College Lib. 9 Oct. 2004. web29.epnet.com.

Scharrer, Erica. "An 'Improbable Leap': A Content Analysis of Newspaper Coverage of Hillary Clinton's Transformation from 1st Lady to Senate Candidate." *Journalism Studies* 3 (2002): 393–406.

Schenken, Suzanne O'Dea. *From Suffrage to the Senate: An Encyclopedia of American Women in Politics*. 2 vols. Santa Barbara, CA: ABC-CLIO, 1999.

Schindehette, Susan, and Jane Sims Podesta. "Street Fighter." *People* (4 Feb. 2001). 8 May 2004. web13.epnet.com/.

Schribman, David. "The Picks of Congress' New Litter." *Fortune* (7 December 1998). 17 Aug. 2004. web9.epnet.com/.

Schroeder, Pat. "Running for Our Lives: Electoral Politics." *Sisterhood Is Forever: The Women's Anthology for a New Millennium*. Ed. and comp. Robin Morgan. New York: Washington Square, 2003.

———. *24 Years of House Work—and the Place Is Still a Mess: My Life in Politics*. Kansas City, MO: Andrews McMeel, 1998.

Schroeder, Pat, with Andrea Camp and Robyn Lipner. *Champion of the Great American Family*. New York: Random, 1989.

Schroeder, Patricia. "Flyaway Robbery." *Cong. Rec.* 22 Feb. 1990. *Thomas*. Library of Congress. 13 Apr. 2004. thomas.loc.gov/.

———. "The Revlon President." *Cong. Rec.* 10 Oct. 1989. *Thomas*. Library of Congress. 13 Apr. 2004. thomas.loc.gov/.

———. "Trickled On." *Cong. Rec.* 7 Mar. 1990. *Thomas*. Library of Congress. 13 Apr. 2004. thomas.loc.gov/.

———. "Wave the Flag, Burn the Taxpayer." *Cong. Rec.* 13 June 1990. *Thomas*. Library of Congress. 13 Apr. 2004. thomas.loc.gov/.

"Schroeder, Patricia." *Current Biography*. New York: H. W. Wilson, 1978. 13 Apr. 2004. vnweb.hwwilson.web.com/.

Schultz, Jeffrey D., and Linda van Assendelft, eds. *Encyclopedia of Women in American Politics*. American Political Landscape Ser. Phoenix, AZ: Oryx, 1999.

"Sebelius, Kathleen." *Current Biography*. Ed. Clifford Thomas. New York: H. W. Wilson, Nov. 2004.

Seltzer, Richard A., Jody Newman, and Melissa Voorhees Leighton. *Sex as a Political Variable: Women as Candidates and Voters in U.S. Elections*. Boulder, CO: Lynne Rienner, 1997.

"Sen. Snowe: 'First Priority Must Be to Enhance Security of Our Maritime Transportation System.'" *States News Service*. 24 Mar. 2004. *LexisNexis*. 11 Aug. 2004. web.lexis-nexis.com/universe/.

"Sen. Snowe Speaks at Women's Business Owners Breakfast." *States News Service*. 2 Mar. 2004. *LexisNexis*. 11 Aug. 2004. web.lexis-nexis.com/universe/.

"Senate Allows Hospitals to Decline to Perform Abortions." *Human Events* 19 Apr. 1996: 362–63. *Academic Search Premier*. Linfield College Lib. 10 Oct. 2004. web5.epnet.com/.

"Senate Asserts *Roe v. Wade* a Correct Ruling." *Human Events* 5 Nov. 1999: 27. *Academic Search Premier*. Linfield College Lib. 10 Oct. 2004. web5.epnet.com/.

"Senate Confirms Dellinger; Napolitano Still on Hold." *Congressional Quarterly Weekly Report* 16 Oct. 1993: 2821. *Academic Search Elite*. Linfield College Lib. 11 Aug. 2004. web7 .epnet.com/.

"Senate Passes $2.2 Trillion FY 2004 Budget Resolution with Smaller Tax Cut Backed by Snowe." *States News Service*. 26 May 2003. *LexisNexis*. 11 Aug. 2004. web.lexis-nexis .com/universe/.

"Senate Rejects Separate Male/Female Barracks." *Human Events* 10 July 1998: 23. *Academic Search Elite*. 11 Aug. 2004. web5.epnet.com/.

"Senate Votes to Fund Foreign Abortions Nix Reagan Policy." *Human Events* 28 July 2003: 31. *Academic Search Premier*. Linfield College Lib. 10 Oct. 2004. web5.epnet.com/.

"Senator Barbara Boxer Holds News Conference on *Roe v. Wade* Decision." *FDCH Political Transcripts*. eMediaMillWorks. 22 Jan. 2003. 12 Aug. 2004. web0.epnet.com.

"Senator Maria Cantwell Isn't Doing So Badly." *Seattle Post-Intelligencer* 6 May, 2001, final ed., sec. P-I Focus: D7. *LexisNexis*. Linfield College Lib. 26 Oct. 2004. web.lexis-nexis .com/universe/.

Shaheen, Jeanne. "Announcement of EXCEL New Hampshire." *Governor Jeanne Shaheen . . . Making a Difference for New Hampshire Families*. 7 Feb. 2001. 27 Feb. 2001. www .shaheen.org/.

———. "Biennial Budget Address 1999." *New Hampshire Office of the Governor*. 11 Feb. 1999. 27 Feb. 2001. www.state.nh/us/governor/.

———. "Biennial Budget Address 2001." *New Hampshire Office of the Governor*. 15 Feb. 2001. 27 Feb. 2001. www.state.nh/us/governor/.

———. "Governor's Radio Address of February 3, 2001." *Governor Jeanne Shaheen . . . Making a Difference for New Hampshire Families*. 3 Feb. 2001. 27 Feb. 2001. www.shaheen.org/.

———. "Inaugural Address 1997." *New Hampshire Office of the Governor*. 9 Jan. 1997. 27 Feb. 2001. www.state.nh/us/governor/.

———. "Inaugural Address 1999." *New Hampshire Office of the Governor*. 7 Jan. 1999. 27 Feb. 2001. www.state.nh/us/governor/.

———. "Inaugural Address 2001." *Governor Jeanne Shaheen . . . Making a Difference for New Hampshire Families*. 4 Jan. 2001. 27 Feb. 2001. www.shaheen.org/.

———. "Jeanne Shaheen: Biography." *New Hampshire Office of the Governor*. n.d. 19 Feb. 1999. www.state.nh/us/governor/.

———. "Remarks—Vision 2000: The States and Small Business Conference." *New Hampshire Office of the Governor*. 9 Dec. 1998. 27 Feb. 2001. www.state.nh/us/governor/.

———. "Speech: Every Kid Covered Campaign Lunch." *New Hampshire Office of the Governor*. 22 Aug. 2000. 27 Feb. 2001. www.state.nh/us/governor/.

———. "State of the State Address, 1998." *New Hampshire Office of the Governor*. 7 Jan. 1998. 27 Feb. 2001. www.state.nh/us/governor/.

———. "State of the State Address, 2000." *New Hampshire Office of the Governor*. 3 Feb. 2000. 27 Feb. 2001. www.state.nh/us/governor/.

Shanley, Mary Lyndon, and Carole Pateman, eds. *Feminist Interpretations and Political Theory*. University Park, PA: Pennsylvania State University Press, 1991.

Shea, Lois R. "Gender Gap in Polls Gives Edge to Shaheen: She's a Role Model to Some Women." *Boston Globe* 6 Oct. 1996, city ed., New Hampshire Weekly sec.: 1. *LexisNexis*. 26 Sept. 1999. web.lexis-nexis.com/universe/.

Sheeler, Kristina Horn. "Christine Todd Whitman and the Ideology of the New Jersey Governorship." *Navigating Boundaries: The Rhetoric of Women Governors*. Ed. Brenda DeVore Marshall and Molly A. Mayhead. Westport, CT: Praeger, 2000.

Shirley, Gayle C. *More than Petticoats: Remarkable Montana Women*. Helena, MT: Twodot-Falcon, 1995.

Short, Brant. "'Reconstructed, But Unregenerate': I'll Take My Stand's Rhetorical Vision of Progress." *Southern Communication Journal* 59 (1994): 112–24.

Sicherman, Barbara, and Carol Hurd Green, eds. *Notable American Women, The Modern Period: A Biographical Dictionary*. Cambridge, MA: Belknap–Harvard University Press, 1980.

Silverman, Amy, and Patti Epler, with John Dougherty and Paul Rubin. "Shades of Green." *Phoenix New Times* 19 Dec. 2002: n.pag. *LexisNexis*. Linfield College Lib. 20 Jan. 2003. web.lexis-nexis.com/universe/.

Simon, Barbara Levy. "Women of Conscience: Jeannette Rankin and Barbara Lee." *AF-FILIA* 17.3 (2002): 384–88.

Skemp, Sheila L. *Judith Sargent Murray: A Brief Biography with Documents*. Bedford Ser. in History and Culture. Boston: Bedford, 1998.

"Sketches of New Governors." *Washington Post* 7 Nov. 1996, final ed., sec. A: A40. *LexisNexis*. 26 Sept. 1999. web.lexis-nexis.com/universe/.

Slevin, Peter. "Women Politicians Grow in Number, Acceptance." *Sunday Oregonian* [Portland, OR] 17 Oct. 2004: A6.

Smart, Barry. *Postmodernity*. London: Routledge, 1993.

Smith, Jeff. "DeGette Compares Troubled Companies: Driven CEOs Led to Woes at Qwest, Healthsouth, She Says." *Rocky Mountain News* [Denver] 7 Nov. 2003, final ed., Business sec.: 4B. *LexisNexis*. Linfield College Lib. 12 Aug. 2004. web.lexis-nexis.com/universe/.

Smith, Margaret Chase. "Woman, The Key Individual of Our Democracy." *Vital Speeches of the Day.* 15 Oct. 1952: 657–59.

Smith, Margaret Chase, with William C. Lewis, Jr. *Declaration of Conscience*. New York: Doubleday, 1972.

Snowe, Olympia J. "About Senator Snowe: Biography." *Senator Olympia J. Snowe: United States Senator for Maine.* n.d. 4 Aug. 2004. snowe.senate.gov/bio.htm.

———. "About Senator Snowe: Committee Assignments." *Senator Olympia J. Snowe: United States Senator for Maine.* n.d. 4 Aug. 2004. snowe.senate.gov/bio.htm.

———. "Floor Statement on Agriculture, Rural Development, Food and Drug Administration, and Related Agencies Appropriations Act, 2004—Conference Report." *Cong. Rec.* 20 Jan. 2004. *Thomas*. Library of Congress. 18 Aug. 2004. thomas.loc.gov/.

———. "Floor Statement on Child Care." *Cong. Rec.* 5 Oct. 2004. *Thomas*. Library of Congress. 25 Oct. 2004. thomas.loc.gov/.

——. "Floor Statement on Community College Teacher Preparation Enhancement Act of 2004." *Cong. Rec.* 2 Mar. 2004. *Thomas.* Library of Congress. 18 Aug. 2004. thomas .loc.gov/.

——. "Floor Statement on Inspector General for Intelligence—S.2515." *Cong. Rec.* 9 June 2004. *Thomas.* Library of Congress. 18 Aug. 2004. thomas.loc.gov/.

——. "Floor Statement on Jumpstart Our Business Strength (JOBS) Act." *Cong. Rec.* 5 May 2004. *Thomas.* Library of Congress. 18 Aug. 2004. thomas.loc.gov/.

——. "Floor Statement on National Dairy Equity Act." *Cong. Rec.* 18 June 2004. *Thomas.* Library of Congress. 18 Aug. 2004. thomas.loc.gov/.

——. "Floor Statement on National Defense Authorization Act for Fiscal Year 2005— Continued." *Cong. Rec.* 23 June 2004. *Thomas.* Library of Congress. 18 Aug. 2004. thomas.loc.gov/.

——. "Floor Statement on Osteoporosis Awareness and Prevention Month." *Cong. Rec.* 10 May 2004. *Thomas.* Library of Congress. 13 Aug. 2004. thomas.loc.gov/.

——. "Floor Statement on Personal Responsibility and Individual Development for Everyone Act." *Cong. Rec.* 29 Mar. 2004. *Thomas.* Library of Congress. 18 Aug. 2004. thomas.loc.gov/.

——. "Floor Statement on Small Business Progress Extension Act." *Cong. Rec.* 12 Mar. 2004. *Thomas.* Library of Congress. 18 Aug. 2004. thomas.loc.gov/.

——. "Floor Statement on Women's Sustainability Recovery Act of 2004." *Cong. Rec.* 29 Apr. 2004. *Thomas.* Library of Congress. 18 Aug. 2004. thomas.loc.gov/.

——. "October—A Month Fighting Breast Cancer." Weekly Senate Update. *Senator Olympia J. Snowe: United States Senator for Maine.* 15 Oct. 2004. 4 Aug. 2004. snowe .senate.gov/.

——. "Snowe Calls Commission's Title IX Report 'Deeply Flawed' Backs Minority Report, Calls for Action on Her Bill to Collect Data on Participation in High School Athletics." *Congressional Press Releases.* FDCH e-Media. 26 Feb. 2003. *LexisNexis.* 11 Aug. 2004. web.lexis-nexis.com/universe/.

——. "Snowe Introduces Legislation to Create Independent Inspector General for Intelligence." News Release. *Senator Olympia J. Snowe: United States Senator for Maine.* 14 June 2004. 4 Aug. 2004. snowe.senate.gov/.

——. "Snowe Statement on Release of Intelligence Committee Report on Pre-war Intelligence Asssessments." News Release. *Senator Olympia J. Snowe: United States Senator for Maine.* 9 July 2004. 4 Aug. 2004. snowe.senate.gov/.

——. "Speech to the John F. Kennedy School of Government." 3 June 1997. *Gifts of Speech.* 12 Aug. 2004. gos.sbc.edy/s/snowe/html.

——. "The Time Has Come for More Affordable Prescription Drugs." Weekly Senate Update. *Senator Olympia J. Snowe: United States Senator for Maine.* 23 Apr. 2004. 4 Aug. 2004 snowe.senate.gov/.

——. "Up from Silence." *True to Ourselves: A Celebration of Women Making a Difference.* Ed. Nancy M. Neuman. San Francisco: Jossey-Bass, 1998. 59–67.

"Snowe, Olympia J." *Current Biography Yearbook.* Ed. Judith Graham. New York: H. W. Wilson, 1995. 543–47.

"Snowe: 'Passing Prescription Drug Legislation Would Verify Nation's Commitment to Providing for Those Who Walked the Path Before Us.'" *States News Service*. 17 June 2003. *LexisNexis*. 11 Aug. 2004. web.lexis-nexis.com/universe/.

Soja, Edward W. *Thirdspace: Journeys to Los Angeles and Other Real-and-Imagined Places*. Cambridge, MA: Blackwell, 1996.

Solochek, Jeffrey S. "Brown-Waite Builds Her Profile in Washington." *St. Petersburg Times* 9 Feb. 2003, sec. Hernando Times: 1. *LexisNexis*. Linfield College Lib. 24 Sept. 2004. web.lexis-nexis.com.

———. "Brown-Waite Ousts Rep. Thurman." *St. Petersburg Times* 6 Nov. 2002, sec. City & State: 6B. *LexisNexis*. Linfield College Lib. 24 Sept. 2004. web.lexis-nexis.com.

———. "Brown-Waite Prevails." *St. Petersburg Times* 2 Nov. 2002, sec. Metro & State: 1B. *LexisNexis*. Linfield College Lib. 24 Sept. 2004. web.lexis-nexis.com.

———. "Freshman's Votes Toe Party Line." *St. Petersburg Times* 5 Sept. 2004, sec. Pasco Times: 1. *LexisNexis*. Linfield College Lib. 24 Sept. 2004. web.lexis-nexis.com.

———. "Know Your Candidates: 5th Congressional District." *St. Petersburg Times* 24 Aug. 2004, sec. Special: 5G. *LexisNexis*. Linfield College Lib. 24 Sept. 2004. web.lexis-nexis .com.

———. "Lawmaker Gets Comfortable in New Role." *St. Petersburg Times* 3 Feb. 2003, sec. Pasco Times: 1. *LexisNexis*. Linfield College Lib. 24 Sept. 2004. web.lexis-nexis .com.

"Speaking with Jennifer Granholm." *Lansing State Journal* 24 Oct. 2002. 4 Nov. 2002. www .lsj.com/editorials/021024_granholm_interview.html.

Spender, Dale. *Women of Ideas and What Men Have Done to Them: From Aphra Behn to Adrienne Rich*. London: Routledge and Kegan Paul, 1982.

Squires, Chase. "Brown-Waite Chats with Voters." *St. Petersburg Times* 19 Feb. 2003, sec. Pasco Times: 6. *LexisNexis*. Linfield College Lib. 24 Sept. 2004. web.lexis-nexis.com.

———. "Brown-Waite Says Tallahassee Lessons Will Help on the Hill." *St. Petersburg Times* 22 Jan. 2003, sec. Pasco Times: 5. *LexisNexis*. Linfield College Lib. 24 Sept. 2004. web.lexis-nexis.com.

Squitieri, Tom. "Democratic Attorney General Fought Hard in 'Ugliest Race.'" *USA Today* 12 Nov. 2002, news sec.: 8a. *Academic Search Elite*. Linfield College Lib. 11 Aug. 2004. web7.epnet.com/.

Sreberny, Annabelle, and Lisbet van Zoonen, eds. *Gender, Politics, and Communication*. Cresskill, New York: Hampton, 1996.

"State Accelerating Campaign against Sex before Marriage." *Associated Press State and Local Wire*. 24 May 2004. *LexisNexis*. 11 Aug. 2004. web.lexis-nexis.com/universe/.

"Statewide Elective Executive Women 2005." Fact Sheet. New Brunswick, NJ: Center for American Women and Politics, Eagleton Institute of Politics, Rutgers University, 2005.

Stevens, Allison. "The Strength of These Women Shows in Their Numbers." *CQ Weekly* 25 Oct. 2003. 28 June 2004. web17.epnet.com/DeliveryPrint Save.asp?tb=1&_ug= sidE183EC66-7164-40C3-A551.

Stineman, Esther. *American Political Women: Contemporary and Historical Profiles*. Littleton, CO: Libraries Unlimited, 1980.

"Stirring the Soup." *Economist* 19 Mar. 1994: 34. *Academic Search Elite* 11 Aug. 2004. web18 .epnet.com/.

Stolberg, Sheryl Gay. "A Day of Firsts, Even for Some Veteran Lawmakers." *New York Times* 8 Jan. 2003: A18.

Sullivan, Patricia A. "Women's Discourse and Political Communication: A Case Study of Congressperson Patricia Schroeder." *Western Journal of Communication* 57 (1993): 530–45.

Symons, Joanne L. "How Will the New Congress Treat Working Women?" *Executive Female* 18.1 (1995): 59. *Academic Search Elite* 11 Aug. 2004. web18.epnet.com/.

Talbott, Basil. "Braun's Back with Strong Performance." *Chicago Sun-Times* 23 Oct. 1992, late ed., News: 4. *LexisNexis.* Linfield College Lib. 13 Nov. 2004. calvin.linfield.edu:2092/ universe/.

Tanner, Robert. "Women Seeking Governor Position." *Statesman-Journal* [Salem, OR] 23 Aug. 2002, nation report: 4A.

Tarullo, Hope. "Napolitano, Janet." *Current Biography.* Ed. Clifford Thompson. New York: H. W. Wilson, Oct. 2004. 49–55.

Thomas, Sue. *How Women Legislate.* New York: Oxford University Press, 1994.

———. "The Impact of Women in Political Leadership Positions." *Women and American Politics: New Questions, New Directions.* Ed. Susan J. Carroll. Oxford: Oxford University Press, 2003.

Thomas, Sue, and Clyde Wilcox, eds. *Women and Elective Office: Past, Present, and Future.* New York: Oxford University Press, 1998.

Thompson, Wayne. "Salem Dodgeball." *Oregonian* [Portland, OR] 15 Apr. 1991: B6.

Thonssen, Lester, ed. *Representative American Speeches: 1968–1969.* New York: H. W. Wilson, 1969.

"The Times Require Granholm's Talents." *Saginaw News* [MI]. 27 Oct. 2002. 4 Nov. 2002. www.mlive.com/news/sanews/.

Todd, Alexandra Dundas, and Sue Fisher, eds. *Gender and Discourse: The Power of Talk.* Advances in Discourse Processes. 30. Norwood, NJ: Ablex, 1988.

Tolchin, Susan J. *Women in Congress: 1917–1976.* U.S. 94th Cong., 2nd Sess. Washington, D.C.: U.S. Government Printing Office, 1976.

Tolchin, Susan J., and Martin Tolchin. *Glass Houses.* Cambridge, MA: Westview, 2001.

———. *Clout: Womanpower and Politics.* New York: Coward, McCann and Geoghegan, 1974.

Tolleson-Rinehart, Sue. "Do Women Leaders Make a Difference?" *The Impact of Women in Public Office.* Ed. Susan J. Carroll. Bloomington, IN: Indiana University Press, 2001.

Tomasky, Michael. *Hillary's Turn: Inside Her Improbable, Victorious Senate Campaign.* New York: Free Press, 2001.

Toner, Robin. "Bucking Bush, Senator Takes a Thorny Path." *New York Times* 5 May 2003, late ed., sec. A: 1. *LexisNexis.* 11 Aug. 2004. web.lexis-nexis.com/universe/.

Tronto, Joan. *Moral Boundaries: A Political Argument for an Ethic of Care.* New York: Routledge, 1993.

Unger, Nancy C. "Rankin, Jeannette Pickering." *American National Biography.* Ed. John A. Garraty and Mark C. Carnes. Vol. 18. New York: Oxford University Press, 1999.

United States. Cong. House. Office of the Historian. Commission on the Bicentenary of the U.S. House of Representatives. *Women in Congress, 1917–1990.* Washington, D.C.: U.S. Government Printing Office, 1991.

United States. Cong. Senate. *Acceptance and Dedication of the Statue of Jeannette Rankin.* Washington, D.C.: U.S. Government Printing Office, 1987.

"U.S. Senator Patrick Leahy (D-VT) Holds News Conference on Federal Marriage Amendment." *FDCH Political Transcripts.* FDCH e-Media. 14 July 2004. *Ebsco Host.* Linfield College Lib. 12 Aug. 2004. web9.epnet.com/.

Valenty, Linda O., and Ofer Feldman, eds. *Political Leadership for the New Century: Personality and Behavior among American Leaders.* Westport, CT: Praeger, 2002.

Vandettei, Jim. "Clinton Emerges. The NY Senator's Growing Role Fuels Talk of Her Future." *Washington Post* 10 Mar. 2003, national weekly edition: 14.

Van Dijk, Teun A. *Ideology: A Multidisciplinary Approach.* Thousand Oaks, CA: Sage, 1998.

Vavrus, Mary. "Working the Senate from the Outside In: The Mediated Construction of a Feminist Political Campaign." *Critical Studies in Mass Communication* 15.3 (1998): 213–35.

Verhovek, Sam Howe. "Senate-Elect Arises from Limbo." *New York Times* 20 Dec. 2000, late ed., sec 1: 52. *LexisNexis.* Linfield College Lib. 26 Oct. 2004. web.lexis-nexis.com/universe/.

Weinstein, Joshua. "Snowe on List of World's Most Powerful Women." *Press Herald Online* [Portland, Me.] 25 Aug. 2004. *Senator Olympia J. Snowe: United States Senator for Maine.* 25 Oct. 2004. snowe.senate.gov/articles/.

Weir, Sara J. "The Feminist Face of State Executive Leadership: Women as Governors." *Western Washington University.* Dept. of Political Science. n.d. 7 Mar. 2001. www.ac.wwu.edu/~sweir/womengovs98.htm/.

Weisberg, Jacob. "Kay Bailey Forehead." *New Republic* 18 Oct. 1993. 28 Oct. 2004. web33.epnet.com/.

Weissman, Art. *Christine Todd Whitman: The Making of a National Political Player.* New York: Birchland-Carol, 1996.

Weissman, Pete. "Speechwriting Secrets from the Senate." *Vital Speeches of the Day.* 15 Jan. 2003. 4 July 2004. web17.epnet.com/.

White, Hayden. *The Tropics of Discourse: Essays in Cultural Criticism.* Baltimore: Johns Hopkins University Press, 1978.

———. "The Value of Narrativity in the Representation of Reality." *On Narrative.* Ed. W. J. T. Mitchell. Chicago: University of Chicago Press, 1981. 1–23.

Whitman, Christine Todd. "Biography." *Office of the Governor.* n.d. 10 June 1998. www.state.nj.us/governor/ctwbio.html.

———. "Deerfield Commencement." 28 May 1995. *Gifts of Speech.* 3 Nov. 2004. gos.sbc.edu/w/whitman.html.

———. "Effective Policy Making: The Role of Good Science." Address to the Symposium on Nutrient Over-Enrichment of Coastal Waters. 13 Oct. 2000. *Gifts of Speech.* 12 Aug. 2004. gos.sbc.edu/w/whitman2.html.

———. "My Moral Compass." *True to Ourselves: A Celebration of Women Making a Difference.* Ed. Nancy M. Neuman. San Francisco: Jossey-Bass, 1998. 131–35.

———. "Remarks at the Land Trust Conference." 20 Oct. 1998. *Gifts of Speech.* 12 Aug. 2004. gos.sbc.edu/w/whitman4/html.

———. "Republicans, Democrats, Feminists, and Post-Impeachment Politics." Address to the National Press Club. 3 March 1999. *Gifts of Speech.* 3 Nov. 2004. gos.sbc.edu/w/whitman5.html.

———. "Second Inaugural Address." *Office of the Governor.* 20 Jan. 1998. 29 Jan. 2000. www.state.nj.us/governor/speeches/inaug988.html.

———. "Statement of Governor Christine Todd Whitman before the VA, HUD and Independent Agencies Subcommittee of the Committee on Appropriations." *Academic Search Elite.* Linfield College Lib. n. d. 9 May 2001. web26.epnet.com/.

"Whitman, Christine Todd." *Current Biography.* New York: H. W. Wilson, 1995. 3 Nov. 2004. vnweb.hwwilsonweb.com/.

"Who Gets Elected?" *Guide to Congress*, 5th ed. Vol. 11. Washington, D.C.: Congressional Quarterly Press-Congressional Quarterly, 2000.

Wides, Louise. *Edith Green: Democratic Representative from Oregon.* Ralph Nader Congress Project Citizens Look at Congress. Washington, D.C.: Grossman, 1972.

Wilgoren, Jodi. "New Governors Discover the Ink Is Turning Redder." *New York Times* 14 Jan. 2003. 14 Jan. 2003. www.nytimes.com/2003/01/14/politics/14GOVS.html?todaysheadlines.

Wilson, Marie. *Closing the Leadership Gap: Why Women Can and Must Help Run the World.* New York: Viking-Penguin, 2004.

Winans, Dave. "Plainspoken and Honest." *NEA Today* May 2004. *Academic Search Elite.* Linfield College Lib. 11 Aug. 2004. web5.epnet.com/.

Windt, Thodore Otto, Jr. *Presidents and Protesters: Political Rhetoric in the 1960s.* Tuscaloosa, AL: University of Alabama Press, 1990.

"With Highway Reauthorization Approaching, Snowe Works for Improvements in Highway Safety." *States News Service.* 11 June 2003. *LexisNexis.* 11 Aug. 2004. web.lexis-nexis .com/universe/.

Witt, Linda, Karen M. Paget, and Glenna Mathews. *Running as a Woman: Gender and Power in American Politics.* New York: Free Press-Macmillan, 1994.

Wolbrecht, Christina. *The Politics of Women's Rights: Parties, Positions, and Change.* Princeton, NJ: Princeton University Press, 2000.

Wollstonecraft, Mary. *A Vindication of the Rights of Woman: An Authoritative Text Backgrounds the Wollstonecraft Debate Criticism.* 2nd ed. Ed. Carol H. Poston. New York: W. W. Norton, 1988.

"Women Guv: Re-election Rates." *Campaigns & Elections* 18.10 (Dec. 1997/Jan. 1998): 13. *Ebsco Host.* Linfield College Lib. 12 Aug. 2004. web15.epnet.com/.

"Women in Congress: Chronological List of Members." *U.S. House of Representatives.* United States Cong. House. 2005. 2 Feb. 2005, bioguide.congress.gov/congresswomen/chrono.asp.

"Women in Elected Office 2005: Fact Sheet Summaries." *Center for American Women and Politics.* New Brunswick, NJ: Center for American Women and Politics, Eagleton Institute of Politics, Rutgers University, 24 Jan. 2005. www.rci.rutgers.edu/~cawp/Facts/Officeholders/cawpfs.html.

"Women in the U.S. Senate 1922–2004." Fact Sheet. *Center for American Women and Politics*. New Brunswick, NJ: Center for American Women and Politics, Eagleton Institute of Politics, Rutgers University, 2004. www.rci.rutgers.edu/~cawp/.

"Women Serving in the 109th Congress 2005–07." *Center for American Women and Politics*. 2005. New Brunswick, NJ: Center for American Women and Politics, Eagleton Institute of Politics, Rutgers University, 24 Jan. 2005. www.rci.rutgers.edu/~cawp/Facts/Officeholders/cong-current.html.

Woods, Harriett. *Stepping Up to Power: The Political Journey of American Women*. Boulder, CO: Westview-Perseus, 2000.

Wright, Frances. "Of Free Enquiry: Considered as a Means for Obtaining Just Knowledge." *Course of Popular Lectures*. New York: G. W. and A. J. Matsell, 1836. 41–62.

Wymard, Ellie. *Conversations with Uncommon Women*. New York: Amacom-American Management Assoc., 1999.

Young, Iris Marion. "Impartiality and the Civic Public: Some Implications of Feminist Critiques of Moral and Political Theory." *Feminism: The Public and The Private*. Ed. Joan B. Landes. Oxford Readings in Feminism. Oxford: Oxford University Press, 1998. 421–47.

Young, Louise M. "Caraway, Hattie Ophelia Wyatt." *Notable American Women 1607–1950: A Biographical Dictionary*. Ed. Edward T. James. Vol. 1 of 3 vols. Cambridge, MA: Belknap-Harvard University Press, 1971.

Index

About the Authors

Molly A. Mayhead is professor of speech communication at Western Oregon University in Monmouth. She received her Ph.D. from Penn State University in 1988. Her research interests include Supreme Court rhetoric, women's political discourse, and First Amendment issues. She collaborated with Dr. Brenda DeVore Marshall to write and edit *Navigating Boundaries: The Rhetoric of Women Governors*, published by Praeger in 2000. She teaches courses in argumentation, public speaking, rhetorical criticism, freedom of speech, and the rhetoric of the women's movement. Molly is very active in the faculty union where she serves as chief grievance officer. She lives on a five-acre farm with her husband, renowned presidential scholar Ed Dover.

Brenda DeVore Marshall, professor and chair of theatre and communication arts at Linfield College in McMinnville, Oregon, received her Ph.D. from Southern Illinois University–Carbondale. Her research interests include women's political rhetoric and the rhetorical nature of the arts. With Dr. Molly Mayhead, she coedited and contributed to *Navigating Boundaries: The Rhetoric of Women Governors*. She teaches courses across the speech communication discipline as well as feminist theory in the college's Gender Studies Program. The recipient of Linfield's Edith Green Distinguished Professor and Samuel Graf Faculty Achievement awards, Brenda participates actively in faculty governance, including service as chair of the Faculty Executive Council, Title IX officer, and faculty trustee. She enjoys gardening, reading, and walking along the Oregon coast with her husband, Ty.